The Speaker's Handbook

Fifth Edition

The Speaker's Handbook

Fifth Edition

Jo Sprague
San Jose State University

Douglas Stuart

Harcourt College Publishers

Fort Worth Philadelphia San Diego New York Orlando Austin San Antonio
Toronto Montreal London Sydney Tokyo

Publisher	**Earl McPeek**
Acquisitions Editor	**Stephen Dalphin**
Market Strategist	**Laura Brennan**
Developmental Editor	**Peggy Howell**
Project Editor	**Jon Davies**
Art Director	**April Eubanks**
Production Manager	**James McDonald**

ISBN: 0-15-508137-3
Library of Congress Catalog Card Number: 99-63075

Speeches adapted with permission for use in Appendix by John Poulakos, Karen Lynn McNeil, Patrick Kan Wong, Jade Pham, and Raymond W. Smith.

Address for Domestic Orders: Harcourt College Publishers, 6277 Sea Harbor Drive, Orlando, FL 32887-6777. 800-782-4479

Address for International Orders: International Customer Service, Harcourt, Inc., 6277 Sea Harbor Drive, Orlando, FL 32887-6777. 407-345-3800, (fax) 407-345-4060, (e-mail) hbintl@harcourtbrace.com

Address for Editorial Correspondence: Harcourt College Publishers, 301 Commerce Street, Suite 3700, Fort Worth, TX 76102

Web Site Address
http://www.harcourtcollege.com

Harcourt College Publishers will provide complimentary supplements or supplement packages to those adopters qualified under our adoption policy. Please contact your sales representative to learn how you qualify. If as an adopter or potential user you receive supplements you do not need, please return them to your sales representative or send them to: Attn: Returns Department, Troy Warehouse, 465 South Lincoln Drive, Troy, MO 63379.

Printed in the United States of America

1 2 3 4 5 6 7 8   039   9 8 7 6 5

Preface

The Speaker's Handbook, Fifth Edition, is at once a reference guide for the individual speaker and a textbook for use in the public speaking course. It is a compendium of principles, examples, and exercises that covers the issues one commonly confronts in preparing and delivering a speech. What distinguishes *The Speaker's Handbook* from other books on public speaking, though, is its flexibility: Each of the twenty-nine chapters stands by itself, so that speakers need consult only those parts of the book covering the aspects of speechmaking with which they need further help.

About the Handbook Approach

In a sense, a book about public speaking is a contradiction. Public speaking is a lived, performed, embodied event that draws its special qualities from the immediate context, the personality of a particular speaker, and the response of a certain audience. Is there really any useful general advice about so specific an act?

Apparently so. For as long as people have felt the need to speak in public, they have turned to others for advice on how to do so more effectively. Early evidence from Egyptian tombs shows that leaders gave serious thought to the choices they faced in speaking to their followers. The oral tradition captured in Homeric legend hints that the giving and taking of this advice predated the written word. The increasing supply of information about the ancient cultures of China, India, and the Americas shows that these peoples had culturally distinctive ways of speaking, which some analyzed and discussed. These observers then formulated advice for others in their culture. Such advice usually came in two forms: Those who had vast experience as speakers told stories about what worked for them; others looked beyond what worked and theorized about why it worked.

Both forms of guidance are still present. Leading platform speakers write books about their experiences. The popularity of such books year after year suggests that people find benefit in the personal and experiential approach. At the same time, university libraries continue to accumulate academic treatises on rhetoric and communication. Here, too, the vitality of these lines of research after thousands of years suggests that much is left to be said and investigated.

There is a third form, one that we differentiate from both those kinds of books and place within another venerable tradition that is over two thousand years old. This form is neither a narrative account of personal success stories nor a scholarly theoretical tome. This is the *handbook*. The first written handbooks for speakers were probably produced by the Sophists in the Greece of 200 BCE. In any field, a handbook represents a particular blending of theory and practice displayed in a concise format. There are scouting handbooks and birding handbooks and managing handbooks and meditation handbooks. In all these cases, a handbook is a distillation of the experience and theory of many people and many eras.

The particular usefulness of handbooks can be found in their characteristics.

Handbooks are brief.
They fit in a person's hand. They are supposed to be as small as practicable to remove the impediment of size for easy carrying, storing, and referencing. The implication of this is that we have tried to distill the most meaningful advice, avoiding bulking the book out. The sample speeches in the **Appendix** are called on over and over again in the text in both examples and exercises. Putting in as many sample speeches as usual in standard textbooks, interspersed throughout the body of the book, would defeat the advantages offered by the handbook format. Cartoons and photographs, likewise, take up too much space.

Handbooks are reference books.
The contents of a handbook are meant to be used in any order. The progression of the chapters, as we have arranged them, is not random, but then again, a reader or teacher does not necessarily have to follow that order. We have written the chapters to be as self-contained as possible to make the book more adaptable to the differing needs of its various users. Long before the information superhighway or menu-driven computers or the invention of the phrase *random access,* people liked to learn things as they needed them.

Adult learners have their own way of designing their learning programs, whether they are setting up a computer or understanding a new job. Most people who buy a computer do not take a course on how to use it. They try a few things, glance at the manual, and work until they get into trouble. Then they look at the manual again, but only for the specific information they need to get beyond the current problem. In effect, they don't worry about the things they don't have to worry about, but they won't know that a thing to worry about exists until they discover it. Public speaking is like that. Until people start speaking, they cannot be sure of all the areas in which they may need improvement. Therefore, users should approach this handbook with a spirit of flexibility, taking what they need in the order they need it. Each teacher brings to the classroom a different experience set and an understanding of the values, needs, and capabilities of the students who attend a particular institution. Therefore, each teacher may choose to assign chapters in an order that fits his or her perception of the best way to increase the skills of those students. Whether users are teachers, students, or businesspersons, we think that they will find some benefit in every chapter of this handbook, but we don't dictate to them in what order they find that benefit.

Handbooks are handy.

When people haul out the book that came with their computer, they want to find the section on changing printer types quickly, not read about the architecture of the system to find the bit that refers to communications between the computer and printer. A good user guide compartmentalizes related information and then tries to make that information as accessible as possible through a variety of pointers and references, using design tools to make things easy to find. We have included aids to let users get to where they want to be, from the quick index and checklists on the end-papers to the use of color and typeface weight in the text itself.

With this compartmentalization, users do not have to read everything at once. A student may be preparing to give an informative speech for a class and is thinking of including some humor. The student could jump ahead and read Chapter 16a(4). It is not that long. A businessperson may be giving a presentation to the board on the adoption of new technology but feel uncertain if he or she has covered everything and in the most effective order. That person could read Chapter 7 on transforming his or her ideas into points and Chapters 19 and 20 on informative and persuasive strategies.

We do have a few specific recommendations, however, on preliminary steps that will help students and other readers get the most out of this book. First, such users should read Chapter **1**. It provides an orientation to communication and helps them crystallize their self-definition as speakers. It helps them diagnose their skill level and gives them an approach to mapping out a skill-development plan for themselves. The format of this book is based on the assumption that speakers cannot be conscious of everything at once. In designing a skills-development program, speakers *should not* be conscious of everything at once. Trying to do everything, in parallel, will frustrate their purpose and inhibit their skill-building. As we say in **1e,** speakers should avoid being overly conscious of their manner of speaking or their message's exact language. But if a speech is different from just another conversation, as we also say, how do public speakers become *just enough more conscious* of the craft of speaking to improve their skill without breaking the conversational bond? The secret lies in having a very clear plan of what their priorities are and in deciding on a limited number of goals to pursue consciously at any one time. The handbook approach lets users pick one or two important skills to work on, and when those are mastered, move to another set.

About Writing This Book

We approached this writing task with an unusual combination of perspectives. In her twenty-five years of teaching public speaking, visiting the classes of other teachers, and consulting, Jo Sprague has observed that there are many "right ways" to approach a course. Doug Stuart, as a vice president of a technical and marketing publications department, has learned how to take even the most complex material and make it clear and accessible to readers. It became evident to us that there was a need for a different kind of book on speaking, one based on what we knew about how adults learn. *The Speaker's Handbook* proceeds from the premise that people like to focus first on the area of greatest concern and then design their own learning experience outward from that point.

About the Fifth Edition

We have been gratified with the response to the first four editions of *The Speaker's Handbook*. And we are pleased that the handbook format worked for students and their instructors, as well as for people who give presentations in their business or community roles. In this edition, we have once again responded to user suggestions on how to make the information even more accessible. We have streamlined both the book and the **Appendix.** Material on humor, for instance, is now incorporated into **16,** Attention and Interest. The Guidelines for Special Occasions **(22)** have been limited to the kinds of occasions that users have identified as truly special. In the **Appendix,** we have included only those sample speech materials that most concisely illustrate the key principles of the book.

As this edition has been trimmed, it has also been updated. Throughout, we have tried to capture the changing contexts and topics for public speaking. We address directly the opportunities (and the risks) posed by information technologies like the Internet and new presentation aids.

Practice Sessions has been made its own chapter **(24),** and moved to the Presentation section, where it serves to guide speakers through the important process of rehearsing, receiving feedback, and orally refining their ideas.

The greatest substantive change from earlier editions is the new chapter on Speaking Ethics, **21.** Here we pull together implications from all aspects of preparing and delivering a speech, inviting readers to think about the obligations they take on when they assume the power of a speaker. The chapter does not provide simple answers to complex ethical questions, but rather emphasizes the importance of respect—for oneself, one's audience, and the integrity of ideas—while balancing short-term effectiveness and long-term integrity.

Finally, though we have received compliments on the inclusiveness of the first four editions, we strive to make each subsequent edition of the *Handbook* more attuned to the diversity of contemporary life. In our treatment of language, reasoning, and vocal and physical delivery, we attempt to show how social forces shape, and are shaped by, speech. What is appropriate, or clear, or persuasive constantly changes as society changes. The effective speaker will be open to the subtle cultural variations in speech situations. If there were no differences between people, communication would be unnecessary. If there were no similarities, it would be impossible. The great strength of oral communication is that its many dimensions offer people ways to seek out connections in the midst of difference; its immediacy allows for on-the-spot adjustments.

About Listening

Being a good speaker and being a good listener go hand in hand. If speakers master the techniques in this "speaker's" handbook, we guarantee that they will be better listeners. They will be more appreciative of good speaking when they hear it, recognizing the art and craft that come into play to create a successful and satisfying speaking event. They will also be more critical of speaking that fails to measure up to the standards they insist upon for themselves. Also, they will begin to notice what they admire in effective speakers and what works and what does not work for them as a part of the audience. Being a good, critical listener is a powerful tool for moving toward speaking competence.

Chapter **13** and sections **14d, 18d,** and **20e** and **f** are particularly relevant to learning to be a critical listener. Empathic listening enters into the skills discussion in Chapters **4** and **29** and in section **5d**. In fact, every chapter of this handbook has implications for listening as well as speaking.

Acknowledgments

With each new edition, the list of people to whom we owe our gratitude grows. First, we acknowledge Peter Dougherty, who initially approached us with the idea for a *Speaker's Handbook,* and the other fine editors who guided us through the previous four editions. We thank the editorial team for the fifth edition: Steve Dalphin and Peggy Howell helped to shape this revision and encouraged us through the process. The production was ably assisted by project editor Jon Davies, art director Michelle Krabill, and production manager James McDonald. It is due to these people, along with the enthusiastic marketing and sales personnel, that we value our continuing association with Harcourt Brace.

We are grateful to Mary Kay Switzer, California State Polytechnic University; Lawrence A. Hosman, University of Southern Mississippi; Philip W. Hoki, University of Texas—San Antonio; Ray Nelson, Mount Hood Community College; Charles Zelden, Nova Southeastern University; Kathleen German, Miami University; Joel L. Bailey, Mountain Empire Community College; Jackie Czerepinski, Idaho State University, who provided helpful comments and suggestions for this edition. We thank also the reviewers for the previous edition: Deborah Smith-Howell, University of Nebraska at Omaha; Lawrence W. Hugenberg,

Youngstown State University; Nancy Keeshan, Duke University; Stacey Reid, Pearl River Community College; Joseph H. Rust, Rend Lake College; Elaine Stenger, Thomas More College; and Ralph B. Thompson, Cornell University. In addition, there are many loyal users of the *Handbook* who have generously shared their comments with us. Without them, we might have changed too much. Thanks for letting us know what works as well as what can be improved. We are grateful for the support of our colleagues at FirstTel Systems Corporation and in the department of Communication Studies at San Jose State University, especially the teaching associates, who have been a continual source of feedback. Neeley Silberman provided invaluable research assistance on this revision as well as taking the lead on the fifth edition of the accompanying Instructor's Manual.

Our partners, Gary Ruud and Samantha Schoenfeld, have given us space, time, support, and help throughout the fifth cycle of this handbook's history. In this complex context, we send them uncomplicated love and thanks.

Jo Sprague
Douglas Stuart

Brief Contents

Part 1. Preparation   **1**

Chapter 1. Understanding Speaking   **3**
Chapter 2. Planning   **17**
Chapter 3. Topic Selection and Analysis   **25**
Chapter 4. Audience Analysis   **44**
Chapter 5. Research   **58**
Chapter 6. Overcoming Fear of Speaking   **73**

Part 2. Organization   **81**

Chapter 7. Transforming Ideas into Speech Points   **84**
Chapter 8. Arranging Points   **96**
Chapter 9. Outlining   **105**
Chapter 10. Transitions   **119**
Chapter 11. Introductions   **124**
Chapter 12. Conclusions   **139**

Part 3. Development   **147**

Chapter 13. Supporting Materials   **150**
Chapter 14. Reasoning   **169**
Chapter 15. Language and Style   **208**
Chapter 16. Attention and Interest   **226**
Chapter 17. Credibility   **237**

Chapter 18. Motivational Appeals 245

Chapter 19. Informative Strategies 257

Chapter 20. Persuasive Strategies 263

Chapter 21. Speaking Ethics 284

Chapter 22. Guidelines for Special Occasions 294

Part 4. Presentation 307

Chapter 23. Modes of Delivery 311

Chapter 24. Practice Sessions 321

Chapter 25. Vocal Delivery 336

Chapter 26. Physical Delivery 351

Chapter 27. Adapting to the Speech Situation 358

Chapter 28. Visual Aids 366

Chapter 29. Answering Questions 377

Contents

Part 1. Preparation   1

Chapter 1. Understanding Speaking   3

1a.   **Understand what it means to be a speaker.**   3

1b.   **Ground your approach to effective public speaking in a meaning-centered view of communication.**   4
    (1) Do not confine your view of communication to information transmission and reception.   4
    (2) Think about communication as the joint creation of meaning.   5

1c.   **Approach public speaking by drawing on three familiar communicative resources.**   6
    (1) Draw on your conversation skills.   7
    (2) Draw on your writing skills.   8
    (3) Draw on your performance skills.   8
    (4) Combine some features of these three communicative resources for an effective public speech.   9
    (5) Avoid relying exclusively or excessively on any one of these resources.   10

1d.   **Beware of common misconceptions about public speaking that may interfere with efficient mastery of the skill.**   11

1e.   **Understand the role of consciousness in skill learning.**   13

Chapter 2. Planning   17

2a.   **To design a unique message, allow time for the four phases of creativity.**   17

2b.   **Make a realistic timetable for your speech preparation.**   18
    (1) List the tasks you will need to complete to prepare the speech, and estimate the time needed for each.   19

(2) Determine which tasks depend on the prior completion of other tasks. 19

(3) Set intermediate deadlines for the major phases of preparation and practice. 20

2c. Make your speech preparation an oral and collaborative process. 22

2d. To present a speech that achieves the flavor of enhanced conversation, focus on different resources at different phases of preparation. 22

2e. Avoid these planning pitfalls. 23
(1) No time for incubation 24
(2) No margin for error 24
(3) "Writer's" block 24
(4) "Speaker's" block 24

Chapter 3. Topic Selection and Analysis 25

3a. Select a speech topic. 25
(1) Draw the topic from your own experience, expertise, and interests. 26
(2) Select a topic appropriate to the audience and occasion. 28
(3) Select a topic that is both timely and timeless. 28

3b. Narrow your topic. 30
(1) Determine the number of ideas you can cover in the time allotted. 31
(2) Select a few main ideas based on thorough analysis of the audience, the occasion, and your own strengths as a speaker. 31

3c. Clarify the purpose of your speech. 33
(1) Identify the general purpose of your speech. 33
(2) Determine the specific purpose of your speech. 34
(3) Specify the desired outcomes you seek from your listeners. 35

3d. Develop a clear thesis statement to guide your analysis of the topic. 37
(1) Frame a thesis statement as a single declarative sentence that states the essence of your speech content. 37
(2) Analyze your topic by breaking your thesis statement into a list of questions to be answered. 39

3e. If necessary, select a speech title. 41

Chapter 4. Audience Analysis   44

4a. Develop an understanding of your audience by seeking information through as many channels as possible.   45

4b. Analyze the demographic characteristics of your audience as an aid to predicting their orientation.   47
   (1) Age/Generation   48
   (2) Sex/Gender   49
   (3) Race/Ethnicity   51

4c. Try to understand what is meaningful to your audience.   52

4d. Determine the audience's attitudes toward your topic.   54

4e. Anticipate your audience's expectations by gathering details about the specific speech situation.   55
   (1) What do they know about your topic?   55
   (2) What do they think about you?   56
   (3) What is the history of your audience as a group?   56
   (4) What is the program surrounding your speech?   56

Chapter 5. Research   58

5a. Have a research strategy.   58
   (1) Fit your research to the time allotted.   59
   (2) Approach your topic so that you progress from the general to the specific.   59
   (3) Develop a lexicon of the terminology peculiar to your topic.   60
   (4) Use the analysis questions developed in 3d(2) to direct your research.   61

5b. Use the library.   61
   (1) Talk to a librarian.   62
   (2) Use the catalogs to locate books and articles on your topic.   62

5c. Use electronic information retrieval.   63

5d. Seek information directly from other people.   65
   (1) Finding human resources   65
   (2) Interviewing   67

5e. Maintain a complete record of your sources.   69

5f. **Capture the information and ideas in discrete units to facilitate retrieval and organization.** **70**
   (1) Notecards from print and electronic sources   70
   (2) Notecards from interviews and surveys   72
   (3) Grouping your cards   72

Chapter 6. Overcoming Fear of Speaking   **73**

6a. **Put your fear of speaking into perspective.**   **73**
   (1) Accept some fear as normal.   73
   (2) Analyze your fear as specifically as possible.   74

6b. **Build your confidence through thorough preparation and practice.**   **75**

6c. **Cope with the physical effects of fear by using techniques of relaxation and tension release.**   **76**

6d. **Use positive self-suggestion to combat your anxiety.**   **77**
   (1) Visualize success.   77
   (2) Replace negative internal statements with positive ones.   78

6e. **If none of the preceding suggestions works, seek outside help.**   **79**

Part 2. Organization   **81**

Chapter 7. Transforming Ideas into Speech Points   **84**

7a. **Assemble all the possible ideas and information that could go into your speech.**   **84**

7b. **Use a variety of organizational tools to identify potential points and examine their relationships.**   **85**
   (1) A rudimentary, working outline   85
   (2) Concept mapping   86
   (3) Manipulating moveable components   86

7c. **Choose main points that taken together correspond exactly to your thesis statement.**   **88**

7d. **Select main points that are mutually exclusive.**   **90**

7e. **Have at least two, but not more than five, main points in the average speech.** **93**

7f. **Express main points and subpoints to reflect coordinate and subordinate relationships.** **93**
   (1) Subordinate points and subpoints should fit inside, or support, a larger idea.   94
   (2) Coordinate points and subpoints should be of equal importance.   95
   (3) Each subpoint should directly relate to the point it supports.   95

Chapter 8. Arranging Points   96

8a. **Arrange main points in a pattern that arises inherently from the subject matter or from the requirements of the thesis sentence.** **97**
   (1) The chronological pattern orders ideas in a time sequence.   97
   (2) The spatial pattern arranges points by location.   98
   (3) In the cause-effect pattern, the speaker moves from a discussion of the origins of a condition to the ways it manifests itself.   99
   (4) The problem-solution pattern examines the symptoms of a problem and then suggests a remedy.   99
   (5) The topical pattern of organization divides a speech into elements that have no pattern exclusive of their relationship to the topic itself.   100

8b. **Group subpoints according to a pattern, but do not feel compelled to echo the pattern of the main points.** **102**

Chapter 9. Outlining   105

9a. **Use the conventional outline format.** **106**
   (1) Follow a consistent set of symbols.   106
   (2) Show the logical relationship of ideas through proper indention.   107
   (3) As a general rule, develop each level of subordination with two or more parts.   108
   (4) Each symbol should designate *one* point only; every point should have a symbol.   108

9b. **Use a full-sentence outline to ensure coherent development of your speech.** **109**

9c. **Phrase the main points of the outline in a way that directly forecasts the subpoints that will be developed.** **114**

Contents

9d. Phrase main points and subpoints in clear, effective, and parallel language.   **116**

9e. Supplement your logical outline with marginal notations of the rhetorical devices used.   **118**

Chapter 10. Transitions   **119**

10a. Select transitions that reflect the logical relationships among ideas.   **120**

10b. Make use of internal previews and summaries.   **122**

Chapter 11. Introductions   **124**

11a. Frame your opening sentences carefully to engage your audience's attention.   **125**

11b. Provide a psychological orientation.   **127**
    (1) Establish a relationship with your audience.   127
    (2) Motivate your audience toward your topic.   130

11c. Provide a logical orientation.   **132**
    (1) Establish a context for your speech.   132
    (2) Orient the audience to your approach to the topic.   135

11d. Make your introduction as compact as possible by combining or omitting steps when appropriate.   **136**

11e. Avoid these introduction pitfalls.   **137**

Chapter 12. Conclusions   **139**

12a. Provide logical closure.   **139**
    (1) Summarize the main ideas of the speech.   139
    (2) Reestablish the connection of your topic to a larger context.   140

12b. Provide psychological closure.   **142**
    (1) Remind the audience how the topic affects their lives.   142
    (2) Make an appeal.   142

12c. End your speech with a clincher.   **144**

12d. Avoid these conclusion pitfalls.   **145**

Part 3. Development 147

Chapter 13. Supporting Materials 150

13a. Define unfamiliar words and concepts. 151
(1) Logical definition 151
(2) Etymological and historical definition 152
(3) Operational definition 152
(4) Definition by negation 153
(5) Definition by authority 154
(6) Definition by example 154

13b. Make frequent use of examples. 155
(1) Use factual examples to illustrate and document your points. 155
(2) Use hypothetical examples for clarification, speculation, and adaptation to the immediate situation. 156
(3) Determine the appropriate amount of detail to include in your examples. 157

13c. Use statistical evidence to quantify, clarify, and prove your points. 159
(1) Check the accuracy of statistical evidence by applying the tests of *who, why, when, how.* 159
(2) Avoid misleading statistics. 161
(3) Make your numbers and statistics clear and meaningful to your listeners. 162

13d. Draw on testimony from authorities. 163
(1) Evaluate the credibility of the authorities you cite when you use testimony as proof. 164
(2) Take care, when editing quotations, to retain key points without distorting their meaning. 166

13e. Weave supporting materials smoothly into the speech. Cite your sources. 167
(1) Cite the sources of your supporting materials. 167
(2) Use a variety of lead-ins for stylistic effectiveness. 168

Chapter 14. Reasoning 169

14a. Identify each point in your preliminary speech outline where reasoning is needed to provide an essential link. 170
(1) Evidence does not necessarily lead to a certain claim. 171

Contents

(2) In linking evidence to claims, people look for patterns of regularity that fit with what they have observed in the world.   171

14b. Use an inductive pattern of reasoning when your argument consists of combining a series of observations to lead to a probable conclusion.   **174**

(1) Look before you "leap": Be sure the instances on which you base your inferences are sufficient and representative.   174
(2) Recognize the degree of probability of your claim.   175
(3) Demonstrate the cost/reward analysis that led you to accept or reject the probable claim.   176

14c. Use a deductive pattern of reasoning when your argument consists of demonstrating how the relationships among established premises lead to a necessary conclusion.   **178**

(1) In a formal deductive syllogism, be sure that there are only two terms and that the major premise sets up an absolute relationship.   179
(2) When using a modified deductive form of reasoning, make it clear that probable premises can lead only to probable conclusions.   181
(3) As a general rule, explicitly lay out all the premises of a deductive argument.   182

14d. Use causal reasoning to demonstrate that one event results from another.   **185**

(1) Test the validity of the causal relationships you claim.   186
(2) Do not oversimplify causal relationships.   187
(3) Explain your causal claims fully and fairly.   189

14e. Use reasoning by analogy to draw conclusions about unknown events, based on what you know about similar events.   **190**

(1) Be sure that when you reason by analogy, the two cases are similar in all relevant and important respects.   192
(2) Do not confuse a literal analogy, which is a form of reasoning, with a figurative analogy, which is used only in a descriptive function.   193

14f. Avoid these reasoning fallacies: **193**

(1) Attacking the person rather than the argument (*ad hominem*)   194
(2) Setting up a straw figure   194
(3) Extending an argument to absurd lengths (*reductio ad absurdum*)   195
(4) The slippery slope   195
(5) Circular reasoning   196

(6) The semantic fallacy 196
(7) False dichotomy 197
(8) Faulty reversal of an if-then statement (affirming the consequent or denying the antecedent) 197
(9) Hasty generalization 198
(10) Confusing sequence with cause (*post hoc, ergo propter hoc*) 199

14g. Through organization and word choice, make it clear to your listeners exactly how your reasoning links your evidence to your claim. **200**
(1) Organize points to show the logical relationships. 200
(2) Use words, phrases, and transitional sentences that spell out what your evidence means and how the parts of your argument are linked. 202

Chapter 15. Language and Style **208**

15a. Understand how oral style is different from written style. **209**

15b. Strive for clarity in your language. **211**
(1) Be precise. 211
(2) Use specific and concrete language. 213
(3) Be economical in your language. 213

15c. Use appropriate language. **215**
(1) Suit the formality of your language to the occasion. 215
(2) Be judicious in your use of jargon or slang. 216
(3) Avoid substandard usage. 217
(4) Use language that is respectful and inclusive. 218

15d. Use vivid, varied language. **219**
(1) Employ imagery. 219
(2) Use stylistic devices. 220
(3) Use fresh language. 222
(4) Vary the rhythm of your sentences. 223

15e. Synchronize your language with that of your listeners. **224**

Chapter 16. Attention and Interest **226**

16a. Engage your audience's attention by making extensive use of techniques that enliven your speech. **227**

(1) Use materials that are concrete and close to home.   228
(2) Keep your audience involved.   229
(3) Keep the energy level of your speech up through variety and movement.   231
(4) Use humor in appropriate situations.   232

16b. Convert attention to interest.   **233**
(1) Emphasize the link between your topic and the listeners' self-interest.   233
(2) Incorporate some of the techniques of effective storytelling.   234

16c. Avoid these attention pitfalls.   **235**
(1) Avoid inappropriate stories, humor, and other attention "grabbers."   235
(2) Don't let a story or joke consume your entire speech.   235
(3) Do not tell jokes unless you have mastered the techniques of joke telling.   236
(4) Be careful that audience participation does not cause you to lose control.   236

Chapter 17. Credibility   **237**

17a. Conduct an honest assessment of your speaking image.   **238**
(1) Are you perceived as *competent?*   238
(2) Are you perceived as *concerned* about your audience's welfare?   238
(3) Are you perceived as *trustworthy?*   239
(4) Are you perceived as *dynamic?*   239

17b. Build your credibility prior to the speech.   **240**
(1) Provide the contact person with adequate information about your qualifications.   240
(2) Help the person introducing you to set a favorable tone.   240
(3) Be aware of your image in all dealings with the group prior to the speech.   240

17c. Bolster your credibility through your speech content.   **240**
(1) Present your credentials.   241
(2) Demonstrate a thorough understanding of your topic.   241
(3) Be sure your material is clearly organized.   242
(4) Make a special effort to present a balanced and objective analysis.   242
(5) Explicitly express your concern and goodwill toward the audience.   243

17d. Use your speech delivery to increase your credibility.   **243**

Chapter 18. Motivational Appeals   245

18a. When developing the content of your speech, be conscious of the emotional impact you want to create or avoid.   245

18b. Relate your speech to the needs of your listeners.   247

18c. Relate your speech to the values of your listeners.   248
    (1) Incorporate appeals to the general values of the culture.   249
    (2) Identify and relate to the core values of your audience.   251
    (3) Forge strong, logical links between the issues of your speech and the values of the audience.   253
    (4) Use motivational appeals to broaden your listeners' sense of history and community.   254

18d. Avoid excessive and inappropriate use of emotional appeals.   255

Chapter 19. Informative Strategies   257

19a. Base your speech on an understanding of how people acquire, process, and retain information.   258
    (1) Avoid information overload.   258
    (2) Give listeners a framework for organizing the information.   258
    (3) Move from the simple to the complex.   258
    (4) Move from the familiar to the unfamiliar.   259

19b. Adhere to these principles of clear explanation.   259
    (1) Use organizers.   259
    (2) Use emphasis cues.   260
    (3) Use examples liberally.   260
    (4) Use analogies.   261
    (5) Use multiple channels and modes.   262
    (6) Use repetition and redundancy.   262

Chapter 20. Persuasive Strategies   263

20a. Clarify the goals of your persuasion.   264

20b. Base your persuasive efforts on sound analysis.   265
    (1) Identify whether your persuasive goal requires you to establish a proposition of fact, of value, or of policy.   266

Contents

(2) Use stock issues, when possible, to help you analyze your topic. 268

20c. Adjust your speech content in light of your audience's attitude toward your topic and you. **270**
    (1) Favorable audience 270
    (2) Neutral audience 273
    (3) Unfavorable audience 275

20d. Organize your points for optimal persuasive impact. **277**
    (1) Use the motivated sequence to engage your audience. 278
    (2) Compare the advantages of two alternative proposals as a way of organizing your speech. 280

20e. As a general rule, place your strongest points first or last. **280**

20f. In addition to presenting your own viewpoints in a persuasive speech, you may often find it advisable to deal with opposing arguments. **281**
    (1) Address the opposing arguments directly, using refutation techniques. 282
    (2) In most cases, answer counterarguments after developing your own position. 283

Chapter 21. Speaking Ethics **284**

21a. Be aware of the ethical implications of all human choices and the way these play out in public speaking. **285**

21b. Respect the integrity of your own core values. **286**

21c. Respect the integrity of your audience. **286**

21d. Respect the integrity of ideas. **287**
    (1) Don't plagiarize. 287
    (2) Don't lie. 287
    (3) Don't oversimplify. 289

21e. Understand that ethical decisions often involve weighing complex factors and competing goals. **289**
    (1) Balance the value of using language in a lively and forceful manner against the risk of causing pain and offense. 289

(2) Balance the importance of appealing to your audience at an
emotional level against the risk of abusing emotional appeals.   290
(3) Balance the right to use compelling persuasive appeals against the
obligation to avoid simplistic persuasive techniques.   290

Chapter 22. Guidelines for Special Occasions   294

**22a. On ceremonial occasions, follow the traditional
patterns but adapt them so they are immediate
and personal.**   **294**

(1) Follow these guidelines when presenting an award or honor.   296
(2) Follow these guidelines when delivering a eulogy or
memorial address.   296
(3) Follow these guidelines for a toast.   297
(4) Follow these guidelines when accepting an award or tribute.   297

**22b. When participating in a panel, symposium, forum,
or debate, tailor your individual presentation to the
group format.**   **298**

(1) Be sure of the format of the program, and clarify expectations
about your responsibilities.   298
(2) Prepare as carefully for a group presentation as for a speech.   299
(3) Be aware of your nonverbal communication throughout the
entire group presentation.   299
(4) Follow these guidelines for a public debate.   299

**22c. Prepare carefully when you chair a program or
meeting. Clarify the format, coordinate the
participants, and anticipate contingencies.**   **301**

(1) Plan the agenda carefully.   301
(2) Be sure all participants in the meeting or program understand
the agenda and the roles they are expected to play.   302
(3) Be prepared for all contingencies.   303
(4) Follow these guidelines when moderating a forum, panel,
or debate.   303
(5) Follow these guidelines when acting as emcee of a ceremony
or banquet.   304
(6) Follow these guidelines when introducing a main speaker.   304

**22d. Prepare for a group interview as if it were a
public speech.**   **304**

(1) Analyze your audience.   305
(2) Prepare an opening statement.   305

(3) Answer questions directly and concisely.   306
(4) Maintain effective delivery skills throughout an interview.   306

Part 4. Presentation   **307**

Chapter 23. Modes of Delivery   **311**

23a. For most speaking situations use the extemporaneous mode.   **311**

23b. Avoid impromptu speaking. But learn to cope with the situation if it is thrust on you.   **313**
(1) Keep your composure.   314
(2) Select a theme.   314
(3) Select an organizational framework.   315
(4) Whenever possible, plan your first and last sentences.   315

23c. Speak from a manuscript when precise wording and exact timing are essential to the situation. Maintain oral style and conversational delivery.   **316**
(1) Prepare an easily readable manuscript in the oral style.   317
(2) Be familiar enough with your manuscript to look and sound as though you are speaking extemporaneously.   317

23d. Memorize a short, important speech only on those occasions when holding a manuscript would be out of place.   **319**
(1) Memorize the structure of the speech before memorizing the speech word for word.   319
(2) Read the speech aloud several times and then work on learning it paragraph by paragraph.   320
(3) As you practice, visualize giving the speech.   320
(4) Do not go into a trance when delivering the speech.   320
(5) If you go blank, switch to the extemporaneous mode and recall the structure of the speech rather than groping for the next word.   320

Chapter 24. Practice Sessions   **321**

24a. Optimize your sources of effective feedback.   **321**
(1) Whenever possible, form a support group of other learners or a network of colleagues and friends.   321
(2) Set guidelines for effective feedback and speech criticism.   322

24b. Use three stages of practice sessions to convert your speech from outline to finished product. **323**
   (1) Use early practice sessions to flesh out your outline. 325
   (2) Use one or more middle practice session for receiving feedback. 326
   (3) Use the last few practice sessions for refinements of style and delivery. 328

24c. Prepare speech notes to act as a guide and a safety net. **329**
   (1) Speech notes should consist of key words and phrases and material that is to be cited directly. 329
   (2) Prepare your notecards in a format that aids your delivery. 330

24d. Fit your speech into the time limit. **331**

24e. Save the hours just before the speech for one final run-through and for getting into the proper, relaxed frame of mind. **333**

24f. Avoid these practice pitfalls. **334**
   (1) "Mental" practice rather than oral practice. 334
   (2) Too many critics. 334
   (3) Overpreparing. 335
   (4) Self-consciousness rather than audience-consciousness. 335

Chapter 25. Vocal Delivery **336**

25a. Identify and eliminate distracting characteristics of your vocal delivery. **337**
   (1) Identify problems of voice quality. 337
   (2) Identify problems of articulation. 338
   (3) Identify vocalized pauses and other irrelevant sounds and phrases. 339
   (4) Identify repetitious patterns of inflection. 340
   (5) Eliminate your distracting habits through a systematic self-improvement program, or by seeking professional help. 340

25b. Speak so that you can be heard and understood. **342**
   (1) Speak loud enough to be heard by the entire audience. 342
   (2) Speak at a rate your audience can follow. 343
   (3) Enunciate words distinctly and naturally. 343
   (4) Make special adjustments, if necessary, to compensate for having an accent that your audience may have difficulty understanding. 344

25c. Reinforce meaning and make your speech more interesting through vocal variety.   **345**

(1) Vary your pitch.   346
(2) Vary your rate of speaking.   346
(3) Vary your volume.   347

25d. Use standard, acceptable pronunciation.   **347**

(1) Identify words that you habitually mispronounce.   347
(2) Check the preferred pronunciation of unfamiliar words.   349

Chapter 26. Physical Delivery   **351**

26a. Be conscious of your appearance.   **351**

26b. Eliminate distracting mannerisms.   **352**

26c. Stand or sit with a relaxed but alert posture.   **352**

26d. If you move about during the speech, make the action purposeful and relevant.   **353**

26e. Keep your hands free so you can gesture if it feels natural.   **354**

26f. Maintain eye contact.   **355**

26g. Use facial expression to reflect or forecast mood and tone.   **356**

Chapter 27. Adapting to the Speech Situation   **358**

27a. Adapt to the audience response as you give your speech. Plan alternative strategies for reactions you may receive.   **359**

(1) If your audience seems bored or restless, consider the following.   359
(2) If you are not getting the agreement you expected, consider the following.   359
(3) If your audience is less informed than you expected, consider the following.   360
(4) If your audience is more informed than you expected, consider the following.   360

(5) If your audience is more heterogeneous than you expected,
     consider the following.   360

27b. Take several steps to prevent distractions. If distractions do occur, be familiar with the strategies to deal with them.   361

(1) Check your presentation's setting and equipment to detect
     possible sources of distraction.   361
(2) Fleeting or low-level distractions during your speech are best
     dealt with by not acknowledging them.   362
(3) Sometimes distractions can be turned to your purpose by
     incorporating them into your speech.   362
(4) When it is actually necessary to interrupt the continuity of
     your speech, do so as quickly as possible and then draw
     your listeners back in.   362

27c. Do not hand control of the situation over to the verbal or nonverbal heckler. Respond to such interruptions calmly and firmly.   363

(1) The verbal heckler   363
(2) The nonverbal heckler   364

Chapter 28. Visual Aids   366

28a. Select a visual aid appropriate to the point you wish to illustrate or clarify.   367

(1) The object or a physical reproduction of it   367
(2) Pictorial reproductions   367
(3) Pictorial symbols   367

28b. Prepare clear and manageable visual aids.   370

(1) Prepare visual aids large enough to be seen by the entire
     audience.   370
(2) Keep your visual aids simple and clear.   370
(3) Design visual aids for maximum audience impact.   372

28c. Introduce your visual aids so that they blend smoothly into the speech.   373

(1) Practice with your visual aids.   373
(2) Maintain eye contact.   373
(3) Keep talking.   374
(4) Do not let your visual aids become a distraction.   374

28d. Understand the benefits, constraints, and perils of using presentation software. **374**

(1) Keep your text slides simple. 375
(2) Maintain consistency. 375
(3) Be judicious in your use of clip art. 375
(4) Do not become secondary to your slides. 376

Chapter 29. Answering Questions 377

29a. Come prepared for a question-and-answer period. **378**

29b. Invite and answer audience questions in a straightforward manner. **378**

29c. Do not allow self-indulgent questioners to distort the function of the question-and-answer period. **379**

(1) The person who wants to give a speech 380
(2) The person who wants to have an extended dialogue 380
(3) The person who wants to pick a fight 380

Appendix 382
Index 413

Part 1

Preparation

---

1 Understanding Speaking
2 Planning
3 Topic Selection and Analysis
4 Audience Analysis
5 Research
6 Overcoming Fear of Speaking

Introduction

Some speakers give little attention to the preliminary stages of preparing for a speech, subscribing to the misconception that "I know how to talk, so I must know how to give a speech"—thinking the task should be easy, that sitting down a few minutes ahead of time to gather thoughts will be enough. Others neglect the preliminary stages because they are fully aware of the difficulties they face and are impatient to get started—even before they know where they are going.

If you focus on the final *product*, a speech, rather than on the *process*, creativity, you experience an urgency to produce something. When you are asked (or told) to give a speech, your immediate impulse may be to grab the first topic that enters your mind and start to practice expressing your ideas on the subject. After "sitting down" in this fashion, you may discover gaps in your knowledge that require a trip to the library. Once at the library, you can find it difficult to decide in which direction to press your research, especially if you are not sure of the audience you will be addressing. Later, back "sitting down," you find that much of the information you have collected is not relevant to the purpose of your speech as it has evolved during this time.

At this point you may stop to wonder if the experienced speakers you have heard ever go through such wheel spinning. After all, they make speaking in public seem so effortless that surely their preparation also must be free of perspiration. Let us assure you that their performance, like that of expert athletes and musicians, reflects a mastery of skills and techniques built on careful planning and hard work. These experienced speakers save time and avoid duplicated and wasted effort by organizing their preparation. They understand that the creative process progresses unevenly and that if they persist through all its steps a creditable product will result.

Chapters **1–6** address the preliminaries that should precede the actual composition of your speech. Examine your approach. *Understanding speaking* and the communicative resources you have at hand are the foundation on which you will build. Allot enough time for *planning.* The security of a sound master plan promotes effectiveness and increases your confidence as a speaker. It is obvious that you cannot start to prepare a speech before you know what you are going to be talking about. It is less obvious that you also need to know *why* you are going to speak. When you *select and analyze your topic,* the later steps of preparation will be easier because your topic will be more focused and your goals more concrete. Drafting a clear thesis statement and teasing out the questions implicit in that statement help direct your research and provide cues for organizing your information. When you envision the preparatory research for your speech, the tendency is to dwell on the amassing of data, examples, and arguments that deal with the topic itself. An important but frequently overlooked type of research is *audience analysis.* Through direct and indirect methods you can obtain information about their characteristics and attitudes that will help you plan your speech. Knowing *research* techniques and sources gives you access to a wide information base. Thorough preparation is just one of the techniques to use in *overcoming fear of speaking.*

Chapter 1

Understanding Speaking

Understand that public speaking is the act of creating meaning with your listeners, and approach your role as a speaker by consciously combining communicative resources you already have at hand.

1a. Understand what it means to be a speaker.

For many people, the first mental image that forms when they hear the words *public speaking* contains a lectern, a podium, and an auditorium—the components of a classic, big-S Speech. This image can be frightening for some, invigorating for others. It is also very narrow. In this handbook, we deal with a wider picture of what speaking means and of when a person becomes a speaker. This picture includes the big-S Speech, and we hope that users of this book will become more skilled in that context, but it includes more. You are a speaker when you stand behind the lectern at the awards banquet or when you approach the floor microphone at a planning commission meeting or when you sit at a table with three other members of your work group and present your proposal for tackling a particular problem. You are a speaker in class, you are a speaker at work, you are a speaker at times among friends and family. And when you are a speaker in one of these settings, you are a different speaker from the speaker you'd be at another.

   Having said this, having broadened the context, we must also ensure that we do not become too broad. Not all oral communication in a group is public speaking. Perhaps the distinguishing characteristic of public speaking is that it is an event when a contract is reached among a group of people where one person, the speaker, is given consent to direct the event.

Many people tend to think that a gulf separates speakers from listeners, with meaning being created by the former and transmitted to the latter. This can promote the view of an adversarial relationship between speakers and listeners: Audiences are people who judge you or receive your thoughts or can be manipulated by you. Actually, communication theorists stress that meaning is socially constructed in a transaction that occurs between speakers and listeners.

Looking at speaking this way does not relieve the speaker of certain basic responsibilities. This does not mean that every speaking situation is an improvisation. To uphold your end of the contract you are obliged to invest energy into creating an effective and efficient event. You should understand that as the speaker you are an originator and inventor—that you bring something that is uniquely you to the transaction and that this is not an option but a condition for effective speaking.

1b. Ground your approach to effective public speaking in a meaning-centered view of communication.

Of course, public speaking is a subset of the broader human activity called *communication*. Even in a practical handbook, it is worth taking a minute to think about your own assumptions about the nature of communication. Working from a view that is too narrow or mechanical will hinder your effectiveness as a public speaker.

(1) Do not confine your view of communication to information transmission and reception.

For decades after the emergence of the Information Age, *communication* was defined in terms of the clear transmission of information from a sender to a receiver. For some kinds of speaking and some parts of speech preparation, these notions are very useful (see **19**). As a general approach, though, comparing speaking to making a phone call or delivering a package has severe limitations. These metaphors tend to direct your thinking toward discrete, sender-controlled, steps. "Giving a speech" becomes a matter of selecting ideas, packaging them, shipping them efficiently, and verifying their receipt. For most purposes, speakers are better served by embracing a more collaborative and complex model of communication.

(2) Think about communication as the joint creation of meaning.

The metaphor of collaborative creation calls up a very different set of images. Think about a group of filmmakers at work, or a software design team, or two textbook authors, for that matter. At any given time, one may be putting forth ideas while the others listen and react. The end product is a composite that emerges from the interaction; it did not exist in any one person's mind at the outset. For us, the distinction between these two approaches to communication is not a trivial one. The shift in emphasis from messages (speaker controlled) to meanings (jointly created) has some important implications.

Meaning is social.

This implies that no one individual, either sender or receiver, can control "the true meaning" of a statement. A speaker who has violated a social norm cannot get off the hook by saying, "I did not intend that to be offensive, so it wasn't." Neither, though, can a single receiver unilaterally control what a statement or action really means. A thin-skinned listener is not justified in overreacting to a rather innocent comment by declaring, "I just felt offended, so that statement was offensive." Probably most of us have been involved in these fruitless and frustrating arguments in which one person tried to insist on his or her meaning of a communication event.

Meaning is contextual.

Similarly, few disputes about meaning are settled by pulling out a dictionary. This implies that words or messages alone cannot tell us "the true meaning" of the communication. *Con-text* is that which surrounds a text. Words take their meanings not just from a dictionary but from all that surrounds them as they were uttered. A message can be repeated identically, but its meaning will never be identical if the context has changed. Thinking about meaning this way takes into account when and where a statement was made, who was present, what happened before as well as the tone of voice and expression that accompanied the utterance.

Meaning is contingent.

This implies that no sentence or act frozen in time has acquired its "true meaning." What something means has to be interpreted within a chain of events. A speech may begin with a story that sounds authentic and is later exposed as an example of what the speaker opposes. Meaning becomes clear as it unfolds in the interplay between speakers and listeners. Often we do not know what something meant until we reflect back on an entire encounter.

Ultimately, meaning is negotiated by discourse communities.

In cases where the "true meaning" of a message is contested, appeals to the words themselves, or to the speaker's intentions, or to the listeners' response have all been shown to be inadequate. Therefore, meanings are worked out over time by larger groups who share some common agreements and who come to build others. What counts as sexual harassment in the workplace, for instance, is not settled by a single court case or congressional hearing. The meaning of the term is hashed out in speeches, letters to the editor, and countless conversations in offices. Groups whose meanings included every friendly comment found their definition rejected. So did those whose meanings excluded everything except direct physical assault. Gradually, a range of meanings of the term within contemporary U.S. culture comes into general understanding. Because these meanings are social, contextual, and contingent, they will continue to change.

1c. Approach public speaking by drawing on three familiar communicative resources.

Public speakers who approach communication as creating meaning with their audiences are off to a good start. Now think of all the times you have successfully created meaning with different groups of people, in different contexts, and on different topics. When you enter into the contract that designates you as a "speaker" it turns out that you are not required to master a brand-new skill. Rather, your challenge is to draw together and adapt several communication skills that *you already have* in your repertoire: conversation, writing, and performance.

Take stock of the communicative resources already at your disposal, available for you to call into use as a speaker (see Figure 1–1).

FIGURE 1–1   Three Communicative Resources

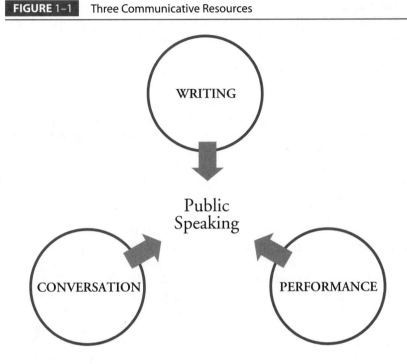

(1) Draw on your conversation skills.

In everyday conversations you do certain things that make you effective. Probably you are relaxed and spontaneous, responsive to the situation and naturally expressive of your changing feelings. Your attention is centered on the person or people to whom you are speaking and the general ideas you want to get across. You do not worry about the exact words to say because the event is highly interactive, with meaning clarified in the give-and-take.

Conversation is a form of risk taking—you are not sure of the outcome at any point. Most of the time this uncertainty does not prevent you from conversing, even if you know that disagreement will be part of it. A lot of apprehension about public speaking can be dissipated if you can carry this aspect of the conversational model into the speaking event.

One of the highest compliments that can be paid to a speaker is to call her or him "conversational." These, then, are the skills drawn from conversation that are useful to a public speaker: to speak in a comfortable and confident manner, to listen and take in the perspective of others, to be open to adapting constantly as you receive feedback.

(2) Draw on your writing skills.

The written word enables us to distance ourselves from our ideas and to freeze them on paper. This distancing allows us to craft and tinker, experiment with alternative forms and play them out in our imagination. This takes much longer than a conversational exploration of ideas, where "you know what I mean" to a close friend can substitute for quite a bit of groundwork.

In writing, you pay close attention to word choice and organization to produce a carefully crafted message. Vocabulary is more precise than in conversation. You have the time to enjoy word play, to explore nuance, and to find elegant phrasing that makes the message unforgettable.

One benefit of writing is that it gives you the opportunity to put enough distance between you and your ideas to see them objectively, test them for logical coherence, see how well they fit together. In writing you can weave in multiple voices of authorities along with your own.

From writing, then, a speaker draws on the attention to language, the order of ideas, the internal unity of the speech. Good writing means not settling for the first thing set down, but rather spending time polishing for the most economical and impactful way of getting a message across.

(3) Draw on your performance skills.

Most people would say they are not performers, since they have not starred in a Broadway show or a rock concert or even community theater or the company talent show. This is a narrow definition of *performance*. Actually, we are all performers. In one sense, performance occurs whenever we do something in contrast to just thinking about it. So you might plan a phone call to a friend and then perform it. When you play volleyball or tell a story to your family you are performing. In this handbook, when we talk about your performance skills we mean the ways you have learned to use your physical presence—tone of voice, gestures, movement—to create a focal point for a group.

To many, performance connotes drama and virtuosity: the electric "presence" of a violin virtuoso, the flash of a track star, or the understated passion of an actor in a revelatory scene. In context, and in appropriate forms, drama and virtuosity are not bad things for a speaker to manifest. Communication can be more complete if you do what you are doing well, with a sense of the emotional needs of your listeners.

So strong has been the emphasis on conversation that *performance* has become a dirty word among speech teachers. That is because for some time performance was seen as an end in itself rather than as an essential human activity. To downplay the performative aspects of public speech is to deny the essential power that makes a speech more than conversation, more than an outline or transcript. *Performance* does not refer to display or phoniness but to an enactment, one that creates an event between speaker and listeners that transcends the message or exchange of information. This transcendence is what makes people say, "you had to be there."

From performance, skills useful to the speaker are the ability to pay attention to the entire effect, the setting and timing, and the capacity to turn a collection of individuals into a cohesive group. Performers know how to make use of all the senses. They tie together visual effects, lighting, sound, music, humor, and drama. They have superb sense of timing and understand how to direct emotional buildup and choose the right moment for climax. Speakers can make use of these skills by learning to visualize the impact they want to have and carefully planning details that contribute to that overall impact.

(4) Combine some features of these three communicative resources for an effective public speech.

Implied in the descriptions of the positive influences of these three skills is the proposition that public speaking would not be successful if it omitted the conversational, the compositional, or the performative qualities. A speaker needs the adaptation of conversation, the preparation of writing, and the engagement of performance to deserve the undivided attention of an audience. This is not to say that each merits equal emphasis in all situations for each speaker. Understanding the positive qualities described above, you need to come up with a unique blend for each time and place. You also need to understand the negative side: **1c(5)** describes some of the perils of leaning too heavily on any one resource.

How you combine these resources, or whether you are aware of them at all, depends on your level of consciousness of your competence (see **1e**), or perhaps on the kinds of feedback you receive in your practice sessions (see **24**). Starting with the assumption that, either through self-awareness or feedback, you are mindful of how you currently call on the communicative resources, let's look at some things to consider as you decide how to combine these elements of conversing, writing, and performing to create an effective public speech.

Consider the demands of the situation and the expectations of the audience.

The type of speech and the situation determine how you blend the skills of communication in various speeches. Often a more formal occasion and a larger audience would demand that a speaker give some of the writer's attention to word choice and unity of a speech. Being invited to moderate a discussion would call on the listening skills that come with conversation. A festive occasion may cry out for a larger-than-life demonstration.

Chapter **4**, Audience Analysis, gives some suggestions on how to learn more about the people to whom you will speak. Refer to Chapters **22** and **27** for guidelines about occasions and situations.

Consider your own personality and distinctive speaking style.

Even on the same occasion and topic, there will be differences among speakers. It is not automatically bad to rely on one resource over another if it is well matched to who you are and how you work best. If you are one of those speakers who is folksy and conversational and puts an audience at ease, you will draw most heavily on those skills.

If you are a great storyteller or have a dramatic flair, you should use that resource to the extent that it is appropriate. If you know that you have trouble being spontaneous, let alone dramatic, in front of a group, you work extra hard on developing the content of your speech so that your words and your message may bond you to your listeners.

(5) Avoid relying exclusively or excessively on any one of these resources.

A speaker needs to draw some behaviors out of all three of these domains. Though ratios may vary, it is just as bad to overuse conversation, writing, or performance orientations as to neglect them. Too much reliance on conversation leads to:

- uneconomical use of time and language
- spontaneous blunders

- failure to control delivery habits that might be distracting
- disorganization, doubling back to repeat points already made
- going off on tangents, a lack of focus

Too much reliance on writing leads to:

- unnatural use of language, unnatural inflection: a "canned" sound
- lack of flexibility, an inability to adapt to an audience on the spot, with many missed opportunities for specific adaptation
- a one-way transmission of a message
- writing to a general audience
- an almost inevitable tendency to read or memorize the text

Too much reliance on performance leads to:

- an opening for stage fright
- an egocentric, melodramatic exhibition that minimizes the transaction between speaker and listeners
- a credibility problem, with the audience doubting the sincerity of expressed emotions, and hence also doubting the accuracy of facts presented
- the message getting lost in a stagy, overly planned speaking event
- the contrast to natural conversation creating embarrassment for you and the audience

1d. Beware of common misconceptions about public speaking that may interfere with efficient mastery of the skill.

There are many approaches to teaching public speaking and much folk wisdom about how effective speakers get that way. Mastery of speaking will come more quickly if you can avoid being affected by misinformation and oversimplified truisms.

Misconception 1: Good speakers are born, not made.

It does seem as though some people are born speakers. In fact, they are people who have a number of component speech skills already in their repertoire or people who learn speech-related skills very quickly. Regardless of appearances, no one is born an effective speaker any more than one is born a good tennis player or a violinist. Inborn predispositions and early learning mean that some will learn faster and go further. However, anyone who has moderate coordination, adequate motivation, and sound instruction can learn to play a game of tennis or a simple tune on the violin. Virtually anyone can learn to give a very decent, clear, effective public speech.

Misconception 2: Good speaking should be easy right away.

When we watch world-class figure skaters, we are fascinated by the apparent ease with which they perform what we know are extremely difficult moves. However easy they make it look, we do not think that on our first time out on the ice we can immediately perform triple axels. We can understand that years of training, dedication, and discipline have gone into making it seem so effortless. Not everyone figure skates. Everyone communicates. We all have our share of good ideas and transmit them more or less successfully in our everyday encounters. This success may lead us to underestimate the difficulty in making the transition to more formal and public modes of expression. Many speakers think, "I know how to talk, so I must know how to give a speech." When this fallacy is recognized after a speech that fails badly, they become very discouraged. In addition, the discouragement may be compounded by Misconception 3.

Misconception 3: Speaking will always be as difficult as it is when you are first learning it.

Preparing an oral message on a substantial topic for a live audience *is* demanding. When at first you must spend hours preparing for a short presentation, there is a real temptation to say, "Who needs it? I can't invest this much time and effort every time I have to talk before a group." Remind yourself that skills requiring effort and attention while being learned become much simpler, almost automatic, once you reach a certain level of mastery. Remember how hard tying a shoelace was at first? Or driving? Or dribbling a basketball? Now that you have mastered one of these skills, you just think of the goal you want to achieve; the individual operations necessary to reaching the goal happen on their own unless an unforeseen situation forces you to pay conscious attention. When you get discouraged with a speech outline that just will not fit together or phrasing that keeps coming out wrong, remember: It *will* get easier.

Misconception 4: There are simple formulas for effective speaking.

Communicating with an audience is an incredibly complex and sophisticated act. Every public speaking event is unique. The speaker has a distinctive style and personality; the audience has idiosyncratic needs and preferences; situations differ from case to case. How these three factors interact creates the meaning in any speaking event. No one can give you an all-purpose recipe for preparing or delivering a speech. With this in mind, be wary of books at the supermarket checkout stand or of one-day workshops that promise instant speaking success. The quickest way to do something is not automatically the best way. When you want to learn a skill well enough for it to become habitual, it is obviously worth taking the time to develop good habits. To return to the example of driving, you were fortunate if you were taught solid fundamental techniques. In the area of public speaking, we have some basis for agreeing on the fundamentals. Certain basic principles date back two thousand years to Aristotle's *Rhetoric* and continue to be refined through social science research.

We have confidence in these principles. The advice in this handbook is not based on what is easiest or fastest, but rather on what has proven to be the soundest. It is more difficult to do a thorough audience analysis than to prepare a speech for all occasions. It takes longer to develop a full-sentence outline than to jot down points in the order they occur to you. It is harder to sound conversational and look poised standing and speaking from notes than it is to read while leaning on a table. But, having learned these sound techniques, you will be more flexible and effective than if you had nothing but the all-purpose recipe.

Although the chapters of this handbook are written as prescriptions, you will not find simple *do*s and *don't*s to apply automatically to every situation. The fundamentals of speaking are stated simply, but the application and combination of these principles depend on your good judgment about each speaking situation.

1e. Understand the role of consciousness in skill learning.

We learn complex skills differently than we learn simple facts. A skill like public speaking involves the combination of a number of intellectual and physical operations. Most of these operations are already in your repertoire. You know how to breathe, how to raise and lower your voice, how to move your hands, how to define a new term, how to group ideas into categories. What you may not know is how to put all of these skills together to make an effective public speech.

The learning of skills is said to progress through four stages:

1. **Unconscious incompetence.** In this stage a person is not aware that he or she is making errors in some area, and may even be unaware that there is a skill to be learned.
2. **Conscious incompetence.** A person in this stage has made the realization that she or he is doing something ineptly and that there is room for improvement. In many cases this awareness creates anxiety, which actually increases incompetence.
3. **Conscious competence.** In this stage a person has taken a skill in which she or he feels incompetent, has improved, and then devotes a portion of consciousness to performing it competently. The absence of such vigilance is likely to mean a regression to more comfortable but less competent patterns. However, if a person perseveres, the awkwardness of the new behavior diminishes and the need for self-monitoring lessens.
4. **Unconscious competence.** Now a person has integrated the learned skills well enough that she or he need not devote conscious attention to maintaining competence—it comes naturally. The skill becomes relatively effortless, and maybe even fun.

    At this level as a speaker you can do more than just talk; you have the freedom to pay attention to audience response and make spontaneous adjustments to enhance the quality of the communication.

A great deal of your communication behavior is unconscious. You do not think about how you move your lips to make sounds or why you use one kind of vocabulary with your best friend and another with your boss. These may be areas of unconscious competence. At the same time, you may not be aware that you mispronounce "escape," twirl your hair when you are nervous, and often commit the fallacy of hasty generalization. These are examples of unconscious incompetence.

When do your communication behaviors receive your conscious attention? Usually when you are learning new skills or when you run into difficulties in communicating. As soon as a skill is mastered or a communication problem is solved, your behavior becomes unconscious again. This is a very efficient system. You are constantly freeing yourself to direct your conscious attention to something more challenging.

Being aware of this process is important, we think, because it makes it possible for you to be conscious of your consciousness. As a developing speaker you can set priorities for learning and decide where to focus your attention. Several of the misconceptions listed in **1e** can be understood in terms of this approach to skill development. The person who thinks speaking should be effortless usually wants to jump straight to Stage 4, unconscious competence, without going through the difficult process of discovering weaknesses and practicing new ways of communicating. The person who thinks speaking is impossibly hard does not trust that Stage 3, conscious competence, will eventually lead to Stage 4. It is uncomfortable to become conscious of what is usually an unconscious act. Things may seem even to get worse before they get better. But if increased competence is the goal, the process is necessary and it does pay off. Before you know it, the new, formerly awkward, behaviors are as habitual as the old ones . . . but they work better for you.

An imbalance in drawing on the skills of conversation, writing, and performance can result in an inappropriate focusing of consciousness. Although it is beneficial to highlight one of the skill areas over the others at various stages while creating the speech (see Chapter 2), if you rely on one skill area disproportionately you place impediments in the way of becoming competent in speaking.

The person relying too heavily on the performance model is being too conscious of the physical and vocal delivery of ideas rather than being conscious of the ideas themselves. The speaker holding this view who sees herself as consciously incompetent can become paralyzed by self-consciousness and anxiety. At the other extreme is the speaker who is overly conscious of what he sees as competence in delivering a speech. He is so enamored with his own gestures and voice that the result is an affected and often showy style. The speaker's attention is on the presentation of self rather than on the presentation of ideas.

Those who overly rely on writing skills misdirect their awareness in the opposite direction. They think too much about what they are saying and very little about how they are saying it. These are the speakers who can go on talking to the formulas on the blackboard while the audience snoozes or who totally lose coherence when someone asks a question that pulls them off their intricately constructed train of thought.

The speaker who thinks little of writing and performance skills while concentrating on conversation can end up being very personable in a speaking event that covers nothing of substance in an unremarkable way. If a speaker, however, has been able to use writing and performing skills to develop the speech, the conversation skill can and should come to the fore during the speech itself. To see a speech first and foremost as inter-personal communication should keep you from being disproportionately conscious of either your manner of speaking or the exact language of your message. In day-to-day interaction you are usually conscious of very basic things: your reason or goal for speaking, the essential message that you want to get across, your relationship with the other communicator, the response you are receiving. These are the same things you should be aware of when you speak in public.

Exercise 1. Which misconceptions do you think are most widespread? Which do you personally tend to hold? Are there other misconceptions about public speaking of which you are aware?

Exercise 2. Identify a skill that you have mastered and describe how you progressed through the four stages of skill learning.

Exercise 3. Can you think of an example in any area of your life where you improved your effectiveness not so much by increasing your skill as by taking control of your consciousness and restructuring where you did and did not pay attention?

Exercise 4. What are some of your areas of conscious competence as a public speaker? Conscious incompetence? Unconscious competence? Can you speculate about some areas of unconscious incompetence or remember examples from the past?

Exercise 5. Assess the resources you have to draw upon as a public speaker by thinking about your strengths and weaknesses as (1) a conversationalist, (2) a writer, (3) a performer. Which of these areas promises to be the most transferable to your public speaking success? Which of these areas will be difficult for you to transfer? Which resource might you tend to draw too much from as a speaker?

Chapter 2

Planning

Have a schedule to structure the preparation of your speech. Allow time to progress through the phases of creativity.

Preparing a substantial public speech is not a mechanical act like preparing the outside of your house for a new coat of paint. It is a creative act where you bring into being something that never existed before and that no one but you would have designed in exactly this form. Taken this way, speech preparation is much more like painting a picture or writing a short story. A perspective that involves creativity has implications for how you choose to manage your time.

2a. To design a unique message, allow time for the four phases of creativity.

It has been proposed that there are four phases to the creative process: preparation, incubation, illumination, and refinement.[1] For speakers the preparation phase includes the gathering of materials, the analysis of the

---

[1]Based on Catherine Patrick, *What Is Creative Thinking?* (New York: Philosophical Library, 1955): 1–48.

topic and audience, and the first stabs at putting the parts together. Incubation is a phase marked by frustration, even despair, when the problems seem insoluble and the speech is set aside. During this phase, your unconscious mind and your peripheral awareness work on the problems. Suddenly, in a moment of illumination, the pieces fit together—or, there may be a dawning awareness that grows in intensity. Illumination may occur while you are working on the project, but it is just as likely to occur when you are driving down the freeway, taking a shower, or even sleeping. Exhilaration and relief accompany this phase. You work eagerly and fluidly. In a few hours it is possible to accomplish more than you have in several days. Then the time comes for refinement. After the creative spurt, there follows a comparatively long period of checking details, fine tuning, and polishing. Like the preparation phase, this phase is largely cognitive and requires concentration and discipline. Many creative products have never been shared with the world because the creator gave up during the refinement phase. Other fine ideas have failed to be appreciated because the speaker presented them directly after the illumination phase, without spending the needed time on refinement. This delineation of the four-phase creative process is provided to stress the importance of allocating time for *each* phase.

2b. Make a realistic timetable for your speech preparation.

At one university, a group of public speaking instructors informally survey their students at the end of each term, asking what advice they would pass on to the new students coming into the class the next term. Overwhelmingly, the surveyed students' response was, "Start early." They all regretted underestimating the time necessary to prepare a speech that reflected what they knew they could do. To know what is "early" enough for you, you need to spend the time to make a realistic timetable.

When professionals plan major projects—whether it is organizing a sales convention, designing a recycling campaign, or tooling up to manufacture a new product—they use a number of structured time-management techniques. While there is no need to get into the intricacies of PERT systems or Gantt charts, there are a few valuable principles that the public speaker can borrow.

(1) List the tasks you will need to complete to prepare the speech, and estimate the time needed for each.

Be sure that you include intellectual tasks such as analyzing your topic and not just physical tasks like going to the library or making your visual aid. For each task jot down the most optimistic and least optimistic estimate of the time. Mentally run through some of the bleaker scenarios. What if all the periodicals you need are checked out of the library the first time you go? What if your phone rings a dozen times the afternoon you had set aside for working on the outline? Remember that certain parts of the creative process cannot be rushed. When setting a timetable for preparing your speech, always provide extra time to allow for emergencies. Speech research and rehearsal can go on when you have a headache or when you are in an emotional funk, but the creative aspects of speech organization require physical and psychological alertness.

Invest time right at the beginning to gather whatever information you need on schedules and availability of resources so that you can come up with an honest estimate of the time you will need for each task.

(2) Determine which tasks depend on the prior completion of other tasks.

This is what professional project managers call *determining the critical path*. It is not enough to schedule three hours to practice your speech and call that "planning." Those three hours must occur after the speech outline is completed. The outline cannot be completed until you have articulated your speech purpose and goals, and so on. When you lay out the entire project in this linear fashion and add up the time estimates for each task, you will see if it is possible to reach your goal. Often you realize that the only way to succeed is to move the starting date sooner (usually to today!). Perhaps your speech is three weeks away and you had planned to work on it the week before. The bulk of your work can probably be done then, but you find that certain preliminary steps must be taken *now*. Or, to take this further, what if your speech is due in three weeks and the critical path adds up to five weeks? If your plans are unrealistic, it is better to discover that now than two days before the speech. In rare cases, the speech can be rescheduled for a later time, but more frequently you must scale down your plans. Perhaps you will have to conduct two or three telephone interviews instead of eight personal ones. Perhaps you will have to go ahead with the best statistics you can find locally and not wait for the materials that are being mailed from Washington. Perhaps you will have to substitute handdrawn transparencies for the professional slides that take several days to process. Most important is for you to decide at the outset on a schedule you can meet. Otherwise you will end up skipping the final and crucial steps of practice and refinement altogether.

(3) Set intermediate deadlines for the major phases of preparation and practice.

In Figure 2-1 speech planning and practice is divided into four phases: initial decisions and analysis, research, developing speech materials, and practice. For each phase the central tasks are contained in a box with a solid border. The related but less time-bound tasks are surrounded by a broken border. Generally, time flows downward and to the right in this table. The figure shows the transitions between phases where deadlines fall naturally. That is, the central tasks of one phase cannot really be started until the central tasks of the next-earlier phase are completed. At some point you must settle on the preliminary decisions of a narrowed, focused topic, purpose, and thesis, and get on into your serious research. At some point you must stop gathering material and put the speech together. If you do not have a speech outline soon enough, you cannot begin the first phase of practice. There is no point in timing your feedback practice sessions so late that you will not be able to take advantage of the feedback.

However, there are times when you must briefly retrace your steps. For instance, this would happen when new evidence presents itself, or when feedback sessions show that more visual aids are needed. Such movement should be minimal, and under almost no circumstances should you be returning to tasks "way back." We feel very strongly that you should not be making any substantive changes to the speech at the last minute. During the last several practice sessions you should have complete mastery of the organization and basic content so your consciousness can center on refinement of phrasing, delivery, timing, and desired audience response.

FIGURE 2-1 Planning and Practice

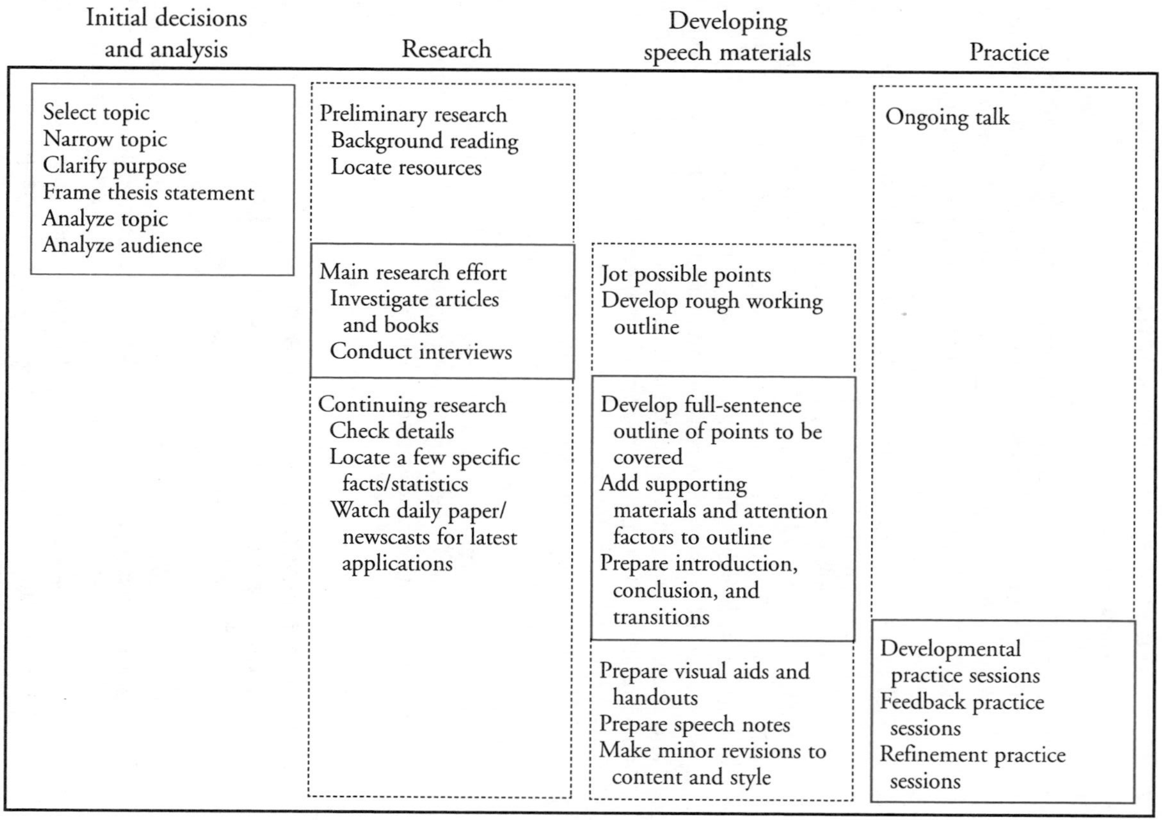

Initial decisions and analysis	Research	Developing speech materials	Practice
			Ongoing talk
Select topic	Preliminary research	Jot possible points	Developmental practice sessions
Narrow topic	Background reading	Develop rough working outline	Feedback practice sessions
Clarify purpose	Locate resources		Refinement practice sessions
Frame thesis statement		Develop full-sentence outline of points to be covered	
Analyze topic	Main research effort	Add supporting materials and attention factors to outline	
Analyze audience	Investigate articles and books	Prepare introduction, conclusion, and transitions	
	Conduct interviews		
	Continuing research	Prepare visual aids and handouts	
	Check details	Prepare speech notes	
	Locate a few specific facts/statistics	Make minor revisions to content and style	
	Watch daily paper/newscasts for latest applications		

21

2c. Make your speech preparation an oral and collaborative process.

Since a speech is delivered orally, it should be composed orally. Since the meaning of a speech is dependent on the interaction of the speaker and the listeners, it should be created collaboratively. Keep the "speech as conversation" theme foremost even during those parts of preparation that require you to draw on your skills as a writer or performer.

Although you cannot practice "the speech" until your basic outline exists, there is a form of oral preparation that begins with your first idea. This is the ongoing talk suggested by the large, dotted section in the "practice" column of Figure 2-1. Talk to yourself about your topic. Talk to other people. Try out your ideas and words, seeing if they make sense. You are not, however, practicing your speech in front of other people. Work your ideas into conversations over lunch and chats with colleagues and friends. You do not need a reaction to every idea from each individual you talk to. After talking to a number of people, you will find that you have begun to word the speech.

No person speaks in a single voice. Even when you sit alone at your desk preparing your speech, the ideas and intonations of your collaborators influence you. This is natural and should be used to your advantage.

If you are fortunate, you may be able to add continuity to this oral and collaborative process by structuring it to embrace a more formal method for feedback and support. See **24**.

2d. To present a speech that achieves the flavor of enhanced conversation, focus on different resources at different phases of preparation.

The first chapter of this handbook established that most speakers already have at their disposal substantial resources as conversationalists, writers, and performers. During the planning and practice stages of a speech these are deployed in different ratios at different times to achieve a successful final presentation. Each of the resources is always present, or at least should be, throughout the process, but emphasis and attention shift according to the phase of the process. Figure 2-1 illustrates these changing priorities. Generally, during the preparation phase writing skills come to the forefront. *This does not mean that you write out your speech!* This means rather that your conscious competence is directed toward issues of selecting points, arranging them, choosing your support, and thinking of apt illustrations. You give attention to transitions between sections and begin to refine the language of the speech.

Once "the speech" exists in some form, you move into a practice phase, and the importance of performative elements increases. Through oral practice you can experiment with vocal and physical dynamics to emphasize certain points and to create certain effects. You will also introduce visual aids, props, movements to begin to see how the entire presentation will come together to fully engage your audience.

If these resources are fully explored during preparation and practice, the writer and performer will recede during the actual speech and the conversationalist will come forth. We use the term *enhanced conversation* to describe the general tone that is effective for almost all speech situations. You will seem conversational and natural, and your conscious attention will be centered on the give-and-take with the audience. Because of the time spent drawing on the writer's resources during preparation and on the performer's resources during practice, however, the conversation will be greatly enhanced over what would likely occur spontaneously. Your thought is more focused, your language is more graceful, your voice is more expressive, and your physical energy is more directed than in everyday talk—but naturally so. That is because the enhancements were internalized during the conscious-competence work of preparation and practice and are revealed as unconscious competence during presentation. The nature of these changes is detailed in various chapters of the handbook (**15a, 23, 25, 26**).

2e. Avoid these planning pitfalls.

The errors that speakers make in their planning are fairly predictable; they reflect common human tendencies, such as procrastination. Being alert to the pitfalls listed next will go a long way toward preventing you from accidentally sabotaging your efforts. Your topic, whatever it is, deserves the best development, and your audience deserves the fruits of that development.

(1) No time for incubation

Remember that the creative process cannot be forced. Be sure to schedule your preparation to give yourself time for reflection before settling down to the job of composing your speech. The best ideas come to you when you live with your topic for a while and let your unconscious and conscious minds interact.

(2) No margin for error

If you overrate your efficiency, you may time your preparation so close that even minor interruptions endanger the success of your presentation. And if a major catastrophe occurs you may not be able to fulfill your commitments at all. Put together a schedule that gives you some breathing room.

(3) "Writer's" block

Although we stress the ways that speech preparation differs from writing, this pitfall is much like the paralysis that many writers face. As authors we know all about the tendency to do a little more research, a little more thinking about it, a little more desk straightening, finally a little more floor scrubbing if that is what it takes to avoid that awful moment of facing a blank sheet of paper. For your speech to be a success you must stop getting ready to create, and begin to create—well before the final deadline.

(4) "Speaker's" block

Do not put off working orally until the last moment. Unless you are one of the world's greatest speakers, the first time you give any particular speech aloud will not showcase its strengths. Make sure this is not in front of an audience, by starting talking early in the process.

Chapter 3

Topic Selection and Analysis

Select an interesting and manageable topic and determine what response you hope to evoke with that topic. To provide an even sharper focus for your preparation, distill your entire message into a concise thesis statement.

Do not settle on the first topic that occurs to you. Consider a number of different topics and examine their various facets. When you have chosen a promising one, narrow it down and crystallize your reasons for speaking about that subject.

3a. Select a speech topic.

As a speaker you will find that you have varying degrees of freedom in topic choice, according to the situation. At one pole there is the office manager who is told to give an oral report on the effectiveness of the current secretarial assignment system. At the other pole is the respected speaker who is given carte blanche to speak on a topic "you feel is important," or the speech student who is told, "Friday morning you will speak third and persuade us to do something, anything."

Most speaking situations fall between these extremes. You may be asked to welcome delegates to a conference or to speak to the Rotary Club about the economy. In these cases it is still up to you to select a theme for your talk. Even when the general topic is set, you will need to home in on an approach that will fit you, the audience, and the situation.

(1) Draw the topic from your own experience, expertise, and interests.

You come to a speech situation with a body of knowledge already. Perhaps it is because of this that you have been asked to speak: "Could you speak to us about your experiences in the Peace Corps [stock market, Blue Angels]?" Other times your background is the springboard for discovering a topic or a slant on a topic that can be developed into a compelling and substantial speech. There are a number of questions you should ask yourself to help you do this.

In answering the questions that follow, do not stop to evaluate every answer as you write it down. You want to generate a list of possible topics by brainstorming. In this technique you do not let your internal censor dismiss any idea as not being good enough for a speech topic. The principle behind brainstorming is that any unworkable idea may trigger a good one, and a group of mediocre ideas may combine to make a great one; so you should not judge any one idea until you have amassed a list of many. Answer these questions in as many different ways as you can think of, even if some seem silly. Later, you will select your best topic in terms of audience and occasion.

What unusual experiences have you had?
Consider places you have traveled, jobs you have held, events in which you have become enmeshed. Perhaps you have ridden in a hot air balloon or held a subcabinet post or were a hostage in a bank robbery. Obviously, these are stories worth telling in the right context. However, do not overlook aspects of your experience that you take for granted but that might be interesting to others. If you are one of seven children or have always been self-employed or grew up speaking one language at home and another at school, you can increase your audience's understanding of events unfamiliar to them by sharing your experiences with them.

What special knowledge or expertise do you have?
Each of us has developed mastery in certain areas. How do you make your living? If your knowledge of the real estate field has provided you with a good income, you can be certain that there will be an audience eager to hear about your techniques. Yet, a job need not be high paying or prestigious to generate speech topics. People like to know how things work. People are often quite interested in hearing about procedures, even

ones that are considered mundane by the persons performing them. Jokes aside, how is your baggage routed from one airport to another? What goes on backstage at a concert? Or, instead of talking about the mechanics of your work, you can build a speech around the people you meet in that context. If you enjoy observing people and have a flair for describing their behavior, you could become an informal anthropologist and social psychologist. You can give special insights into human nature or some aspect of our culture through topics like: dog owners as seen through the eyes of a letter carrier, the curious tribal customs of the used car lot, and patterns of interactions observed in a dentist's waiting room.

Your course of study in school has increased your knowledge in areas that perhaps are obscure to your potential audience. Think, too, about the talents, hobbies, and skills you have developed. Could you build a speech around rewiring your house, playing a musical instrument as relaxation therapy, preparing gourmet meals for backpacking, or describing the British class structure as conveyed through mystery novels? You may have researched in depth topics that appeal to you: Woody Allen movies, holographic technology, varieties of beer, Sudanese history, cults.

What strong opinions and beliefs do you hold?

Say you are at a party and suddenly find yourself arguing fervently about gun control. The conversation up to this point had dealt with a number of equally controversial subjects, but your contributions had not been so impassioned. Which are the topics that stir you up in this way? These issues, which probably touch on your core values (see **18c**) frequently make good speech topics. You will be less self-conscious if you are speaking from a deep conviction. The audience will be more generous in spirit, even when they are in opposition, if they see you are speaking from the heart.

Besides those issues that can provoke you into heated debate, there are others that fascinate you intellectually. Do you have a pet theory about the decline of the nuclear family, why relationships fail, what makes a good manager, or whether there is other sentient life in the universe? Explaining the basis of your beliefs can make an excellent speech.

What would you like to know more about?

You may, ever since signing the note for your most recent business loan, have been curious about the workings of the Federal Reserve System. After reading about shifting alliances in central Europe, you might have become interested in the roots of the breakup of the Soviet Union. Coming out of the movie theater after seeing the most recent space adventure, you might have made a resolution to go to the library and look up information on NASA's plans for a space station. Use the occasion of giving a speech as an opportunity to research some topics that have piqued your curiosity.

(2) Select a topic appropriate to the audience and occasion. See also Chapter 4.

By brainstorming through the questions in **3a(1)**, you have created a possible subject list of great variety. To choose the one topic on which you will speak, you next need to think about the audience and the occasion. Two more questions you can ask yourself at this point are:

Audience: What are *these* people's expectations?
Occasion: What are these people's expectations *now?*

Knowing who the audience is and why its members are gathered together can help you rule out a number of topics. A speech on the fluctuating silver market could be interesting, but not to a seventh-grade class. Japanese architecture would probably not be the best subject for a speech given to the American Medical Association. Selling a product, promoting a candidate, or proselytizing for a faith would be out of place in a eulogy.

When you have removed the inappropriate subjects from your list, you then need to find the *most* appropriate of the remainder. Empathy is your best tool. Imagine sitting on those hard chairs in the boardroom or classroom. What would you sit still to hear?

(3) Select a topic that is both timely and timeless.

You may still have more than one possible topic on your list, even after going through the processes in **3a(1)** and **3a(2)**. Other things being equal, the best topics are those that are both timely and timeless. There are certain issues that have always been and always will be part of human discourse. The rights of the individual versus the rights of the group and the need for security versus the need for adventure were being discussed

1,000 years ago, 100 years ago, and this past year; they will continue to be discussed by our descendants. When you tie a contemporary event to one of these enduring human dialogues, you link the timely and the timeless. Neither one of these conditions by itself is an indication that the topic would be a good one. Consider the criterion of timeliness. If an event has been taking up three front-page newspaper columns a day for two weeks, a speech on that topic may be timely. But unless you can tell your audience what it all means in more universal terms, there probably is little for you to give them that they do not already know. You have wasted their time. The reverse is true also: Your audience can miss or fail to be interested in the profundity of your topic if you do not tie it into the fabric of their current existence. A profound, timeless topic should have a timely application. A timely speech should point out the timeless implication of the subject.

Table 3-1 shows how topics that are too narrowly contemporary or too broadly universal may be altered to meet these criteria. Notice the different kinds of speeches to which the timely/timeless standard can apply.

Exercise 1. Suppose that each of the following five topics is of great interest to you and that you are qualified to speak about them:

1. The martial arts
2. Try mediation before litigation
3. Problems of our Social Security system
4. How television commercials are made
5. Western misconceptions about Islam

Which would be best for each of the following audiences? Select more than one if you wish, but justify your answers.

    a. A speech class where the assignment is to support a thesis with factual and statistical evidence from several different sources
    b. A community service club luncheon
    c. A junior high neighborhood youth group
    d. A current events study group
    e. A keynote address at a business conference

Exercise 2. Explain how each of the five topics above could be developed to reflect both timely and timeless concerns.

TABLE 3-1	Arriving at Timely and Timeless Topics	
Timely (but Potentially Trivial)	Timeless (but Potentially Diffuse)	Timely and Timeless
There was a major confrontation last week when the Ku Klux Klan held a rally downtown.	Freedom of assembly must be protected for everyone.	Last week's confrontation over the Ku Klux Klan rally raised important questions about what restrictions, if any, should be placed on freedom of assembly.
My trip to Quebec.	Travel helps people understand diversity of human cultures.	My trip to Quebec helped me to understand my own culture by contrasting it with another.
Our company has adopted a new profit-sharing plan.	The best management philosophy is one that treats the employees like partners.	Our new profit-sharing plan will benefit the employees directly and reflect an enlightened philosophy of management.

3b. Narrow your topic.

One of the old public speaking jokes goes as follows:

A: I'm giving a speech at the annual banquet tonight.
B: What are you going to talk about?
A: Oh, about 15 minutes.

Speaker A's answer is not wholly facetious. It acknowledges the important principle that the selection of a topic is not complete until that topic has been narrowed to accommodate the constraints of time.

The main advantage of limiting a topic is to ensure depth of analysis. To avoid superficiality, you have to keep one eye on the clock while preparing your speech. To get into a topic, to get under the surface, you have to limit yourself to the number of points that can be adequately developed in the time available. You can expedite your research and preparation by narrowing your topic from the beginning. Instead of looking up all the books and articles about higher education, you can focus on those related to the financing of community colleges, or pass/fail grading, or coed dormitories.

(1) Determine the number of ideas you can cover in the time allotted.

The average speaker speaks between 100 and 150 words per minute. If you speak very rapidly or very slowly, you may fall outside this range. Chances are, though, that your rate of speaking is somewhere near 125 words per minute. If you want to check your rate, see **25b(2)**.

A typical journalistic paragraph of simple sentences runs about 125 words. Thus, a very general rule of thumb is that an average speaker speaks about one short paragraph per minute. If your material is highly technical or interspersed with statistics, dialogue, and dramatic pauses, or if you speak slowly, you had better allot two minutes per paragraph. This system is very rough, but it allows you to do some realistic narrowing of your topic.

For instance, if you plan on speaking informatively for eight to ten minutes on the criminal justice system in the United States, you will need to set aside at least one to two minutes for the introduction and one minute for the conclusion. This leaves six or seven minutes for the body of your speech. If you choose to talk about the history of the criminal justice system, the causes of crime, the way crime statistics are calculated, the workings of the probation department, and the difficulties of recruiting police officers, you could spend about one to one and one-half minutes on each subject. But could you do the subjects justice? By narrowing the topic to one of these areas you could develop two subpoints for three minutes each or three subpoints for two minutes each—a more realistic plan.

The same principle can be applied to longer speeches, business presentations, and lectures. A 20-minute speech can be thought of as 20 short, simple paragraphs or 10 longer, more developed paragraphs. Table 3-2 shows how something like that could be broken down.

Exercise 3. The Poulakos speech in the **Appendix** has 2,900 words. Roughly how long would it take to deliver?

(2) Select a few main ideas based on thorough analysis of the audience, the occasion, and your own strengths as a speaker.

In the preceding section, knowing that the criminal justice speech should be cut to one or two main points does not tell you *which* one or two to select. Consider the following questions; they can help you develop your ability to narrow a topic effectively.

TABLE 3-2	Time Allotment of Speech Elements
	Minutes

Inroduction	
Welcome audience	1
Tell anecdote about Uncle Bob	1
State topic and preview main points	1

First main point	
Explain and define	1
Subpoint	2
Subpoint	2

Second main point, etc.	
	—
	—
	—

Conclusion	
	2
	20

Which aspects of your topic are best covered in the public, oral mode?
Is it wise to spend five minutes reading a list of numbers? Probably that data should be handed out for further study, and the *meaning* of the key numbers discussed instead.

Also ask yourself: Is this an important topic to discuss in a public speech? A speech should not be used to transmit routine information, to discuss specialized problems of a small portion of the audience, or, of course, to indulge the speaker's ego.

Which aspects of your topic are best suited to this audience and occasion?

Let audience analysis direct the emphasis of your speech. Select those points that relate most directly to the needs, attitudes, knowledge, and expectations of your listeners. See **4**.

Which aspects of your topic can you present most effectively?
Select those points on which you have the most knowledge and in which you have the most interest. Do you excel at explaining complex material,

or making abstract ideas personal? Are you better with human-interest stories than statistics, or vice versa? Select those points that best fit your speaking personality.

Exercise 4. Select a speech from the **Appendix.** Suppose that you were allotted one-third the time needed to give *that* speech. How would you limit the topic?

Exercise 5. Look at the outline on comic books in **8b.** If you were to present that speech to avid comic collectors, how would you limit the topic? Look at the outline on women in the labor force in **9b.** How would you limit that topic if you were given fifteen minutes to speak to a high school social studies class?

3c. Clarify the purpose of your speech.

(1) Identify the general purpose of your speech.

What is your intention?

> Are you trying to change people's minds?
> Are you trying to teach them something?
> Are you trying to entertain them?

For instance, if you have decided on Jazz as your topic and have narrowed that topic further to Jazz Saxophone Players, there are several possible speeches you might give. Do you want to explain the harmonic theories of Ornette Coleman to your audience? Or do you want to convince them that Sonny Criss has not been given the attention he should? Or perhaps you will choose to inspire your audience by telling of the comebacks of Stan Getz and Art Pepper after these two musicians overcame drug problems.

The general purpose of a speech can be classified in one of these three ways:

Inform:	A speech designed to explain, instruct, define, clarify, demonstrate, teach.
Persuade:	A speech designed to influence, convince, motivate, sell, preach, stimulate action.
Evoke:	A speech designed to entertain, inspire, help listeners relive, celebrate, commemorate, bond.

The *speech to evoke* is often called the *speech to entertain,* but we feel that that word unfortunately has come to connote snappy patter and one-liners, which is much too narrow a definition. An evocative speech elicits a certain feeling or emotional response. The emotion or feeling can be one of fun, escape, and diversion—entertainment, if you will—but it can also be solemn and serious as in a eulogy, where a sense of community and an appreciation of individual worth may be evoked.

You will quickly discover that no speech has only one purpose. Most have a combination, but with one purpose usually dominant. For instance, a classroom lecture is used primarily to teach, but can at the same time be used to shape attitudes. The purpose of a campaign speech is to get the folks to vote for the candidate, but the speech can also entertain. An excellent sermon might do all three: inform, persuade, and evoke.

Exercise 6. Describe how each of the following topics could be made into a:

1. Speech to Inform
2. Speech to Persuade
3. Speech to Evoke

Topics:
  Trains
  Natural Childbirth
  Investing in Gold
  Men's Fashions

(2) Determine the specific purpose of your speech.

Knowing which of the three purposes—to inform, persuade, or evoke—is predominant in your speech will help you in the next step: deciding what you really want to accomplish with your topic. In phrasing this purpose, isolate the central reason for speaking. You will have many incidental goals, but you cannot select and organize your materials without a very clear set of priorities. Be both specific and realistic about the purpose you set for yourself. Do you want to teach your listeners all about chess in a 10-minute speech? Or do you want to give them the basic principles of the game? Do you want them to buy your company's telecommunications system, or agree to have you demonstrate it to a group of managers? Do not go any further until you can complete this sentence:

If there were one goal I would like to achieve in this speech, it would be . . .

At this point your topic should have a clear focus:

Not:	My specific purpose is to inform the audience about politics.
But:	My specific purpose is to inform the audience about the role of the two-party system in American politics.
Not:	My specific purpose is to persuade the audience against drunken driving.
But:	My specific purpose is to persuade the audience of the need for stiffer penalties for drunken driving.

(3) Specify the desired outcomes you seek from your listeners.

Once your goal is phrased in the terms of what *you* want to do, turn it around and phrase it in terms of what you want your *audience* to do:

If there were one action I'd want my listeners to take after my speech it would be . . .

In other words, if my speech is a success what will my audience do? This is called the *primary audience outcome*.

Not:	My desired outcome is to sell this product.
But:	My desired outcome is to have you buy this product.
Not:	My desired outcome is to explain photosynthesis.
But:	My desired outcome is to have you understand the workings of photosynthesis.

After you have identified the single most important audience outcome that you are looking for, your speech goals can be clarified even further. Implicit in every general goal statement are many contributing subgoals that may also be phrased as concrete audience behaviors. If your overall goal is to persuade the members of the audience to take up the guitar, you want them first to *decide* that it is a good idea, second to *purchase* a guitar, third to *sign up* for lessons, and last to *continue* to practice.

Notice the significance of the verbs in each case. The emphasis is on the behavior you want the audience to adopt. This sort of goal analysis has proved effective in recent years in both education and business. Teachers learned to phrase their previously fuzzy goals as concrete behavioral objectives. Both teaching and learning have improved. In the business world, the Management by Objectives movement helped employers and employees analyze tasks and set definite goals and deadlines.

The same procedures will help you plan your speech. Break the primary audience outcome into components, paying particular attention to using phrasing with verbs that describe overt behavior rather than general states of mind.

"I want my audience to *appreciate* art" is fine for a primary audience outcome, but you must go further and ask yourself how you will know if you have succeeded. What, exactly, are people doing when they are appreciating art? If you think about the specific behaviors or operations that contribute to appreciating art, you will come up with a list like this:

- *Go* to galleries.
- *Read* books on art.
- *Create* pieces of art themselves.

Observe how speech purposes and outcomes can be crystallized for each type of speech:

General Purpose: To inform.
Specific Purpose: To inform the audience of the steps of a successful job interview.
Primary Audience Outcome: I want my audience to become familiar with the steps of a successful job interview.
Contributing Audience Outcomes: I want my audience to:
- *distinguish* between the job interview and other types of interviews.
- *understand* what the interviewer expects.
- be able to *list* the four phases of the typical employment interview.
- *recognize* the importance of appearance and body language.

General Purpose: To persuade.
Specific Purpose: To convince the audience that changes in individual behaviors are needed to protect our environment.
Primary Audience Outcome: I want my audience to commit themselves actively to environmental concerns.
Contributing Audience Outcomes: I want my audience to:
- *use* public transportation, when possible.
- *minimize* the use of nonbiodegradable materials.
- *recycle* paper, glass, aluminum, and steel.
- *make* their dwellings energy efficient.
- *support* environmentally oriented political candidates and *contribute* money and time to environmental causes.

General Purpose: To evoke.
Specific Purpose: To celebrate the successful conclusion of a complex project and honor the individuals responsible for the success.

Primary Audience Outcome: I want my audience to experience a sense of community with all those who participated in the PowerCom software development project.

Contributing Audience Outcomes: I want my audience to:

- *recognize* the contribution and achievement of each group: engineers, designers, writers, testers, trainers, and support staff.
- *feel* pride in their individual contribution.
- *relive* some of the intermediate successes.
- *identify* with each other by laughing at "in jokes" that only someone involved in this project would understand.
- *share* in the warmth felt for Annette, the "spark plug" of the development group.

Note: The specific outcomes do not necessarily have to echo the language of the speech purpose. Sometimes, for instance, it is essential to inform the audience about specific points before they can be persuaded, or to lighten a primarily informative speech with some entertainment. As a rule, though, the majority of the audience outcomes should be compatible with the general purpose of the speech.

Exercise 7. Look at all of the speeches in the **Appendix.** Identify them by their type—informative, persuasive, or evocative. State the one-sentence specific purpose you think each speaker had.

Exercise 8. List at least four contributing audience outcomes that might be developed for each of the following primary outcomes. Use specific, concrete verbs to describe the behaviors.

I want my audience to learn about genetic engineering.
I want to have my audience experience the thrills of a trip to the Galápagos.
I want my audience to drive more safely.

3d. Develop a clear thesis statement to guide your analysis of the topic.

(1) Frame a thesis statement as a single declarative sentence that states the essence of your speech content.

Many management consultants talk about the necessity of an organization's coming up with a short mission statement to focus the energy of its staff, giving them something concrete against which to gauge the appropriateness of any contemplated action. In a similar vein, your topic analysis needs a thesis statement that gives you something concrete against which to test ideas. In contrast to your "purpose" and "outcomes," your thesis sentence states your topic as a proposition to be proved or a theme to be developed. This sentence, sometimes referred to as the *central idea*, gives your speech this focus. It helps you make the transition from thinking about where you want to end up (your goal) to how to get there.

A thesis sentence should not merely announce your topic. It should capsulize what you plan to say about the topic. The rationale for insisting on the complete sentence is the clarity of thought that comes when you must delineate both what you are talking about (the subject of the sentence) and what you are saying about it (the predicate of the sentence). A thesis sentence of "Today I will talk about roses" makes *you* the subject and makes the fact that you *are talking* the predicate—hardly the essence of your speech content. However, "Roses are beautiful" makes the topic serve as subject (roses) and the point being made about it (they are beautiful) the predicate. See **9b** for further discussion of the role of propositional phrasing in testing the relevance and completeness of ideas.

Be sure that the thesis statement includes enough information to differentiate your approach from other possibilities.

Informative Speech

Not:	My speech is on gangs.
Or Even:	Young people find gangs attractive.
But:	There are a number of sociological and developmental reasons for gangs being attractive to youth.

Evocative Speech

Not:	We are here to dedicate the new hospital wing.
Or Even:	The opening of this wing is a great day for O'Connor Hospital and the community.
But:	This new surgical wing reflects the efforts of many dedicated fund-raisers and increases the quality and quantity of medical care available in our community.

Persuasive Speech

Not:	Something must be done about tuberculosis.
Or Even:	Drug-resistant TB is on the increase and should be combated.

But: The threat of a resurgence of TB requires a major govern-
                        mental program of education, research, and treatment.

(2) Analyze your topic by breaking your thesis statement into a list of questions to be answered.

When chemists analyze a substance, they identify its components. As a
speaker you go through a similar process when you break up a topic to
find all the subtopics within it. In persuasive speeches this takes the form
of a fairly structured issue analysis discussed in **20b**. Informative and
evocative speeches require analysis as well. By committing yourself to
developing a thesis, you take on an obligation to discover and answer a
set of questions. These questions are the ones your listeners will be asking themselves before they accept your thesis. These questions are the
ones you should identify before proceeding with your research.

Do not be restricted by the wording of your thesis. In analyzing the
grammatical structure of a sentence, you probably learned to fill in the
understood subjects and predicates. "Pick up that book and then let
go" has to be seen as "(You) pick up that book and then (you) let go
(of it)." Consider this thesis for a persuasive speech: *Like other industrialized nations, the United States has a castelike social system based on race, sex,
and age.*

Embedded in this thesis are five questions your audience will be asking as they listen:

Does the United States have a castelike system?
Is the stratification based on race?
Is the stratification based on sex?
Is the stratification based on age?
Are these characteristics shared by other industrialized nations?

If you wanted to speak about comic books, you might develop the following thesis sentence:

With their scope, history, and influence, comic books are an interesting
    component of American popular culture.

For this informative speech, four questions present themselves:

What is the scope of comic book themes?
What is the history of the comic book?

What influence have comic books had?
Are comic books an interesting component of American popular culture?

Even in an evocative speech at a retirement dinner, you might cap-sulize your message into this thesis sentence:

> Because of Braulio Fuentes's contributions to our organization and his personal qualities, we will miss him but wish him well in his retirement years.

As you think about developing this talk, you will find that there are four questions you ought to investigate:

> Exactly what contributions has he made?
> What personal qualities do we value in him?
> In what ways will he be missed?
> What specific good wishes do we have for his retirement?

To answer these, you can look into Mr. Fuentes's history with your organization. Ask those who work with him what they will miss most, and find out if he plans to travel, raise rare orchids, or start a consulting firm.

The answers to these questions will not necessarily be the main points of your speech, and you might not develop your ideas in this order. How-ever, the analysis serves to direct your research and prevents you from being guilty of any glaring oversights.

Exercise 9. Read one or more of the speeches in the **Appendix** and formulate a single declarative sentence that best sums up the content. You may find the actual sentence in the speech itself, or you may, in the case of an implicit thesis, have to draft a sentence of your own.

Exercise 10. Evaluate the following as thesis statements for a speech. If they are not effective, rewrite them.

What shall we do about the problems of the cities?
Cambodia—its history, its people, its problems—will be the topic I will cover today.
The need for mandatory drug testing for athletes!
Taxpayers should not have to subsidize art that is pornographic or unpa-triotic.
How to make a Caesar salad.
There are three causes of congressional gridlock.

Exercise 11. Look at the thesis sentence in each of the speeches in the **Appendix.** Identify the questions implicit in each. Do the speakers address each issue?

Exercise 12. Identify the questions embedded in each of these thesis sentences:

Grading on the curve is inaccurate, unfair, and elitist.
A cruise is an educational way to relax, make friends, and see the world.
Because the property tax is essentially regressive, it is an uncertain and inequitable source of revenue for the city.

3e. If necessary, select a speech title.

While every speech needs a thesis and a purpose, not every speech needs a title. Those instances in which a title is necessary are: when there is to be advance publicity; when there is a printed program; and usually, when the speaker is going to be formally introduced. Unless there is a definite deadline to announce your title, you can defer selecting one until after the speech is composed.

A title can take any grammatical form. It can be a declarative sentence, a question, phrase, or fragment.

"Freedom of Speech Is in Jeopardy"
"Is Free Speech Really Free?"
"Threats to Free Speech"
"Free Speech: An Endangered Species"

Note: Do not confuse the thesis statement with the speech title. The thesis statement is a declarative sentence essential for the organizing and composing of the speech. The title is not.

An effective title should pique interest in your subject and make the audience eager to listen. Sometimes a metaphor, quotation, or allusion that is central to the speech can be part of the title:

"Who Will Be David to This Modern Goliath?"
"Social Security: A House of Cards"
"With Malice toward All"
"No Past, No Future, The Present Does Not Exist"[1]
"Feeding Problems, Starving Opportunities"[2]

"From Little Rock to a Hard Place"[3]
"Satellites, Soap, and Succotash"[4]

In an effort to be clever or profound, do not devise a title that will totally mystify your audience, like:

"Babaloo!"

or

"The Heraclitus of Sycamore High"

Nor should you select a title that promises more than you deliver. That is false advertising. Do not announce:

"How to Double Your Income While Working Two Days a Week"

and then give a speech on how to make one's first investment in income property. Likewise, a title such as:

"Digging Up Dirt at the White House"

might lead your audience to think that your speech has more titillating content than your recollections of work as a gardener in the White House Rose Garden. This may sell tabloids at the supermarket, but it is not considered good speaking technique.

Keep the title concise. Avoid the sort of title initiated by eighteenth-century novelists:

The Fortunes and Misfortunes of the Famous Moll Flanders & c. Who was Born in Newgate, and during a Life of continu'd Variety for Threescore Years, besides her Childhood, was Twelve Year a Whore, five times a Wife (whereof once to her own Brother), Twelve Year a Thief, Eight Year a Transported Felon in Virginia, at last grew Rich, liv'd Honest, and died a Penitent, Written from her own Memorandums . . . by Daniel Defoe.

and perpetuated by academics:

"A Quasi-experimental Investigation of Latency of Response, Self-disclosure and Turn Taking in Same Sex Dyads: Etiology, Manifestations and Implications."

Do not give your speech in your title.

Exercise 13. Evaluate the titles of the speeches in the **Appendix**. Are they effective?

Select titles for the speeches outlined in **8b** and **9b**.

Exercise 14. Find the lettered examples that match each of these categories:

1. General Topic
2. Narrowed Topic
3. General Purpose
4. Specific Purpose
5. Primary Audience Outcome
6. Contributing Audience Outcome
7. Thesis Statement
8. Analysis Question
9. Title

a. Have more lives been saved when a CPR-trained person has been present?
b. To convince the audience that the greater the number of people who know CPR, the better the chance of more lives being saved every day
c. Encourage friends to take a class in CPR
d. Cardiopulmonary resuscitation (CPR)
e. I want my audience to actively work toward increasing the number of people who know CPR.
f. Learn CPR and Make the World a Safer Place
g. As many people as possible should learn CPR to increase the probability that a person trained in this life-saving technique will be available in the event of a heart attack or similar medical emergency.
h. To persuade
i. The value of learning CPR

Chapter 4

Audience Analysis

Base your speech preparation on thorough audience analysis.

A speech is not an intention in the mind of a speaker nor is it a text that exists in a vacuum. Speakers do not give speeches *to* audiences, they jointly create meaning *with* audiences. The ultimate outcome of any speech situation is a product of what the speaker actually says and how the listeners process and interpret what is said. Audience analysis therefore is much more than a step in planning a speech. It is the constant awareness of those who are the "coauthors" of your speech.

You speak to a particular group of people because you want a certain response from them. If you do not know the composition of that group, you cannot make intelligent decisions about what to include, what to emphasize, how best to arrange and present your ideas. Research your audience thoroughly. Their age, sex, attitudes, expectations are all relevant to your planning.

The composition of audiences varies. The members of one may have many similarities; the majority of another, little in common. Within a given audience the degree of homogeneity or heterogeneity can differ for each of the characteristics discussed in this chapter. For instance, an audience can be fairly homogeneous in terms of sex—predominantly female, say—and heterogeneous in its composition of people who agree or disagree with your position.

We approach each of these characteristics as a discrete factor and describe the techniques to be used with various kinds of homogeneous audiences. *You* will have to "mix and match" these techniques as you uncover the actual composition of your potential audience.

Later in the process of preparing your speech, you will use the information to adapt your materials to the audience.

4a. Develop an understanding of your audience by seeking information through as many channels as possible.

When you ask an audience to listen to your ideas, you are asking them to come partway into your experience. It is your obligation to go partway into theirs. Probably you and your listeners belong to some common, broad speech community, or you would not be interacting. Yet every person is also a member of multiple discourse communities that are tied to cultural heritage, geographical location, occupational groups, and so on. Each of these communities has its own code of conduct and specialized vocabulary. By observing and reflecting on your audience from different perspectives, you can discover what communication links are already present between you—and what gaps need to be bridged.

Do not limit yourself to any one of the following:

Direct observation. This is the most reliable source of information about an audience. The easiest audience to analyze is a group of which you are a member. You know what will interest them, convince them, or make them laugh. With an unknown audience try, if you have enough lead time, to observe them either functioning as a group or functioning as an audience. Observing a group's business meeting or watching how they respond to another speaker can tell you a great deal about them.

Systematic data collection. One excellent way to become informed about your audience is to ask them about themselves. Politicians and advertisers spend millions on public opinion and market surveys. Such research reveals who their audiences are and how they feel. Do not discount even a simple form of data gathering like having a three- or four-item questionnaire distributed at a meeting before the one where you will speak. You might arouse interest and curiosity while you gain information.

Selected interviews/focus groups. When you cannot get information on the whole audience, then arrange to talk to one or two members of the group. If that is not possible, talk to someone who shares characteristics with your potential listeners. For a speech to a group of teenagers, talking to one teenager—even if she or he is not going to be a member of that audience—can provide you with useful information. The same applies to interviewing someone who manages a department at IBM other than the one to which you will speak; and, similarly, you will benefit from conversing with your friend Renea, active in the local chapter of the National Organization for Women, at whose regional conference you will speak.

In these interviews, try to find out not just *what* people think, but also *how* they think. Ask open-ended questions and encourage respondents to expand on their answers by framing follow-up questions in a nonargumentative tone. Ask them for examples and stories. Listen also to the language they use to address your topic. You can gain understanding to what is most meaningful to people by tuning in to the words they choose and the metaphors they use. See **15e**.

The contact person. The person who asked you to speak has certain expectations about the interaction between you and the audience, otherwise you would not have been invited. Ask this contact person to elaborate on his or her perceptions of the audience. Do not be reluctant to ask as many specific questions as occur to you; both you and the contact person have a stake in the success of your speech.

Intelligent inference and empathy. When you do not have any specific information about an audience, draw on your general knowledge of human behavior and groups. What are reasonable assumptions about an audience that would be found at a Fourth of July block party, or about those at an open seminar on investment strategies? These need not be obscure; certain intelligent inferences could easily be made about the audience at a National Rifle Association conference.

Do not use just your reasoning powers; let empathy round out the image. Get outside yourself and adopt your listeners' frame of reference.

Even if you cannot relate to the specific details, try to recall a situation in your life when the same underlying emotion was present. With all the big issues you face as a city councilperson, it can be hard to see why this neighborhood homeowners' group to which you will speak is so upset about changing one-way streets to two-way streets. Stop and remember those times when you perceived something in *your* neighborhood as a threat to your property value and the security of your family. It may not always be relevant to say: When have I been in this situation? But you can usually say: When have I felt this kind of feeling?

4b. Analyze the demographic characteristics of your audience as an aid to predicting their orientation.

There is no such thing as an average audience. A speaker would be more than a little surprised to stand before a group of listeners whose composition followed exactly the distribution of the last census in regard to age, sex, race, socioeconomic status, and religion. Obtaining each audience's vital statistics will enable you to make certain general predictions about their responses. Some pertinent questions might be:

What is the average age of the audience members?
What is the age range?
What is the sexual breakdown of the audience?
What racial and ethnic groups are represented, in about what proportions?
What is the socioeconomic composition of the group?
What occupations are represented?
What religious groups are represented?
What is the political orientation of the group?
How homogeneous (similar) or heterogeneous (diverse) are the audience members for each of the above characteristics?

Obviously, all of these demographic characteristics are not equally important for any given speech. The religious configuration of your audience would be important to have while preparing a speech on abortion. The age distribution would similarly be important for a speech on Social Security reform. Or, religion and age might have no bearing whatsoever on a third topic. Despite differences in relative importance to a particular topic, each demographic characteristic should be noted, if only to give you a general picture. It is disconcerting to face a roomful of ethnically diverse teenagers if you had expected middle-aged professionals of northern European descent.

Holding an image of your audience in mind as you prepare and practice your speech will affect dozens of minor decisions not related to your overall strategy. Just on the basis of your general cultural awareness, you will adapt your language usage, humor, and style of delivery to what you know about your audience. In addition, Chapter 20 will help you plan more specific adaptations.

Caveat: Very few generalizations can be made on the basis of demographic factors. The studies from which evidence is drawn are often flawed. Also, social change occurs so rapidly that by the time this research is reported the situation has changed. By the time the findings have reached the average layperson through synthesis or summaries, even more time has elapsed. Social science research, even when carefully controlled and well designed, tells us how one group *on the average* differs from another group *on the average*. For example, with respect to almost any trait you might select, the differences among individual women and among individual men are far greater than the differences between the average man and the average woman.

Still, it is naive to say that because people are individuals group data tell us nothing. If you know that an audience is all female or all over 65 or all Asian American, you do know more than if you had no information about the audience at all. Demographic data let you make some *probability statements*. You can say that many people in an audience are likely to respond in a certain way. You cannot say that any individual in that audience definitely *will* respond in a given way.

Understanding the limitations of such analysis, you should be aware of various demographic characteristics that may affect your audience's response—including the following:

(1) Age/Generation

Maxims like "you're as young as you feel" and "age is a state of mind" tell us to be careful when we make assumptions based on chronological age. Most of us have been exposed to octogenarians who routinely question authority and are open to new experiences, and to eighteen-year-olds who have already ossified their thought patterns. Despite these exceptions, some generalizations can be justified. Current theory holds that psychological development does not stop at the threshold of adulthood, but continues through life in fairly predictable stages. Works by Erikson and Sheehy can offer insight into the most common crises and value realignments of people in their twenties, thirties, forties, and so on.[1] For our purposes, *younger* refers generally to people going through adolescence, formal education, or the early phases of establishing career direction and of confirming life goals.

- Younger people tend to be idealistic. They respond positively to arguments based on change and innovation. They are impatient about social change and want to see results in the near future.
- They are strongly affected by the values of their peers.
- Young people like a speech to be organized in a fluid, narrative fashion. They prefer a rapid, exciting tempo of delivery, employing several media or channels of communication.
- Older people are more conservative. They are responsive to appeals to traditional values. They tend to have a stake in the status quo and are reluctant to risk major changes. They are more patient in waiting for results.
- When listening to a speech, older people prefer a linear, highly structured organization with clear previews, transitions, and summaries. They are most comfortable with a slow, deliberate style of delivery.

In addition to thinking about the life stage of your audience, you can infer from the members' ages certain specific experiences they have had, based on their generational identity. In other words, it's not just that your audience members (at the turn of the century) are fifty years old that is important. Unlike other fifty-year-olds of the past and future, they were children during the post–World War II prosperity, students during the idealistic Sixties, disillusioned young adults during the Watergate era, and so on. This is a different audience from one of fifty-year-olds in the mid-1970s, who had been adolescents during the Great Depression and had come of age during World War II. Think about what current events have inspired and traumatized the particular audience you are addressing. What movies, TV shows, songs, and sports figures were central to their lives? What generational stereotypes might they have become weary of?

(2) Sex/Gender

Sex is the demographic category that relates to biological maleness or femaleness. *Gender* refers to the socialized roles we have learned as appropriate for our sex. There may be a very few experiences that are directly

---

[1]See, for example, Erik Erikson, *Identity and the Life Cycle* (New York: Norton, 1980), and Gail Sheehy, *Passages: Predictable Crises of Adult Life* (New York: Dutton, 1976).

linked to sex; a speech on breast feeding or circumcision might take the actual male-female composition of an audience into account. Far more commonly, however, gender issues enter into audience analysis. The issue is not how many males and females are present, but how the audience members (of either sex) think about masculinity and femininity. These gender expectations are highly culture bound and change rapidly in contemporary life.

Traditionally, women were socialized to be nurturant, sensitive, compassionate, and emotional. So, in the past, appeals to home, family, and the safety of loved ones have usually been effective with traditional women. Traditionally, men were socialized to be dominant, aggressive, ambitious, and unemotional (except when it came to sports). So a speech to a predominantly traditional male group used appeals to power, success, competitive values, and cold, hard logic.

In recent decades many more women and men have come to a new consciousness of the way sex-role socialization has limited their avenues of expression and growth. They are experimenting with new roles and divisions of labor in public and private life. Both men and women undergoing this process bridle when presented with stereotypical assumptions about roles and power matrices.

As a speaker you are well advised to avoid statements that may offend a sizable portion of your audience. Women, especially as they become aware of past oppression, are naturally sensitive to slights to their dignity and their role as autonomous adults. Many object to being referred to as *girls, gals,* or *ladies*—or to overly cute designations such as *distaff side* or *the fairer sex*—which tends to trivialize their status. Many women believe that references to their clothes and appearance, however complimentary and well meant, focus on women as sex objects or decorative accessories. To be on the safe side with any audience, avoid such comments as:

> I was chatting at dinner with your lovely vice president, Professor Ruhly. Now why didn't they have teachers like that when I was in school?

> To Mr. Davis's left, the charming young lady in the pretty blue dress is our regional sales manager, Linda.

Avoid examples that assume that everyone fits into traditional roles.

> Tomorrow morning as your wife serves you breakfast, ask her about the prices she finds at the grocery store. [In some households men cook breakfast and shop for groceries.]

If you had a son about to take over your business, wouldn't you tell him . . .
[Why not a daughter?]

Especially if you are female, do not perpetuate the myth of female incompetence in ways that may offend other women.

Now, about the direction of market trends. [giggle] I'm not very good with figures, but I'm sure you men can make some sense out of these charts.

(3) Race/Ethnicity

As with women and men, the differences between ethnic groups are not innate. The differences that do exist result from variations in socialization and experience. In the authors' home state we daily encounter newcomers who came here voluntarily to be with their families or to enhance their opportunities, or who came involuntarily as refugees. Conversations with such diverse members of our communities encourage those of us who have been in the United States longer to remember why our ancestors came: some seeking opportunity, some escaping economic hardship or political and religious oppression, some involuntarily as slaves.

The expanding ethnic and cultural diversity can be seen as either a problem or an interesting opportunity. In the past, when there were three or four predominant ethnic groups in an area, it might have been a reasonable goal to become somewhat expert on the cultural values and symbols of those groups. Today, when dozens of cultures are part of a single community or organization, this approach to audience analysis becomes overwhelming.

To further complicate the challenge, it is not just that audiences are multicultural groups, but also that they are composed of individuals who are themselves multicultural persons. It is increasingly rare to find someone whose heritage is monocultural in any real sense. It is not uncommon to meet a person who has one European parent and one South American parent and who has lived on four continents. Others may be part of an ethnic group that has largely been oppressed but may personally have had a very privileged upper-middle-class lifestyle and education. A third-generation Korean American will share most of the cultural experiences of other native-born U.S. citizens, but will have some experiences that may derive from having a Korean name or features that are related to by some as "Asian."

Because people's experiences, not their traits, shape them as listeners, there are no prescriptions for how to relate to predominantly white, African-American, Native American, Latino/Latina, Hispanic, or Asian-American audiences. Instead, you will need to familiarize yourself as far as possible with the experiences of each group. The common experience of nonwhite racial groups and most other ethnic minorities in the United States has included discrimination and oppression. Members of these groups, like women, are justifiably sensitive to any communication that reduces their status or reflects old stereotypes. Forms of address, both collective and individual, are very important. Never refer to people by first names, diminutives, or nicknames unless invited to do so. Especially, do not address white males by titles such as mister, doctor, or colonel while addressing anyone else more casually. Find out what group designations your audience prefers and respect their wishes.

Beyond showing sensitivity to the relationship of dominant and non-dominant cultural groups, a speaker can also demonstrate an appreciation of cultural diversity. People of any ethnic group can tend to look at things from the standpoint of the group's own history and culture. Taking the time to investigate other cultural views can open up a number of refreshingly different avenues to good communication. Making the effort to pronounce unfamiliar names and phrases correctly and avoiding the most stereotypical cultural generalizations shows your goodwill and openness.

This kind of investigation is worthwhile only if it is put to appropriate use. The superficial approach, equivalent to the politician who is photographed eating his way through every ethnic restaurant in his constituency, results in a speech that rings false. The focus should be on the factors that influence communication, such as: What constitutes a credible image? What level of eye contact is appropriate? How much controversy or intensity becomes discomforting?

4c. Try to understand what is meaningful to your audience.

Since speakers are not transmitting information, but rather jointly constructing meanings with listeners, no part of audience analysis is as important as learning *how a particular group of people makes meaning*. The demographic data you have collected can be useful, but only if treated within the context of this complex process. We know that a person's age, race, and sex all contribute to her or his interpretation of the world. But so do religion, social class, educational level, economic status, sexual orientation, health, physical ability, and many other factors. One thing that the incredible diversity and constantly changing profile of U.S. society have made clear is that no formula could ever be devised to tell a speaker how each of these variables relates to a particular topic, let alone how they all interact together. In a sense, you as a speaker have been freed from the unrealistic goal of making predictions based on static traits of your listeners. Instead, your task is to thoughtfully consider how they engage in a constant process of constructing, and reconstructing, the world. (See Table 4-1.)

This third and most useful way of understanding audiences requires both empathy and intellect. From this perspective, you can begin to grasp how it is that different people can observe the same events but interpret them "logically" to come to opposite conclusions (see **14a**). In this sort of audience analysis you are trying to glimpse what some describe as *core values* (see **18c**) and what others might call *worldviews, personal construct systems, frames of reference, informal theories,* or *master narratives.* What do your listeners draw on to organize their experience and make sense of it?

There are two sources of such information. You can learn about cultural and group differences by reading, traveling, being exposed to literature and

TABLE 4-1	Relating to an Audience
Level of Understanding	Analysis
Being oblivious to audience (poor understanding)	Here is how I see this issue. You should see it the same way.
Adapting to audience's traits (better understanding)	Because you are male, you are probably competitive and would respond to statements about being a winner. Because you are older, you may be conservative and would be skeptical about sudden change.
Understanding and respecting how audience interprets the topic (best understanding)	Because of your experiences (which may or may not be linked to your demographic traits), you have this set of values and this way of defining yourself. I can see how your worldview makes sense to you, and here is how my position overlaps and resonates with what is most meaningful to you.

art forms that shake up your own category systems. You can also learn by listening openly and participating in dialogue with the people you want to understand. Many times people can tell you explicitly about their beliefs and attitudes, but often the processes by which they make meaning are taken for granted and are difficult for them to articulate. You may not get the insights you want through questionnaires or traditional interviews, but may need to rely on extended observation and careful attention to the ways their talk reveals their values, priorities, and conflicts. See **15e.**

4d. Determine the audience's attitudes toward your topic.

If you were to think of every possible reaction that a person might have to the thesis of your speech, you could spread those reactions across a continuum that ranges from extreme disagreement to extreme agreement. Much social science research is based on asking people to clarify their attitudes on scales like this one:

Strongly disagree	Moderately disagree	Slightly disagree	Neither agree nor disagree	Slightly agree	Moderately agree	Strongly agree

If your goal were to bring about some specific act, your listeners' responses would range across these categories:

Opposed to action	Uninclined to act	Ready to act	Taking action

If the majority of your audience falls on the left of either continuum, that audience should be considered an *unfavorable* audience. If at the middle, they should be termed *neutral*. To the right, *favorable*. Most speakers would agree that knowing the audience's predisposition toward the topic is the single most important bit of information in planning their speech strategy. If your speech deals with a controversial topic, it is particularly important to interview people who are different from you in terms of attitude and experience. Listen carefully and respectfully to their account of the world. At the information-gathering stage, your goal is not to plan a strategy for changing them, but rather to try to see how their views and yours might be connected. This means letting go of your predispositions and judgments about people who disagree with you.

When you find out whether your audience is favorable, neutral, or unfavorable, you will be able to follow the specific suggestions offered in **21**. Although attitudes toward your topic are most obviously relevant to persuasive speaking, they can influence the speech to inform or evoke as well.

4e. Anticipate your audience's expectations by gathering details about the specific speech situation.

We have stressed the importance of knowing your purpose in speaking, but what is your audience's purpose in listening? Why are they sitting there giving you their valuable time? Perhaps they are required to as part of a class or part of a job assignment. Maybe they are present voluntarily, but for a reason unrelated to you or your topic—for example, they enjoy the social contacts of an organization and tolerate a speech as part of the meeting. Or perhaps, if you are very fortunate, they are there because of an interest in what you have to say. In any audience, you will find combinations of these and other motivations. Knowing the predominant audience expectation is vital to the preparation of your speech. An excellent speech can fail miserably if the audience expected a different sort of talk altogether.

This is not to say that you must be bound by the audience's expectations. You can lead them to a new mental set; but to do that successfully you need to discover what they know and expect to begin with. Start with these questions about your listeners and the occasion:

(1) What do they know about your topic?

Overestimating or underestimating the sophistication of your audience can be disastrous. No one likes to be "talked down to" or to waste time listening to what she or he already knows. It is equally frustrating for an audience to try to follow a technical or complicated talk that assumes a background and vocabulary they do not have. In both cases your listeners will first become irritated and then tune out. People listen best and learn best when exposed to information that is just beyond their current level of understanding. Then they are neither bored nor overwhelmed. Make no blanket assumptions about that level, use the techniques of audience analysis to find it.

(2) What do they think about you?

Learn what your audience has heard, read, or assumed about you. If they believe you are an unquestioned expert, a misguided fanatic, or the funniest speaker their program chair has ever met, it will surely influence how they listen to you. You will want to build on their positive expectations and overcome their negative ones. As **17a** explains, knowing what your credibility is before the speech helps you decide how much you need to do to bolster it during the speech.

(3) What is the history of your audience as a group?

Audiences come in many different forms, with varied levels of group cohesion. An example of an audience with a low level of group cohesion would be the people who showed up after reading about your speech in the coming events section of the newspaper. Most audiences, though, have some common history, which may vary from a long association in a business or club to a few weeks together in a classroom. Learn all you can about this collective history. What projects have they undertaken? What lighter, social events have they shared? What problems do they face? What have they accomplished as a group? What other speakers have they heard? You may find possible connections to your speech topic.

(4) What is the program surrounding your speech?

To understand an audience's expectations of you, it is essential to learn your speech's place in the context of their immediate situation. Whether you are part of a three-day conference or a high school assembly, familiarize yourself with the agenda and where you fit into it. Did your listeners just arrive from home, or have they been sitting in session since eight this morning? How long a speech do they expect? Have they had a cocktail hour or eaten a big meal? The overly relaxed or sated audience can be a challenge to a speaker, but so can the thirsty or hungry one. Have they just listened to a long treasurer's report, endless head table introductions, or a stand-up comedian? Is your speech the main event, or are they anticipating the election of officers, the juggling act, or the speaker to follow?

You obviously cannot have control over these conditions, but that makes it all the more important to get answers to as many of your questions as possible beforehand. Then you can direct your time to preparing a speech ideally suited to the occasion.

Exercise 1. Suppose you are the contact person for a speaker who will talk about defense spending. Prepare an audience profile at least two paragraphs in length that summarizes the most relevant demographic and attitudinal data. If you are enrolled in a speech class, use the class as the audience you will describe. Otherwise, describe a group you know well, such as your department at work or an organization you belong to.

Chapter 5

Research

Research your topic.

Say that you are gratified to have been asked to give a talk on your life history. Pretty easy to do, you think; who knows you better than you? Just a matter of spinning off tales as they come to you: "And then, in the summer of '96—or was it '95?" Start again with a different supposition: A professional biographer has become interested in your life and wants to include it in her lecture tour repertoire. She would interview you and find out what happened in the summer of '96—or was it '95?—and then also interview your parents, siblings, children, professors, friends, and colleagues and pore over files in the library. Granting that you and the biographer have equal speaking skills, which speech would give the audience more accurate information and analysis? Which would have a more balanced perspective? This facetious example is put forward to demonstrate that there really is not a speech topic, no matter how close to your heart, that could not benefit from research.

5a. Have a research strategy.

Plan a research strategy that optimizes your effort for the time allotted. This requires you to reflect upon your topic and the situation before dashing off to research it. How much time do you have? What facts are you compelled to look up just from the nature of your topic? What themes require investigation? What are the objectives of your research? Other questions center on where you will get your information. What can be best found in the library? Which research can be done with a computer, using CD-ROM, or connection to online services and the Internet? What people can you approach to discuss your topic?

(1) Fit your research to the time allotted.

The approach you take to research can vary widely according to the time you have to prepare and the nature of your topic. Chapter **2** advises having a realistic timetable for preparation. With one day's notice you cannot make an exhaustive study of the literature, but you can draw from general references like encyclopedias, whether at the library, on CD-ROM, or online. With more time a broader effort is possible, starting with the information gleaned from general resources and using that as a direction finder as you progress through other, more specific sources.

(2) Approach your topic so that you progress from the general to the specific.

Start with an investigation of the "big picture." You do not want to commit yourself prematurely to only one avenue of research; you may miss hints of other areas important to your topic. As you move further into your research, you can get more specific, knowing what you can afford to ignore, but also knowing that if other areas unexpectedly become pertinent you have enough general understanding to be able to follow those trails effectively.

As the planning chart in Chapter **2** indicates, there is a round of preliminary or exploratory research that precedes a speaker's main research effort. With a topic about which you know very little, you are going to have to do some general research anyway before you can develop your topic analysis. For a familiar topic you will need this preliminary research to crystallize in your mind the focus of your analysis as well. There are two basic sources to tap for research: other people and recorded information. Unless you are fortunate enough to have unlimited access to an expert as a family member or a good friend, ordinarily it is best to start with the recorded information, saving the use of human resources for later when you know how best to take advantage of their expertise. Here, too, is where the general references become your initial and primary resource.

One of the most useful talents to have in the early stages of research is the ability to skim read. Even if you had unlimited time to prepare, it would not make sense to grab the books and articles whose authors' names begin with *A* and read them from start to finish, then go onto the *B*'s, and so on. Before checking any books out from the library (or buying them, for that matter), look through a number of them quickly. Since you will not have time to read everything, try to get a feel for the most important approaches and theories. To do this, look at the tables of contents, skim the first and last chapters of a book, or read the first and last paragraphs of a chapter or article. Make note of the names of the key scholars and public figures who are frequently cited. Notice recurring concepts and studies. Do not feel obligated to read every single sentence.

You will need to develop a similar discipline as you search online, the ability to skim-"surf." Especially on the Web it is easy to get seduced down a long set of links that are fun and interesting but have absolutely nothing to do with what you are researching.

As you begin, look for summary or state-of-the-art articles and books that synthesize current thought on your subject. Pieces that trace the history of your topic are also useful. Quite often these sources are readily identifiable by their titles:

"What is a working woman?" [H. H. Stipp, *American Demographics*]
"The lasting changes brought by women workers" [*Business Week*]
Women in the American Economy [Juanita M. Kreps, Prentice-Hall]
"Women and the workforce" [Alice Kessler, *The Reader's Companion to American History*, via Web search]

Skimming several sources and reading a few general ones will give you a good overview of your topic. You can then further narrow your topic and focus the remainder of your research.

(3) Develop a lexicon of the terminology peculiar to your topic.

Beginning to study a new topic is almost like learning a new language. As you start exploring your topic, make a list of key terms that come up. In researching women in the labor force, for example, you will find that you need to understand the distinctions made between *equal opportunity, affirmative action,* and *comparable worth.* You will notice that certain phrases such as *glass ceiling, queen bee syndrome,* and *pink-collar workers* have been coined by earlier writers and are widely used in the discourse on this topic. Familiarity with the language of your topic will be essential as you continue your research, since you will need to identify key words as you search through the literature.

(4) Use the analysis questions developed in 3d(2) to direct your research.

When you've made one pass through for background research, but before you launch your main research effort, go back and analyze your topic. Consider whether you want to narrow your topic, adjust your speech objectives, or fine tune the wording of your thesis sentence. Carefully follow the suggestions in **3d(2)** to list what it is that your audience will want to know. These questions become the basis of your research objectives. Suppose that your thesis is *Since the beginning of the Industrial Revolution, women in the United States have been exploited as a cheap and expendable source of labor.* Your audience will want to hear the answer to questions like: Are women a cheap source of labor? Are women an expendable source of labor? Can the labor practices appropriately be labeled as exploitation? Has the treatment of women been rather consistent since the Industrial Revolution? Clearly then, your list of research objectives would include goals like these: Find out how women's salaries compare with those of men who do the same job. Find specific examples of women having been treated as an expendable source of labor. Find an expert definition of *exploitation.* Find out how women's work changed at the time of the Industrial Revolution. And so on. Like a shopping list that you take to the store, this set of questions can provide focus and direction. Armed with this list of research objectives, you are ready to make the best use of your research time and to ask for the help you need.

5b. Use the library.

The first library appeared in the United States 300 years ago. The first free public library appeared 200 years ago. For all these decades, libraries have existed to provide clarification to those who wish to know more about any topic. Even the smallest library usually has a connection to a larger system through which it can order what you need. In addition to the standard lending libraries there are special libraries or collections that have a particular theme as a focus. If the library gives tours of the facility, be sure that you go on one.

(1) Talk to a librarian.

Librarians are service-oriented information specialists, and contrary to the image presented in popular culture, are not there merely to shush people who forget to whisper. They are there to help you find the materials you need. Do not hesitate to ask them questions. They want the challenge of understanding your requirements and directing you to the answers you seek, whether you have questions about key terms, what general resources for a particular topic are best, what databases are best to use, and more.

(2) Use the catalogs to locate books and articles on your topic.

The book catalog
In most libraries the book catalog is a computer database. These database systems let you search for entries a number of ways. For instance, you may choose to search by some combinations of subject, author, and title. Or you can focus on topics as they are grouped in the Dewey decimal system or the Library of Congress classifications. Or you can search by keywords or *descriptors,* words or short phrases that the database uses to identify entries on related topics. (In our hypothetical example of women in the labor force, some keywords might be: Labor market, Women, Wages & salaries, Sex discrimination.) Or in some cases you may make a *free text* search, where the computer will not limit itself to defined descriptors, but rather will look for words and combinations of words that you have chosen within the titles and content summaries of the books in the database. The lexicon you developed in **5a(3)** will be extremely helpful in both keyword and free text searches.

In libraries without computers the book catalog is the card catalog—banks of drawers containing small cards that cite each book in at least three places: by author, by title, and by variations of its subject. The subject cards are generally equivalent to the keywords of the computer database.

Special collections may have separate catalogs; check with the librarian to see which catalogs you have access to.

Periodical indexes and databases

You can locate magazine, journal, and newspaper articles on your topic using the periodical indexes and databases available at the library. This may entail perusing bound volumes, scanning a microfilm reader, or searching a computer database, such as InfoTrac. Some of the indexes and data bases are general in their coverage; others can be quite specific to a field or area of interest. Whether it be criminal justice, religion, engineering, business, music, essays, tax law, or any one of a multitude of topics, there is a very good chance that a specialized index or database will exist for it. Once again, do not hesitate to approach the librarian to ask for guidance in finding these sources.

There also are indexes for many major newspapers. Size of the library and closeness of the major city are usually the factors determining the availability of such indexes.

Special dictionaries, encyclopedias, and similar resources

Special dictionaries and encyclopedias are useful tools, especially for clarifying terms and concepts as they are used in fields of which you may have little knowledge. Many such reference works cover world history, finance, law, medicine, science, philosophy, music, literature, and other subjects of significance.

Depending on its size, the library may have many other possible sources of information available, including filmstrips, microform, records, compact discs, cassettes, film, and videotapes.

5c. Use electronic information retrieval.

There are a number of ways for you to retrieve information electronically. You can use an institutional search service that provides access to databases at remote sites. You can use a computer terminal at the library that provides access to databases on site. You can use a personal computer to dial up an online service you subscribe to. You can use a computer to hook up to an Internet Service Provider. These choices run from the very structured (the institutional search service) to the very unstructured (the Internet).

LEXIS-NEXIS, DIALOG, BRS (Bibliographic Retrieval Service), and Wilsonline are services that provide information retrieval. The database you use can depend on your topic and which system is subscribed to by the search service you deal with. A service can have hundreds of databases to choose from; each of the data bases can cover more than 100,000 separate articles and papers. You can get access to one of these systems in a number of ways. Many public libraries subscribe to at least one service. College and university libraries are likely to have a search service, usually available only to students, staff, and faculty. Many companies have access to at least one of the major systems.

Online services accessible by personal computer can offer information in a variety of areas, from an online edition of an encyclopedia or news magazine, to stock market performance, to government statistics, to news on sports and entertainment, and so on.

Seeking out information may be more esoteric on the Internet, where you may use such things as Gopher servers and the World Wide Web to track down what you are looking for. There are a number of ways you gain access to the Internet, and once there, a number of ways you move around in it; its combination of flexibility and arcane global structure can make it a daunting prospect for casual users. You can lessen the grief if you approach the available search engines with a search technique that maximizes focus and minimizes ambiguity. Use Boolean operators (this AND that, this OR that, this NOT that), if the search engine allows, to keep from being overwhelmed by results that number in the tens of thousands of "hits." If you searched for "Finland" in hopes of finding some information on Finnish exports in 1996, you may have to wade through Web sites extolling Grandmother Kovanen's cookie recipes, Bob and Diane's trip to Helsinki, and so on, before finding anything useful. Many engines permit the user to specify that one word in the search should be near another, and use other tools ("wildcards," required terms, for instance) to be as precise as possible at the beginning.

For the most efficient use of any of these electronic resources, you must create a concise search strategy by narrowing your topic after considering different avenues of approach. See **5a.** Then you can decide what are the most likely categories, keywords, and search texts to identify information related to your topic. Coming prepared to do a search will save you time by avoiding going down blind alleys and investigating topics before discovering their lack of relevance.

Caveat: Scrutinize Web-based materials with special caution. Although *any* information you gather in the course of research should be subjected to tests of credibility and reliability as described in **13,** the wide-open nature of the World Wide Web invites a particularly critical eye. In contrast to the various review processes applied to getting ideas into print or onto film, all it takes to mount a Web site is the software and a server. Many Web sites are the equivalent of an opinion forcefully stated at a party: the authority resides in the volume, not the merit.

5d. Seek information directly from other people.

Research is more than delving into piles of books, papers, and printouts. You are surrounded by potential sources of information in the form of other people—either as individuals or as members of informal or formal information networks. These sources can complement and supplement your library and electronic research. They are not a substitute for it. No matter how compelling any single narrative, you do not want to be completely seduced away from those piles of book, papers, and printouts. The speech you give must still be *your synthesis* of ideas and facts from many sources—not just a report of someone else's ideas.

(1) Finding human resources

Your acquaintances, family, and coworkers can be sources of information.
As you start developing ideas on your topic, begin to talk about them with the people you come in contact with every day. You may encounter surprising sources of expertise. The person with whom you play tennis may turn out to know quite a bit about computers, or your dentist may have gone to China last summer. On many topics, what these people can offer you is not so much expertise as a lay perspective that you will not find in any book. Talk to any five friends and you can compile a list of amazing computer foul-ups. Did any of your acquaintances ever find someone worth dating in a singles bar? What do they think is the most urgent economic problem the country faces?

You might turn this into an informal survey, or even go a step further and develop a brief written questionnaire.

Seek out experts.
In every community there are people with specialized expertise in your topic. They can make a significant contribution to your research in that

they often can tell you of unpublished data, local applications, or local examples of your subject, or they can direct you to obscure sources. Try:

Educators. At whatever level—high school, trade school, college, or university—educators are usually very approachable experts. Dissemination of information is their business. If you do not already have a specific person in mind after your research to this point, call the appropriate department or school. They will direct you to someone knowledgeable.

Public officials and agencies. People elected to public office consider it one of their duties to make information available to their constituents. Most have staffs whose job it is to locate and send out government documents, copies of bills pending, and so on. In addition, scores of public agencies are staffed by experts who are ready to help you. If you do not know where to start, call the main switchboard of the local or regional government and outline the direction of your research. They can tell you the department with which to begin.

Independent agencies and special interest groups. Groups such as the American Cancer Society, Planned Parenthood, and the National Hot Rod Association can be excellent sources of information. Be aware that such groups often represent a limited perspective. Talk to a spokesperson from the National Rifle Association, or the Sierra Club, but weigh the information you receive against the standard of objectivity that you have developed (it is hoped) through previous comprehensive research. When possible, interview experts with differing orientations toward your subject, especially if the subject is controversial.

A useful resource for making contact with these groups is the *Encyclopedia of Associations,* available at the library. This encyclopedia contains descriptions of the groups and where to get in touch with them. Many of the groups listed have a toll-free telephone number that you can call.

Potpourri. Judges, athletes, businesspeople, police officers, doctors, merchants, accountants can all be experts. If you do not know a person in the particular field, see if you have a one-step link to one through a colleague or friend. Failing that, be alert to people mentioned in the newspapers. Chances are that if they were interviewed once, they would be willing to answer other questions. If you have no contacts in a monolithic organization, start with the public relations officer. However, when you know to whom you want to talk, there is no harm in calling that person's office and explaining your request. Maybe you will not get an appointment with the mayor, the chief of police, or the coach of the football team, but you may be able to meet with a top aide or assistant.

Look also for experts who may have credentials of a less formal sort. A homeless person is an expert on certain dimensions of homelessness. In short, do not skip a potential source of useful information and possibly a fresh viewpoint by limiting your definition of *expert*.

Along with the local community, there is also the electronic community accessible by computer. You can tap into an enormous pool of talent. The newsgroups and conferences available online can introduce you to knowledgeable human resources at a national, even global, level. Thousands of forums exist, covering just about every area of interest you could think of, and probably many that you would never think of, from Celtic music to calculus to corporation law, bicycling to boycotts to Barbie. In these groups and message boards people carry on extended dialogue on many issues. Questions are asked and answered, challenged and rebutted. Join in by asking your own questions and engage in the multifaceted discussion that can result.

Before asking a specific question, check to see if it is one that has come up many times before. Questions of this sort, and their answers, are usually posted in a Frequently Asked Questions (FAQ) file. If there is such a posting in your area of interest, read it first—you may find many answers immediately, and you may also find answers to questions that you had not yet thought of asking.

(2) Interviewing

Prepare for the interview.

Do not go into an interview cold. Analyze who the person is and ask yourself in what ways she or he can best contribute to your research. If the person has written an article or book on the subject, read it. You should devise a list of questions that are specific enough that you will not be wasting this person's time by asking for information that you could have gotten out of the encyclopedia. You want to prepare open-ended questions rather than yes-no questions or simple factual queries, but at the same time you do not want to be so vague that you give the person no starting place. For instance, you are studying the history and present condition of women in the labor force and you are directing your questions to the chair of the County Commission on the Status of Women:

Not:	"How many women are there in the work force in this county?" [The figure could have been looked up before.]
Not:	"What are the problems working women encounter?" [too vague]
But:	"I've read that in this county the average woman's salary is 32 percent less than the average man's. To what do you attribute this?"

During the interview.

Spend the first few minutes establishing rapport and setting a context for the interview. Explain who you are, why you need the information, and how far you have gotten. Also, confirm your understanding of the time available. This may be a recapitulation of your initial phone call or letter. If you wish to tape the interview, ask permission at this point, but be ready with a notepad in case you do not get it. At any rate, you ought to take notes even if you do tape. Notes will help you keep track of potential questions and needed clarifications as you go along, and you will have a written record to assist you in finding important points when you later go over the tape.

When you begin to ask questions be sure to let the expert do most of the talking. Do not interrupt, disagree, or hold forth on your opinions. Be supportive verbally and nonverbally: Nod, smile, express interest and concern with your posture and facial expression. Encourage the person with short noninterruptive comments, such as "mm-hmmm," "I see," "that's interesting," "Then what happened?" and so on.

Check your understanding of the points being made by paraphrasing and clarifying: "In other words, what you are saying is . . ." "Would this be an example of what you are talking about? . . ." "Are you using the term 'discrimination' with the connotation of conscious intent?"

As the expert answers the open-ended questions, follow up with more-specific questions in response to those answers: "You said a minute ago that the issue of comparable pay for women may be more important in the long run than the Equal Rights Amendment. Why do you say that?"

Also, use questions to summarize and direct the interview: "So far you've talked about four problems working women face—unequal pay, lack of training, sexual harassment, and inadequate child care. Are there others?"

Allow for a closing phase for the interview. Respect the interviewee's time limit, and if you are approaching it, stop—even if you have gone through only half of your questions. Summarize your perspective of the interview. Often it is productive to ask if the person would like to make a wrap-up statement. In some cases you can ask, "What's the question I haven't asked that you wish I had?" And, of course, thank him or her.

5e. Maintain a complete record of your sources.

Form the habit of identifying the source for every piece of information you use and of recording complete bibliographic information for each source. Think about the battering your credibility will take if you are questioned about a bit of evidence and your only reply is "I found this in my research, but I don't remember exactly where," or, "Somebody told me this, but I don't remember who." With electronic catalogs your task often will be easier—you may be able to print out the bibliographic information for each of your potential sources or perhaps download it onto diskette. In other situations you will need to record it yourself. Writing down volume numbers of journals or the city of publication or the telephone number of your interviewee—details that you will never mention in your speech—may seem like unnecessary work, but routinely recording all information will help you retrieve sources if you need to check them again. If you later develop your speech into a written report or article, your research notes will be priceless.

Since you are recording all the details about your sources anyway, we recommend you master one of the standard formats for citing references. Then, if you need to append a reference list to an outline or decide to produce a handout for your audience, the sources of your research will be appropriately laid out. Three of the most popular formats are found in *The Chicago Manual of Style,* the *MLA Style Manual and Guide to Scholarly Publishing,* and the *Publication Manual of the American Psychological Association.* These vary in layout, but they all require an alphabetical listing that includes author, title, date, and publication details. In addition to the conventions for citing books, articles, chapters and abstracts, there are correct ways to cite interviews, personal correspondence, TV shows, Web sites, and e-mail.

5f. Capture the information and ideas in discrete units to facilitate retrieval and organization.

In the process of doing your research, you will want to gather and record your information and ideas in a way that makes it as easy as possible to find things when you look for them later and to work with them creatively. The ability to photocopy whole chapters of books, or download pages and pages of text from the Web does not make it any easier to review the information you have. Smaller, more manageable units will promote creative flexibility as you arrange and rearrange, structure and restructure your thoughts and data.

We talk about "notecards" in this section, but the important thing is not the media, the cardstock, but the activity—if you use an outlining tool or idea development software on a computer these suggestions are as pertinent. That said, 4″ × 6″ notecards are easy to manipulate and don't require a power source nearby.

(1) Notecards from print and electronic sources

As you read the book or article, jot down each discrete idea or bit of information on a separate card, being sure you add the identifying code and page number. Use only one side of each card. There are three kinds of data you might record: direct quotations or citations (Figure 5-1), paraphrased ideas (Figure 5-2), and references for later use (Figure 5-3). Do not neglect to do this for materials gotten online; even if you have a print-out, it is valuable to go through the process of paraphrasing or quoting so that you will have isolated and internalized the key points that drew you to that source in the first place.

If you decide now or later that the table mentioned in Figure 5-3 is valuable, you may want to photocopy it rather than tediously transcribe it by hand. If you photocopy lists, diagrams, tables, and other technical material, immediately head the sheet as you would a notecard.

For each source, select a one- or two-word identification code that refers to that source and no other. Usually the author's last name is sufficient. "Berch." If there is another book by Berch among your references, you may need to use "Berch, 1982," "Berch, 1986." Or if there are two sources from that author and year: "Berch, *Endless Day,*" "Berch, *Work and Worth.*" Or, of course, if you have different authors with the same last name: "Berch, B.," "Berch, F."

| **FIGURE** 5-1 | Direct Quotations or Citations |

Berch, p. 50.

On protective labor legislation for women (early 1900's):

"The ideology of protection seems only to have reinforced the difficulties working women faced. It left women isolated from the trade union movement. It pushed women out of the industrial sector of the economy, which was covered by legislation, into the service and clerical field, reinforcing existing tendencies toward occupational segregation. And with all that protection by the state, women still barely earned a living wage."

| **FIGURE** 5-2 | Paraphrased Ideas |

Berch, p. 148

Cites research that shows no discernable differences in aptitudes of the sexes in 14 "key skills." Shows that women surpass men in 6 skill areas (e.g. observation) and men surpass women in 2 areas (e.g. grip).

FIGURE 5-3   References for Later Use

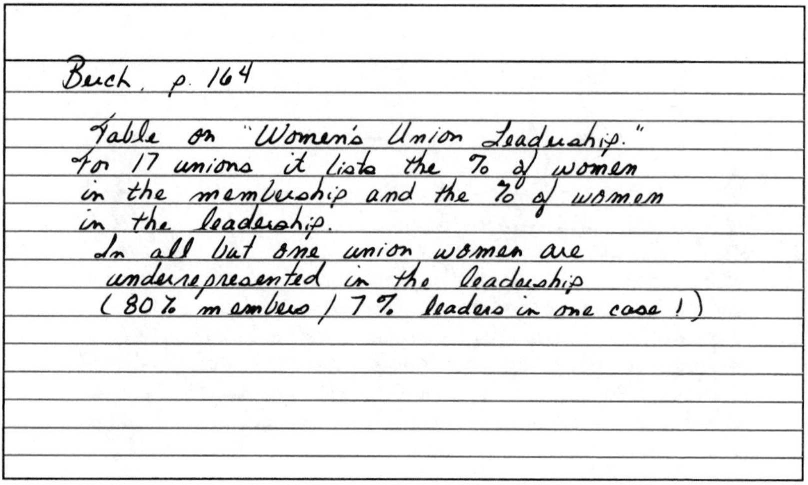

Buch, p. 164

Table on "Women's Union Leadership."
For 17 unions it lists the % of women
in the membership and the % of women
in the leadership.
In all but one union women are
underrepresented in the leadership
(80% members / 7% leaders in one case!)

If you copy entire articles or chapters, be sure to make a bibliography card for each. Many people find it helpful to photocopy the title page and copyright page of the book or periodical.

(2) Notecards from interviews and surveys

The suggestions in **(1)** relate to printed information, but are easily adapted to information acquired through interviews and surveys. Make a bibliography card for each interview, citing the person interviewed, his or her qualifications, the date of the interview, and that person's telephone number or address. As you listen to the tape or go over your notes, transcribe the information on cards.

(3) Grouping your cards

When you have gathered many notecards, you may want to stack them under cover cards with titles such as _history, causes, solutions,_ or you may decide to put these key words in the upper right corner. As you will see in the section on organizing, this grouping of ideas and naming of categories usually occurs later in the process of preparing your speech.

Chapter 6

Overcoming Fear of Speaking

Understand, analyze, and accept your fear of speaking. Combine thorough preparation with relaxation and visualization techniques to increase your confidence.

6a. Put your fear of speaking into perspective.

(1) Accept some fear as normal.

Many speakers try to be completely calm in every speech situation. This is unrealistic. Whether they call it stage fright, shyness, or speech anxiety, all speakers feel some fear. One out of five people experiences rather serious fear, enough to adversely affect performance. One out of 20 people suffers such serious fear of speaking that he or she is essentially unable to get through a public speech. For most of us, though, the fear can be managed and sometimes even turned to positive effect. People who perform in the public eye—actors, athletes, musicians . . . and speakers—have learned to function while concealing their fear. Despite their discomfort, they can use the rush of emotion to energize their performance.

The more speeches you give, the more confident you will become. You will recognize that fear is usually worst just before the speech and through the introduction. Once your speech is under way and the audience responds to you, negative emotions are often replaced by exhilaration.

(2) Analyze your fear as specifically as possible.

"I'm scared to death" is a common statement and it describes the emotional intensity of stage fright. Although one survey found that people list the fear of public speaking ahead of the fear of death, few people really expect the experience to be fatal. Just what are we afraid of? An amorphous, ill-defined fear cannot be dealt with. Dealing logically with the fear requires examining its components so you can isolate a number of specific problems to be solved.

It is helpful to list your fears on paper. Be as specific as possible. If you write statements like "I'm afraid I'll make a fool of myself," ask yourself these follow-up questions: How will I do that? ("I'll forget my speech"); What will happen next? ("The audience will think I'm dumb"). Use this format for your list:

> I am afraid that [specific event] will occur and then that [specific result] will follow.

When you have generated your list, you can classify the fears you have.

For items like "I'm afraid my visual aids won't be clear," the solution is simple. Check out the clarity of your visual aids with a few people and, if there is any problem, redesign them. As **6b** points out, many fears result from inadequate preparation. The mere act of writing the fears down makes them manageable and often points immediately to a solution.

Other fears on your list may relate to physical responses. "I'm afraid my hands will shake and my voice will crack." If many of your concerns fall into this category, pay special attention to the suggestions in **6c**.

Probably a number of items on your list deal with your failure to meet your own high standards. Recognize this fear as a positive motivation to do the best you can. Realize, too, though, that the power of suggestion is great and that dwelling on failure can cause it to happen. Use some of the visualization and verbalization techniques recommended in **6d** to create positive self-expectations.

If your fears are so pervasive you could not even verbalize them, or if you could list literally dozens, or if the consequences you dread are extreme ("I might collapse in the middle of the speech"), consider some of the more formal options mentioned in **6e**.

Finally, look at your list and decide which consequence is the one you are most afraid of. For most of us, like the college teacher who regularly lectures to a large student audience but quails at the thought of presenting a paper to twelve colleagues, the greatest fear is the fear of negative evaluation, particularly by peers or authority figures.

This fear of negative evaluation will translate into fear of your audience. As a group they seem threatening and critical. Remind yourself that an audience is merely a group of individuals and that a speech is just an enlarged conversation. If it would not be frightening to speak to any three or four of them, then it should not be frightening to speak to all of them together.

Of course, there are a few harsh, critical people in the world, but we have found that most listeners are charitable and supportive. They would just as soon hear a good speech; so they will, in effect, be rooting for you. Particularly, they want you to be confident. Recall how you felt when listening to very nervous speakers: Your discomfort and embarrassment were almost as great as theirs. This is testimony to the basic empathy of most audiences. Listeners will pick up the speaker's emotional tone, so that, for instance, a tense speaker will create a tense audience. On the other hand, you can actually feel an audience relax when a speaker who gets off to a shaky start hits his or her stride and the speech begins to roll.

If there is one technique that has helped people cope with stage fright, it is reconceptualizing the role of the audience, from "critic" to "recipient." A speaker must break out of the self-absorption of speech fright: "How do I look? Will they like me? Is my speech good enough?" Remind yourself that you are not there to perform, but to share. Center your thoughts on hypothetical audience members who are sincere and responsive. What do you have to give these people? How will the ideas and information you offer enrich their lives?

All of this advice comes back to the importance of the conversational resource at the time of speaking. There are some recent research findings that suggest that the best way to reduce communication apprehension is to change how you look at the public speaking event. It is not easy, but if you can think of yourself more as "talking with" the listeners and less as "performing for" them, you will feel much more comfortable.

6b. Build your confidence through thorough preparation and practice.

Why do sky divers think they can reach the ground in one piece? Preparation and practice allay their fears. Why do investors risk large sums of money? Preparation and practice have given them a clear view of the consequences. As we note elsewhere, the fact that good speakers make speechmaking look effortless does not mean that it is easy or uncomplicated. Their seeming lack of effort is based on extensive preparation over a period of time. The confidence they exude is also a result of preparation—not genes or fate or dumb luck. Nearly anyone can be poised and confident giving a speech. The speaker who has prepared thoroughly can be as confident as the sky diver who has exhaustively checked all his gear or the investor who has studied innumerable projections.

If you feel uncertain about getting your speech started, perhaps your introduction needs more work. If you are fearful of losing the continuity of the speech, you may need to practice it aloud several more times to internalize the flow of ideas. If you find yourself becoming generally anxious, use this as a stimulus to go over your preparation yet again. Drill yourself on the particulars of your supporting material. Go over your outline a number of times. Whatever else you do, remember that time wasted fretting about the outcome could better be used in positive action to ensure a positive outcome.

As you prepare, follow the suggestions on practice sessions in Chapter **24.** Avoid making last-minute changes in the speech and avoid memorizing your speech and practicing it so much that the ideas become stale and your delivery mechanical.

6c. Cope with the physical effects of fear by using techniques of relaxation and tension release.

When we are fearful or anxious, our bodies react by tensing the muscles to brace for attack and by releasing extra adrenaline to prepare us to fight or flee. These "fight-or-flight" responses, which are helpful when confronting a bear in the woods and were adaptive for our prehistoric ancestors, are not appropriate when the threat is psychological. When fear of speaking triggers our primitive sense of danger, we experience such symptoms as rapid heart rate, dizziness, butterflies in the stomach, trembling, perspiring, and dryness of the mouth. Muscular tension in the throat can cause a voice to quaver, sound strained, or even produce the unpredictable squawks of distant adolescence.

These physical symptoms will probably diminish with time as your successful experiences as a speaker make disaster appear less probable. But some degree of physical discomfort is likely to persist. You can master techniques to help you feel more comfortable.

When too much adrenaline makes you jumpy, physical activity usually helps to mitigate the effect. Of course, heavy exercise before a speech is impractical and overstimulating. A brisk walk around the block or a little pacing in the hall can be enough to bring your body back to normal. If you have a few moments of privacy, light exercise will feel good—just a few knee bends, arm swings, and neck rolls. If you remain in sight of your audience before the speech, you may be able unobtrusively to clench and unclench your hands, but do not risk your credibility by going through any bizarre preparatory rituals. Once the speech begins, take advantage of the extra energy that the adrenaline provides to make your delivery more vigorous. Appropriate, dynamic gestures will help you discharge the nervous residue.

You can also handle symptoms of nervousness by learning to use relaxation techniques. Relaxation, like any other skill, is achieved through practice. Using any of a number of books or tapes on stress, tension, and relaxation, you can learn first to isolate the areas of your body that are tense and then to relax them. Try meditation, biofeedback, or self-hypnosis. Explore such methods as tightening, then relaxing, certain muscle groups; visualizing serene settings; or imagining sensations such as warmth or heaviness in parts of your body. There are great individual differences in people's responses to these techniques. Continue to experiment until you find one or more that are effective for you. After learning and practicing such techniques, you should be able to achieve relaxation, even lower your pulse and blood pressure, while taking a few deep breaths before you speak.

Chemical aids to relaxation—alcohol, drugs, tranquilizers—are not advisable. Most have side effects that impair your mental and physical performance during a speech, not to mention fabricating a false sense of security.

6d. Use positive self-suggestion to combat your anxiety.

(1) Visualize success.

Psychologists have discovered the tremendous power of visualization in influencing performance. When you experience fear, you are visualizing the most negative outcome for your speech. The more powerful your imagination, the more horrible and graphic are the disasters you can dream up. It is possible, however, to turn these fantasies around. For example, tennis players, field goal kickers, and concert pianists, among others, have found it helpful to visualize what they are striving for. When preparing a speech, do not let yourself think about failure. When you detect those thoughts in your mind, replace them with a positive scenario: "I will approach the lectern calmly, smile at the audience, and begin. My voice will sound strong and confident." Do not set unrealistic standards of perfection. Build some contingencies into your fantasy. "If I forget a point I'll look down at my notecard and concentrate on the main idea I am conveying." Run through these positive visualizations a few times a day before you speak. As you practice, picture the audience responding favorably to the speech. Just before you get up to speak, tell yourself about the general tone and image you wish to project. "As I go up there I am going to communicate my sincerity and concern in a warm, natural, confident manner."

(2) Replace negative internal statements with positive ones.

One approach to reducing fears is based on a therapeutic technique called *cognitive restructuring.* In essence, it probes our mental commentaries and identifies the unrealistic or irrational statements that cause fear, replacing them with more positive, logical, and realistic beliefs. We all have constant narrations running through our minds, voices chattering in the background. These commentaries are so familiar that we are barely conscious of them. With some introspection you can bring them to the front of your mind and examine the effect they have on your behavior. It is helpful to remember that these are not statements of fact, but are statements that you yourself have created and that you can choose to replace if they interfere with your efficient functioning. Once you become fully aware of the commentaries that govern your response to public speaking, you can work on replacing the unproductive beliefs with more positive ones. See Table 6-1.

Your unproductive responses are habitual and will not change easily. At first you will have to repeat the replacement sentences mechanically, over and over, as you might learn a new formula or equation. Because the replacement sentences are so reasonable and logical, a large part of your mind will want to accept them. The reassuring nature of the words often helps you to become physically calmer, and this more comfortable sensation acts to reinforce the new beliefs.

TABLE 6-1	Replacement Statements
False Belief	**Positive Replacement**
My speech will be a failure unless everyone in the audience likes it.	I will be successful if most people present respond favorably.
A good speaker never says, "Uh" or "Er."	A few nonfluencies aren't even noticed unless attention is called to them.
I'm going to go blank.	I've practiced several times. I know the basic structure of this speech.
I can't handle this tension!	Even though I feel uncomfortable, I'm able to cope with tense situations.
Someone will ask me a question that exposes my ignorance.	I'm not ignorant. I've research this topic and I'm prepared for any reasonable question.

6e. If none of the preceding suggestions works, seek outside help.

Some fear of speaking is too deeply rooted to be remedied by the methods suggested here. If your fear of speaking is almost paralyzing, you may need help in coping with it. Research shows that even severe fear of speaking can usually be reduced to a manageable level when treated by a qualified professional. It is not necessary to commit yourself to a long-range course of therapy that fully explores all the causes of your anxiety. Training programs for speech fright may deal directly with the symptoms by adapting techniques used for overcoming phobias such as fear of snakes, spiders, flying, and so on.

Many colleges and universities offer special sections of speech classes for fearful students. Others offer ungraded workshops to supplement regular classes. These programs use systematic desensitization (a method that combines relaxation exercises and visualization), cognitive restructuring, skills training, or a combination of these and other methods. Psychologists and speech consultants also offer programs to help reduce fear of speaking. Such programs may be publicized under the names of stage fright, communication apprehension, speech anxiety, reticence, or shyness.

Part 2

Organization

---

7 Transforming Ideas into
Speech Points
8 Arranging Points
9 Outlines
10 Transitions
11 Introductions
12 Conclusions

Introduction

Of the four phases of the creative process, most speech training emphasizes preparation and refinement because these are logical, rule-bound processes. Incubation and illumination are rarely mentioned because they do not lend themselves to systemization. These middle steps touch the emotions. The process of creating a poem, a story, a painting, a symphony, or a speech produces intense feelings of discouragement and excitement. After you have analyzed your audience and topic, and have thoroughly researched your subject, you discover that when you start to outline and organize your ideas, composing a speech is not always straightforward and systematic. Even with adequate preparation, you will find yourself pacing the floor, staring into space, filling your wastebasket with false starts. Rest assured that you are not the only one to whom this happens.

In writing this book, we did not sit down at the computer, type the title *The Speaker's Handbook,* and then proceed unerringly through to the last page. The naming and arranging of categories took hours: Should practice be dealt with as an aspect of preparation? Can style be separated from content? Does the motivated sequence fit under patterns of organization or under motivational appeals? Even when we had settled on a general outline, the details of that outline were altered again and again as the actual writing progressed. At times the topics seemed so interconnected that we felt we were trying to untangle a skein of yarn rescued from the attentions of the cat. Would it ever come out in one straight line? This frustration is an inherent part of the creative process. When you have read only one article on a topic, it is easy to write a summary of it. When you have researched and analyzed a topic fully, you begin to suffer from information overload. First, you are overwhelmed by the amount of information; second, you see so many connections among the facets of the topic that you have trouble dividing it. See this frustration as a sign that you have gone beyond the "book report" stage and are beginning to impose your own creative structure on the topic. In effect, you are saving your audience from the agony of information overload by experiencing it yourself and then struggling until you have drawn something clear and meaningful out of the morass.

The analysis and synthesis of information have appropriately been called *invention*. *Analysis* is the taking apart of a topic, a process that follows specified rules. *Synthesis* is the remolding of the parts into a new whole—truly creating or inventing an interpretation that did not exist before. There are no set rules for synthesis. While many people could collect the same information and divide a topic into certain logical parts, no two people could prepare the same speech. The synthesis that you create reflects your personality, your values, and your individual approach to life.

Chapters 7–12 suggest ways to organize and structure your material to provide a unified speech. Out of the many ideas you encounter in your research, it is necessary to *transform them into points* that best reflect your purpose in speaking. A set of parallel, clearly stated, mutually exclusive main points will be easy for you and your audience to remember. There are several effective ways to *arrange these points*. The speech *outline* is not just an arbitrary and tiresome exercise imposed by teachers; preparation of a complete outline gives you a logical blueprint for your speech. Also important are the *transitions* that form the bridges between the parts of the speech. When the body of your speech is structured, you will want to devise an *introduction* to lead your listeners into your topic, and, later, wrap it up for them with a *conclusion*. (See the Speech Structure Flowchart.)

SPEECH STRUCTURE
FLOWCHART

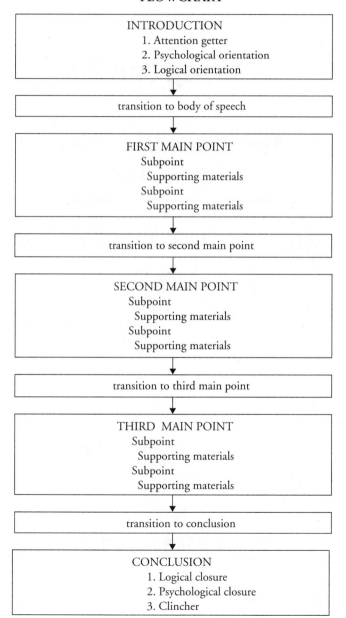

INTRODUCTION
1. Attention getter
2. Psychological orientation
3. Logical orientation

↓

transition to body of speech

↓

FIRST MAIN POINT
Subpoint
  Supporting materials
Subpoint
  Supporting materials

↓

transition to second main point

↓

SECOND MAIN POINT
Subpoint
  Supporting materials
Subpoint
  Supporting materials

↓

transition to third main point

↓

THIRD MAIN POINT
Subpoint
  Supporting materials
Subpoint
  Supporting materials

↓

transition to conclusion

↓

CONCLUSION
1. Logical closure
2. Psychological closure
3. Clincher

Chapter 7

Transforming Ideas into Speech Points

Look for logical groupings of ideas that could be developed as points of your speech.

You may have lots of good ideas, but you need a procedure to assess which are important and where you want to go with them. The act of sifting all your ideas on your speech topic and coming up with a satisfactory pattern, a coherent synthesis, is a demanding, multistep process that cannot be given short shrift. In essence, the process of organizing entails:

1. Generating many ideas
2. Grouping them into clusters
3. Labeling each cluster
4. Reworking, adjusting, and culling the ideas until you have two to five major groupings that cover the most important ideas and that can be developed in your allotted time

7a. Assemble all the possible ideas and information that could go into your speech.

When you begin to prepare a speech, do not limit yourself. Begin to jot down every item you might possibly cover in your speech, whether drawn from your research or from ideas you have been percolating. Follow the techniques of brainstorming; go for quantity rather than quality at this point. Do not judge or dismiss any idea. Write it down. There is no need yet to impose any order on what you are writing. Work quickly and do not worry if some ideas are variations on the same theme or wildly divergent. You cannot start the process of organizing until you have some raw material to organize.

7b. Use a variety of organizational tools to identify potential points and examine their relationships.

Look back over the brainstorming list you made and consider how you might cluster the entries. Are there any that stand out as possible main points? Are there any that seem obviously to fit together? Are there any that fall naturally under others?

There is no one correct way to group these ideas. Almost certainly there are some ideas that will get omitted altogether, others that have to be forced a bit to fit into any category. You may notice points you grouped together that are not all of equal importance. Sometimes one or more of the ideas from your brainstorming list serve as a category around which to group lesser points. Sometimes you will group several minor ideas first and then devise a superordinate heading.

You can use a number of different techniques to begin your organization, choosing one or a combination that suits how you work best, whether visually or textually.

(1) A rudimentary, working outline

Perhaps the most traditional technique of speech organization is to arrange ideas in the hierarchical, indented outline format. At this stage of development, however, you do not want to be constrained by the requirements of the formal full-sentence outline (see **9a** and **9b**). The full-sentence outline has a very important role in ensuring that you properly elaborate your points and subpoints, but a less rigid form, the *topic outline,* is more useful at this point. Examples of both types of outlines are shown in **9b**, on the subject Working Women in the United States.

Because you are likely to experiment with several alternative groupings of ideas, don't spend time on phrasing or format. Just try fitting ideas under one another, nesting them in various ways until you discover a pattern that seems to make the most sense.

If this is a comfortable method for you, you will have a head start on developing the full-sentence outline. However, even this loose form of outlining may be premature if it blocks your thought processes. There are other, more spatially oriented ways to marshal your thoughts, which we describe next.

(2) Concept mapping

Concept mapping is a visual method of taking your ideas and showing how they relate to each other. At its most basic form you quickly draw a simple diagram made of labeled circles and squares, connecting them with lines.

Start with your central idea, your topic, and write it in a box or circle in the center of a sheet of paper. Think about the points from your brainstorming list and print some major ones around the topic, leaving enough room to add more subpoints. Your ideas will start to cluster around certain points; as you write each new one down, draw a line to connect it to its related point. This doesn't have to be done hierarchically, however. Subpoints might come to you before a broader point does. You can redraw as new relationships become clear.

There are a variety of styles for doing this, under the names of clustering, mind-mapping, branching, and ballooning. See Figure 7-1 for an example of a simple concept map, one that could have been part of the organizational process that led to the comic book outline in **8b**.

(3) Manipulating movable components

This can be similar to concept mapping in that you organize things spatially, or it can be similar to outlining in that you put things together in linear form; it depends on the components you use. For example, you can jot your ideas on 3″ × 2″ self-sticking notes and stick them to a wall or desktop. You can cluster them according to themes, moving ones from group to group until you are happy with the total grouping. Or, if you prefer to look at things more linearly, you can use the self-sticking notes to make a rudimentary outline on whatever surface you're using, complete with indention of subpoints.

FIGURE 7-1   Simple Concept Map

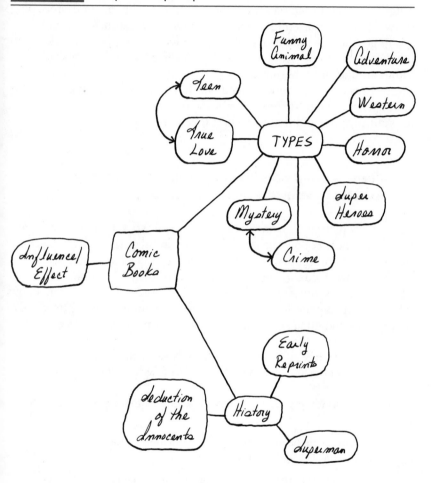

Another possibility is to start with your research notecards and supplement them with cards on which you've written your own thoughts. In **5f** we suggest grouping the research notecards under subject cover cards. From this beginning you can write ideas, transitions, and syntheses on more cards and shuffle them in where you think they fit. As with the sticky notes, you can easily change the organization to experiment with a variety of approaches to your subject.

These two paper-based approaches can also be duplicated on a computer, using, at the simplest end, the outlining facility of word processing software, or specialized idea development software at the other end.

To get the full benefit of each of these techniques, do not lock in too quickly to any one pattern. Leave yourself enough freedom to move things around until they click.

As a result of this process, you will have a set of potential points for your speech. The next step is to choose the points that are most suitable for your purpose and that work best together.

7c. Choose main points that taken together correspond exactly to your thesis statement.

To decide which main points to include in your speech, first look at your thesis sentence. Follow the steps discussed in **3d** to identify the essential questions you must answer. For persuasive speeches that develop propositions of fact, value, or policy, consult **20b** for information on how to identify the essential questions with more precision. Once you know what a complete development of your topic requires, use the thesis sentence as a standard against which to test your main points. Ask yourself:

> Is there any part of my thesis that is not developed in the speech?
> Is there any main idea of the speech that is not reflected in the thesis?

Look at the following thesis sentence and the main points selected to develop it.

> Thesis statement: The jojoba plant is an effective energy source capable of eliminating U.S. dependence on foreign oil.
>
> I. The jojoba plant is a virtually untapped source of energy.
> II. Energy can be produced from the jojoba plant efficiently and safely.
> III. Given an adequate educational program, the public would come to accept jojoba plant energy.

Obviously something is missing. Either the thesis sentence should be changed by deleting the last phrase or another main point should be added establishing the ability of jojoba plant energy to eliminate U.S. dependence on foreign oil.

Here is another set of main points developed from the same thesis sentence.

Thesis statement: The jojoba plant is an effective energy source capable of eliminating U.S. dependence on foreign oil.

   I. The jojoba plant is a safe, efficient, marketable source of energy.
  II. The jojoba plant could create sufficient energy to eliminate U.S. dependence on foreign oil.
 III. The jojoba plant can be used as a source of protein.

In this case the final main point has nothing to do with the thesis sentence. This idea might be mentioned in passing as a part of the introduction or conclusion, but should not be a main point unless the thesis sentence were broadened to include the jojoba's value as a food source.

The following set of main points corresponds exactly to the thesis sentence; nothing essential is missing, nothing superfluous is included.

Thesis statement: The jojoba plant is an effective energy source capable of eliminating U.S. dependence on foreign oil.

   I. The jojoba plant is a virtually untapped source of energy.
  II. The jojoba plant is a safe, efficient, and marketable source of energy.
 III. The jojoba plant could create sufficient energy to eliminate U.S. dependence on foreign oil.

When appropriate, you may adjust your thesis sentence to reflect the refinement of thinking that has resulted from the organizing process.

Exercise 1. Do the following sets of main points correspond to the thesis sentence? If not, rewrite the outline and/or thesis sentence so that the correspondence is exact.

Thesis: Cats make better pets than dogs.

   I. Cats are neater than dogs.
  II. Cats are more independent than dogs.
 III. Cats have an interesting life history in mythology and literature.
 IV. Cats are loyal and affectionate.

Thesis: A four-day work week would be beneficial to our company.

   I. Employees will enjoy longer weekends.
  II. Employees will miss rush hour traffic jams.
 III. Employees can share child care more equitably.

Thesis: Homosexuals are discriminated against in every area of their lives.

   I. Homosexuals are victims of discrimination in housing.
  II. Homosexuals are victims of discrimination in employment.
 III. Homosexuals have made valuable cultural contributions throughout history.

7d. Select main points that are mutually exclusive.

It is no accident that *main* points are so labeled. As explained in **7c** they are those few ideas that are central and indispensable to the development of the thesis.

Main points should be mutually exclusive for maximum clarity. Each category should exclude the ideas that are subsumed by any other category. Put more simply, this rule is a version of the maxim "a place for everything and everything in its place." The challenge for the speaker lies in finding a scheme where each idea fits in just *one* place.

Sometimes when you are grouping ideas under potential main points you will find that many will fit into two or more categories. When this overlapping occurs, you know that you have not yet found an effective system for classifying your ideas. Settling on a single organizational pattern is essential. If you do not know where an idea fits, your audience certainly will not. If you were unsure of your pattern, the result might be an outline like this:

Topic: Great Films
   I. Drama
      A. One Flew Over the Cuckoo's Nest (1975)
      B. The Adventures of Robin Hood (1938)
      C. The Wild Bunch (1969)
  II. Comedy
      A. Annie Hall (1977)
      B. Singin' In The Rain (1952)
      C. The Producers (1968)
 III. Black & White Film
      A. Raging Bull (1980)
      B. The General (1927)
      C. Stagecoach (1939)

A quick look shows that the topic was not completely thought through before the speaker began to lay out the structure of the speech. It appears that the speaker has not yet been able to decide whether the discussion on film will form along lines defined by dramatic category or by color or the lack of it. Since whether a movie was shot on color or black and white stock does not have any intrinsic relationship to the subject (being more a matter of the history of the technology), having the three main points be Drama, Comedy, and Black & White Film presents a problem: The three main points are not distinct categories. Ideally, with a system of mutually exclusive main points, you would know how to classify any kind of film and put it under one point only. If we put the sample outline to the test, however, we encounter uncertainty. "Raging Bull," for instance, is a drama, but there it is under Black & White, not Drama. If we take a film not yet listed, like "Bringing Up Baby," which is a black & white comedy from 1938, the uncertainty continues. There is no basis to exclude it from either the Comedy or Black & White categories. So, although each main point taken alone seems a plausible way to classify some movies, the three main points taken together do not constitute a sensible way to look at the topic. It is like trying to add fractions to decimals.

Here is another example of an outline on the same topic:

Topic: Great Films
I. Black & White
    A. Drama
       1. Stagecoach (1939)
       2. Touch of Evil (1958)
       3. The Manchurian Candidate (1962)
       4. Raging Bull (1980)
    B. Comedy
       1. The General (1927)
       2. Bringing Up Baby (1938)
       3. Some Like It Hot (1959)
       4. A Hard Day's Night (1964)
II. Color
    A. Drama
       1. The Adventures of Robin Hood (1938)
       2. Rear Window (1954)
       3. The Wild Bunch (1969)
       4. One Flew Over the Cuckoo's Nest (1975)
    B. Comedy
       1. Singin' In The Rain (1952)
       2. The Producers (1968)
       3. Annie Hall (1977)
       4. Tootsie (1982)

In the preceding example the topic is divided into main points along a single dimension: color, or lack of it. These main points are each broken down into two categories that then are repeated for each main point.

This same topic could be divided many other ways. For instance, the main points might also form along chronology, like:

I. 1920s
   A. Drama
      1. Greed (1924)
      2. Sunrise (1927)
   B. Comedy
      1. The Gold Rush (1925)
      2. The General (1927)
II. 1930s
   A. Drama
      1. All Quiet on the Western Front (1930)
      2. The Adventures of Robin Hood (1938)
   B. Comedy
      1. It Happened One Night (1934)
      2. Bringing Up Baby (1938)

or English-Language and Non-English, or by director, or by genre, and so forth.

What is so important is that you choose *one* classification scheme for your main points that gives you a rule by which to include each item under one and only one main point.

Note: There will often be a few cases that fall between categories or are difficult to classify. For a general audience it is usually best to narrow your topic to exclude these unusual cases and discuss them in the question-and-answer period if necessary. Be sure in laying out your categories to use such language as "westerns, in general, can be classified as . . ." or "with a few exceptions . . ."

For a technical topic with a sophisticated audience, you may discuss the borderline cases in your introduction, conclusion, or transitions or create a catchall category:

Theories of Language Development
   I. Chomsky's Linguistic Competence Theory
   II. Skinner's Behavioral Theory
   III. Other theories

7e. Have at least two, but not more than five, main points in the average speech.

Although this rule sounds arbitrary, it is not as restricting as you may think. As a speaker, you should be able to cluster your ideas around a few main themes. If every thought is treated as a main point, there will be no opportunity left to *develop* any of them. With many random subpoints, you never extract meaning from an unorganized barrage of information. On the other hand, if you have only one main point, you basically have your topic and no organization to speak of, either.

Understand, too, that your audience is not going to be able to remember more than a few main points.

7f. Express main points and subpoints to reflect coordinate and subordinate relationships.

Ideas of equal importance or of parallel logical function are called *coordinate points*. Points of lesser significance that support, explain, or contribute steps of logical development to other ideas are called *subordinate points*.

The relative importance of main and other points must be very clear in your own mind. Every point in the speech is subordinate, coordinate, or superordinate to every other.

If you were to classify methods of transporting goods you might come up with:

Transportation of Goods
    Trains
    Trucks
    Airplanes
    Ships

In this example, Trains, Trucks, Airplanes, and Ships bear a coordinate relationship to each other and a subordinate relationship to the larger, or superordinate, category Transportation of Goods. Each mode of transportation in turn may have more specific divisions. For instance:

Types of Trucks
    Tractors
    Vans

> Dumps
> Tankers
> Flatbeds

Here each type of truck bears a subordinate relationship to the heading Types of Trucks and a coordinate relationship to each other type.

Logical relationships are similarly shown through subordination and coordination, as in this example:

> Trucks are an efficient means of transporting goods.
> [because]
> They have a wide network of destinations.
> [because]
> They have a great versatility of design.
> [and because]
> They are relatively cheap to operate.

It is evident that the reasons are subordinate to the points they establish.

(1) Subordinate points and subpoints should fit inside, or support, a larger idea.

Sometimes ideas slip in that are "too big" for the points they are supposed to be supporting. Consider the following example from a speech on the role of aircraft carriers in World War II and think about the fit of these points.

> I. Aircraft carriers were instrumental in winning the war in the Pacific.
>   A. The successful use of aircraft carriers at the battles of the Coral Sea and Midway blunted the Japanese drive across the Pacific.
>   B. Planes launched from aircraft carriers were able to inflict damage to enemy bases out of the range of land-based aircraft.
>   C. Antisubmarine warfare was the major use of aircraft carriers in the Atlantic.

In this case Subpoint C is not related to the major idea nor is it subordinate in importance. The use of aircraft carriers in the Atlantic does not fit under their use in the Pacific. The two ideas bear a coordinate relationship, and the statement in Subpoint C should probably be Main Point II.

(2) Coordinate points and subpoints should be of equal importance.

Another problem occurs when an idea is "too small" to fit with the others at its level. In the following outline the main points are not coordinate:

   I. Aircraft carriers were instrumental in winning the war in the Pacific.
      A. The successful use of aircraft carriers at the battles of the Coral Sea and Midway blunted the Japanese drive across the Pacific.
      B. A number of new aircraft carriers were named after carriers sunk earlier in the war.
      C. Planes launched from aircraft carriers were able to inflict damage to enemy bases out of the range of land-based aircraft.

Subpoint B jars when compared to the other two subpoints. There may have been some initial benefit from the confusion that such naming would cause the intelligence services of the Japanese, but it would hardly be "instrumental."

If you have one main idea that seems much less important than the other, (1) omit it, (2) create another main point so this less important idea can become a subpoint, (3) mention the idea as part of the introduction or conclusion, (4) occasionally consider a catchall main point, such as: "There are several other factors . . ."

(3) Each subpoint should directly relate to the point it supports.

Do not group unrelated subpoints.

   I. Aircraft carriers were instrumental in winning the war in the Pacific.
      A. The successful use of aircraft carriers at the battles of the Coral Sea and Midway blunted the Japanese drive across the Pacific.
      B. The F4F fighter was redesigned to have folding wings so that aircraft carriers could carry more planes.
      C. Planes launched from aircraft carriers were able to inflict damage to enemy bases out of the range of land-based aircraft.

Subpoint B is interesting and probably appropriate as a subpoint somewhere in this speech, perhaps supporting a superordinate point dealing with steps that were taken to make the carrier forces more efficient. Clearly, though, Subpoint B has no *direct* relationship to the point about the war in the Pacific.

Chapter 8

Arranging Points

When you arrange your points, consider the traditional patterns of speech organization, and select or create the one that is best suited to your topic and purpose.

When the main ideas of a speech are selected, it is necessary to arrange them in the order that will maximize effectiveness. In some cases the decision is virtually made for you. For an argument to seem logical to an audience, the premises must be unfolded in a certain order, as explained in **14g.** Debate speeches or closing arguments to juries, for example, have such strict requirements that they almost always unfold according to stock patterns, as shown in **20a.** Many ceremonial or special occasion speeches are so stylized that they follow a formula. See Chapter **22.** One can expect a commencement speaker to begin by congratulating the graduates and their parents and then move to enunciating a challenge for the future. And it is safe to predict that at a retirement dinner the speaker will begin by summarizing the honoree's achievements and subsequently will speculate humorously about the honoree's coming leisure time. For the usual informative or persuasive speech, though, there is no given pattern. You, as a speaker, must select the best arrangement of ideas.

8a. Arrange main points in a pattern that arises inherently from the subject matter or from the requirements of the thesis sentence.

There are several traditional patterns of speech arrangement: chronological, spatial, cause-effect, problem-solution, and topical.

(1) The chronological pattern orders ideas in a time sequence.

Probably the most ancient form of extended discourse is the narrative unfolding of a story. A time-ordered format still undergirds many contemporary speeches. *Historical* development is the most common chronological pattern. If you were giving a speech on the course of European music 1600–1900, you might arrange it this way:

I. The Baroque period (1600–1750)
II. The Classical period (1720–1810)
III. The Romantic period (1800–1900)

Also look at the outline on women workers in **9b**.

Another chronological pattern divides a topic into *past-present-future*. In a speech on automobile propulsion, you might arrange your ideas in this manner:

I. In the days of cheap oil, auto engines did not need to be energy efficient.
II. Today, redesigned engines provide increased efficiency.
III. We can look forward to new technologies that may even replace the need for fossil fuel–burning engines altogether.

A third way to look at a subject chronologically is to analyze a process *step by step*. The topic How to Keep Fit through Aerobic Exercise could generate this outline:

I. Determine the resting and working heart rate for your age.
II. Begin each session with stretching exercises and low-level cardiovascular warm-up.
III. Through vigorous exercise maintain your working heart rate for 30 to 40 minutes.
IV. Allow at least 10 minutes for cool-down and stretching exercises.

(2) The spatial pattern arranges points by location.

The spatial pattern is often based on geography. This can encompass the globe or the two blocks around your house.

> Topic: Crime
>   I. Crime on the Eastern Seaboard
> II. Crime in the Midwest
> III. Crime on the Pacific Coast

Other geographical arrangements might divide this topic into Crime in Europe, Crime in Asia, Crime in Latin America; or Crime in Manhattan, Crime in Brooklyn, Crime in the Bronx.

Geography need not refer just to areas on a map but can show up as other ways of dividing the world spatially.

> Topic: Crime
>   I. Rural crime
> II. Urban crime
> III. Suburban crime

The spatial pattern might also be applied to much smaller areas, such as the floor plan of a house or the arrangement of a library. The following example of a spatial pattern describes a very small area indeed:

> Topic: An aircraft instrument panel
>   I. Instruments needed to maintain controlled flight are on the left side of the panel.
>   A. Compass
>   B. Altimeter
>   C. Artificial horizon
>   D. Turn and bank indicator
>   E. Air speed indicator
> II. Instruments providing information on the operating condition of the aircraft are on the right side.
>   A. Tachometer
>   B. Manifold pressure gauge
>   C. Oil temperature gauge
>   D. Oil pressure gauge
>   E. Fuel gauge

(3) In the cause-effect pattern, the speaker moves from a discussion of the origins of a condition to the ways it manifests itself.

This pattern is used to show that events that occur in sequence are in fact causally related. A cause-effect structure is well suited to a speech where the goal is to achieve either understanding or agreement rather than overt action.

   I. There has been a sharp increase in housing costs over the last generation.
     [as a result]
  II. It is extremely difficult for a one-income family to purchase a house.

Occasionally the pattern may be reversed to an effect-cause sequence.

   I. It is extremely difficult for a one-income family to purchase a house.
     [this is because]
  II. There has been a sharp increase in housing costs over the last generation.

Of course, when using the cause-effect pattern, you must be sure that the causal relationship you propose is a valid one. See **14d.**

(4) The problem-solution pattern examines the symptoms of a problem and then suggests a remedy.

This pattern is used in persuasive speeches that advocate a new policy or a specific course of action.

   I. The current system of financing health care in the United States is inadequate.
     [to remedy this]
  II. A system of national health insurance would provide medical care to all citizens.

On rare occasions a speaker might choose to use a solution-problem pattern.

   I. A system of national health care insurance would provide adequate medical care to all citizens.

[this is necessary because]

II. The current system of financing health care in the United States is inadequate.

The psychological and stylistic weaknesses of this pattern should be evident. Most audiences would resist accepting a program of change before hearing the justification for that change.

(5) The topical pattern of organization divides a speech into elements that have no pattern exclusive of their relationship to the topic itself.

This is the most frequently used speech pattern. It is also the most difficult in that you cannot rely on a predetermined structure, but rather must understand the range and limitations of the subject itself in order to select an effective pattern. Some topics obviously fit a time or space sequence; many subjects, however, do not lend themselves readily to any of the arrangements discussed so far. In these cases you need to generate an original system for structuring the speech. Since a pattern intrinsic to one subject will not work with another, the application of any topical pattern you select will be unique to that one speech.

Often the best structure for a speech is the listing of the components of a whole or the listing of reasons that add up to the thesis sentence. The following is an example of a topical pattern that lists reasons for a conclusion.

Thesis: Capital punishment should be abolished.

   I. Capital punishment does not deter crime.

  II. Capital punishment is ultimately more costly than life imprisonment.

 III. The risk of executing an innocent person is morally unacceptable.

Sometimes topical patterns may combine aspects of other organizational patterns. For instance, a *cause* leads to an *effect*, which is seen as a *problem* and therefore requires a *solution*.

   I. Children watch a great deal of television.
   [therefore]

  II. Children are not developing skills in reading and creative play.
  [and this is a problem; so to remedy it]

 III. Parents should limit children's viewing time.

Other topics easily suggest their own arrangements, such as grouping the pro and con points on a controversial issue or answering questions that have been laid out checklist-style by some expert on your subject.

When you are building a speech that supports a controversial thesis, as in most persuasive speeches, arranging your main points is more complex than just choosing a pattern. Your speech will consist of an *argument* for your thesis, and the main points may be parts of that argument or may be a series of smaller arguments that add up to your overall conclusion. You will have important decisions to make about how best to lead your audience through your reasoning pattern. For an unfavorable audience (see **4d**), this requires spelling out every step of the process. Besides these logical considerations, you will often need to think about the psychological impact you are attempting to create. These more advanced organizational patterns are discussed in Chapters **13** and **20**.

Note: Sometimes two or more organizational patterns will seem to fit your topic equally well. In that case try to understand your audience's frame of reference to determine which sequence will be clearest and most persuasive to them. Suppose, for instance, you were giving an informative speech on a vegetable-processing plant. You could arrange the speech chronologically from when the produce arrives to when the cartons of packaged food are shipped away. Or you could arrange the speech spatially, leading the audience through the front offices and around the floor of the plant. For an audience familiar with food processing, either sequence might be fine. For an uninformed audience, though, the spatial arrangement, which might start out in the quality-control section, could be confusing. The chronological pattern, starting with the vegetables arriving from the fields, would be preferable.

Exercise 1. By generating separate sets of main points, show how each of these topics could be presented in three different organizational patterns.

Smoking and Lung Cancer
National Parks
Racial Discrimination in the United States
Terrorist Attacks on Airliners
Oriental Cooking

8b. Group subpoints according to a pattern, but do not feel compelled to echo the pattern of the main points.

After your main ideas are set, look at the subpoints under each. These, too, need to be arranged in some effective order—topical, chronological, whatever. You do not have to repeat the pattern used for the main points; you can choose the format that makes the most sense for each set of subpoints. Notice the different arrangements in the detailed outline that follows:

> Thesis: With their scope, history, and influence, comic books are an interesting component of American popular culture.
>
> I. Comic books are not merely "comic," but rather explore a range of subject matter.
> - A. Funny animal comics and kid comics are parables and parodies of the human condition.
>   1. Elmer Fudd and Bugs: Tradition versus the pioneering spirit.
>   2. Barks' ducks: Epic adventure and human foibles.
>   3. Harvey's rich kids: Capitalism with a human face.
> - B. True love and teen comics present a hackneyed, boring, and sometimes disturbing picture of male/female relationships.
>   1. True love girl meets, loses, gets, marries boy (and vows never to be so stupid as to put her needs above his again).
>   2. Teen comic girl fights other girls for the favors of a jerk male like Archie, who her father thinks is a twerp.
>   3. True love and teen comics foster the "Us versus Them" view of the male/female world.
> - C. Western and adventure comics concentrate on the triumph of good over evil.
>   1. Western cattle barons learn that six-gun-slinging saviors arise naturally from oppressed common folk.
>   2. Adventure stories pit virtuous types against the blind malice of uncaring nature.
> - D. Horror and mystery comics investigate ethics and morality while titillating and scaring readers.
>   1. Eternal punishment for an unethical choice is a recurring theme of horror comics.
>   2. The tempting hedonism of wrongdoers is graphically displayed in mystery comics—until the ironic twist of fate on the last page.
> - E. Superhero comics manifest the unspoken and sometimes frightening fantasies and aspirations of the American people.

Topical

1. Superman is the supremely powerful spokesman and policeman for the American definition of the "right way."
2. The jackbooted hero, Blackhawk, was created in World War II to fight totalitarian fire with fire.
3. Mar-Vell personifies the desire for total knowledge and the wisdom needed to use it.
4. Spider-Man is the embodiment of the perennial underdog triumphant.

II. Comic books started as anthologies of another medium but soon grew into a separate art form developing along a path of its own.
  A. Early comic books were mostly reprints of Sunday newspaper comic strip sections.
    1. "Foxy Granpa" was reprinted in a number of comic books just after the turn of the century.
    2. The following decades saw strips like "Mutt & Jeff," "Little Orphan Annie," and "Moon Mullins" reprinted.
    3. Reprint books in the thirties included such titles as "Tarzan" in *Tip Top Comics* and "Terry and the Pirates" in *Popular Comics*.
  B. By 1938 the majority of comic books contained original work and, with the appearance of Superman, the golden age of comics began.
    1. *Detective Comics* was the first single-theme, all-original comic.
    2. Superman, the first costumed superhero, was featured in *Action* no. 1.
    3. More than 150 titles were in print by the end of 1941.
  C. During the decade after the war, comic books for the most part went into a slump.
    1. With the Axis powers defeated and the Cold War not yet focused, the perceived need for superheroes lessened and the sales of their books slacked off.
    2. Many horror, mystery, superhero, adventure, true love, and teen comics fell before the wave of censorship following the publication of *Seduction of the Innocent*.
    3. Funny animal comics and kid comics retrenched behind the strongest series.
  D. By the late fifties comic books had started to recover, overcoming their tarnished image.
    1. In creating the Comics Code Authority, publishers hoped to reassure worried parents and legislators.
    2. The silver age of comics began with the reintroduction of long-idle golden age characters.
  E. In the early sixties the trend toward emphasizing characterization, motivation, and involvement with issues initiated a new and

Chronological

still-developing era in superhero comics, the effects of which were eventually felt in the other comic genres.

1. The Fantastic Four, Spider-Man, and the Hulk were the first fallible and self-questioning superheroes.
2. Comic books became accepted by a wider, more literate audience.
3. Concern with ethical and even political questions became more evident, even in kid comics and funny animal comics.

III. Comic books have an effect beyond their entertainment value.

A. Comic books are a unique and vigorous art form.
 1. Comic books have developed exciting and innovative methods for transcending the static nature of the panel format (series of distinct pictures across and down the page) to produce a sense of motion and drama.
 2. The art of comics is not confined to the work within a single panel, but also touches the arrangement of panels on a page.
 [as a result]

B. Comic books can be seen to influence other media.
 1. Many filmmakers' use of split screen and quick cuts demonstrates a stylistic adaptation of the comic panel format.
 2. Camp and pop art drew heavily on comic book themes and styles.
 [and as a result]

C. Comic books are in demand with collectors.
 1. Some issues of rare comics can bring prices in the thousands of dollars.
 2. Every year there are many large conventions around the United States where comics can be bought, sold, and traded.

Cause - Effect

Chapter 9

Outlining

Use a formal outline as an organizational tool.

The speech outline is an indispensable tool of speech organization. A clear outline will help you keep track of the points you want to cover; using one will also increase the chances that your audience will retain the gist of your message. The act of outlining, laying your ideas out on paper, forces you to select the points that support your thesis and to demonstrate how they fit together. Until you have something concrete in front of you, how can you say you truly know what you are going to talk about? As the planning and practice table in Chapter 2 illustrates, you must develop a logical outline of your points and supporting materials before you can finalize the oral version of your speech.

Only through this outline development can you avoid falling into one of these familiar traps: either overestimating your preparedness or underestimating it. In the first case you might say, "I've researched this subject so much that I've got it down cold." Until you give the speech—or begin writing down your ideas—how can you be sure? In the second case you might say, "I'll never understand this topic, even though I've spent weeks in the library!" An outlining session could surprise you by making evident your unconscious understanding of the subject. In short, the written outline gives you some distance from the thoughts that are spinning around in your mind. Freezing these ideas on paper makes them accessible for you or others to evaluate. A teacher, colleague, or peer group can tell you if the connections you make are clear and compelling.

It is important that you understand the concept of outlining that appears in Chapter **9**. Some outline formats include the introduction and conclusion as main points of the speech. We do not recommend this. Rather, outlining as used here refers to the ordering of the *basic* ideas in the body of the speech. Also, do not confuse the formal speech outline with informal research notes (see **5f**), preliminary organizational tools (see **7b**), or speaking notes (see **24**). While any of these may take an outline form, the *outline* referred to in the following sections is a detailed, logical plan of the speech.

It is essential to begin laying out your formal outline at the correct point in the planning process. Full-sentence outlines especially are so much like writing that they must not be used too early in the process (thus producing writer's block) or too late (thus resulting in a speech delivered in a written rather than an oral style). Oral composition and oral practice should surround this one excursion into writing.

9a. Use the conventional outline format.

By following these rules of outlining, you will be able to visualize the relationships among the ideas of your speech:

(1) Follow a consistent set of symbols.

It is conventional to use roman numerals to label the main ideas of the speech and to alternate from letters to numbers for each successive level of subordination, in this manner:

I.   Main point
   A. First level of subordination
     1. Second level of subordination
       a. Third level of subordination
         (1) Fourth level of subordination
           (a) Fifth level of subordination

Do not skip levels. If your speech has only main points and one level of subpoints, use I, II, III and A, B, C. If your outline includes a second level of subordination, you must also use 1, 2, 3. Do not indulge in idiosyncratic systems of labeling levels such as:

```
1—Dogs
    *Hunters
  a:  Spaniels
    b—Retrievers
```

Dashes, colons, and inversions of the standard progression may make sense to you. It would be to your benefit, however, to get into the habit of using the universally accepted format. Not only is this format simple (though still allowing you to go to the fifth level of subordination), but also most people find it familiar and easy to understand because of its long, widespread use.

(2) Show the logical relationship of ideas through proper indention.

Each subordinate idea should be indented several spaces to align with the first word—not the labeling numeral or letter—of the point it supports. This makes the relationship among ideas visually obvious.

Wrong:
I. Bagpipes are not solely a Scottish instrument.
   A. Bagpipes originated in Asia Minor.
     B. There are various forms of bagpipes in Ireland and Spain, for example.
       1. Spanish bagpipes are similar in construction to Scottish pipes, with the sizes of the parts different.
        2. Uilleann bagpipes in Ireland differ from Scottish pipes in that the piper uses bellows under the arm to keep the bag full rather than blowing into the bag.

Wrong:
I. Bagpipes are not solely a Scottish instrument.
A. Bagpipes originated in Asia Minor.
B. There are various forms of bagpipes in Ireland and Spain, for example.
1. Spanish bagpipes are similar in construction to Scottish pipes, with the sizes of the parts different.
2. Uilleann bagpipes in Ireland differ from Scottish pipes in that the piper uses bellows under the arm to keep the bag full rather than blowing into the bag.

Right:
I. Bagpipes are not solely a Scottish instrument.
    A. Bagpipes originated in Asia Minor.

B. There are various forms of bagpipes in Ireland and Spain, for example.
   1. Spanish bagpipes are similar in construction to Scottish pipes, with the sizes of the parts different.
   2. Uilleann bagpipes in Ireland differ from Scottish pipes in that the piper uses bellows under the arm to keep the bag full rather than blowing into the bag.

Note how in the last example your eye was directed down the levels of subordination. Your outline should not look like a piece of prose. Your outline exists only to illuminate and clarify the structure of your ideas.

(3) As a general rule, develop each level of subordination with two or more parts.

English teachers are fond of saying, "Never have a *1* without a *2* or an *A* without a *B*." Generally this is good advice. The concept of dividing an idea into parts—subordination—becomes nonsensical if a major point is "divided" into only one subpoint. Categories are useful because they encompass several related things. Suppose a main point of your speech were outlined as follows:

I. Redwood City is the best California city in which to live.
   A. It has the best climate.
II. ....

If Redwood City's climate were your only example, you would be in trouble. A good climate is hardly enough to justify the conclusion you have drawn. You might be guilty of hasty generalization. To avoid this fallacy, outline your speech following the rule of having *at least* two supporting points at each level of subordination. It is far better to develop a few points fully than to cover many points superficially. The rule *no 1 without a 2, no A without a B* is a good one to ensure depth of analysis.

(4) Each symbol should designate *one* point only; every point should have a symbol.

Do not combine two or more ideas in any point of your outline. Give each separate idea its own logical heading. By the same token, your outline should not contain any free-floating words or phrases. Every idea should be firmly anchored to a symbol in the hierarchy of points.

WRONG:

Causes

A. Both economic and sociological factors contribute significantly to urban decay.
B. Political factors are of minor importance.

RIGHT:

I. Urban decay has a number of causes. — **Free-floating header made into a main point**
  A. Economic factors are the major cause.
  B. Sociological factors are also significant. — **Old Point A split into two points**
  C. Political factors are relatively minor.

Exercise 1. Outline one of the speeches in the **Appendix.** How many levels of subordination does the speaker use? Are there cases of a *1* without a *2,* or an *A* without a *B?*

9b. Use a full-sentence outline to ensure coherent development of your speech.

The thesis statement (see **3d**), the main points, and at least the first level of subpoints should be stated as declarative sentences. The declarative sentence is, in effect, a proposition. As such it can be proved or disproved, accepted or rejected.

Look at the following sentence:

I. Secondhand smoke harms nonsmokers.

If this sentence were presented to you on a true-false test, you could, with adequate knowledge, answer one way or the other. It is the black-or-white condition of the declarative sentence that makes it such a useful tool.

What would you do if you read this item on a true-false test?

I. Nonsmoker's rights

or this:

I. What is the effect of secondhand smoke on nonsmokers?

Obviously an answer of true or false to either of these examples would be impossible. It would be equally absurd if a stranger approached you and asked, "Do you agree with me about the growth of the Welfare State?"

Your inevitable retort would be, "Well, what *do* you think about the growth of the Welfare State?"

Far too many speeches are constructed around just such vague phrases, questions, and uncompleted ideas. The listener knows the speaker's general topic, but cannot always recognize the specific points the speaker is trying to make.

Wrong:	I. What are the causes of crime?
Right:	I. Crime is caused by a combination of sociological and psychological factors.
Wrong:	I. History of the feminist movement in the United States
Right:	I. U.S. feminism can be divided into four historical periods.
Wrong:	I. Buying a house will have tax advantages. You will also build equity. House ownership is fun and fosters pride.
Right:	I. House ownership builds equity, provides tax benefits, and gives pleasure.
	or
	I. There are both economic and emotional benefits to owning a house.

Besides rendering the speech more coherent for your audience, the use of declarative sentences in your outline forces you to become conscious of the exact points you want to make and forces you to frame them explicitly. As you begin to research any topic, you will find scores of interesting details and perspectives. How do you decide which ones to include in your speech and which ones to leave out? Once the thesis and main points are stated in propositional form, they will provide a basis against which you can test all other speech content.

The following outlines deal with a topic—The History of Women in the U.S. Labor Force—that could fill, and has filled, many volumes. Observe how the use of a thesis sentence and full-sentence main and secondary points in the first outline provides a basis for the speaker to decide what to include.

Full-Sentence Outline

Thesis: Since the beginning of the Industrial Revolution, women in the United States have been exploited as a cheap and expendable source of labor.

   I. In preindustrial colonial settings, the boundaries between men's and women's spheres were indistinct.

    A. Colonial women ran self-sufficient domestic factories.
      1. Women produced the major source of artificial light, candles.
      2. Clothing and bedding were manufactured.
      3. The making of soap was a major contribution.
    B. The rigors of frontier life decreed a more equal division of labor between women and men than found on the rapidly industrializing Eastern Seaboard.
      1. Men and women shared long hours of joint farm work.
      2. Women were often left alone for long periods to run the farm.
 II. Between the Revolution and the Civil War, increased industrialization led to increased exploitation of women workers.
    A. Factories undercut home production.
    B. When the western migration caused shortages of male workers, women became a cheap source of labor for the factories.
      1. The percentage of women in the work force increased.
      2. Women, in 1829, earned one quarter of what men did.
    C. Women workers' efforts to improve their lot were not successful.
      1. The first women's strike was in 1824, but poor organization made it and others ineffective.
      2. Associations of women workers failed because of the women's isolation and inexperience.
III. In spite of increasing unionization between the Civil War and World War II, women's position in the work force remained inferior.
    A. Women were an unwelcome minority in trade organizations.
      1. Male union leaders did not believe in equal pay for equal work.
      2. Women were barred from union offices, men said, because "no conveniences were available."
    B. Attempts by women before 1900 to organize among themselves met with failure.
      1. Women's unions were not taken seriously.
      2. Women workers were usually too impoverished to strike successfully.
    C. Important gains by women workers in the first decades of the twentieth century yielded little net improvement.
      1. Women's situation had improved in some areas.
        a. Unionization of the garment industry was successful.
        b. New job classifications were opened to women during World War I.
      2. Women workers still had neither security nor equality.
        a. Men got their jobs back after the war.
        b. Women received one half of comparable men's pay.
IV. During World War II and after, women were used as a dispensable and secondary source of labor.

A. Traditional views of femininity were conveniently set aside according to economic needs.
   1. Three million women were recruited to replace our fighting men.
   2. "Rosie the Riveter" became a mythic ideal.
B. After the war, labor, government, and industry cooperated to push women out of their new jobs.
   1. Although most women wanted to keep working, by 1946 four million were gone from the work force.
   2. When plants began to rehire men, women's seniority was often ignored.
   3. With the unions' tacit approval, many jobs held by women during the war were reclassified as men's jobs.
   4. Many of the laid-off women were denied unemployment insurance.
   5. Articles and pamphlets exhorted women to return to their "primary role."
      a. Women were needed to provide a haven for returning men.
      b. Women were needed to nurture the nuclear family.

Here is a *topic outline* on the same subject.

Topic Outline

Topic: Working Women in the United States

I. Preindustrial
   A. Colonial women
      1. Soap
      2. Clothing
   B. Frontier women
      1. Indian attacks
      2. Farm work
II. Increased industrialization to Civil War
   A. Women in factories
      1. Smaller hands suited to weaving
      2. One dollar per week, less lodging
   B. First union attempts
      1. 1824
      2. Lady Shoe Binders, Lynn, Massachusetts.
III. Post–Civil War to pre–World War II
   A. Growth
      1. 225,922 in 1850
      2. 323,370 in 1870

B. Conflicts
   1. Male union leaders
   2. Strikes
C. The struggle for suffrage
   1. Elizabeth Cady Stanton
   2. Susan B. Anthony
D. World War I
   1. New jobs
   2. Department of Labor Women's Bureau
IV. World War II era
  A. Rosie the Riveter
    1. Three million women
    2. Patriotic appeals
  B. Women in the military
    1. WASPS
    2. Army nurses
  C. The feminine mystique
    1. Home as haven
    2. Rise of suburbia

At first glance the topic outline seems to be a coherent, tidy arrangement of points. All the main points appear to relate to the topic, and all the subpoints appear to relate to the main points; but can you form a sharp image of what the speaker is saying about working women in the United States? For example, the first main point of the speech is "Preindustrial." Preindustrial what? The preindustrial *era,* presumably. Yet the term "preindustrial" is so broad that it could include the first humans to appear in America, thousands of years ago. In fact, this point will probably deal with the work that women did between the first European colonization and the advent of the Industrial Revolution, but it ought to be phrased to leave no doubt. This is only half the job, though. No matter how refined, a subject still needs a predicate. Although a speaker can delimit a subject with precision, using sufficient modifiers and qualifiers, it will not be clear what she or he means to say *about* that subject. Even if the speaker refines Point I of the second outline to describe a specific group of women in a specific era (e.g., "Colonial life for women, 1620–1783"), you cannot pinpoint what idea is being developed: that there were many working women? that their lives were hard? or that they participated in all spheres of work? As these questions are raised and answered, the speaker transforms a loose phrase into a full sentence. If it turns into something like Main Point I in the first outline, the speaker would probably decide that stories about Indian attacks, however interesting, do not belong in this speech.

Exercise 2. Now compare the remaining main points of the two outlines and specify which subpoints are extraneous and which need to be modified.

The use of a full-sentence outline is important in informative and evocative speeches as well as in argumentative and persuasive speeches. In a speech to evoke or to inform, you do not literally *prove* a thesis or its main points, but you do have an obligation to cover topics fully. Using sentences rather than phrases will focus your speech development and will provide you with clearer criteria for deciding which points to include and which ones to leave out. Full-sentence outlines are not extra work, they are a needed tool to demonstrate logical relationships in the speech. Once these issues are thought through, you can proceed to a more spontaneous and fluid oral form of expression, confident that the underlying structure of your speech is sound.

9c. Phrase the main points of the outline in a way that directly forecasts the subpoints that will be developed.

It is not enough to have an outline that has full sentences as main points. The sentences must logically encompass the main ideas of the speech. Suppose a speech outline had the following as a main point:

    I.   Many people are unaware of the origins of the paper they use every day.

If this were *really* the main idea being developed in this section of the speech, the subpoints should look something like this:

    A. Ursula is utterly unaware of the origin of paper.
    B. Clint is clueless about where paper comes from.
    C. Ned never thought about paper for a minute.
    D. . . . and so on . . .

Obviously, the speaker does not intend to spend this whole portion of the speech exposing the ignorance of the general public. More likely, she or he will be talking about where paper did come from. The main point should reflect that. The phrase "many people are unaware" does not have to be jettisoned altogether, but it can become just a transitional lead-in, not an essential component of what is to follow.

Because main points of a speech can be thought about as subthesis sentences, the tests that were introduced in **3d** can be applied to their phrasing. Recall that a thesis sentence was required to answer two simple questions about the speech: "What's it about?" and "What about it?" Each main point should be cast so that it answers these same questions about the section of the speech that is being covered.

Wrong:

I first would like to take a few minutes to discuss the origin of paper.

What's it about?	A speaker talking for a few minutes.
What about it?	The topic being talked about is the origin of paper.

Wrong:

Another interesting point is the origin of paper.

What's it about?	The origin of paper.
What about it?	It is interesting.

Right:

The origins of paper can be traced to the use of papyrus in ancient Egypt.

What's it about?	The origin of paper.
What about it?	It can be traced to papyrus in ancient Egypt.

Do not include transitional phrases that might be part of your oral presentation in the outline. They make for pseudosentences. Also, do not include your supporting evidence in the phrasing of a main point.

Wrong:

A study done by Dr. Wilson showed that in three major companies in our area 148 people were diagnosed with carpal tunnel syndrome last year.

What's it about?	A researcher did a study.
What about it?	The study found that carpal tunnel syndrome affected 148 people at three companies.

Right:

Carpal tunnel syndrome is one of the most common forms of repetitive strain injuries.

What's it about?	Carpal tunnel syndrome.
What about it?	It is a very common form of repetitive strain injury.

It is highly unlikely that this one study is a *main* point of a speech. Keep statistics, testimony, and examples at the subordinate levels. Your main points should express the more general ideas of the speech; these are supported by evidence or data.

9d. Phrase main points and subpoints in clear, effective, and parallel language.

Once you have framed your main ideas so they are logically and grammatically complete, take time to recast your points in language that will highlight them for your audience. In this final phase of refining the outline, you move from one of the writer's resources—organizing points logically—to another aspect of composition skill—sometimes called "writing for the ear." This step forms the bridge from completing the outline as a blueprint to beginning to imagine the oral performance that will ultimately occur. Of course, you will not be reading or memorizing your full-sentence outline, and you may never state the points as they are written out. But you will want to phrase the key ideas so they stand out from the overall flow of your presentation. When you express your main points in parallel language—that is, when you present them in sentences that repeat a certain syntactic structure or repeat a particular grammatical form—you make them more easily identifiable. This augments the techniques of signposting, previews, and reviews covered in Chapter 10, all of which you use to make your organization clear to your listeners.

Ideas that are phrased in concise, colorful, parallel language are more likely to be remembered both by speaker and by listeners. See also Chapter 15. Look at the following main points from a speech on higher education:

Wordy and Unparallel

I. The skills you will learn in college will add to the probability of your earning more money, not only in your first job, but throughout your entire lifetime.

II. Through higher education one can also gain a perspective on many aspects of life, to enrich the nonworking hours and provide for a more creative use of leisure time.

III. While they are in college, most students have a variety of social and interpersonal experiences and make new friends through extracurricular activities and informal exchanges.

These are declarative sentences, as they ought to be, and they do show three separate, important arguments in favor of the thesis that a college education is valuable. The points, though, are too wordy and redundant to stand out clearly from the general flow of the speech.

Here they are made considerably more concise without sacrificing their basic meaning:

More Concise

I. Your earning power will be increased by a college education.

II. One can prepare for a richer use of leisure time by attending college.

III. In college, students meet new friends and enjoy worthwhile social experiences.

Still, these main points can be made more memorable and effective. The sentences lack parallelism; one is in the passive voice, two are in the active voice; one is in the second person, two are in the third person; one is plural, two are singular. Listeners are not as quick to see the relationships between the points when the perspective and the focus keep changing like this. Whenever possible, strive for grammatical consistency of structure, person, number, and voice:

Concise and Parallel

I. A college education will enhance your earning power.

II. A college education will enrich your use of leisure time.

III. A college education will expose you to new people and social experiences.

Exercise 3. Rephrase the following main points so that they are concise and parallel.

Thesis: The United Nations is essential to world peace and harmony.

I. The United Nations serves the useful function of providing all countries with a place where they might air their grievances or propose courses of action they consider desirable.

  II. It would be better if all countries could articulate their hopes for the future and use the United Nations to direct their energies toward a common goal.

  III. With the world "getting smaller," everybody is beginning to realize that we are all one big, human family and that we need the United Nations to help us keep in touch with other "family members."

Thesis: Advertisers use a variety of techniques to influence consumers.

  I. Tone and mood can be established through color.
  II. Many advertisers use symbols effectively to attain their goals.
  III. You can manipulate shapes for visual impact.

9e. Supplement your logical outline with marginal notations of the rhetorical devices used.

Every speech has a psychological as well as a logical structure. A formalized content outline helps you to crystallize the relationships between propositions and support. You can also use the outline to chart the relationships between speaker and audience. Chapters **13–20** explain how to use many rhetorical devices to enhance your speech. Make marginal notations on your outline, showing where you plan to use various rhetorical devices. This will help you see what you are doing so you can improve the audience appeal of your speech. Is all the humor clustered at the beginning and end of an hour-long lecture? Perhaps some humor can be shifted to the middle. Do you support every main point with a fact followed by a hypothetical example? Perhaps you can vary the forms of support.

Chapter 10

Transitions

Transitions should link points to provide unity and express relationships among ideas.

Transitional sentences, phrases, and words serve as bridges between points. They also signal to the listener how two ideas are related. The connective words can completely change the impact of a message. Observe the not-so-subtle differences in these three sentences:

> He plays the piano, *and* I invited him to my party.
> He plays the piano, *so* I invited him to my party.
> He plays the piano, *but* I invited him to my party.

Clear and evocative transitions are more important in speaking than in writing because the spoken message is ephemeral (see **15a**). In this book, for example, we show you the relationships among ideas by indenting, capitalizing, and using different punctuation and typefaces. But, as a speaker, you do not have access to these devices. You need to use verbal signposting techniques to show how your points relate. Keep your listeners informed about the overall structure of your speech by the generous use of phrases like:

> My next major point is . . .
> The third cause of inflation is . . .
> To show you what I mean, let me tell you three stories.
> In summarizing this entire argument . . .

The final point we should consider is . . .
What, then, is the solution to this three-part problem I have outlined?

Do not worry about using too many signposts. Your audience will appreciate them.

10a. Select transitions that reflect the logical relationships among ideas.

The transitions you choose should illuminate the basic organizational structure of the speech. Without even seeing their content you can tell what pattern these speeches follow:

Thesis:

     I say that for three reasons. First,
  I. ....
     This situation is also due to
  II. ....
     Last of all, we can attribute the problem to
  III. ....

or

Thesis:

     Initially,
  I. ....
     Next,
  II. ....
     Finally,
  III. ....

The transitions alone tell you that you are hearing an effect-to-cause speech in the first case and a chronologically arranged speech in the second.

Points can be related in a number of ways. Crystallizing those relationships and expressing them through appropriate transitional phrases will enhance your clarity. Try to use a variety of transitions instead of linking all your ideas with "OK, now let's look at . . ." or "First of all," "Second of all," "Third of all," and "Last of all." The following list provides examples of the many transitional words that can be used to tie main points to one another, main points to subpoints, subpoints to one another, supporting evidence to arguments, or introductions and conclusions to the body of the speech. Transitions are needed in all these places (Table 10-1).

Notice how Carnegie Foundation President Ernest L. Boyer used simple transitional words and phrases in his speech on the importance of

TABLE 10-1	Transitional Words that Signal Relationship
Relationship	Transitional Words
Chronological	First, second, third, Next, then After . . . Following . . .
Cause-effect	So, since, thus, Therefore, hence, Consequently, as a result Due to . . . Because . . .
Part-to-whole	One such . . . Another . . . The first (second or third) of these . . . For instance, for example, Illustrative of this, A case in point: Let me give you an example . . .
Equality	Similarly, additionally, Another . . . Of equal importance . . . Also, Moreover,
Opposition	But, though, however, On the other hand, Conversely, on the contrary, Yet . . . In spite of . . . Nonetheless, nevertheless,

preserving the arts in education.[1] He stated at the end of his introduction that lifelong learning in the arts is crucial for several reasons, then, after developing his first point, Boyer said:

> *Besides* expressing feelings and insights words cannot convey, the arts are necessary to extend the child's ways of knowing and bring creativity to the classroom.

After a few paragraphs of development, he used a combination summary and preview to bridge to his third point:

> The arts extend language. They encourage creativity and give children new ways of knowing. *But we also need the arts* to help students integrate learning and discover the connectedness of things.

Boyer's fourth point was introduced with this transition:

> *Further, the arts, while essential for all, have special meaning* for children who are socially insecure, emotionally distressed, or physically restricted.

Notice that the italicized words and phrases serve to tie the parts of the speech together and provide a sense of unity to Boyer's speech.

10b. Make use of internal previews and summaries.

The importance of previews in speech introductions and of summaries in conclusions is emphasized elsewhere (see **11** and **12**). Sometimes transitions between main points should take the form of internal summaries or internal previews that pull together two or three main points.

Internal Preview

Once your résumé is prepared, the next step in job seeking is to prepare a list of specific job openings. The three best sources here are newspaper listings, your campus placement service, and word-of-mouth recommendations. We will examine the pros and cons of each of these.

---

[1] Ernest L. Boyer, "Lifelong Learning in the Arts," *Vital Speeches of the Day* 61, no. 1 (15 Oct. 1994): 15–18. (Emphasis added in extracts.)

Internal Summary

Since the problems in our department were affecting morale and since we had found they were caused by poor communication, we instituted an unusual training program. Let me tell you about it.

Internal Summary and Preview

I've told you why we need to reduce our dependence on the automobile, and I hope I've convinced you that a light rail system is the best alternative for our city. Now, you're probably asking two questions: "What will it cost?" and "How will it work?" I want to answer both these questions. First, the question of cost.

Caveat: Do not forecast the end of your speech prematurely by bluntly saying "In summary," anywhere but in the conclusion. See **12d**. Carefully qualify your internal summaries by using phrases like, "So, to summarize this first idea" or "Let me review the points so far."

Exercise 1. Write transitions to connect the main points of the women workers outline in **9b** and of the comic book outline in **8b**.

Identify the transitional sentences, phrases, and words in one or more of the speeches in the **Appendix**.

Chapter 11

Introductions

Use an introduction to establish a relationship with your audience and to orient them to your topic.

After you have outlined the body of the speech according to the organizational techniques described in the previous chapters, compose an introduction that will prepare your listeners to deal with you and your topic. Both the speaker and the audience need a period of adjustment before getting to the meat of the speech.

It is important to realize that your speech really starts before you utter the first word and that *that* first word is crucial to the success of the speech. The moment the attention shifts to you—whether you are sitting at the head table or in the first row of seats or standing to the side of the board-room—you need to begin to develop a rapport and prepare your audience to listen to you. For the most part they want to like you and want to listen, and there is some tension as a result. Because you know how important these initial moments are, you will have planned your first few sentences very carefully. Your listeners will relax when they see you know what you are doing, that you are obviously in control.

Engage the audience.
Perhaps you have witnessed speakers who start talking halfway up from their seats, continue talking while walking to the podium, and *then* notice the audience. When *you* become the center of attention, stand up and, if necessary, move confidently to the position from which you will speak;

then pause to *engage the audience.* Look at them and acknowledge non-verbally the fact that you and they are together.

The main thing you want to do in these first few moments is to survive them. You know from experience as an audience member how long it takes to get used to a speaker's appearance, style of talking, and mannerisms. If you are feeling self-conscious during this part of the speech, it is probably appropriate: Chances are the audience is paying more attention to you personally than to your ideas. Your task is to shift their attention from you to the topic.

This chapter identifies and explains the important features of an introduction that will propel you through the uncomfortable moments and into the body of your speech.

11a. Frame your opening sentences carefully to engage your audience's attention.

Even experienced speakers who do not worry beforehand about the exact wording of the body of their speech tend to plan and prepare their introduction carefully. Because you will be occupied with all the things that are going on at the beginning of your speech, do not risk leaving your opening sentences to the inspiration of the moment. You need strong and basic material that will carry the speech forward.

Start with a sentence that leaves no doubt that you are beginning. Avoid false starts, apologetic or tentative phrases: "Is the mike on?" "Well, here goes nothing," or "Let's see, where shall I start?" Tone is almost as important as content here. Your immediate purpose is to command the attention of your audience. Several methods of gaining attention are discussed in **16a.** Techniques such as suspense, novelty, humor, and conflict are effective and you will probably use them throughout your speech; they are almost mandatory in your introduction.

You may begin the attention-getting phase of your introduction by telling a joke, relating a story, citing an apt quotation, making a startling statement, or asking a provocative question. Be imaginative; it is even all right to be a little dramatic; but do not go too far. An attention getter should emerge logically from your topic and have at least a reasonable connection. Avoid a contrived and gimmicky opening such as flicking off the room lights and asking, "Are you in the dark about . . . ?" Your attention getter should be consistent with your personality and the situation. What is perfectly normal for someone else may seem unnatural for you. Adopting an unnatural style is doubly troublesome; not only are you uncomfortable, but also your audience will sense that you are not yourself.

With this in mind, consider the following possible attention getters for the comic book speech in **8b**.

A humorous or light way of introducing the topic may suit you best:

> Did you ever want to leap a tall building in a single bound? I did. Did you ever want to be more powerful than a locomotive? I did. Did you ever want to be faster than a speeding bullet? I did. As you can tell, I was warped early by the influence of comic books . . .

Or perhaps you are more comfortable with a dramatic attention getter:

> On a May afternoon in Washington, Frank Salacuse and John Snyder wrapped up their negotiations and shook hands. Both were happy with the result. Snyder walked away with $17,500, and Salacuse's syndicate now had a mint copy of *Marvel Comics*, no. 1, a comic book with the 1939 price of 10 cents on its cover.

A straightforward conversational approach to the topic can still get attention:

> In the 10 years I've been collecting comic books, I've learned that they are more than escape or entertainment. As I read the 13,000 comics in my collection, their contribution to popular culture has become clearer and clearer.

As this third example illustrates, attention getters need not be unduly catchy or clever. However, it is essential that you begin your speech with a few well-planned sentences that say, in effect: I know where I'm going and I want you to come with me—it will be worth your while.

Exercise 1. Do all the speeches in the **Appendix** have clear attention-getting steps? What devices are used?

Exercise 2. Write an engaging attention getter for the speech on women in the labor force in **9b**.

11b. Provide a psychological orientation.

Attention, once gained, must be transformed into interest. Before you can ask your audience to concentrate on the substance of your message, you need to orient them psychologically. This orientation has two parts: establishing a good relationship with your listeners and interesting them in what you have to say.

(1) Establish a relationship with your audience.

Speakers can seem remote and aloof, cut off from the audience by role and status. Use your introduction to create a personal bond with your listeners. You can do this with references to everyday, common occurrences. If your audience can visualize your going to the dentist, seeing a movie, losing your keys, or playing with your kids, they will be conscious of you as a human being, not just a dispenser of information.

In addition to establishing a relationship that is warm and friendly, you want the introduction to set a tone of collaboration with your audience. For the most part people learn better when they are active than when they are passive, and they have more of a commitment to a decision in which they have participated. You can therefore appreciate that a collaborative tone will aid you in achieving your speech goals. Here are some ways to create a sense of dialogue even in a speech that is primarily a monologue:

- Acknowledge your audience's expertise. "As managers, you could give me a dozen examples of what I've just said."
- Admit your own fallibility. "One issue I'm still struggling with is . . ."
- Ask for their help. "I hope that during the discussion period later you'll share some of the solutions you've found to these problems."

In general, the idea you are trying to project is: "Although I'm doing the talking now, I'm here to learn from you as well as instruct you. I hope to influence your thinking, but I'm willing to have you influence mine."

Caveat: Some speakers are so intent on seeming human that they become gratingly humble. They lose credibility altogether by such bumbling comments as: "I'm a little nervous being up here," "Now, where are my notes?" or "I'm not really the one who is qualified to be telling you this."

127

When deciding how to build a positive relationship with your audience, you should ask two questions:

What relationship do I have with these people now?
What relationship do I need to have in order to accomplish my speech purpose?

In effect, you are conducting one of the phases of audience analysis described in **4d**. The answers to these questions will help you decide which combination of the following techniques can be used in your introduction to build rapport with your listeners.

Establish credibility.

The judgments the members of the audience make about you as a person influence the judgments they make about your topic. Chapter **17** on credibility says that to be respected and believable a speaker should be perceived as having good sense, goodwill, and good character. The chairperson's glowing introduction may leave no doubt about your expertise on law enforcement, but to meet your goal of persuading these students to consider careers as police officers you need to establish your goodwill. On the other hand, you may be speaking to a group of friends who like and trust you but wonder: What does good old Joe know about nuclear energy? In this case, you would use the introduction to bolster your credibility in the area of good sense.

Establish common ground.

Emphasize similar background, experience, interests, goals to show what you and your audience share. Observe how William A. Dimma builds common ground as a part of his introduction to a speech sponsored by York University in Toronto:

For over the past twenty-three years I've been associated with York as a part-time student, an alumnus, a professor, an academic administrator, a longtime governor, the father of a student and, as of last Saturday evening, the father of a graduate with a bright new B.F.A. degree. [1]

---

[1] *Vital Speeches of the Day* 56, no.9 (1990): 283.

Refer to the setting or occasion.

One way to demonstrate your personal connection to the immediate speaking situation is to refer directly to the time and place. Jeanne Wakatsuki Houston, coauthor of *Farewell to Manzanar,* began a college commencement speech this way:

> Many years ago—forty-three to be exact—when I stood on the ground where De Anza College now stands, I looked out onto lush orchards, fragrant with blossoms in springtime and laded with plump fruit in summer. I viewed the acres of foliage carpeting the earth with green—patches of beans, tomatoes, and squash, and long furrows of strawberries glistening red under their leafy canopies.
>
> In those days, I knew this area well, for I had spent several summers picking those berries at a large strawberry ranch called Esperanza, located not far from here. *Esperanza,* the Spanish word for "hope," was farmed by Japanese families. . . . [After briefly recounting her family's experience as part of the U.S. government's internment of Japanese Americans in World War II, she continued:] Why do I tell you this? I tell you this because when I picked those berries I never dreamed I would be speaking at a college that someday would rise up within view of where I knelt in the dirt. It was beyond my imagination. But here I am sharing with you some thoughts and insights I have accrued since those days in the strawberry fields more than forty years ago.[2]

Flatter your audience.

Everyone likes to be complimented, as long as it is personalized and not too heavy-handed. An audience who perceives that you like and admire them is more likely to reciprocate.

In a speech presented at a workshop for teachers, one of the authors used this approach:

> Those of you who gave up your Saturday morning to be here are not a typical group of teachers. Study after study reveals that the teachers who show up voluntarily to in-service workshops on teaching skills are the very best

---

[2]Jeanne Wakatsuki Houston, "A Tapestry of Hope: America's Strength Was, Is, and Will Be Its Diversity." *San Jose Mercury News,* 19 June 1994: 1C, 4C.

teachers. Just look around you. The ones who most need this workshop aren't here today, are they? But a brush-up is always helpful. "A" teachers want to learn to be "A+" teachers. And maybe together we can find some ways to reach those "C–" teachers who didn't come.

Refer to the person who introduced you or to some other person present.

One good way to build a relationship with a group is to demonstrate that you relate successfully to one of its popular members.

> Thank you, Jack, for that very flattering introduction. You know, it's said of some speakers "this person needs no introduction." I'm not one of those. I need all the introduction I can get. Recognizing that, Jack was kind enough not to mention that he's had to bail me out, both figuratively and literally, many times in the fifteen years we've known each other.

Use humor.

A similar sense of humor is a good basis for a relationship, both interpersonally and on a larger scale. Show your audience that you and they laugh at the same things. However, this is a particularly perilous technique. See **16c** for cautions about its use.

In a business communications course, Ellen Watrous started her speech on historical cost accounting versus replacement cost accounting in this fashion:

> A French balloonist once floated across the English Channel and landed in a field of wheat. He spotted an Englishman and said, "Excuse me, sir. Can you tell me where I am?" The Englishman replied, "Certainly. You are in a basket in a field of wheat." "You must be an accountant," said the balloonist. "Amazing," said the Englishman. "How did you know?" "Easy," replied the balloonist. "Your information is typical: totally accurate but absolutely useless."

(2) Motivate your audience toward your topic.

This motivational step is one of those most often overlooked in speechmaking, but it is *the* pivotal step of the introduction. Your speech, in spite of the enthusiasm you hold for the topic, can be derailed by your audience's "what's-it-to-me?" attitude. This attitude is not limited to the hostile audience; it is characteristic of nearly all audiences. You need to reassure your listeners that there are good reasons for them to be warming seats, that your topic—whether it be of an informative, persuasive, or evocative nature—has a link with their own experiences and is thereby worthy of their attention. The speech on accounting, cited above, was presented to a class of undergraduate students in various fields of business. The speaker went on to say:

> Everyone here destined to work for business enterprises is in the same basket with the lost balloonist. In fact, many of you will become the balloonist. You will be the person who makes investment and credit decisions through which business enterprises obtain financing, accumulating capital for production and marketing of goods and services. And you will depend on information provided by financial statements to make those investment and credit decisions which will inevitably affect your working lives. Yet financial accounting suffers from the same malady that the Englishman in our story suffers. That is, accounting fails to provide relevant information about the effects of inflation and price changes on the financial statements of business enterprises.

Sometimes a two-step link is necessary—not every speech topic can be sold to your audience on the grounds that it will make them rich, save them time, help them succeed, or make them popular. When you cannot make a direct link to a basic need, motivating your audience depends on a step-by-step exposure of connections that lead from your topic to some core value. At the outset of your speech, your listeners may not be immediately stimulated by your topic of African Firewalking. They may not care about foreign cultures as such, but you can make a two-step link. Step 1: Explain firewalking so that your audience understands its place in African culture. Step 2: Show the audience that the world is changing and that they will need to understand diverse cultures (like African culture) so that they can learn how to deal productively with people coming from backgrounds that vary from the audience's own.

Understanding the information in **16** (Attention and Interest) and **18** (Motivational Appeals) will be especially useful.

Exercise 3.   Analyze how psychological orientation is provided in each speech in the **Appendix.** What steps, if any, do the speakers take to establish a relationship? To motivate the audience?

Exercise 4.   Suppose you were speaking to the following audiences on the topics indicated. How would you go about building a positive relationship? How would you motivate them to listen further?

a. A civic organization of businesspeople about the need for reducing the dependence on private automobiles for daily commuting
b. A group of fire fighters about public speaking
c. A college speech class about kinds of running shoes

11c. Provide a logical orientation.

Now that your audience is motivated to listen, you must be sure they are prepared to listen. In the logical orientation you show your listeners how you will approach and develop your topic—in effect, giving them an intellectual road map.

"Logical" is used here, in its broadest sense, in contrast to "psychological" as used in **11b**. The emphasis has shifted from an orientation generated by consideration of the audience to one that grows from your subject. The essence of logic is part/whole relationships. In this phase of your introduction you show the larger whole into which your speech fits and how you have partitioned your topic.

(1) Establish a context for your speech.

Give your audience a perspective on your topic by using one or more of the following:

Fit your topic into a familiar framework.

> San Jose is located fifty miles south of Oakland and fifty-four miles southeast of San Francisco, about thirty miles inland from the Pacific Ocean.

Here we are relating the unknown in terms of the known, in a geographical sense. You can also relate your topic to some schema, chart, organizational structure, or process with which your audience is already familiar. In this case, if your listeners know where the Pacific Ocean and San Francisco are, they can start to think about San Jose.

In the next example the speaker places the object of discussion in its relationship to a known organic structure:

> As you know, the federal government is divided into three branches: the Legislative, the Judicial, and the Executive. When we think of the Legislative branch we think of the Congress. However, there are several other parts of this

branch. Today I want to describe to you the workings of the Speech Writing Division of the Legislative Reference Service, part of the Library of Congress.

The speaker can also connect an unfamiliar topic to the familiar by using analogy:

> When the traffic lights break down on a busy corner, you see a traffic cop standing in the middle of the intersection, blowing a whistle and telling impatient motorists where to go. In effect, that is what I do as Crisis Manager at the Metacom Corporation.

Place your topic historically.

Another way to provide perspective on your topic is to describe its historical context. It helps listeners to know the background and what events led up to the situation as it stands at the time of your speech. One of the most famous speeches by an American, Abraham Lincoln's "Gettysburg Address," used this simple form of introduction:

> Fourscore and seven years ago our fathers brought forth on this continent a new nation, conceived in liberty and dedicated to the proposition that all men are created equal. Now we are engaged in a great civil war, testing whether that nation or any nation so conceived and so dedicated can long endure. We are met on a great battlefield of that war. We have come to dedicate a portion of that field, as a final resting place for those who here gave their lives that that nation might live. It is altogether fitting and proper that we should do this.

On far less momentous occasions, whenever an audience needs to be briefed or reminded about the background that forms the context for a particular speech, a historical recounting can be effective.

> Last June, following the series of gang-related incidents in the Ravensbrook and Southside neighborhoods, our mayor appointed a special task force to explore the scope and causes of increasing gang violence in our city and to make recommendations to the city council. Throughout the summer eleven of us on that task force held a series of briefings by experts and scholars. Then between September and January we held eight "town hall" meetings throughout the community. To complete our data analysis we also conducted over one hundred interviews. Tonight's meeting is the first open hearing on the preliminary draft of our recommendations. I am now going to present and explain

those recommendations; our purpose is to get your reactions and suggestions to these ideas before we finalize our draft to submit to the council next month.

You might also want to place your topic in a broader historical context. For example, in the introduction of a speech dealing with some aspect of the French Revolution, mention can be made of what was happening in America, the rest of Europe, or the Far East at that time in history, thereby providing the listeners with the larger picture.

Caveat: We are talking here about a brief historical recapitulation. In many speeches a fairly extended narration of past events is important, and in such a case "History" should be a main point of the speech. Look at your thesis sentence and see what it dictates. It might state: "Past injustices require us to provide compensatory educational experiences for minorities." That would demand a main point dealing with the history of the particular minorities.

Place your topic conceptually.

Just as you can place your topic in time or space, so can you locate it in the world of ideas. By showing your listeners how your speech fits in with certain familiar theories, concepts, and definitions, you help them prepare to listen. For example:

> You're familiar with the law of supply and demand as it relates to goods and services. Let me review this basic market mechanism with you, because I want to ask you to apply these same essential principles to our system of information exchange.

Provide new definitions and concepts.

If you are going to use unfamiliar terms and concepts in your speech, or familiar terms in unfamiliar ways, prepare your audience. Related to this, if you feel the need to use a term or phrase that has been co-opted as a slogan or rallying cry by some group, with all the attendant distortion of meaning, you had better be sure to define early exactly how you plan to use it.
Introduce an unfamiliar term:

> *Operations Support Systems* for a telecommunications service provider are software applications that deal with four broad areas: Billing and Customer Care, Provisioning, Planning and Engineering, and Network Management.

Define a familiar term used in an unfamiliar way:

> Often when people speak of a system of restitution for criminals, they refer to a program where prisoners contribute wages to a collective pool of some sort. The restitution system I will be talking about involves direct compensation from individual criminals to their victims.

In introducing her topic, Carol W. Kinsley, executive director of the Community Service Learning Center, took care to clarify her topic:

> Here is a definition: Community Service Learning is an educational process . . . that involves students in service experiences with two firm anchors: First, their service is *directly* related to academic subject matter; and second, it involves them in making positive contributions to individuals and community institutions.[3]

(2) Orient the audience to your approach to the topic.

The second step in a logical orientation—once you have shown how your speech fits into some larger context—is to preview the structure of your speech. If your listeners have been given a framework on which to attach your points as your speech unfolds, their comprehension of your topic and thesis is made that much easier.

Reassuring your audience of what you are going to cover will reduce anxiety and internal counterarguing. Suppose you declare, "I will discuss the background of the problem, and discuss my solutions to it, and then I will answer those objections most often raised against my position." Hearing this, your audience will be more patient, not raising those arguments in their minds to block out your position before you have stated it.

In most introductions you will explicitly state one or more of the following: your topic, thesis, title, or purpose. For example: "I would like to persuade you to change your vote on this bond issue." The circumstances that would make this strategically *not* the thing to do are discussed in Chapter **20** on persuasive strategies. At times you also want to tell what you are *not* talking about—essentially explaining to your audience how you have narrowed your topic.

Here is an example, derived from the comic book outline in **8b**, of a speaker spelling out what the speech will not cover:

---

[3]Carol W. Kinsley, "What is Community Service Learning?" *Vital Speeches of the Day* 61, no. 2 (1994): 40–42.

I am not going to tell you which comic books are currently the best invest-ment. Nor am I going to explain how to treat and store comic books so that the acid in the paper won't turn them into yellow confetti. I *am,* however, going to tell you some things about comic books that will help you better understand their place in American popular culture.

Another choice you have is whether to give an exact preview of the points you are going to cover or just a much more general sketch of your topic. Explicit previews are useful in the majority of speeches and absolutely essential for speeches with fairly technical or complex topics. The speaker gives his or her listeners a reassuring road map to carry through the speech, one that they can refer to if they start to get lost. When should you not use an explicit preview? If your speech is built around a dra-matic, climactic sequence, you should not ruin the effect by giving it away in a preview. Rather, summarize your ideas in the conclusion. In a case where each point builds on the audience's understanding of the pre-vious points, a detailed preview might do more harm than good. Very short, simple speeches rarely need previewing.

Exercise 5.   What methods are used by the speakers in the **Appendix** to provide logical orientation? Would any of these speeches be more effective if they did or did not include a specific preview?

Exercise 6.   Write a logical orientation for either the comic book outline in **8b** or the outline on women in the labor force in **9b.** Include a specific preview of the main points. Rewrite it, substituting a more general preview that paraphrases and capsulizes the main points. Under what circumstances would each form be most effective?

11d. Make your introduction as compact as possible by combining or omitting steps when appropriate.

Generally, plan an introduction that is between 10 and 15 percent of your speaking time. If your introduction included all the steps in **11a, b,** and **c** as discrete units, it might be longer than the speech itself. Do not progress mechanically through these steps; your introduction would be choppy, disjointed, and overlong. Organize the introduction in a natural narrative style, keeping in mind the *functions* of getting attention and pro-viding psychological and logical orientation. Whenever possible, select material that fulfills several of the functions of an introduction.

In addition to combining parts of the introduction, it is often appropriate to omit steps altogether. A presidential speech can begin, "My fellow Americans, tonight I want to talk about the serious problem of international terrorism." Attention, credibility, and motivation to listen are assumed.

When attention is already riveted on you—as when you are about to announce the long-awaited results of a competition—a lengthy opening story is out of place, maybe even hazardous to your health. Likewise:

- If you are a minister speaking to your own congregation, or a candidate addressing a rally of your campaign workers, you certainly do not need to waste time building a relationship.
- With a group of angry property owners gathered to protest a tax increase, it serves no real purpose to tell them how important the topic is.
- A study group that meets regularly to hear lectures on a certain topic needs very little logical orientation. You can jump quite directly into the substance of your speech.

Examine your audience, the occasion, and your speech purpose to see what aspects of an introduction can be combined, handled with a passing sentence or indirect reference, or omitted altogether. Just be sure that, by the time you begin your first main point, you can answer all these questions in the affirmative:

Are they listening?
Do they want to keep listening to me?
Do they want to know more about this topic?
Do they understand where I'm coming from?
Do they understand where I'm going?

Exercise 7. Examine each of the speeches in the **Appendix.** Are all of the steps of an introduction present in each? What steps are omitted? Do you think the omissions are justified? What functions are combined?

11e. Avoid these introduction pitfalls:

Don't begin with, "Before I start I'd like to say . . ." You have already started. See opening paragraphs of **11.**
Don't ever begin with an apology like: "I'm not really prepared" or "I don't know much about this, but . . ." See **11a.**

Don't read your introduction. Or, if it is "almost memorized," be sure it does not sound mechanical. This is a time when your eye contact should be maximized and your inflection natural and conversational. See **25c**.

Don't be dramatic to the point of assuming a whole new identity or persona. Leave that to the cabaret impersonators and give *your* speech as *yourself.* See **11a** and **15c**.

Don't use an attention getter that has no real link to your topic. Avoid the temptation to stretch a point so you can start with an unrelated joke you think is hilarious. Similarly, firing a starter's pistol in the air at the beginning of a speech on "How to Get a Running Start on Your Competition" would do more to distract than attract your audience. See **11a**.

Don't make your introduction seem disproportionately long. See **11d**.

Don't use stock phrases like "Unaccustomed as I am to public speaking" or overworked apocryphal stories. Ask a friend to give a brutal critique of your trove of expressions and stories. See **15d**.

Don't name-drop in building your credibility. You do not want your audience to think that you are just gratifying your ego. See **17c**.

Don't startle your audience by coming out of a yogalike trance into an explosion of oral energy. This is a favorite of high school orators. Engage your audience before you start. See opening paragraphs of **11**.

Don't start with a long quotation that leaves your audience wondering where the quotation ends and your words begin.

Chapter 12

Conclusions

Use a conclusion to provide logical and psychological closure.

Many speakers make the common mistake of not leaving enough time for a proper conclusion. It is not enough to finish developing your last main point and then mumble, "I guess that's all I wanted to say." Just as you led your audience into your topic step by step in the introduction, so must you lead them out again in a conclusion, tying all the threads together, leaving your audience with a sense of completeness or closure. Like the introduction, the conclusion should be precisely planned, almost to the point of memorization. You should choose your words carefully: Social scientists tell us that people are most likely to remember what they hear last.

12a. Provide logical closure.

Although you have already demonstrated the interconnectedness of your points and ideas in the body of the speech by the use of transitions and internal previews and summaries, you still need to tie it all together for your audience at the end.

(1) Summarize the main ideas of the speech.

In all but the shortest of speeches you are well advised to include a fairly explicit restatement of your thesis and main ideas. Most of the reasons why you might be reluctant to state your thesis and main points in your introduction do not apply to the conclusion. For instance, at the end of your speech even an unfavorable audience may as well know that your intent has been to persuade them. The argument or dramatic sequence you did not want to reveal at first has now been unfolded, and it will be helpful to recapitulate.

In a technical or argumentative speech it can be particularly useful to restate your thesis and main points exactly. For instance:

> So, in this speech I have shown you why conjugal visits should be allowed in prisons. I first explained the system of conjugal visits that has been adopted successfully in some penal institutions. Second, I made the point that conjugal visits contribute directly to the morale and rehabilitation of prisoners. Finally, I documented that the visitation system is beneficial to society as a whole.

In some speeches you may think this is too mechanical. You may then choose to paraphrase rather than restate exactly, summing up the content, but not in the identical words.

> Today I have tried to give you some sense of how conjugal visits have worked elsewhere, and of the benefits they would bring to prisoners and to society as a whole.

Only in a short, one-point speech can you safely omit a summary. Otherwise, there is no reason not to summarize—you have nothing to lose and only clarity to gain.

(2) Reestablish the connection of your topic to a larger context.

There can be an integration of the parts of a speech that goes beyond mere summary. In some cases, a conclusion serves to pull together several ideas into a pattern that has been implicit all along. This can be true for either inductive or deductive lines of reasoning, where the final relationship among points needs to be spelled out. See **14.** In other cases, you will want to build on the points you have established to refer to broader implications or ramifications of your topic. There may not be time to address these topics in your speech, but you want to raise the issues for your audience to think about.

In the introduction, you drew your speech topic out of some broader context. After developing your ideas, you may want to show how they tie back to the original larger picture. A speech on the training of teachers may have such a format, as shown graphically in Figure 12-1.

If you have introduced new definitions and concepts, or familiar definitions and concepts in unfamiliar ways, use the conclusion to reinforce your use of them.

FIGURE 12-1   Relationship to the Larger Picture

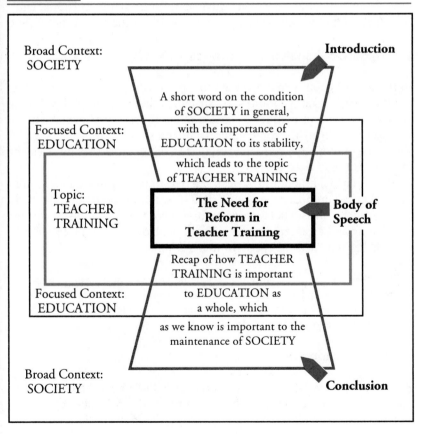

Broad Context: SOCIETY — **Introduction**

A short word on the condition of SOCIETY in general,

Focused Context: EDUCATION — with the importance of EDUCATION to its stability,

which leads to the topic of TEACHER TRAINING

Topic: TEACHER TRAINING — **The Need for Reform in Teacher Training** — **Body of Speech**

Recap of how TEACHER TRAINING is important

Focused Context: EDUCATION — to EDUCATION as a whole, which

as we know is important to the maintenance of SOCIETY

Broad Context: SOCIETY — **Conclusion**

Exercise 1. How do the speeches in the **Appendix** provide logical closure? Do you approve of the speakers' decisions to summarize explicitly, generally, or not at all?

Exercise 2. Write a logical wrap-up for either the comic book outline in **8b** or the outline on women in the labor force in **9b**.

12b. Provide psychological closure.

Making your topic fit together logically for your audience is not enough. They have to go out psychologically satisfied with your speech—you need to have touched them. When you plan your conclusion, think not only about what you want your listeners to understand and agree with, but also about how you want them to be feeling at the end of the speech.

(1) Remind the audience how the topic affects their lives.

In the introduction, you made the topic personal to your audience. During the speech itself, you implicitly sustained that orientation by making your examples and manner of speaking appropriately personal. At the end you must bring the topic home again and show your listeners why it should be of more than academic interest to them—that they have a stake in what you have described.

The financial accounting speech referred to in **11b** moved away from the audience's immediate concerns right after the introduction. The body of the speech consisted of a rather technical comparison of historical cost accounting and replacement cost accounting. However, in the conclusion the speaker returned the spotlight to her listeners:

> Whether you work for a large organization or have your own small business, whether you keep your own books or deal with a cadre of accountants, these two systems will affect you. Understanding the basic logic of each is necessary if you are to make sound decisions.

(2) Make an appeal.

Part of the psychological wrap-up of a speech can be a direct appeal to your audience, especially in a speech to persuade. Ask them directly to behave in a certain way (through adoption, deterrence, discontinuance, or continuance, see **20a**) or ask them to change their attitudes. Robert Kennedy, in a speech to the Democratic legislative dinner shortly after the Watts riots of 1967, ended his speech this way:

> For us as Democrats the responsibility is clear. We must reject the counsel of those willing to pass laws against violence while refusing to help eliminate rats . . .
>
> We must offer that leadership—in every legislature and school board and city hall—which dares to speak out *before* it tests the shifting wind of popular anger and confusion; that leadership which prefers facts to illusions, actions to sullen withdrawal, sacrifice and effort to indulgence and ease.[1]

An appeal can be strengthened by a statement of your own intent: "I plan to give blood tomorrow morning and I hope to see you down there."

In some speeches the appeal makes most sense if it is partitioned. You might make one appeal for long-range action and one for immediate action. Or you might make one appeal telling people what they can do individually and another appeal telling them what they can do collectively. With a large and diverse audience, you might direct different appeals to segments of the audience, as Peter M. Gearhart did in wrapping up his speech on the future of the legal profession:

> In closing, I have separate messages for lawyers and the general public.
>
> For lawyers, my message is this. Our challenge is not public relations, it is human relations. Our challenge is not too much commercialism, it is too little attention to making legal markets work better. Our challenge is not to protect the mystery of the legal profession; it is to *project* its humility. . . .
>
> Ultimately, my message is not to fight change, but to capture change, to make it work *for* the public in the context of professionalism. It will be good for the public, and I think that it will make practicing law more fun.
>
> To the nonlawyers, I add this: We lawyers are here to serve. Call on the best that is in us. You can, and should, expect a legal system that works for you. It is your legal system; ultimately, we are going to put you in control of it. It is precisely because what we do is so central to the American experience, so central to protecting individuality while building the American community, that your expectations should be high. When we fail to meet these

---

[1] *Congressional Record,* 6 Aug. 1967.

expectations, we will try to do better. But *watch us* do better. We have a lot of good still to do.[2]

Exercise 3. What do the speeches in the **Appendix** do to provide psychological closure? Are they effective?

12c. End your speech with a clincher.

It is as important to plan your last sentence as it is your first. Every speech needs a sentence that leaves no doubt that the speech is finished. Speakers who have not prepared this clincher tend to keep summarizing while trying to devise a good exit line. As a result, many of them taper off in dismay and defeat with such frail endings as:

> "I guess that's all I wanted to say."
> "Oops! My time is up, I'd better stop now."
> "Well, I'd like to say more, but I ought to take questions."

Other speakers do not taper, they just stop short, leaving the audience to decide whether the blank air is a pause or the real ending.

One type of effective clincher for a speech ties back to the attention getter used in the introduction: Answer definitively that provocative question you asked initially; reintroduce your opening joke or story and take it one step further—or twist it in the light of your thesis.

> Frank Salacuse's syndicate spent $17,500 for its comic book, but all *you* need is a pocketful of change and transportation to the nearest newsstand or grocery store to rediscover a unique facet of Americana.

Also consider clinching your speech with a proverb, aphorism, quotation, or snatch of poetry. Martin Luther King, Jr., ended his historic "I Have a Dream" speech by evoking the words of an old spiritual: "Free at last, free at last, thank God Almighty, we are free at last."

---

[2]Peter N. Gearhart, "The Future of the Legal Profession," *Vital Speeches of the Day* 60, no. 11 (1994): 347–352.

Do not use "thank you" as a substitute for a clincher. It is not customary to thank your audience after a classroom speech or a business presentation, but only when you have been honored by a special invitation to speak. In this case, "thank you" can be the transition from the other parts of your conclusion into your clincher.

> And so, for all these reasons, I hope you agree that government regulation must be checked.
> Thank you for inviting me to be here and for your kind attention. As you seek solutions to the complex problems of your industry, I hope that you will remember the words of Thomas Jefferson: "The price of liberty is eternal vigilance."

The delivery of your clincher is as important as its content. Do not mumble your last sentence in a throwaway voice or spend the last few speaking moments gathering up your notes and slinking away. Be familiar enough with your clincher that you can deliver it while maintaining eye contact with your listeners. When you finish, drop your eyes briefly, then reestablish contact to indicate willingness to answer questions, or to acknowledge applause. Inevitably, just as in the beginning, you will be self-conscious at this point. You will feel the focus changing from your message back to you. Remind yourself to project a confident image here so that you do not undo the effect of your clincher.

Exercise 4. Evaluate the last few sentences of each speech in the **Appendix.** Does the final sentence of each successfully serve the functions of a clincher?

Exercise 5. Write a clincher for either the outline on comic books in **8b** or the outline on women in the labor force in **9b**.

12d. Avoid these conclusion pitfalls:

Don't end with an apology:
    "I guess I've rambled on long enough."
    "I don't know if I've made this clear."
    "I'm not usually this hyper; it must be the coffee."
Don't trail off. Do your audience the courtesy of wrapping things up and using a clincher. See **12c**.
Don't introduce a whole new point in your conclusion. The body of your speech is the place for that. See **7c**.

Don't read your conclusion. Or, if it is "almost memorized," be sure it does not sound mechanical. Practice moving into your conclusion naturally so that your eye contact remains constant and your vocal presentation is natural and conversational. See **23c(2)**.

Don't make the conclusion disproportionately long. It is a summary and ending.

Don't end a speech in a style or mood that is at odds with the tenor of the rest of the speech. You do your listeners a disservice if you have kept them laughing up to the very end only to hit them with a stark recitation of doom. See **15c**.

Don't use the phrases "in conclusion" or "in summary" in any part of the speech other than the actual conclusion. You will lose part of your audience while they reorient themselves to the fact that the speech is continuing even though they thought it was winding down. See **10b**.

Part 3

Development

13 Supporting Materials
14 Reasoning
15 Language and Style
16 Attention and Interest
17 Credibility
18 Motivational Appeals
19 Informative Strategies
20 Persuasive Speaking
21 Speaking Ethics
22 Guidelines for Special
    Occasions

Introduction

In talking about the power of words, VerLynn Sprague, the father of one of the authors, customarily gave this rebuttal to an old cliché:

> It's been said that a picture is worth a thousand words. Well, I'm not sure how true that is. Some pictures are worth a million words. It depends on the words. Let me choose the words for you: the Twenty-Third Psalm, the Lord's Prayer, the preamble to the Constitution, the introduction to the Declaration of Independence, the "Gettysburg Address," and Shakespeare's Sonnet 18. A person would be hard-pressed to find a picture that means as much to me as those thousand words do.

The next ten chapters deal with words and pictures, and the pictures we draw with words. Of all the choices you make as a speaker, by far the most important is your choice of the message you will send. Too often people tend to think of a speaking assignment as a burden, a block of time to be filled. Approach it more positively! Here is a chance to share something you really believe in. Have you ever thought about the potential power a public speaker has? Look at just one dimension of that power—the amount of time you control as a speaker. If you give an eight-minute speech in a class, that does not seem like much—until you consider that with an audience of thirty people you have been granted four hours of human time and attention. If you give a two-hour training workshop to a dozen coworkers, that is twenty-four human hours—one full day. Or, if you deliver a one-hour keynote address to 150 people at a conference, you have consumed 150 human hours—*almost a week*. This view of the speaking situation dramatizes your tremendous opportunity and responsibility.

Being entrusted with these precious hours of human time motivates you to prepare extensively. You will not want to waste your listeners' time by underestimating their intelligence, stating the obvious, boring them, or taking twice as long as necessary to make a point. Remember, you are not doing all this work for an eight-minute result, you are getting set for four hours of potential influence.

It probably took VerLynn Sprague at least an hour to select and count the thousand words that would best illustrate the point about their power. He knew his ratio of preparation time to speaking time was going to be sixty to one, but he felt it was worth it to formulate the material that was original, effective, and memorable.

We believe that a speaker, to show good faith with an audience, has an ethical obligation to respect their interests as well as his or her own. Of course, the speaker has a purpose in speaking, but the power of the platform should not be abused. If you are very skilled, you can use personal charisma, emotional appeals, and loaded language to have an almost hypnotic effect on some listeners. We cannot say that these techniques are ineffective. We do make the judgment that they are unethical.

A good speech should never substitute emotion for reason. When you presume to command people's time and attention, you owe it to them to know what you are talking about. Your message should be logical, factual, and coherent. Only after developing the sound rational base should you move on to making the message personal and palatable.

Chapters **13–22** guide you through the concepts pertinent to the development of your speech. The first six chapters introduce the concepts. The remaining chapters suggest responsible ways to weave them into strategic tapestries and adapt them to certain specialized situations. Selecting the proper *supporting materials* provides proof and amplification for your ideas. Familiarity with basic principles of *reasoning* helps you establish logical patterns of thought and avoid fallacies. The relationship of *language* and thought influences speech development, which is not complete until ideas are cast in a clear, effective oral *style*. There is a psychological and interpersonal component to speech; it comes into play through sparking listeners' *attention and interest*, through establishing your *credibility* with them, through making *motivational appeals* to their needs and values, and through evoking their delight. "Strategy" may bring to mind calculated moves by generals or gridiron game plans, but in speech it carries none of the combative or manipulative and tricky connotations of these images. A speech strategy is this only: a master plan for combining your content with other elements of speaking to meet a certain goal. Depending on the nature of that goal, you can formulate effective *informative strategies* or *persuasive strategies,* always within a framework of *speaking ethics*. When the skills and perspective associated with these elements are mastered, you can apply them not only to routine speaking assignments, but to the requirements of *special speaking occasions* as well.

Chapter 13

Supporting Materials

Clarify and justify each of your points with a variety of supporting materials. Be sure these materials meet the tests for sound evidence and are smoothly integrated into the speech.

When you have set up the basic structure of your speech, you then turn to selecting the materials—whether gleaned from research or from your thinking processes—that will make up its real building blocks. The process can be thought of as analogous to "fleshing out" a skeletal drawing of a figure, or to adding the siding to the frame of a building. These supporting materials are crucial to the success of your speech. They are the "stuff" it is made of. They probably determine whether your listeners characterize your utterances as valid or invalid, interesting or boring.

The forms of support you use can be selected only in reference to a basic structure. It is impossible to judge the appropriateness of supporting materials unless you are very clear about what you are supporting. We are appalled to hear some speakers say, "My first point is the Chicago example. My next point is the study done by the Harvard sociologist." Example of what? Study proving or explaining what principle? It is extremely important, as we stress in 3 (Topic Selection and Analysis) and 7 (Transforming Ideas), that you measure every component of your speech against a logical outline. If your point is *Crime is on the increase,* then the story of a single crime, however graphic and compelling, should not be chosen for your development. To *support* that point you need comparative data—examples collected from at least two periods of time must be presented to establish a trend.

Supporting materials may take the form of clarification or of proof. Often, especially in speeches to inform or evoke, these materials amplify, clarify, or expand on ideas. In other cases materials are used to bolster controversial claims for which a speaker seeks acceptance. Although the philosophical notion of ever proving a point completely could be questioned, we speak of supporting materials as proof because they can serve to justify an idea, adding to the probability of its acceptance. Frequently a single piece of support, such as a statistic, functions as both clarification and proof of a point. Some kinds of support, though, like hypothetical examples or definitions, can be used only as amplification; they never serve to prove anything. For a more extended and advanced discussion of methods for clarifying ideas refer to **19** (Informative Strategies). For further advice on proving controversial claims, see **20** (Persuasive Strategies).

Select the support for your ideas first on the basis of relevance, then soundness, and then interest value. Avoid the rut some speakers fall into when they use mostly examples, or mostly testimony, or mostly explanation. Form the habit of using a variety of the following methods to develop your speech.

13a. Define unfamiliar words and concepts.

We all have had the experience of listening to speakers who used so many unfamiliar terms that they might as well have been speaking in a foreign language. In other cases we may have had a hazy notion of the speaker's meaning but craved reassurance: regressive taxes *(poor people pay more— no—less?)*; left brain function *(is that the logical side?)*; deglaze the pan *(something like sauté, probably)*.

There are many methods of definition you can use to save your audience from this kind of experience. Select one or more of the following, depending on which type best suits your situation.

(1) Logical definition

Logical definition, also known as genus-species or dictionary definition, has two steps. It first places the concept to be defined into a category; then it explains the characteristics that distinguish that concept from all other members of the category. For example:

ANTHROPOLOGY is a	
Step1	*formal field of academic study* that studies the human species	[not a religion or a political system or a health food]
Step 2	*as a whole* to develop a *comprehensive understanding of human nature and history.*	[which differentiates it from physics, sociology, biology, psychology]

Some speakers make the mistake of skipping Step 1. Listening to a description of the *Spitfire* as being "more effective, certainly, than the *Boulton Paul Defiant,* and faster and more agile than its predecessors and contemporaries," will not be enlightening if the listener is not told that the *Spitfire* is in the category WWII British Fighter Aircraft. Note that the category is fairly specific. It provides a better focus than the less specific category Airplane, which can bring to mind images of everything from the *Wright Flyer* to a Boeing 767.

(2) Etymological and historical definition

One way to clarify a word's meaning is to explain how the word was derived, either as linked to some historical event or as drawn from root words in an older culture:

Etymological

Anthropology is drawn from the Greek *anthropos,* meaning "human being," and *ology,* meaning "the study of."

Historical

In 1880 Charles G. Boycott, an English land agent in Ireland, refused to reduce rents. In response, his tenants refused to pay them. The word *boycott* has entered the language to mean the act of refusing to engage in social or economic interaction with some entity, either to coerce or to express disapproval.

(3) Operational definition

One way to explain a term is to tell how the object or concept referred to works or operates. Such operational definitions may simply indicate the steps that make up a process:

The *mean* is what you get when you add up all the scores and divide by the number of scores.

Logging on to the computer consists of specifying the system, giving your user ID number, and designating the form your data will take.

Social scientists use operational definitions to explain how conceptual terms are measured:

A *physically active person* will be defined as someone who spends at least six hours a week participating in a vigorous form of exercise.

A *good supervisor* will be defined as a person receiving a score of 25 or higher on the supervisor rating index.

Returning to the anthropology example, you might define the field by telling what an anthropologist does:

An *anthropologist* makes systematic observations about past or present human behavior and then synthesizes these observations into generalizations about human nature and history.

(4) Definition by negation

Socrates said, "Nobody knows what justice is, but everyone knows what injustice is." In many cases the best way to clarify a term is to explain what it is not. Abstract notions such as fairness, clarity, and power can sometimes be better defined by describing actions that are unfair, relationships that are unclear, or people who are powerless.

Reference to opposites can be used to explain concrete terms, too:

Hypoglycemia is something like the opposite of diabetes.

Anthropologists do not amass specialized data on a whim—digging for bones because they need the exercise or living among the natives because the indigenous fish are delicious.

This sort of definition can be powerful and intriguing. For a well-rounded picture, however, negation is best combined with other forms of definition.

(5) Definition by authority

This method of defining is useful for controversial or vague terms where a choice must be made among plausible alternatives. The arbiter of meaning becomes the person with the most credibility or the most power (see also **13d**).

> I don't know what *you* mean by "a little late," but the boss says anything over 15 minutes goes on your record.

> Free speech cannot be suppressed unless a "clear and present danger" exists. The Supreme Court has defined it thus: "No danger flowing from speech can be deemed clear and present, unless the incidence of the evil apprehended is so imminent that it may befall before there is opportunity for full discussion. If there be time to expose through discussion the falsehood and fallacies, to avert the evil by the processes of education, the remedy to be applied is more speech, not enforced silence. Only an emergency can justify repression."

In the anthropology speech you could cite the renowned Margaret Mead:

> She characterizes anthropology as a latecomer, and an uncommitted discipline that spans several fields: "It does not fall, with relentless traditionalism, into any category of science or of humanities or of social science. . . . It is in this very anomalousness that I believe anthropology can make a unique contribution to a liberal education."[1]

(6) Definition by example

Among the many supporting roles played by examples (see **13b**), definition by example is a common and effective means to make terms concrete. The speaker explains something by pointing at it, verbally or literally.

> When I talk about a charismatic leader, I mean someone like John Kennedy, Martin Luther King, Jr., or Adolf Hitler.

> The weapon used in Kendo is a bamboo practice sword called a *shinai*. Here is one [hefts *shinai*].

---

[1]Margaret Mead, "Anthropology and Education for the Future," *Readings in Anthropology,* 3rd ed., eds. Jesse D. Jennings and E. Adamson Hoebel (New York: McGraw-Hill, 1972), 3–6.

There are two basic ways to cause the strings of the guitar to vibrate: strumming, which sounds like this [strums], and picking, which sounds like this [picks].

Anthropology includes such works and studies as L. S. B. Leakey's archeological research in the Olduvai Gorge, Margaret Mead's description of sex roles of the Tchambuli society, Noam Chomsky's treatise on transformation linguistics, and Konrad Lorenz's arguments for the innateness of human aggression.

Observe that the examples chosen to define *anthropology* were familiar and diverse, representing four distinct areas of anthropological research.

Exercise 1. Define each of these terms by two different methods.

Cross training
Love
Collective bargaining
A tachometer
Sibling rivalry

13b. Make frequent use of examples.

Few words can perk up an audience better than "Now let me give you an example." Beyond the universal appeal of a good story, examples provide the audience with a chance to check their perceptions of a speaker's message. When concepts are brought down to actual cases, the listener can see if his or her images coincide with those of the speaker. As a speaker you will need to make decisions about whether to use real examples or hypothetical ones and about how brief or how extended these examples should be.

(1) Use factual examples to illustrate and document your points.

A fact is an assertion that is universally accepted. Sometimes it is directly verifiable, as in "Sandra Day O'Connor is a justice of the Supreme Court." Even if you were not at the swearing-in, there is enough corroborative evidence from many sources to satisfy you that this is a factual statement. "The earth is 93 million miles from the sun" is another assertion accepted as a fact, although it is not *directly* verifiable through any of the five senses. We do accept it, however, because we have constructed theoretical frameworks around consistent results of observation and can make predictions of near-absolute certainty. Knowing the speed of light in Einsteinian space/time, the distance of the earth from the sun can be checked with instruments that extend the senses.

When you use such examples for explanation, it is essential that you imbue them with clarity, relevance, and variety. When you use examples to prove a point, though, specific logical tests must be met. This is the essence of inductive reasoning as discussed in **14b**.

Are sufficient examples given?

To establish the point that high schools in your county are failing to provide basic literacy skills, it would hardly suffice to tell about a few functionally illiterate graduates you know personally. The more examples you give, the less likely your listeners will dismiss the phenomenon as the product of chance.

Are the examples representative?

Even if you gave a dozen examples of local graduates who were functionally illiterate, the conclusion would be suspect if all the cases were from the remedial class at one school. To be credible, examples should represent a cross section of students in the county.

Are negative instances accounted for?

Your conclusion about the failure of the schools might be countered by someone citing the example of her niece who was a National Merit Scholar or pointing out that test scores at Arbor Estates High School were above the national average. When you reason by example, you must look into and account for dramatic negative examples. Perhaps the niece has an IQ of 175. Maybe Arbor Estates High School has a cadre of charismatic English teachers. Your obligation, if you wish to carry your point, is to show how these examples are atypical, why they should be excluded from a consideration of the general status of most students in most schools in the county.

(2) Use hypothetical examples for clarification, speculation, and adaptation to the immediate situation.

Sometimes, when no factual example quite suits your purpose, or when you are speculating about the future, you may choose a brief or extended hypothetical example:

How should you develop an investment portfolio? Well, let's imagine that you have a monthly household income of $4,000 and that your expenses run about $2,800. Let me show you how to calculate what portion of the remainder should go into fairly liquid low-risk areas like the money markets or short-term T-bills, and what portion can go into higher-risk areas like commodities.

Picture a young woman—let's call her Katie—heading toward her car after working overtime. Because she's so tired, she doesn't hear the footsteps behind her until she's some distance from the building. Katie quickens her pace . . .

Hypothetical examples do not have to be extended ones:

What would happen if this tax law were to pass? Well, Miguel over there couldn't deduct his business lunches. Audrey wouldn't be able to depreciate her buildings. You, Tom, with kids about to start college . . .

Obviously, hypothetical examples cannot *prove* anything. They are useful for clarification because they can be tailored to fit the subject exactly. As the previous example demonstrates, hypothetical examples allow you to bring the members of your audience into your speech. When you design your examples, follow the suggestions in **16a**.

Be aware that the examples you pick reflect a set of assumptions about the world. Be sensitive to racist or sexist implications of your illustrations. Are all the bosses men, the secretaries women; do all the laborers have Polish names and all the drunks Irish? If your examples imply that you see the world in these inaccurate stereotypes, understand that some members of your audience will be offended. If, however, you believe we have a pluralistic and rapidly changing society, mix up the names, sexes, races, and roles to reflect that diversity.

(3) Determine the appropriate amount of detail to include in your examples.

Examples in a speech are often short when the speaker can safely assume that the audience already accepts them. What this means is that you may point quickly to several familiar examples. To clarify an idea you might say: "The employee benefits manager handles all of the forms of reward that are not wages—medical insurance, dental insurance, bonuses, profit-sharing plans, company scholarships, for example." To prove a proposition you would also point to familiar and accepted cases. "In the early campaigns in Virginia, the generals of the Confederacy repeatedly demonstrated superior tactics. Think, for example, of Jackson's Valley Campaign, or Lee and the Seven Days' Battles and Second Bull Run." But, obviously, these brief examples would not be effective with listeners who had never heard of profit sharing or who knew nothing of the Civil War. In such cases more detail would be needed.

When a succession of quick references will not illuminate a point for your listeners, extend the example into an illustration:

> Let's look at one example of the tactical superiority of Confederate generals: Lee's Campaign of Second Bull Run. With daring and skill, Lee kept his opponent, Pope, off balance. Lee first sent Jackson around to capture the Union base of supplies twenty miles to Pope's rear. When Pope predictably went after Jackson, Jackson eluded him. During this time Lee moved his army to put it into a position where, when Pope did finally find and attack Jackson, Lee was able to make a devastatingly decisive flank attack.

Though these scenarios take time to develop, they create vivid images that might make the point with more emphasis than would shorter examples.

When you use examples, you must decide how long or short to make each one. This is an area of unconscious incompetence for many speakers. Some use only such brief references that we are left mystified by their cryptic allusions to "what happened in New Jersey" or the "Browne affair." Others tell every detail of every case. For instance, we end up knowing not only that the software product works, but also the color of the diskette package, the thickness of the plastic wrapping, the cleanliness of the monitor screen, the length of time spent waiting at the checkout counter, the name of the salesperson, and so on and on.

Be conscious of the choices you make. Select the degree of elaboration for each example based on audience familiarity with the incident, and based on the effect you want to create and an understanding of the best use of the time allotted to you. Ideally, a speech blends several short examples with a few extended ones. Properly selected, these show the audience both the breadth of your subject and a look in depth at some aspects of it.

Exercise 2. Look at the speeches in the **Appendix.** How many examples are used in each? Label each as *brief* or *extended,* and as *factual* or *hypothetical.* Evaluate the variety of any examples used to establish an inductive line of argument.

Exercise 3. Select one of these topics: Teenage Suicide, Media Impact on Elections, Organ Transplants. Now develop an example in each of the following categories and briefly explain in what sort of speech situation it would be most appropriate.

Brief factual
Extended factual
Brief hypothetical
Extended hypothetical

Exercise 4. Select one of the three topics in Exercise 3 and develop an inductive argument that meets the tests in **13b(1).**

13c. Use statistical evidence to quantify, clarify, and prove your points.

When examples are systematically collected, amassed, and classified, they are reported as statistics. In the case of the literacy topic discussed in **13b(1)**, it would not be feasible to discuss, by name, all the students who illustrate your point. It would simply take too much time to give enough examples to show the seriousness of the problem. This is when you turn to statistical evidence. By examining test scores, conducting follow-up studies of graduates, or interviewing teachers, you could clarify and support your speech with material such as:

58 percent of the seniors in our county high schools did not reach the basic proficiency level on the state reading exams.

One third of our graduates who went to college failed freshman English.

Teachers report that one out of four students has trouble comprehending material written at the seventh-grade level.

(1) Check the accuracy of statistical evidence by applying the tests of *who, why, when, how.*

Who collected the data?
Investigate the qualifications and competence of the researchers. Was the work done by a professional pollster or the host of a call-in radio show? A

graduate student or a noted scholar? An advertising agency or a government task force?

Why were the data collected?

The motivation behind collecting certain information can make the data suspect. Statistics from research done by a candidate's staff, purporting to show massive support for the candidate, may come more from a need to demoralize the opposition than a need to show a true picture to the public. Most people have more confidence in inquiries that grow out of a drive to advance knowledge. Although not totally free of bias, independent pollsters, investigative journalists, scientists, and academics are seen to be more objective than persons committed to selling a product or promoting a cause.

When were the data collected?

Be sure your evidence is up-to-date. Attitudes change as swiftly as prices these days, and sometimes data are obsolete by the time they are published. If you are dealing with a continuously active subject, like the economy, it would not hurt to consult an expert about a source for the most recent data.

How were the data collected?

Find out as much as you can about the design of the research and the details of how it was executed. If a certain statistical finding supports a key point of your speech, do not settle for a one-paragraph reference from *Psychology Today*. Track it back to the *Journal of Social and Experimental Psychology* and learn more about the original study.

First, compare definitions. You may find the title of the study promising, but a closer reading could show that the investigator defines "part-time workers" or "effective leadership" in ways that do not apply to your speech.

Check how the cases were chosen. Subjects and examples should have been selected randomly or through some other logical and unbiased system.

Evaluate the method of data collection—observation, experiment, or survey conducted by phone, mail, or personal interview. If possible, look at the actual instrument used. Are there leading questions or unrealistic forced choices in the interviews and questionnaires?

Even if you are not an expert, you can spot bias introduced into the research method, for example, through the phrasing of directions or the ways the findings are analyzed and presented.

(2) Avoid misleading statistics.

We know that language is ambiguous, but we tend to believe that numbers make straightforward statements; there is no mystery in 2 + 2 = 4. However, numbers *can* be just as ambiguous, with statistical pitfalls to trap the unwary.

The fallacy of the average

A critic once said, with tongue in cheek, that a person could stand with one foot on a block of ice and one foot in a fire and be *statistically* comfortable. While the average is usually a useful tool for analysis, it sometimes can give a picture absurdly at odds with reality.

Less absurd, but just as misleading, might be the report that the Smurge Company has an average of twelve computer scanners per department. In fact, the Art Department has forty scanners, and most other departments have one or none. As this demonstrates, calculating the arithmetic *mean* is not appropriate when one or two extreme cases skew the distribution. The *median* (number or score that falls at the midpoint of the range) or the *mode* (the most frequently occurring score or number) can be more meaningful averages to use in this example, although they, too, can be abused.

The fallacy of the unknown base

When a speaker uses percentages and proportions, he or she can imply that a large population has been sampled. In fact, data are sometimes reported in this manner to give credence to unscientific or skimpy evidence. "Two out of three mechanics recommend this synthetic oil." Most listeners would see this as shorthand for "we polled three hundred mechanics around the country, and two hundred of them recommended this synthetic oil." How valid would this recommendation seem if it came to light that in reality only *three* were polled?

"80 percent of the crimes in this county were committed by teenagers," seems to point to a serious problem. It certainly has more impact than "we had five burglaries this year, and four were committed by teenagers." Four instances do not make a crime wave; 80 percent is an epidemic.

The fallacy of the atypical or arbitrary time frame

Recently an executive of a computer circuitboard company told us that sales in February had doubled over the previous month. These data could be misleading unless you knew that January is always the worst month in the yearly cycle of the small computer industry. If the executive had compared February and November, the month in the cycle where the pre-Christmas home computer and videogame buying frenzy reaches its peak, then the picture would have been quite different. A more valid example to demonstrate company growth would have to compare February with February of the previous year.

By choosing longer or shorter timeframes, this executive could give varying impressions of company health. If he chose November-December-January, with its sharply downward trend, he might convince employees this is no time to talk about raises. Or, he might reassure stockholders by reporting a gradual but steadily upward trend revealed by the figures from the last five Novembers.

(3) Make your numbers and statistics clear and meaningful to your listeners.

The stereotypical dry, plodding speech is the one that is overloaded with statistics. After a short while the audience becomes overloaded, too, and starts to build a dike against the numbers flowing over them. When you do use statistics, round them off. Say "about fifteen hundred" instead of "one thousand four hundred eighty-nine point six." Use comparisons to make the numbers more understandable:

> For the amount of money they propose to spend on this weapons system we could provide educational grants in aid to all the needy students in the eleven western states, or triple the government funding for cancer research, or upgrade the highway system in this state and its three neighbors.

> The immensity of time taxes our ability to perceive it. The universe came into existence 20 billion years ago; our distant mammal ancestors watched the dinosaurs die out 65 million years ago; our closer ancestors came down from the trees 20 million years ago; recorded history began a scant 7,000 years ago. Think of this in terms of a cosmic calendar: The Big Bang set off

the celebration on January first. It wasn't until late on December 30 that mammals began to supplant the giant reptiles, and not until 7 p.m. on December 31 did protohumans start feeling more at home on the ground than in the trees. And recorded history did not begin until three seconds before midnight on that same day.

Avoid overused comparisons. Too many dollar bills have been laid end to end and too many large objects have improbably been dumped onto football fields or placed next to the Empire State Building. Furthermore, audiences are no longer shocked to consider the "five people in this room" who will suffer some fate, or the dire toll of outside events that will be racked up "by the end of this speech" or "by the time I finish this sentence."

Exercise 5. What additional information would you need to have before accepting the following statistical evidence?

Studies show that over two thirds of the total meaning a person communicates is conveyed nonverbally.
Of people who chew gum, four out of five surveyed prefer sugarless gum.
Researchers have found that the average social drinker has eight serious hangovers a year.
Dozens of cases of police harassment have been brought to my attention during my opponent's term of office.

13d. Draw on testimony from authorities.

Often we call on statements from other people to get our point across. Testimony can be looked upon as an outward extension of the speaker's own fact-finding. When we do not have the opportunity to verify something through our own senses, we rely on the observations of others. Even if you have never been arrested or never been a public safety officer, you can be credible giving a speech on the penal system, by making judicious use of testimony.

It might be effective to recite the events of a typical day in prison or to deliver the comments of an inmate on the surroundings. You can draw on the authority of experts or eyewitnesses.

Remembering his five years of incarceration, Mike Carson said, "Every day was the same. We sat in our cells doing nothing but waiting for our hour of exercise or our chance to eat the same lousy food."

Or:

> Based on her study of prison conditions, note criminologist Sarah Jackson reports, "Only a few inmates have the opportunity to attend classes or to hold a job that will teach them a useful skill."

Testimony may be cited directly or paraphrased. One might use a direct quotation in the following manner:

> According to a report of the Second Circuit Court of Appeals: "Beginning immediately after the state's recapture of Attica on the morning of September 13, and continuing until at least September 16, guards, state troopers, and correctional personnel had engaged in cruel and inhuman abuse of numerous inmates. Injured prisoners, some on stretchers, were struck, prodded, or beaten. Others were forced to strip and run naked through gauntlets of guards armed with clubs . . . spat upon or burned with matches . . . poked in the genitals or arms with sticks."[2]

Or, one might paraphrase the statement like this:

> A report of the Second Circuit Court of Appeals catalogs the cruel and inhuman abuse following the Attica riots. When the state regained control, guards and prison personnel subjected the prisoners to harsh physical punishments.

(1) Evaluate the credibility of the authorities you cite when you use testimony as proof.

You do not have to research a controversial topic for very long before you find that there are seemingly authoritative quotations to cover every side of an issue. It is easy to find citations that say almost anything, but it is much more difficult to select those that really provide legitimate support for your points. Test the credibility of the authorities you quote by asking these questions:

Does the authority have access to the necessary information?

A person does not have to be famous to be an authority. The eyewitness to an accident can tell you authoritatively what happened in the intersection. Your neighbor does not have to be a China watcher to report on a

---

[2] Jessica Mitford, *Kind and Usual Punishment: The Prison Business* (New York: Knopf, 1973), 265–66.

trip taken to that country. The farther removed someone is from the source, however, the less trustworthy that person's information. A quotation from the accident eyewitness is preferable to a quotation from an acquaintance telling what the eyewitness said.

Ambiguous descriptions can be misleading. "My brother works for the government and he says there's a massive conspiracy to cover up the cost overruns in the Defense Department" or "It is the opinion of a noted psychologist that the assassin is definitely insane" is testimony that loses its effect when we find that the brother is a postal clerk and the psychologist had only read the newspaper accounts of the assassin's trial. When you use an authority, be sure that the person had firsthand experience, direct observation, or personal access to relevant facts and files.

Is the authority qualified to interpret data?

As stated above, anyone can credibly describe what she or he saw. It is when a person starts making interpretations, forming opinions and conclusions, and proposing recommendations that the standards of credibility become stricter. People earn the right to be considered experts either by holding specific credentials—such as a law degree, Ph.D., Realtor's license—or by having established a record of success and experience.

Is the person acknowledged as an expert on *this* subject?

When the Washington Redskins football team executed a play suggested by then-President Nixon, we saw a peculiar variation of the practice of presenting a sports figure in commercials as an authority on nutrition or automotive engineering. President Nixon's acknowledged expertise in the field of foreign policy did not make him a credible football authority. There are other cases where an expert's opinions have subtly stretched beyond the range of his or her expertise. A tax attorney may be presented as an expert on constitutional law, a social psychologist may express an opinion on the causes of schizophrenia, or a well-known chemist may receive national attention for her or his views on the efficacy of vitamin C. The opinions they express may or may not be valid, but their expertise in a related field makes them, at best, only slightly more credible than an informed layperson.

Is the authority figure free of bias and self-interest?

It is not very surprising when the chair of the Democratic National Committee characterizes the party platform as a blueprint for justice and prosperity, or when a network spokesperson describes a new television show as an incisive and intelligent portrayal of the human condition. It is not surprising, nor is it very persuasive. We would give much more credence to the opinion of a political analyst or a television critic who appears to have no personal stake, ideological or monetary, in the response to the opinion. What would be surprising, and highly persuasive as well, is reluctant testimony. If you were able to find testimony from a person speaking *against* his or her interests, presumably because of honesty or as a duty to a larger concept, then it certainly would be an effective addition to your presentation: "Even the National Committee chair admitted that the platform is fuzzy on foreign policy."

(2) Take care, when editing quotations, to retain key points without distorting their meaning.

Truncating quotations to highlight the basic thrust of the message is perfectly acceptable. What is unacceptable is editing a person's statements to such a degree that they appear to support positions other than or even opposite those supported by the actual quotations. There is the old joke about the movie critic who wrote that "the wretchedness of the acting in this film is nothing short of amazing!" only to find later that an advertisement for the movie quoted him as saying "this film . . . is amazing!"

Do not edit a source so radically that the quotation loses all substance. Virtually content-free quotations are sometimes used as a deliberate tactic to confuse listeners or to overwhelm them with an apparent preponderance of evidence. A common example of this is the recitation of the conclusion reached by an authority without including any of the reasoning that lead to the conclusion. "About the job-retraining program, the mayor has said that it 'is a disappointment.' The president of the Chamber of Commerce stated that it 'has not fulfilled our expectations.' The chair of the Council of Unions labeled it 'a failure.'" The people cited may be authorities on the subject, but it is entirely possible that their reservations result from an analysis that is not at all pertinent to the speaker's point. For instance, they all may be complaining of inadequate funding rather than attacking the concept of the program. It is impossible to tell from these cryptic quotations. It is also possible that these experts could be wrong. A listener would need to hear more about *why* they drew the conclusions they did.

13e. Weave supporting materials smoothly into the speech. Cite your sources.

When you have chosen appropriate definitions, facts, examples, statistics, and testimony, the challenge remains to marshal these supporting materials and present them effectively. You will want to emphasize the quality of your materials, make them clear and understandable, and organize them appropriately in relation to the points they support.

(1) Cite the sources of your supporting materials.

By giving credit for your supporting materials, you build your own credibility, showing the range of your research. You are also providing information your listeners are almost certain to want. Very few audiences will settle for "studies show . . ." or "one researcher found . . ." or "a friend once told me . . ." In order to evaluate these statements, listeners need to know more about where the information came from.

This does not mean that you are required to present regulation footnotes in oral form, citing volume and page numbers. Nor need you recite an authority's complete biography or necessarily explain a study's design intricacies. Although you should know the *who, why, when,* and *how* of every bit of data you use, you will probably mention only a couple of these in introducing the evidence.

How then do you decide which to include? You can follow two basic suggestions. The first one encompasses those questions you predict your audience will have. Put yourself in the listeners' place and adopt a skeptical outlook: What would you question about the data? A hostile audience might want to know whether your expert was objective, a group of social scientists might question whether the opinion poll you cite was scientifically conducted. The second suggestion for selecting details about a source is: Stress what is most compelling and impressive. If you have a thirty-year-old quotation from a Supreme Court justice, but you think the sentiment expressed is timeless, stress the *who* and not the *when.* What is the best feature of the evidence—its recency, the large size of the sample, the prestige of the journal where it appeared?

(2) Use a variety of lead-ins for stylistic effectiveness.

Do not get into the habit of introducing all your illustrations, or all your statistics, and so on, with the same phrase. "Some figures about this are . . . some figures about that are . . ." Be prepared enough that you can employ a number of different lead-ins for each kind of supporting material. There are many possibilities, such as:

> To support this idea . . .
> This point is verified by . . .
> _____ put it well, I think, when she said . . .
> In the words of _____ , . . .
> What causes this situation? One answer to that question was offered by _____ when he wrote last year . . .
> Let me tell you about a survey taken in the early eighties by a Brandeis psychologist . . .
> There are several examples of this. Let me share just two . . .
> I was immediately struck by the similarity to an experience I/she/_____ once had . . .

However you decide to introduce a quotation, do not say "quote, unquote" or wiggle pairs of index and middle fingers in the air to approximate quotation marks. A subtle change in your voice or posture is enough to indicate to your listeners the boundaries of a direct quotation.

Exercise 6. Compare the use of supporting materials in the speeches in the **Appendix.** Note the presence of explanation, definition, examples, statistics, and testimony in each.

Does every speech use a variety of methods?
What are the two favored forms of supporting material in each speech?

Chapter 14

Reasoning

Use sound reasoning to develop your speech. Avoid logical fallacies.

Reasoning is the process by which we come to understand something previously unknown, through analyzing and integrating those things we already know. Your goal in a public speech is to share your insights with your listeners by "thinking" out loud, retracing for them the steps that led you to your conclusions. If you have not fully reasoned out your conclusions, or if you have made gross logical missteps in reaching them, the chance of those conclusions being accepted by an audience becomes exceedingly slim. Any remotely intelligent group of listeners will not be moved by hearing *what* you think; they will want to know *why* you think it. Consequently, the reasoning that should be the foundation of every speech can also be seen as "the giving of *good* reasons."

People reason every time they make links between ideas. We speak in grammatical sentences (at least most of the time) even if we do not know the formal parts of speech or rules of grammar. By the same token, speakers and listeners reason competently a great deal of the time or else they would not have survived to adulthood. When people disagree it is not because one of them does not know the rules of formal or everyday logic. It is rather because they disagree about the facts and evidence or they disagree about the interpretation of it. Making sure that your supporting material is valid was covered in Chapter **13**. Without getting into the intricacies of formal logic, this chapter addresses how to make sure your interpretation of the evidence is valid *and comes across as valid.*

To develop a logical line of thought and test its validity, you will first need to understand a little more about how reasoning functions to link key points of a speech together. Then, you will need to become familiar with standard patterns of reasoning and with a few of the common fallacies. Finally, you can decide how best to use reasoning in putting your speech together.

There are four patterns of reasoning discussed in this chapter: inductive reasoning, deductive reasoning, causal reasoning, and reasoning by analogy. They are not analyzed here in depth as logical forms separate from one another, as in fact most complex reasoning involves a combination of methods. For instance, a causal connection might be established either inductively or deductively. Or perhaps a literal analogy might be used to justify a statement that becomes, in turn, the major premise of a deductive argument. As you read the remainder of this chapter, do not expect to master the intricacies of logical reasoning. Look instead to incorporate into your thinking a general sense of four very common patterns that you can use to structure speech material in a rational way.

14a. Identify each point in your preliminary speech outline where reasoning is needed to provide an essential link.

Every speech involves synthesizing data, explaining ideas, and clustering points. For some topics, developing the points then becomes a matter of just "unpacking" the clusters. If your point is that there were three causes of the Spanish Inquisition, then you need to just list and explain those. In many cases—in all persuasive speeches and some sections of evocative and informative speeches—a far more challenging task confronts the speaker. You must develop lines of argument through reasoning. For instance, if you have a cluster of ideas gathered around the point "reasons for allowing fetal tissue research," just listing and explaining those reasons will never suffice. You will be informing the audience of your reasons, or perhaps you will be informing them of what some experts say, but you will not be convincing them that your list of reasons warrant their acceptance unless you explain why you (and the experts you cite) come to the conclusion you do. This *conclusion* can also be called a *claim*.

Claims are any statements that you need to establish and substantiate because they are not taken for granted by your listeners. Your thesis sentence is a claim, your main points are claims that support *that* claim, and even some of your subordinate points have to be reasoned through before they will be acceptable.

Some of the statements that make up your speech outline may not be controversial (for example, poverty is bad) or may be obvious (for example, most people would prefer not to pay higher taxes). Many other points will need to be supported. The supporting materials, evidence, or data discussed in Chapter 13 bolster your point. At least you think so, or you would not have put those data and that claim together. However, the challenge of reasoning is to show how the data and claim are linked.

(1) Evidence does not necessarily lead to a certain claim.

Suppose that you have a conclusion or claim that you want your listeners to accept, and you have some evidence or data that you believe support that claim. Clearly, everyone who confronts the same facts and figures does not automatically come to the same conclusion that you do. What links the *data* to the *claim,* or *warrants* its acceptance, is the process of reasoning. For example, suppose that two different people are confronted with the fact that more people go to the doctor in countries with national health care programs than in countries with privately funded health care. Person A concludes that this is an argument in support of adopting national health care in the United States. Person B concludes that this is an argument against national health care.

There is no connection between evidence and claim except through the reasoning link that you provide. See Figure 14-1.

(2) In linking evidence to claims, people look for patterns of regularity that fit with what they have observed in the world.

In the health care example given earlier, Person A was drawing on a pattern observed in the past, namely that people who cannot afford a service they need will seek out that service when it becomes affordable. This is perfectly reasonable and logical; we all can think of plenty of common-sense examples.

Person B is also being logical and reasonable in linking the evidence of increased medical visits to the claim that national health care would be

171

FIGURE 14-1   Reasoning Links Evidence and Claim

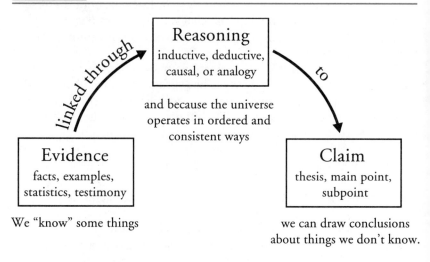

undesirable. This person is drawing on another observed pattern of human behavior—that people who see a resource as free and unlimited may use it inappropriately and wastefully. There is also plenty of support for that.

The issue here is not what the facts are, but what the facts mean. For our purposes, the significance of these opposing views is to show that there are many sensible ways to interpret the same piece of evidence. A speaker who would use evidence to support a claim cannot just present the evidence and hope it speaks for itself. The speaker must explain the relevance of the evidence and justify the link to a particular claim.

The orientation toward communication taken in this book is that speakers do not just transmit information to listeners. Speakers and listeners create meanings together. Therefore, on any complex and controversial topic, you need to show your audience why evidence is meaningful and help them build the argument with you. This is done by spelling out your interpretation of the data and showing how this interpretation fits one of the common patterns of reasoning familiar to your listeners.

Exercise 1. For each of these claims, list at least three pieces of evidence you could use to support it. (For the purpose of this exercise, you can make it up or rely on general knowledge.)

Smoking should be banned in all indoor public places.
Congress should pass a ban on all assault weapons.
Drivers over the age of seventy should have to take a road test every year to renew their driver's license.

After you have listed the evidence, explain how each piece of evidence supports the point.

Exercise 2. Show how the evidence presented here can be linked to the two different claims. What logical pattern does a person draw upon in each case?

Example A
Evidence: The form of government in the United States has existed for over two hundred years.
Therefore
Claim 1: We should maintain our present form of government.
Because
Link or Reasoning: ...

or

Therefore
Claim 2: We should change our present form of government.
Because
Link or Reasoning: ...

Example B
Evidence: Deaths from firearms have increased in the past few years.
Therefore
Claim 1: We need even stronger gun control laws than the ones we have.
Because
Link or Reasoning: ...

or

Therefore
Claim 2: We should get rid of gun control laws.
Because
Link or Reasoning: ...

14b. Use an inductive pattern of reasoning when your argument consists of combining a series of observations to lead to a probable conclusion.

The simplest and most common kind of reasoning is *induction*. Dozens of times a day we draw inferences that go beyond what we observe directly. Induction assumes an orderly universe. We could not function unless we trusted regularities in events, unless we believed that much of what has happened before will happen again. We step in front of oncoming traffic because we believe from previous experience that the cars will obey the traffic signals. After several sleepless nights we stop drinking coffee at bedtime. See Figure 14-2.

(1) Look before you "leap": Be sure the instances on which you base your inferences are sufficient and representative.

Inductive reasoning consists of collecting enough instances to establish a pattern. Remember the logical tests in **13b(1)**. A typical line of inductive thought can be portrayed as follows:

Orchid$_1$ has no fragrance.
Orchid$_2$ has no fragrance.

FIGURE 14-2   Inductive Reasoning Draws Inferences from Observations

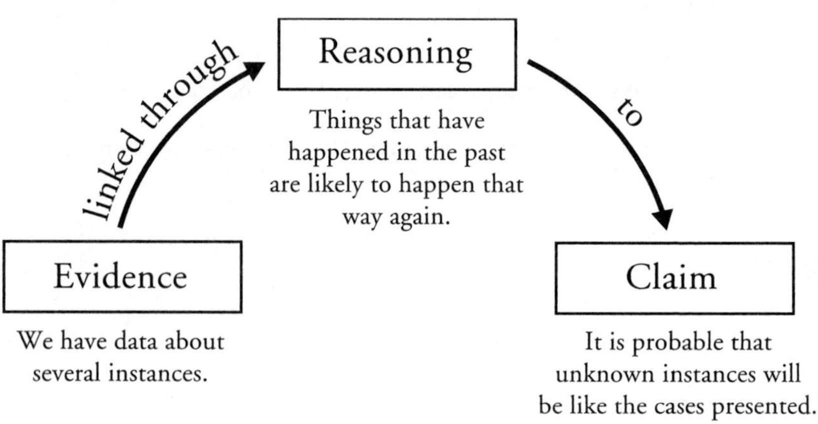

Reasoning

Things that have happened in the past are likely to happen that way again.

linked through

to

Evidence

We have data about several instances.

Claim

It is probable that unknown instances will be like the cases presented.

Orchid$_3$ has no fragrance.

....

....

....

Orchid$_n$ has no fragrance.
Therefore, it is probable that all orchids have no fragrance.

The extent to which you can generalize from such observations is linked to the extent of your sampling. If you smelled only the orchids in one corner of one hothouse, you would be less able to make a general conclusion than had you smelled orchids in different hothouses throughout the country.

By far the greatest problem in this kind of reasoning is determining the value of *n*. Obviously you want to test several cases before drawing a conclusion, but how many are enough? This is the issue of "enoughness." If you drive five Hupmobiles and they all have mechanical difficulties, is that enough to say that Hupmobiles are bad cars? If a researcher finds that 132 out of 150 soap opera fans surveyed do housework while listening, is that enough to justify a conclusion about that group? At best you can say, "It is likely that Hupmobiles are lemons," and "Soap opera fans probably do housework while listening." The conclusions drawn from induction are always *probable* rather than *absolute*. The only way you could say that *all* Hupmobiles are lemons would be if you had tested every one. This would be counting, not reasoning. Reasoning, as you recall, is defined as drawing conclusions about the unknown.

Be cautious in drawing inferences from limited data. How many cases did you examine? Were they selected fairly? Are the contrary instances accounted for? See **13b, 14f**.

(2) Recognize the degree of probability of your claim.

An inductive conclusion can fall anywhere along this continuum:

possible	probable	almost
		certain

The degree of certainty depends on the methods used in making our observations, and on the number of observations made. A conclusion like, "the last two times I've gone to that restaurant the service has been lousy. I'll bet they've changed management," would fall far to the left. Two observations is a very small number, and there are many other viable explanations for the poor service. At the other end of the continuum is a statement like, "Birth control pills prevent fertilization." This conclusion is based on a great many observations collected systematically. We can say we are 99 percent sure it is true, but we still lack complete certainty.

How strong must this probability be before you can consider valid the conclusion of an inductive argument? A 51 percent probability, 75 percent, 99 percent? Unlike deductive reasoning, for which there are agreed-upon tests of validity, the test of an induction varies in every case. There is no mathematical or logical answer to the question. The issue of "enoughness" is more a psychological question of individual perception, as is explained next.

Would you leap off a twenty-foot wall for $1,000? Many would say yes. It is *possible* that you could be killed, but it is probable that you would escape with no worse than a sprained ankle. Would you jump from the roof of a three-story building for $1,000? Most people would say no. It is *possible* you would be unharmed, but not very probable. In both cases you set the acceptable level of probability by weighing the risks against potential gains. Flipping a coin has a 50 percent probability—good enough for a dollar bet, but would you bet your life on a coin toss? When you choose to fly in an airliner, you bet your life, but the probability is 400,000 to 1 you will arrive safely, and the gains of speedy transportation outweigh the minimal risk.

(3) Demonstrate the cost/reward analysis that led you to accept or reject the probable claim.

When induction is used in a public speech, the speaker's task is to convince the audience members that the conclusion arrived at is probable enough to warrant their acceptance. The so-called "inductive leap" is based on an apt image. You lead the listeners to a certain point with the data you have and then ask them to jump across a chasm to the conclusion you see. Here, as in the preceding examples, the level of "enoughness" is contingent on the risks and benefits perceived.

Suppose that you know of a new kind of drug rehabilitation program that has been found to be quite effective in pilot studies in three different communities. In urging its adoption in your city, your line of reasoning might go like this:

The program worked in Community A.
The program worked in Community B.
The program worked in Community C.
Therefore, it is probable that the program is effective and will work here.

Because these other cases were not studied totally systematically (with control groups, random sampling, and follow-up studies, for example), and because there are only three instances, you cannot state your conclusion at a high level of probability. You must recognize that the drug rehabilitation program could fail in your community. Imagine that it were possible to assign concrete levels of probability, and that both proponents and skeptics of the program agreed that there was about a 75 percent chance of its success. A member of your audience might well ask, "Why should we spend $650,000 just for a three-out-of-four chance we might help a bunch of junkies?" You cannot change the 75 percent odds, but what you can do is affect your audience's assessment of the costs and rewards. Tell them how the program, if it works, will benefit the whole community: decrease crime, put former addicts back in productive employment, and lower the temptations for adolescent drug use. Also minimize the costs. "$650,000 sounds like a lot, but it's only $.85 per citizen." When the listeners reassess the costs and rewards, and see them as you do, the 75 percent odds may look more attractive.

Consider another example, where the conclusion's probability is very high.

Nuclear power plant A has had no accidents.
Nuclear power plant B has had no accidents.
Nuclear power plant C has had no accidents.
....
Nuclear power plant n has had no accidents.
Therefore, it is probable that nuclear power plants are safe.

Suppose the conclusion could be granted a 95 percent level of probability. Even so, you or someone else might not feel the evidence was sufficient to make the inductive leap. In explaining this to the audience, you would minimize the rewards—most of the energy we would get can be obtained through other sources—and maximize the risks by describing just how awful a nuclear accident could be. Your argument is: "I'm not willing to subject my family to a five-out-of-one hundred chance of this sort of destruction just to have a few extra electronic luxuries."

In the case of the drug problem, a low probability met the test of enoughness for the speaker. In the case of the nuclear power plant, even 95 percent was not enough. The difference lies in the perception of risk and reward. No level of enoughness is too high or too low—no inductive argument is innately logical or illogical. The validity is negotiated between you and your audience.

14c. Use a deductive pattern of reasoning when your argument consists of demonstrating how the relationships among established premises lead to a necessary conclusion.

Unlike induction, where the emphasis is on collecting observable data, deduction consists of manipulating verbal statements, or premises, according to formal rules. Deduction, then, does not really involve bringing new data into play, but just rearranges what you already know. If this is the case, why do we think we can learn anything new through the process of deduction if we are dealing with the known? Bits of data are useless until we can assign meaning to them by discovering how they fit together. From this are derived scientific breakthroughs, brainteasers, gossip, and the English murder mystery. In the obligatory denouement of the last-named, the detective patiently explains to a roomful of suspects the meaning of the details known but not assimilated by the reader:

> Everyone who had a motive appeared to have an alibi at the time of the murder. Because people cannot be in two places at once, I deduced that the time of the murder must have been earlier than we thought. Remember the maid who discovered the body in the bedroom, saying it was as cold as ice? But the bedroom was quite warm from the fire in the fireplace. A corpse is not as cold as ice unless it has been stored in a very cold place for hours and only later returned to the bedroom. And then there were the cobwebs almost imperceptible against the corpse's silver hair. What place in this manor is both cold and cobwebby? The wine cellar. Only Peters, the butler, had a key to the wine cellar!

Having the clues is not enough, it takes a supersleuth to find the perfect pattern. See Figure 14-3.

In our everyday lives, we have that "Aha!" experience when we suddenly discover the pattern underlying separate facts. Just as you are falling asleep you sit up abruptly and say: "Just a minute! My sweetie

FIGURE 14-3   Deductive Reasoning Finds the Patterns in What You Already Know

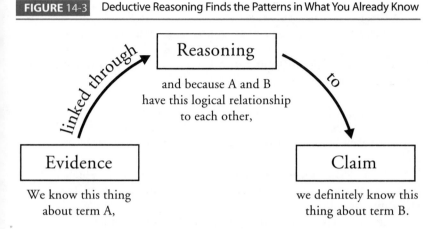

claimed to be at the library all evening, but in our late night phone call mentioned having to drive around the broken power lines on High Street. I heard on the late news that those lines went down just tonight. But High Street is nowhere near the library. It's over by Club Danz Tilyadrop."

This kind of reasoning is quite different from induction, which involves going out and gathering data. Facts that are already known are put together in a way that reveals their implications. In this case, the implication is that:

> If you were at the library, you couldn't know about the power lines.
> You did know about the power lines.
> You were not at the library. (You dirty . . .)

(1) In a formal deductive syllogism, be sure that there are only two terms and that the major premise sets up an absolute relationship.

Because the correctness of deduction lies in whether it follows a form, experts in deductive reasoning learn complex symbolic formulas by which they test arguments. For the purpose of this book, we need only to touch on the basic concept of deduction: If we know certain things about how two terms (concepts, events, characteristics) are related, we can discover other relationships that are logically entailed or implicated.

Term *A* is related in a known way to Term *B*.
We know certain things about *B*.
Therefore, we can draw certain conclusions about Term *A*.

To use deductive reasoning in a speech, you need to transpose this into a series of steps:

Step 1:Establish that a relationship exists between two terms.
Step 2:Establish the actual condition/status of one of the terms.
Step 3:Show how a conclusion about the other term necessarily follows.

Step 1 in deduction—establishing the "major premise"—takes many forms. It always involves an absolute relationship between two terms. Here are examples of four common relationships:
One term may be an intrinsic characteristic of the other.

All ducks have webbed feet.
Conflict is inherent in the collective bargaining model.

One term may be a category that includes the other.

All Volkswagens are motor vehicles.
The Food Stamp program is part of the social welfare system.

One term may be inevitably linked to the other.

If you heat water to 212 degrees at sea level, *then* it will boil.
If corporate taxes are cut, *then* investment will increase.

The two terms may be opposite or exclude each other.

Either that fabric is natural or it is synthetic.
Unless we crack down on drunken drivers, fatalities will rise.

When you have established one of these basic, therefore "major," premises, you have set up a formula that will serve as the linking device at the top of your arc of reasoning. When you move to Step two you establish something about one of the two terms (in what logicians call the *minor premise*). A piece of evidence like "Daffy is a duck" might mean many things, or nothing, in some lines of argument. But in the context of the first major premise illustrated earlier, it is the minor premise, and the resulting, relevant implication is that Daffy has webbed feet.

Feed in the data you have, follow the rules of deductive logic, and certain conclusions are inevitably entailed:

> We did not crack down on drunken drivers, *so traffic fatalities must have increased.*
> This blouse is made of a synthetic fiber, *so it is not made of a natural fiber.*

The beauty of deduction lies in its certainty. If your listeners accept the premises, they must accept the conclusion.

This seems so attractive that one might wonder why a speaker would use any other method. Why waste energy on the probable conclusions of induction, with their floating points of enoughness that allow audiences to capriciously—yet legitimately—reject a 95 percent certain conclusion? Why not stick with deduction, where the rules are clear and the conclusions have to be accepted? The problem with deduction is that in order for its conclusion to be absolute, its premises must be absolute. Unfortunately, most absolute statements of relationships are either untrue or trivial. Who really cares if ducks have webbed feet, or needs to reason about it? The things we do have to reason about, and tend to give speeches about, are complex issues of public policy, human behavior, and social values. In these domains it is rarely possible to find acceptable statements that *"all X is Y"* or that, *"if X, then Y always* follows" or that "either *X* or *Y* and *no other alternative."* The requirement of having an all-or-nothing beginning premise is so restrictive that true, formal deductive reasoning is rather rare. In speaking (if not in logic class) it is acceptable to use a slightly less rigorous form of deduction.

(2) When using a modified deductive form of reasoning, make it clear that probable premises can lead only to probable conclusions.

In the if-then statement about tax cuts, does a reduction on corporate taxes absolutely *have to* result in increased investment? A more honest syllogism would be:

> It is highly probable that a cut in corporate taxes will increase investment.
> Congress is almost certain to cut taxes.
> Therefore, it is highly probable that investment will increase.

But now we have lost the tidy inevitability of deduction. No longer do the rules of logic force our listeners to accept our conclusion. We are back to the same kinds of problems we face in induction, persuading the audience to weigh the probabilities as we do. Our appeal to them would be:

> If you grant this premise as probable,
> and
> if you grant this other premise as probable,
> then it is logical to grant this conclusion as probable.

When you look at deduction this way, you can, as a speaker, take some liberties not available to the logician. You may build a deductively structured argument with premises that are not absolute, recognizing, of course, that the conclusions you derive will not be absolute either. Each point needs to be supported sufficiently to persuade a member of the audience to say, "I'll grant that point; it's reasonable; it's probable." Thus the degree of probability of any conclusion is a product of the degree of probability granted to each premise. (If quantification of probabilities were possible, it would work like this: Major premise that is 80 percent probable × minor premise that is 75 percent probable = conclusion that is 60 percent probable.)

The form of a deductive argument is still an elegant way to justify a conclusion, even when it has been modified to lose the clean force of a true syllogism. In its diluted but more realistic form it provides an effective structure for part of a speech, or for the entire speech. When the conclusion you want your audience to reach can be arrived at through many logical channels, seriously consider arranging your points in a deductive format.

(3) As a general rule, explicitly lay out all the premises of a deductive argument.

One of the real advantages of structuring ideas deductively is that you must state the relationships among the concepts with which you are dealing. When you clearly state the major premise on which your argument rests, you call to your listeners' minds certain values, assumptions, or even logical truisms. The audience can then apply these concepts when you move on to specific cases in developing your minor premise. In the following logical arguments, notice how the major premise serves in each case to direct the listeners' awareness to a statement that the speaker might otherwise have left implicit.

> Anyone who has been elected to high office has had to make a number of political compromises along the way.
> Candidate J has served as governor and U.S. senator.
> Therefore, Candidate J has made a number of political compromises.

> A person denied access to the benefits of society will either become embittered or will turn to crime.
> Many members of ethnic minorities who are denied access have not committed crimes.
> Therefore, many are embittered.

> It has always been the goal of our social welfare system to help recipients become self-sufficient.
> Certain current programs encourage dependency and discourage initiative.
> Therefore, these programs should be changed.

> A good friend is a person who helps you reach your potential.
> Several people in this organization have helped me strive toward my potential.
> Therefore, as I say good-bye, I feel like I am leaving a number of good friends.

Sometimes speakers have so internalized a point of view that they leave out parts of their argument that they see as obvious. When this is done intentionally for persuasive effect because the speaker and listeners share common values, the use of these economical lines of argument (called *enthymemes*) can be powerful. See **20c.** These are rare exceptions. On controversial topics before diverse audiences, however, neglecting to lay out all parts of the argument is dangerous; we find that excellent speeches often take the time to articulate and justify the premises they are based on. Consider the previous examples. The first point of each argument might have been omitted or tossed in as an aside rather than developed. By the same token, in saying, "Of course Thompson should be hired, he has the most experience" or "We couldn't possibly pass this bill, it endangers the free enterprise system," you are assuming that your audience accepts your assumption that "the person with the most experience should be hired," or that "anything that endangers the free enterprise system is undesirable." If they do not accept those assumptions, all your efforts to prove Thompson's experience or the bill's effects are wasted. If they do agree, you will not have lost much time by reiterating those points. Listeners will be more likely to remember your specifics if they have a logical framework for them.

Like the detective with the clues, your task is not just to list the facts, but to demonstrate how they fit together and what they ultimately mean. Often the conclusion of the speech is the place to weave together the threads of a deductive argument.

> So, I've shown that it is our goal to reach full employment and that the only available paths are through direct provision of public sector jobs or through indirect stimulation of private sector jobs. Since I went on to give you several reasons for rejecting the public sector alternative, there is only one conclusion left. To create full employment the private sector must be stimulated.

Exercise 3.   Here are some conclusions that could have been reached either inductively or deductively. Briefly lay out an inductive and a deductive argument that leads to each.

Natural childbirth is best for parents and infant.
More states should institute regulations protecting computer users from workplace conditions that can cause carpal tunnel syndrome and other repetitive strain injuries.
The Academy Awards are rarely given to the best films.

Exercise 4.   What costs or risks would you need to minimize and what benefits would you need to maximize in order to establish a high probability of acceptance for these conclusions?

This new treatment for herpes should be marketed.
Every school bus should be equipped with seat belts.
We should hire only college graduates for our sales department.
You should cut animal fat out of your diet.

Exercise 5.   What unstated assumption or absolute statement of relationship underlies each of these arguments?

She must be doing a good job. She hasn't been fired.
You should buy a condominium. It's cheaper than a house.
Well, it's not a win for labor, so I guess management wins.
I thought he had some self-respect, but now I learn he's on welfare.

Exercise 6. Identify the basic reasoning pattern in each speech in the **Appendix.** Are they inductive or deductive? Can you lay out the underlying argument in three or four sentences?

14d. Use causal reasoning to demonstrate that one event results from another.

Causal reasoning is the backbone of all speeches that deal with policy and problem solving. In most cases, if a person says, "I don't favor your policy (or program, or solution)," what that person is really saying is, "I disagree with you that *X* causes *Y*." What this means is that you must carefully scrutinize the relationship that exists between two events to satisfy yourself that it *is* causal, and then you must provide your listeners with information that indicates how thoroughly you tested this relationship. See Figure 14-4.

Of course, in a problem-solving or policy speech there is rarely *one* cause. To assert that there is would be gross oversimplification and would jeopardize the acceptance of your conclusions. Still, it helps to understand the rigorous tests you would have to apply to a statement if you were to assert a pure causal relationship in it—that is, "one cause leads inevitably to one effect."

FIGURE 14-4   Causal Reasoning Links Cause and Effect

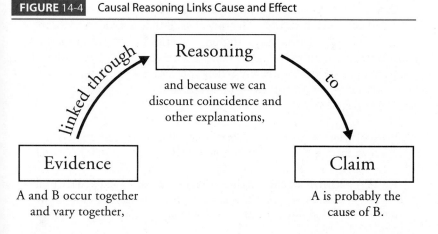

(1) Test the validity of the causal relationships you claim.

A causal relationship is stronger than a mere correlation. It is not coexistence. Two events may occur together or in sequence without one causing the other. For instance, morning sickness and weight gain often occur together, but neither causes the other; they are the result of a third condition, pregnancy. To be sure that the relationship is a causal one, apply these tests:

Do the alleged cause and alleged effect occur together?

To prove that a causal relationship exists, at least two formal comparisons must be made, as with a control group and experimental group. Otherwise mere coincidence or correlation cannot be ruled out. It is not enough to show that the alleged cause is present with the alleged effect, but that also in the absence of the alleged cause the alleged effect does not appear.

> If a rash appears every time you eat tomatoes, and never appears when you haven't eaten tomatoes, this is strong evidence that tomatoes cause the rash.

> There are three groups of arthritis sufferers, matched in all important characteristics such as age, sex, diet, and general health. Group A receives the drug Painaway, Group B receives a placebo, and Group C receives no treatment. Members of Group A experience dramatic relief, and there is no change in the condition of members of Group B and Group C. This supports the claim that Painaway causes a reduction in arthritis symptoms.

To prove a causal relationship, you must show both concurrent presence and concurrent absence. Technically, all that is needed to *disprove* a suggested causal relationship is to point to a case where the alleged cause was present without the alleged effect, or vice versa. So, if you found that your rash occurred occasionally when you had not eaten tomatoes, or if you had once eaten tomatoes and not gotten the rash, a pure causal relationship does not exist.

> Classical economic theory suggests that raising tariffs reduces imports. Yet, when we increased the tariff on Argentine beef, imports remained constant.

> For years I believed the other teachers who said students would read the book only if they were given weekly quizzes. Then one semester I dropped the quizzes and found that students were as well prepared each week as before.

Do the alleged cause and the alleged effect vary together?
Another test of causation is to determine that the magnitude of change in the cause matches that in the effect.

If one bite of tomato gives you a small rash, and consuming many tomatoes gives you a big rash, this is one more bit of evidence to suggest that tomatoes cause your rash.

High school graduates, on the average, earn more than high school dropouts. People with some college education earn more than high school grads, but less than college graduates. People with advanced degrees, taken as a group, have the highest incomes. Though you can think of individual exceptions, research on groups of people shows that each increment of formal education is accompanied by an equivalent increase in earning power.

(2) Do not oversimplify causal relationships.

In the worlds of physics and chemistry, there are some clear, straightforward casual relationships.

An action results in an equal and opposite reaction.

or

Adding silver nitrate solution ($AgNO_3$) to sodium chloride (NaCl) will cause silver chloride (AgCl) to precipitate.

These could be represented as as:

$$C \rightarrow E$$

However, in the areas of politics, psychology, medicine, economics, and the like, more complex patterns usually exist.

Some effects have multiple causes.

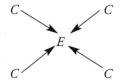

187

If smoking were the single cause of lung cancer, then every smoker would have lung cancer, and every victim of lung cancer would be a smoker. Obviously, this is not the case. Yet research does show smoking to be one causal factor contributing to lung cancer. The simple tests outlined in **14d(1)** cannot be applied to cases of multiple causation. If you speak of issues like poverty, crime, divorce, economic recession as though they had a single direct cause, you will justifiably lose credibility with your audience.

Some causes are also effects, and some effects are also causes in a long causal chain.

When we designate a cause of a certain event, we can look at the immediate cause or a more distant factor. A doctor might say that the cause of a particular death was a cerebral hemorrhage. What, though, was the cause of that? Perhaps a fractured skull, which was caused by going through a windshield, which was caused by the impact of a car with a tree, which was caused by excessive drinking, which was caused by worry over being unemployed . . .

$$C \rightarrow (E/C) \rightarrow (E/C) \rightarrow (E/C) \rightarrow E$$

In a speech you need to discuss enough of these links to give a realistic picture and to demonstrate to your listeners that you understand the complexity of the process, without going so far back in the chain as to be absurd.

It is sometimes important to point out the cyclical nature of certain causal chains. For example, ignorance about a particular group may lead to prejudice, which in turn results in lack of contact with that group, which perpetuates ignorance. This sort of analysis is far more interesting than positing a single cause of racial disharmony.

Some effects result from a one-time cause, and some from ongoing causes.

Effects that are labeled undesirable can be dealt with in two ways, either by treating the effect directly, or by blocking the cause that produces the effect. To decide which strategy makes the most sense in a given instance, you need to determine whether the cause is one-time or ongoing.

Picture a neighborhood with bare dirt for landscaping, glassless windows, broken furniture in the yards, and residents in need of medical care. You are concerned about these symptoms and want to take some action. If you find that a tornado whipped through the area, you may push for emergency relief, rebuilding loans, and intervention by the Corps of Engineers to clear wreckage. However, if you learn that the area is depressed and that poverty is chronic, then you may choose to advocate organizing retraining programs, campaigns to attract large business to the community, or setting up health clinics. A mistake in evaluation, where the effect of an ongoing cause is treated as if it resulted from a one-time cause, will lead to the eventual reappearance of that effect.

To try to remedy problems through minor adjustments in laws and institutions, when the real causes lie in basic attitudes and values, is the worst kind of oversimplification. Nearly as bad is the tendency to advocate "education" as the answer to all social ills. Better to lay out a two-phase solution, with short-range steps to deal with the symptoms, complemented by a long-range attack on the underlying cause.

(3) Explain your causal claims fully and fairly.

Pure, simple causal arguments like those scientific truths cited in the first paragraph of **14d(2)** deal with absolute relationships. In this way they are like the deductive arguments in **14c**. Like deductive major premises, however, valid but nontrivial examples of absolute relationships are rare. More common are lines of reasoning that lead to probable causal claims, like the following:

> X was present in these cases, and Y occurred.
> X was absent in these cases, and Y did not occur.
> Changes in the amount of X have often led to corresponding changes in the amount of Y.
> Therefore, it is probable that X causes Y.

Probable to what degree? To the degree that your examples have been sufficient and representative, and that conflicting examples are minimized or explained. With this sort of causal argument follow the advice in **14b**. Do not overstate your claim. Say, "this is a major cause," not "this is *the* cause." Say, "there is strong evidence of a causal link between . . ." and so on.

The establishment of a probable causal claim requires the same sort of risk/benefit analysis as does inductive reasoning. If it is highly likely that eating red meat causes cardiovascular disease, what are the risks of ignoring this link? What are the benefits of accepting it?

Finally, whenever possible explain the way the causal connection operates. Otherwise, even if you demonstrate perfect correlation between two factors, you may succeed in establishing only that one is a sign, signal, or symptom of the other. Causal reasoning tells more than what is connected, it tells why things are connected. Whenever applicable in your speech, include a brief explanation of *how* the cause leads to the effect. Cite expert testimony, if possible or useful. The more explicit your analysis of causation, the less likely your audience will dismiss your causal claim as mere coincidence.

Exercise 7. Explain two ways you might *disprove* each of the following causal assertions, using principles from **14d(1):**

> Supreme Court rulings on arrest procedures have allowed criminals to go free.
> Unfair laws have caused discrimination against women.
> Strokes are caused by stress.
> Lack of educational expenditure has produced an inferior generation of college students.

Exercise 8. Now, explain how each of the causal statements in Exercise 7 might reflect one or more of the kinds of oversimplification referred to in **14d(2).**

Exercise 9. Identify at least one instance of causal reasoning in each speech in the **Appendix.** Are the causal links valid?

14e. Use reasoning by analogy to draw conclusions about unknown events, based on what you know about similar events.

When we reason by analogy we compare two things that can be placed in the same category. In the process, we assume that since we know that *A* and *B* have a number of characteristics in common, we can conclude that those things we do not know about *B* are highly likely to resemble their counterparts that we *do* know about in *A*. See Figure 14-5.

Reasoning by analogy is a natural and powerful way to make links. People intuitively look to similar examples when they want to understand something. The president's foreign policy advisors are trying to decide whether to intervene in a foreign country's internal struggles. A judge is pondering whether to admit expert testimony on battered wife

FIGURE 14-5   Analogy Compares Two Things in the Same Category

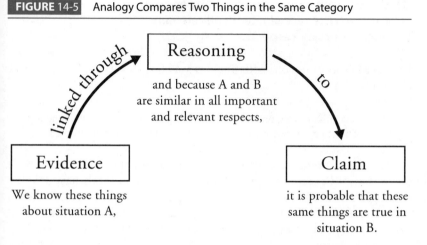

syndrome. You are wondering today whether to take the freeway or surface streets to work. In all these cases, from the most cosmic policy issues to the most mundane everyday decisions, people ask themselves: *What is this like that I already know about?*

That we draw so readily on analogy to make our own decisions impels speakers and advocates naturally to turn to it when they want to make a case for a certain interpretation. Its attraction lies in its naturalness and the understanding that listeners are accustomed to thinking about logical links in its terms.

Like the other forms of reasoning we have explored, analogies can be used to support contradictory claims. Some of the president's advisors will argue that the foreign country is just like Somalia and intervention will be fruitless. Others will insist that it is more like Panama and vital matters of principle are at stake. One lawyer will tell the judge that the case at hand is like the one where such evidence was admitted, but opposing counsel will insist that it is more like another case where expert testimony of this sort was excluded. One member of your carpool claims that today is like other Mondays, when traffic is light on the freeway. Another points out that on other rainy days like today there are often accidents that slow things down on the freeway.

Although reasoning by analogy is so innate—or *because* it is—you need to approach it with a careful eye on the analogies you use.

(1) Be sure that when you reason by analogy, the two cases are similar in all relevant and important respects.

Here is the sort of unconscious analogy we all use everyday. Does it meet the test?

Alternately sulking and throwing tantrums was effective in manipulating my father. Therefore, these same tactics should be effective with my boss, Fred.

There are certain similarities between the father and the boss: Both are authority figures, both are male, both are older, both have trouble dealing with emotions. It is also easy to point out differences. Father is tall, Fred is short. Father drives foreign cars, Fred drives a pickup. No cases are identical, and just pointing out differences does not discredit an analogy automatically. Are there relevant and important ways they differ? In this instance, yes. The relationship with the father was a personal one; that with Fred is professional. In one case a child and an adult are relating; in the other, two adults. Major personality differences between the father and Fred may exist. These stated differences are probably important enough to lead the person to reject the conclusion that sulking and throwing tantrums are effective ways of dealing with the boss.

When comparing cases from different geopolitical areas, be especially aware of cultural differences. The identical institutional changes might be adopted in Scandinavia or Syria or Sri Lanka with radically different impact. Even within a national culture, microcultural differences exist. A university faculty will not respond to management practices the same way as a business organization will. The innocent belief that "people are people" must be modified by our increasing awareness of the role played by gender, social class, race, sexual orientation, and numerous other factors that influence the experiences people have even when living under externally similar conditions.

Reasoning by analogy should also be tempered by accounting for the impact of history. Comparisons between the Vietnam war and the Persian Gulf conflict were often made, yet the very experience of Vietnam irreversibly altered U.S. perceptions of foreign policy, military strategy, and media coverage; any war following Vietnam will be different *because* of Vietnam.

(2) Do not confuse a literal analogy, which is a form of reasoning, with a figurative analogy, which is used only in a descriptive function.

Reasoning by analogy requires a comparison of two members of the same category. Figurative analogy compares the members of different categories.

Convincing my boss, Fred, to adopt a new procedure takes as much persistence, luck, and timing as starting my 1972 Fiat on a January morning.

Going to war in Vietnam was like tap-dancing on quicksand.

These may have stylistic impact, but they cannot support a conclusion. The examples in (1), however flawed in their logic, did make comparisons within the same categories—two human relationships or two wars. The examples in (2) compare a human relationship with a human-machine relationship and a war with a fantastic athletic impossibility.

Exercise 10. Return to Exercise 1 and look at the ways you linked your evidence to the claims. Classify each line of reasoning as inductive, deductive, causal, or analogy.

Exercise 11. Identify at least three similarities and three differences between each pair of following concepts. Now go back and think about how these enter into the way we reason by analogy. Write one argument for each topic where the similarities are sufficiently relevant and important to justify the conclusion. List other lines of reasoning on each topic that would probably be discounted due to the differences you identified.

A football game and a war
A family and a group of employees
"Ethnic cleansing" in the Balkans and racial discrimination in the United States
The national debt and one's personal checking account

14f. Avoid these reasoning fallacies:

Some people commit reasoning fallacies knowingly, with dishonest intent. Others commit them through lack of practice in doing their own thinking. The good public speaker wants to avoid the appearance of either. Once you have built your speech around sound, logical arguments, go through it to detect any constructions that even hint of sloppy thinking. One glaring fallacy in your speech will make all your other conclusions suspect. It is not necessary to learn all the fallacies—over one hundred have been categorized with Latin names—but you should be familiar with the most common of them.

A bonus of learning about these is that you can improve your critical listening. Not only will you be able to construct a logically sound speech, but you also will be able to detect the thoughtless, lazy, or false lines of reasoning that some people may employ.

(1) Attacking the person rather than the argument *(ad hominem)*

This fallacy substitutes character assassination for solid refutation or persuasion.

> Anyone who advocates abortion on demand is a murderer anyway. It certainly wouldn't surprise me to find them taking kickbacks from the clinics that would receive government funds.

(2) Setting up a straw figure

This fallacy consists of creating a weak argument, attributing it to the opposing side, and then proceeding to demolish it. The false implication is that all the opponents' arguments are as flimsy as the "straw figure," and could be dismissed with equal ease if time permitted. A familiar example was the cry of "they'll plunder Social Security!" in every discussion of the Balanced Budget Amendment.

Opponents of affirmative action policies are sometimes heard to raise these objections:

> We can't hire people from underrepresented groups without regard for their qualifications. It's not right to hire a mathematician to teach English just because she's a woman.

This is misleading, because proponents of affirmative action do not advocate disregarding qualifications. The speaker has distorted the issue with these extreme examples to avoid confronting the complexity of the issue.

(3) Extending an argument to absurd lengths (*reductio ad absurdum*)

Similar to the straw figure, this fallacy makes a potentially sound argument appear groundless by extending it to a point where it can be ridiculed. Often this extension goes beyond reasonable interpretation of the original point. In challenging current methods of criminal sentencing, a speaker might say:

> The average criminal is condemned to a bleak cell while top government wrongdoers lounge around in "country club" facilities. The logic is that the latter have already been punished considerably by loss of face, prestige, and professional standing. This seems to say that punishments should be harsher on those who have the least to lose. By this reasoning the senator who commits murder might get off with a citation and public embarrassment, while an unemployed ghetto dweller who shoplifts should be put on bread and water, with regular sessions on the rack.

Pointing out these patently outrageous inequities does not constitute a legitimate attack on the basic concept that the impact of punishment on an offender can be one valid criterion for decisions about sentencing. This kind of fallacy relies on the humor of the cockeyed image it creates. Disarmed by a ludicrous example, the listeners lose sight of the real issue.

(4) The slippery slope

This common fallacy consists of making the false assumption that taking the first step in any direction will inevitably lead to going to dangerous lengths in that direction. The image is of someone sliding down a slope without being able to stop.

> Domino effect: If one country in a region falls into ethnic conflict, all those around will fall.
>
> If you ever take just one drink, you will become an alcoholic.
>
> If we let the government ban the sale and possession of assault rifles, banning all firearms is next.
>
> If we let the government abandon support of the arts, artistic freedom will die.

(5) Circular reasoning

Circular reasoning assumes as one of its premises the very conclusion it sets out to establish. Most of us know the hopeless feeling of trying to deal logically with such dead-end arguments as "you can't get credit unless you have a good credit rating, and you can't have a good credit rating unless you have gotten credit." Often circular reasoning results from granting absolute authority to some source, and thus being blinded to the fact that others might not attribute similar authority to it.

> I know that God exists.
> It says so repeatedly in the Bible.
> And everything in the Bible is true since it's the ordained word of God.

Other instances of circular reasoning come out of definitional word games.

> No sane person would consider suicide, because it's insane to want to take your own life.

> We need a court of equity to resolve labor-management disputes, because collective bargaining results in settlements that aren't equitable. What do I mean by an equitable settlement? I mean the kind of settlement that is arrived at by a court of equity.

(6) The semantic fallacy

The rich, connotative nature of words, which so enhances communication, can also abet fuzzy thinking. When midstream shifts of definition are obvious, they can be funny, as in "blackberries are red when they're green," or "not a single burglar was arrested this month; they must all have been married."

More subtle and dangerous shifts in definition can occur in various critical parts of an argument.

> The free enterprise system, which we all cherish, could not exist without competition. This bill to protect small businesses threatens our whole economic structure. There can be no true competition when one group is given special protection.

In the underlying value premise, the word *competition* is used in the general sense of a market mechanism. In claiming that the bill endangered *competition* the word is used in a much narrower sense, as in "a specific contest between individuals." The semantic fallacy is especially difficult to identify and is frustrating to respond to, because the syllogistic form of the argument appears to be valid. The problem arises from the slight slippage of definition as a term is used with different meanings in different premises.

(7) False dichotomy

It is fallacious to base reasoning on an *either/or* statement when the two alternatives are not really mutually exclusive, or when other alternatives exist. Many speeches set up artificial choices.

> Would you rather have a football program or a band and orchestra at our school?

This can be a false dichotomy. Through careful economic management and marshaling of resources it may be possible to maintain both.

> Either we stand up to naked aggression, or we lose the confidence of our allies.

This basic premise so oversimplifies a complex issue that no conclusions can be drawn from it. Do not set up a deductive argument with a false dichotomy as its major premise.

(8) Faulty reversal of an if-then statement (affirming the consequent or denying the antecedent)

Another kind of deductive reasoning is based on an if *A*, then *B* relationship. A common fallacy is to assume that because *B* necessarily follows *A*, the reverse is also true: that *A* necessarily follows *B*.

> If I hear voices through the wall, *then* there is someone in the next room.
> I hear voices through the wall.
> Therefore, there is someone in the next room.

This is a valid statement. However, its validity in this form does not mean that its reverse will also be true. The following cannot be derived from the original if-then statement:

> I don't hear voices, so there must be no one in the next room.

This problem arises from lazy thinking, where a person knows two factors are associated but has not carefully analyzed which follows from the other, if indeed that sort of relationship exists at all. Guilt by association is the most common manifestation of this fallacy.

> If a candidate agrees with all the principles of an organization, then he or she will receive that organization's endorsement.
> The People's Counterinsurgency Brigade (PCB) endorsed Elizabeth Day.
> Therefore, she must agree with all their principles.

This is a fallacious conclusion, because there is nothing in the first statement that requires an organization to endorse only those candidates who are in 100 percent agreement with its principles. It is entirely possible that Day's opponent shares no values with the PCB, and Day only one, so she receives the endorsement as the lesser of the evils. The conclusion that Day must agree with all PCB principles would be valid only if the original if-then statement were reversed, saying that total agreement necessarily follows from endorsement. That relationship has not been established in this example.

Political candidates so fear this kind of faulty reasoning by voters that they will often publicly repudiate the endorsement of extreme groups and supporters. They cannot count on the electorate to recognize the difference between a group endorsing a candidate and a candidate endorsing a group.

(9) Hasty generalization

This fallacy entails making a premature inductive "leap." See **14b**. It is glorified in the pomp surrounding Groundhog Day, where data from an isolated event is blindly accepted as gospel in relation to a much wider range of events.

This statement has a faulty leap:

> The savings and loan scandal proved that every elected official has a price.

Time may not allow you, as a speaker, to include all your data that led you to a conclusion. It is especially important, then, to have the unused data at your fingertips so that you can deflect any accusations of hasty generalization that may come up.

(10) Confusing sequence with cause *(post hoc, ergo propter hoc)*

The Latin label for this fallacy translates as "after the event, therefore because of the event." It is natural to try to understand the world around us by looking for cause-effect patterns wherever possible. So strong is this motivation that we are frequently guilty of imitating Chanticleer the rooster, who firmly believed that it was his predawn crowing that caused the sun to rise each day.

Perhaps the most famous example of this fallacy in this century is the "Tut Curse." Five months after he had opened the tomb of the Pharaoh Tutankhamen, Lord Carnarvon died in Cairo from complications following an insect bite. At the moment of his death, Cairo experienced a power blackout, and this was interpreted by many to be a manifestation of an ancient curse. Thereafter, if anyone remotely connected to Egyptology died, it was attributed to the mummy's curse, no matter if the agent of this "curse" were heavy traffic or arteriosclerosis.

To avoid this fallacy never assume causation based on time sequence alone. Test every causal hypothesis against the criteria in **14d**.

Exercise 12. Identify the fallacy or fallacies in each statement.

> I'm surprised you health food nuts eat granola packaged in cellophane bags. Aren't you afraid the synthetic chemicals will poison the contents?
> Anyone who drives a foreign car doesn't care about this country anyway.
> You said you could prove the point by sheer logic. Well, I agree. The logic was pretty sheer.
> It always rains on Easter. I remember it has for the last three years.
> Well, either you support your country, or you are critical of the government. Which is it?
> The jury system should be abolished. Last year a jury awarded $3 million to a woman who didn't like the nose job she got. The next month the doctor committed suicide.

Exercise 13. Examine the reasoning in the speeches in the **Appendix**. Do you find any fallacies in reasoning?

14g. Through organization and word choice, make it clear to your listeners exactly how your reasoning links your evidence to your claim.

It is not enough to have a speech that is well reasoned and free from fallacies. The reasoning process must be made clear to listeners. When speakers present just a cluster of evidence or a cluster of reasons for a claim, they are acting as if communication occurs through the simple transmission of messages. The perspective taken in this book is that communication consists of making meaning together. Therefore, as a speaker you will need to show the listener what makes evidence meaningful to you.

(1) Organize points to show the logical relationships.

As explained in **14a**, controversial claims are found at all levels of a speech. How overall patterns of reasoning come into play is determined by how you lay out the speech.

Sometimes the thesis sentence is supported by a line of reasoning and each main point is a part of the argument. For example:

Thesis sentence: Prayer should not be allowed in schools because it violates the doctrine of separation of church and state, which is a central tenet of U.S. society that must be preserved.

I. The doctrine of separation of church and state is a central tenet of U.S. society that must be preserved.
   A. Why we have this doctrine
   B. Why it must be preserved
II. Prayer in the schools violates the doctrine of church and state.
   (Develop through testimony and examples.)
   Therefore: In conclusion, (Restate thesis.)

In other cases, the thesis statement may be an "umbrella claim" that is supported by several separate and somewhat independent claims.

Thesis: Preschool programs like Head Start are economically, socially, and morally justified.

The economic, social, and moral claims are separate main points where most of the reasoning of the speech will be found.

In still other cases, reasoning is necessary at very specific subpoint levels in the speech to justify important claims.

There is no one way to display your lines of reasoning in a speech outline, but it is very important that you phrase points to show the connections. Do not just group "reasons." Show reasoning.

Wrong:

I. The United States cannot afford to have a middle-class tax cut.
   A. Our deficit is huge.
      (Support by testimony and statistics.)
   B. The loss of revenue would hurt vital programs.
      (Support by testimony and statistics.)

Better:

I. The United States cannot afford to have a middle-class tax cut.
   A. To pay for a tax cut we would either have to cut spending or go further into debt.
      (Briefly explain why these are the only alternatives.)
   B. It is not desirable to cut spending.
      (Support by testimony and statistics.)
   C. It is not desirable to go deeper in debt.
      (Support by testimony and statistics.)

Wrong:

I. Having a longer school day does not improve learning.
   A. They tried it at Riverdale High School, and test scores were unchanged.
   B. They tried it at Glenbrook High School, and test scores actually went down.
   C. At Creekside High School test scores have gone up even though their school day has not been lengthened.
   D. Braeburn High School shortened their school day, and test scores did not change.

Better:

I. Having a longer school day does not improve learning.
   A. In cases where the school day was lengthened, test scores did not improve.
      1. Unchanged at Riverdale High
      2. Went down at Glenbrook
   B. In cases where the school day was not lengthened, test scores are not lower.
      1. Improved at Creekside
      2. No change with shorter day at Braeburn

Summary transitional statement: If there were a causal relationship between length of school day and learning as measured by test scores we would logically expect that scores would be higher where the school day is longer and lower where the school day is shorter. I have just demonstrated that this is not the case. Sometimes just the opposite is true. So you can see why I conclude that having a longer school day does not improve learning.

Remember the difference between points and support for the points. See **9c** and the introduction to **13**. Do not use sources in place of reasoning. In the first example that follows a speaker attempts to support a causal claim by saying that experts have agreed with the claim. But the listener does not know why these people came to the conclusion they did. In the second example, the reasoning behind the causal claim is explained, with experts used to back up specific points.

Wrong:

I. The use of sexist language perpetuates discrimination against women.
   A. Dr. Deborah Stone says sexist language causes problems.
   B. Professor Lydia Sorenson says sexist language is the root of many social problems.
   C. Linguist Chris Nupriya states that language affects behavior.

Better:

I. The use of sexist language perpetuates discrimination against women.
   A. Language shapes social perception.
      (Cite experts and studies.)
   B. Speech that leaves women out can lead to people overlooking them.
      (Cite experts and studies.)
   C. If people subconsciously exclude women from certain roles, they discriminate against women.
      (Cite experts and studies.)

(2) Use words, phrases, and transitional sentences that spell out what your evidence means and how the parts of your argument are linked.

In addition to setting up a speech structure that highlights your reasoning, you should give thought to selecting language that illuminates the logical linkages between your ideas. Never just jump from one point to the next. Practice adding phrases that are specific cues to the kind of reasoning you are using.

For inductive reasoning:
Show the strength of your examples.

> One case that supports my claim is . . .
> Another example that adds to this pattern is . . .
> These statistics illustrate a widespread . . .
> These instances are just a sample of the . . .
> Across many levels of income and many parts of the country, the same pattern holds true. For example . . .

Acknowledge the probable nature of your data by using qualifiers.

> Many . . .
> Most . . .
> Virtually every study in the literature . . .
> Evidence strongly indicates . . .
> I can say with near certainty . . .
> From these cases, I feel quite confident in concluding . . .

Demonstrate costs and rewards.

> I'm willing to bet my tax dollars that this program will work . . .
> I think these are good/bad odds because . . .
> This is a gamble we can't afford to take . . .
> The risks, though they do exist, seem minimal compared to the rewards . . .
> Is it worth it to you to . . . ?

For deductive reasoning:
State your premises.

> I base this on a core value of mine that . . .
> Underlying my position is one of the fundamental tenets of our constitutional form of government . . .
> The argument for my claim rests on one basic assumption that I hope you will agree with. It is . . .
> Either . . . or . . .
> If . . . then . . .
> Only when . . . then . . .

Anyone who . . .
To the extent that . . . , then to that extent . . .

Spell out your reasoning.

Since I've shown you X and Y, . . .
Therefore . . .
This entails . . .
From this it follows that . . .
What this means is that . . .
We have no choice but to conclude that . . .
Based on this, I reason that . . .
It seems logical to conclude that . . .

For causal reasoning:
Show how the cause and effect vary together.

In state after state where spending on education went up, crime went
    down . . .
Notice that as soon as that company closed down, pollution was reduced . . .
This is no coincidence. When X occurs, then Y occurs . . .
For every unit of increase in X, notice that there is a proportional increase . . .

Qualify your causal claims if necessary.

There may be many causes, but the one I have identified is a major causal
    factor . . .
It is highly probable that smoking causes these health problems . . .
In the vast majority of cases, X causes Y . . .
At least in middle-class white families where most of the research so far was
    conducted, there seems to be a strong causal link between watching vio-
    lence on television and acting in antisocial ways . . .
Except in small family-owned companies where a different dynamic seems
    to be in effect, employee morale is greatly enhanced by offering a series
    of options for benefits . . .

Explain the mechanism of the cause.

The reason all these experts have concluded that X causes Y is that . . .
I've shown you all these cases where being abused as a child seems to lead
    to being an abusive parent. Let me explain how that happens. . . .

For reasoning by analogy:
Stress the points of similarity.

In Ecuador, as in neighboring Colombia and Peru . . .
At three cities of about the same size and makeup, the same pattern recurred . . .
For eight of the ten other universities in our conference, adding women's sports to the athletic program has led to more alumni support . . .
Likewise, . . .
Similarly, . . .
In a parallel case, . . .

Explain points of difference that your listeners may be concerned about.

Although *Kully vs. California* was tried in district court, the principle still applies here because . . .
Despite differences in size, our company can learn from this story because . . .
I realize that some of these instances happened a long time ago, but I don't think human nature changes much in this respect . . .

Spell out the link.

If it worked in New Jersey and Idaho and Georgia, it will work in the rest of the country . . .
The analogy holds true. We can apply these solutions to our problems. . . .
The other groups who tried such proposals have been disappointed. Let's learn from their mistakes. . . .
Let's not wait too long on planning for earthquake safety. We put off dealing with flood control and the results have been tragic. . . .

As we stated in Chapter **10,** transitional phrases are more important in speaking than in writing because a listener cannot look back at previous points. These cueing phrases play a crucial role in developing an oral argument. In an outline, claims are stated before their supporting reasons and evidence. This is an organizational artifact, and should not obscure the fact that claims are reached only at the end of a line of reasoning. However, for purposes of signposting and keeping your audience informed about the direction you are taking, it is generally a good idea to first state the claim and then explain the reasons for it. Listeners may be easily lost as the steps of an argument unfold, though. By the time you reach the end of your reasoning, they may forget what claim you were trying to support. Therefore, it is also generally a good idea to restate the claim after you have presented the argument.

In the following example, the speaker's thesis is the claim that marijuana should not be legalized. Each main point was a separate claim that was supported by a different form of reasoning. Observe how at the end of each main point she recapitulates her reasoning to show how it led to her claim, which she then restates. These brief statements can make the difference between a speech that makes sense only to the speaker and one that is made meaningful to listeners.

> I. People are dangerous when they are under the influence of marijuana. (examples of accidents that were caused by people who were under the influence of marijuana)
>
> Summary of Main Point 1: These five tragic stories about innocent people who were killed by someone who was under the influence of marijuana provide us with one reason why marijuana should remain illegal: People are dangerous when they use marijuana.
>
> II. Marijuana is a highly addictive drug like cigarettes and alcohol. (testimony from doctors and other experts)
>
> Summary of Main Point 2: We all know how easy it is for some people to get addicted to nicotine and alcohol and the problems they have. Marijuana is very similar. It, too, can be addictive.
>
> III. Smoking marijuana often causes people to use "harder" drugs. (statistics and testimony from drug users and doctors)
>
> Summary of Main Point 3: Therefore, even though many marijuana users do not go on to use harder drugs, many do. These experts claim that contact with the criminal element and experiences with "getting high" serve as significant causal factors in predicting subsequent usage of harder drugs.
>
> IV. Marijuana use reduces intelligence.
>   A. Reduced brain cells lower intelligence.
>   B. Marijuana kills brain cells.
>
> Summary of Main Point 4: Because anything that kills brain cells reduces intelligence, and because marijuana has been shown to kill brain cells, you can see that it follows logically that marijuana reduces intelligence.

Conclusion: (restatement of thesis, showing how the points are linked to it) I have shown that marijuana use puts innocent people in danger, is addictive, leads to use of hard drugs, and reduces intelligence. It seems logical that we should not legalize any practice that has these serious consequences.

Exercise 14. In the marijuana example just given, what kind of reasoning is being used in each of the four statements? Do you see any potential fallacies in the reasoning of the marijuana speech?

Chapter 15

Language and Style

Choose words and constructions that make your ideas clear and memorable. Respect the power of language.

Certain interpretations of classical rhetoric tended to treat language as an adornment to ideas—a sort of gift wrapping put on a package to make it appealing. Some modern communication models give a similar impression by suggesting that an idea is first fully thought out before it is encoded for transmission. Current understandings of language grant it a much more central role in communication: Language is the essence of thought, not a mere vessel for it. We no longer believe that our ways of thinking are universally "programmed in," but rather develop as we interact, linguistically, with others. This means much more than learning to speak English instead of Cantonese. It means that if you had been born in a different time and place you would not just use language differently, you would think differently. So, language not only reflects culture but also shapes our society.

Because of the pervasive and largely unconscious power of language, we are leery of any treatments that relegate language to a single step late in the communicative process. In this handbook we stress the importance of "talking ideas into being" throughout the entire process of speech preparation. Competent speakers are conscious of the ways they develop their ideas through language to achieve an effective speaking style.

Style is a word of many shadings. A "stylish" person is one who conforms to the latest fads and fashions. A "stylized" drawing is one in which the artist includes the least amount of detail needed for comprehension. Style is decorator colors—whatever that means. Style is tight jeans or loose jeans, depending on the year. Style is none of these things to a speaker.

In the context of speaking, style is simply your choice of words and the way you string them together. "Good" style is choosing and combining those words so that your audience can easily understand and assimilate your content. Good style is clear, appropriate, vivid, and varied language.

15a. Understand how oral style is different from written style.

Speech is very much a slave to the fourth dimension, time. Words are uttered, and immediately the resonances and overtones start to fade. Listeners have just one contact with each word; memory is the only instant replay. On the other hand, a written essay exists as a time machine: It allows a reader to return to a place where the eye had been a few seconds or many years before. This quality of the written word has obvious implications regarding comprehension, and while oral style and written style use the same components, a speaker should not think the styles are interchangeable.

Naturalness is a theme that runs through this handbook. The natural-sounding speaker understands how oral style is different and uses that understanding to talk to an audience rather than deliver what appears to be a ten-page quotation. Listeners expect to hear patterns that reflect the norms of conversation, if more refined. The ideal balance between the orality and literacy of a speech depends on the audience and occasion. See **1c(4).** Sometimes you will draw more heavily on the communicative resource of the writer. Other times you can use the language and cadence of conversation.

There are some important ways in which oral style differs from written style. Even with the redundancy built into the language, a speaker is more likely to use repetition to ensure comprehension. In oral style there is a greater frequency of signposting, internal summaries, and internal previews to make the organization clear. See **10.**

Shorter sentences and words of fewer syllables are characteristic of oral style. Sentence fragments are acceptable, as are contractions. Even in

| TABLE 15-1 | Differences between Written and Oral Style |

Written Style	Oral Style
As mentioned above ...	As I said a few minutes ago ...
One cannot avoid individuals with this characteristic.	We can't avoid people like that.
A hypothetical case in point might be a situation where government ...	Imagine this. Suppose Uncle Sam ...
It is unlikely that such will result.	Well. Maybe.
Subjects were randomly assigned to either a control group or one of three experimental treatment groups, pretested for initial attitudes toward the topic, then posttested after each experimental group had received a persuasive message containing one of three levels of fear appeals.	Here's how we did our research. First we randomly assigned the subjects to four groups. Next we gave all four groups a pretest to see what attitudes they held toward the topic. Then three of the groups head persuasive messages. One had a high level of fear appeals, one a medium level, one a low level. Last, we posttested the attitudes of all four groups, including the control group that received no message.

a formal setting, a speech will still be more colloquial than an essay on the same topic.

It would be wrong to think that these qualities of oral style are limitations. To view orality as the mere lack of literacy, Walter Ong says, is equivalent to describing horses as automobiles without wheels. Appreciate the spoken word and take advantage of its unique features. The rhythm and meter of speech aid memory. The physical immediacy creates a bond between speakers and listeners. Attune your ear to the music of the spoken word and use it to your advantage as you phrase your ideas. Drawing on the resources of performance—part of every effective speech to some degree—involves a feel for the power of the spoken word (see Table 15-1).

Exercise 1. Rewrite these segments in a style more appropriate to oral communication.

After having removed the air filter, one can begin to investigate origins of the problem.

All clerical and administrative personnel will undergo semiannual performance appraisals designed to evaluate their competence and clarify objectives for the next appraisal period.

15b. Strive for clarity in your language.

We know that language does more than label objects, concepts, and actions. Words *are* acts. They do things, like promise or threaten; they can even serve to marry or excommunicate people. Because of this power, we sometimes make messages intentionally vague—perhaps to save face or build solidarity. For the large part, though, the clear transmission of information is to be valued over other ends. "Bear come. We go. Now!" may not be subtle or poetic, but it certainly conveyed an important image from one prehistoric human to another. Some modern speakers in love with their own verbiage should do so well! If you understand the priorities of communication, the first question you will ask yourself is "Did my listeners get the picture?" When the speaker and the listeners end up with totally different mental images, something has gone awry. Perhaps the speaker has used words in nonstandard, idiosyncratic ways; or chosen words so general that they evoke many different responses; or buried the significant words in an avalanche of extraneous phrases.

To construct clear messages you must do two things. First, invest some effort in clarifying your own thoughts. Know exactly, not approximately, what picture you want to get across. Second, consider the receivers of the message and what the words are likely to mean to them.

(1) Be precise.

To combat fuzzy and ambiguous communication, you need to seek out the word that means precisely what you wish to convey and use it in a structure that illuminates, not obscures, its meaning.

Use the proper word.
Many words can denote the same object or idea; however, each may have a slightly different focus. Do not say a person was "indicted" for robbery if in fact you mean "arrested" (much less serious) or "convicted" (much more serious). Learn important distinctions and honor them.

Be careful around words that sound similar but have no similarity of meaning. "Allusion" means *a passing mention,* "illusion" means *a false perception.* Some other troublesome near-homophones are *affect/effect, imminent/eminent, casual/causal,* and *aesthetic/ascetic.* Remember that oral language is simpler than written language. Avoid using a precise word when it may seem pretentious. See Table 15-2.

Be quite sure you know what an unfamiliar word means before rushing to use it. Malaprops are funny for the audience, but devastating for the speaker. Imagine the response to a speaker who means to say "The answer I've reached is inescapable" but actually states "The answer I've reached is inexplicable."

Keep your figurative language unmuddled.

See **15d(2).** In attempting to convey your picture vividly, do not confuse the issue by throwing discordant images together.

The wife of an official charged with taking a bribe accused the government of entrapment in this manner:

> The FBI has created the *illusion* of a crime. It's like raping Alice in Wonderland.

No doubt the speaker knew what she meant, but the rest of us were not so lucky. Wonderland is a crazy, illogical world where the powers-that-be are capricious—and that is a good picture to accompany an accusation of entrapment. But used as it was, it only left her listeners deaf to the rest of her words while they tried to pick out the real meaning of the image.

TABLE 15-2	Oral Style Is Simpler	
Pretentious	Better
I was appalled at the feculence that oozed from the typewriter of this so-called greatest living American novelist.	I was appalled at the filth that oozed from the typewriter of this so-called greatest living American novelist.
Then I butted heads with the misoneists of the planning commission.	Then I butted heads with the planning commission, which seems to have a pathological hatred of change.
Hear my obsecration!	Hear my supplication!

(2) Use specific and concrete language.

The more specific and concrete your words, the less is left to your listeners' imaginations. When a speaker says "NCAA academic standards for college athletes are ineffective," one listener may think "Yes, they are racist," while another may think "Yes, they are too low," or another, "Yes, they should be set by the faculty at each college." Yet all of these may be at odds with the intentions of the speaker, who perhaps feels that the standards are too high. Do not have your words name a broader category than they need to. See Table 15-3.

Minimize the use of abstract words such as *love, freedom, justice, beauty*—words that have no tangible, physical referent. When you have no option but to use abstract words, supplement them with concrete examples to make them less cerebral and ethereal:

> What is more important to me than peace? Freedom is more important to me than peace.
> If I weren't able to travel where I wish, if I weren't able to worship as I please, meet to discuss grievances, read and write what I want, then I would struggle to regain all these things.

(3) Be economical in your language.

The bloated language of the bureaucracy, both civil and military, is a common target of ridicule in the schools and media. Unfortunately, all this attention has done little to slow the general acceptance, or at least

TABLE 15-3 Be Specific and Concrete

Do Not Say	If You Really Mean	Or Even
"We need to attract individuals."	"We need to attract customers."	"We need to attract grocery shoppers."
"This will cause problems."	"This will be expensive."	"This will cost us $2,500 we don't have."
"Our committee has studied it."	"Our committee researched and discussed it."	"Our committee read documents, heard testimony, and deliberated for several hours."

tolerance, of wordy, euphemistic language. In the interest of clarity, you should express yourself with the fewest, most straightforward words that still effectively convey your meaning.

Sometimes speakers use long words, extra words, and convoluted constructions for the untenable reasons listed in Table 15-4.

Most often, though, wordiness results from lack of discipline. Editing is not a simple process, and many people shy away from it. These speakers prefer a machine-gun style of word choice, spewing out redundancies while bracketing the target with approximate synonyms. The clear speaker is more like the sharpshooter who takes careful aim and makes every word count.

Wordy

Some individuals express their feeling that it is objectionable to eliminate and remove laws which serve to protect female members of the labor force. No one could really be in favor of doing away with protective laws for workers if the elimination of these laws would lead to the exploitation of the people no longer covered. The question I want to raise, however, is whether there is really any relevance to the sex of those workers who should be protected from exploitation, since wages and working conditions ought to be equitable for all employees.

Economical

There are objections to wiping out laws protecting women workers. No one would condone exploitation. But what does sex have to do with it? Working

TABLE 15-4	Motives for Bloated Language	
	Uneconomical	Economical
To Hide Meaning as with Doublespeak	We sustained losses through friendly fire.	We shelled our own troops.
To Avoid Responsibility, as with the Passive Voice	It has been determined that your services are no longer needed.	I have decided to fire you.
To Soften Unpleasant Messages, as with Euphemism	Jesse has gone on to his reward.	Jesse died.

conditions and hours that are harmful to women are harmful to men; wages that are unfair for women are unfair for men.

—Shirley Chisholm

15c. Use appropriate language.

There is no standard style to use in speaking. Different audiences and topics require different approaches. You must, in the light of audience analysis, make decisions about the degree of formality, which part of your personality to project linguistically, and how deeply you descend into specialized language. Your age, status, and personality also determine what language is appropriate for you. Listeners have expectations about the vocabulary and stylistic level suitable for a senior executive, for instance, that differ from those for a teenager or a poet-in-residence.

Language is not fixed. New words and phrases are always coming into our language and others are dropping out. Meanings change, and standards of appropriateness change. A real presidential speech we heard as we worked on the third edition sounded very much like the fanciful example we chose for the first edition of this text to illustrate unthinkable informality for a presidential address.

(1) Suit the formality of your language to the occasion.

Just as you dress differently for formal and casual events, so should you tailor vocabulary and usage to fit the situation. Might it not be a little startling if the organizer of a PTA bake sale finished an announcement in the following fashion:

> This, then, is my plea to you: For the sake of our children, for the sake of our school, for the sake of our PTA, give of yourself for this culinary endeavor.

Equally inappropriate would be a CEO's annual address to stockholders that began:

> Well, folks, things look kinda grim, but don't get bummed out, we'll be OK if we just hang in there.

In general, the more formal the occasion,

the more serious the tone,
the more subtle the humor used,
the more elaborate the sentences,
the greater the number of figures of speech,
the greater the departure from everyday word choice.

More formal occasions would be policy statements, debates, ceremonial speeches. Less formal occasions would be business conferences, roasts, rallies, and after-dinner speaking. In short, the more formal the occasion the less you can rely on the resource of conversation and the more you must put in the time to incorporate the resources of writing and performance.

(2) Be judicious in your use of jargon or slang.

Both jargon and slang can be used to create a bond with a specialized audience. At times jargon can also allow you to get a point across more quickly. Slang, when called into play at opportune moments, can enrich the texture of your language. But the perils they introduce are substantial. You may confuse your audience with technical terms or sacrifice your credibility by using slang expressions that are offensive or are already out of date.

Notice how this excerpt from a talk on "Preventive Maintenance" is made understandable to a larger audience by substituting plain English in the second version:

Slang and Jargon Version

Let's look at how Jack could have benefited from a little PM. He burned a lot more number two than he needed to before he got around to running the rack on his Slam-bang. A maintenance schedule would have pointed out any problems long before the engine started smoking. Same thing with the front SQ drop-in. He wouldn't have cooked it if he periodically checked and renewed the oil.

Plain English Version

Let's look at how Jack could have benefited from a little preventive maintenance. He burned a lot more diesel fuel than he needed before he got around to adjusting the fuel injection system on his dump truck. A maintenance schedule would have pointed out any problems long before the engine started smoking. Same thing with the drive axle gears. They wouldn't have overheated and failed if he periodically checked and renewed the oil.

(3) Avoid substandard usage.

Remember that the competence of the speaker as perceived by the audience has a great bearing on the credibility they ascribe to him or her. While acceptable usage varies from place to place, there are many words and constructions that are rated substandard by consensus. The speaker who consistently uses *ain't* for *isn't* or who gets sloppy with noun-verb agreement will find that a large percentage of the audience will not give serious consideration to her or his points. Of course, you can sometimes break the rules for dramatic effect, like capping your opposition to a proposal with "Ain't *no* way!"

Where will you find a guide for what is standard? Some of us do not remember all that went on in high school English. Expose yourself to models of literate and graceful usage by reading quality magazines and good literature, and by listening to respected public speakers and commentators. This exposure often leads to an intuitive recognition of correct usage. If you have never heard one of your language models say, "This here's the nexus of the problem," then you would be wise not to say "this here" yourself. See Table 15-5.

Caveat: Not all nonstandard language is substandard. Sometimes when people try to "standardize" the language others use, they are actually trying to change the content or to mold the identity of the speaker. Women should not have to talk like men. People of color should not have to talk

TABLE 15-5   Substandard and Standard English

Substandard	Standard
Ten items or less.	Ten items or fewer.
…said to my friend and I …	…said to my friend and me …
I could care less!	I couldn't care less!
A large amount of people attended the rally.	A large number of people attended the rally.
Where'd you put it at?	Where'd you put it?
He hits the ball good.	He hits the ball well.
They couldn't hardly see what happened.	They could hardly see what happened.
I would have went there myself.	I would have gone there myself.

like their compatriots of northern European descent. You will not feel comfortable or seem authentic if you abandon your own idiom. Strive to find a way to maintain your own cultural, ethnic, and individual identity while still speaking in a way that will not lead to social stigma.

(4) Use language that is respectful and inclusive.

Referring to a group or individuals by the name they prefer is a sign of respect. When changes are made, those changes are often symbolic of a new status or image. For those used to the word *Negro*, the transition to *black* in the 1960s caused some problems, yet now it seems natural and is the baseline that some defend from the transition to *African American*. Today many adult females want to be called *women*, not *girls* or *ladies*. It is not possible to please everyone or to be on top of every trend. (Is it *Mexican American, Chicano, Hispanic, Latino?* Is it *Minority, Third World, People of Color?* Is it *Handicapped, Disabled, Physically Challenged?* There are definite differences in the meanings of these words and preferences as to their use.) What you can do is make a reasonable effort to learn which reference people prefer. You can make a commitment to flexibility. Acknowledge that it is worth the temporary inconvenience of changing a language habit if that change is highly symbolic to the person involved.

A more complex stylistic issue is the use of the generic *he, man, mankind.* Now that attention has been focused on these images, no speaker or writer can feign innocence of their impact. One may not mean to exclude females by such usage, but one should be aware that many male and female listeners now find the generic terms jarring. If you want to avoid distracting, possibly offending, many listeners, consider using "he or she" and replacing "man" with "humanity," "people," or "humankind." Sometimes, in a series of singular examples, alternating pronouns can have the same effect. If you are worried about distracting the dwindling segment of an audience offended by the current trend, you can avoid the issue altogether by using plural and collective nouns instead of pronouns and by replacing words like *chairperson* with *presiding officer* and *mail person* with *letter carrier.*

Exercise 2.   Rewrite the following sentences so that they are clearer. Make them more concrete, economical, correct, and inclusive.

It's a very unique sort of thing how Karen just makes everybody feel sort of good. She's real notorious as the most respected girl on our whole staff of salesmen.

At this time I'd like to say that one point to consider is the fact that we were totally surrounded by smokers who caused us considerable irritation and distress and aggravation.

Plus, I personally feel that we also face a serious crisis of psychological morale. We need to get off our duffs and sit down and talk about this epidemic that has us running on only three cylinders.

15d. Use vivid, varied language.

Keep your listeners attentive and interested by avoiding dull, stale, and predictable language. Your message may never get past their short-term memory if you do not infuse it with vigor and a sense of newness. Why settle for the common and trite? Energize your language by effective use of the following:

(1) Employ imagery.

When you describe something, put the senses and the imaginative capacities of your listeners to work.

Not: The life of the long-haul trucker is rough. Aside from being worn down by the effort of driving, the trucker can get discouraged by the tedium.

But: The long-haul trucker pulls to the side of the road. Throughout the day the road has fought back through the springs and steering wheel. Even though the truck is stopped, his arms up to his elbows still throb to the rhythm of hitting four hundred miles of highway expansion joints. The harsh roar of the engine and the cacophonous flexing of the cab rivets leave him with an infuriating ringing of the ears. After a boring, wholesome dinner the trucker slips into the cramped womb of the sleeper cab, hoping to sleep. In the morning the cycle of noise, sweat, and stress starts anew.

(2) Use stylistic devices.

Enliven your language through the planned use of figures of speech and certain arrangements of words and phrases.

Simile and metaphor

You can add vigor to your speaking by using language that connects objects or ideas to vivid images. A simile makes a comparison between two things ordinarily dissimilar. "When she came in from shoveling off the walk, her hands were as cold as ice." No one would mistake a hand for some ice, but in this case they share the characteristic of extremely low temperature. A metaphor creates a figurative equation that implies two unlike things are the same. "Her hands were ice cubes." Or: "We stand in horror as our money disappears down the gluttonous maw of the federal government." Making the government a shark forms a more compelling image than "We stand in horror as the federal government operates with fiscal irresponsibility."

Personification .

One way to bring objects or ideas to life is to imbue them with qualities of human beings. We know that no room is really "cheerful," that winds do not actually "whisper," and that, being legless, the economy cannot possibly "limp"—but all of these images are potent because we find it easier to identify with reflections of our own behavior.

> Israel now faced the choice of either to be choked to death in her southern maritime approaches or to await the death blow from northern Sinai.
> —Abba Eban

Hyperbole

To emphasize a point, you may deliberately overstate it in a way that is clearly fanciful rather than misleading.

> This paperwork will be the death of me.
> I thought about nothing else for the next three days.
> The governor has repeated this same promise to you a million times.

Repetitive language or structure

Repeat key words or phrases to make your listeners feel that your points are snowballing to a certain conclusion. Use parallel structure to emphasize relationships.

Sometimes a syntactic construction is repeated:

> How serious is the morale crisis? We have lost several key employees. What has caused the problem? Lack of clear upward and downward communication. How can we change things? By hiring an interpersonal and organizational communication trainer for a series of workshops.

Notice that no phrases are repeated, but the question-answer, question-answer format gives a sense of momentum to this paragraph.

You can use repetition to introduce consecutive paragraphs. For instance, a speaker can build a sense of urgency or dedication by repeating the phrase "We must act now to . . ." as each problem is presented.

Within a paragraph you can achieve a similar effect by starting a series of sentences with the same words, or by using a sentence as a connecting refrain.

> You see, I was born to a teenage mother, who was born to a teenage mother. I understand. I know abandonment, and people being mean to you, and saying you're nothing and nobody, and can never be anything. I understand. Jesse Jackson is my third name. I'm adopted. When I had no name, my grandmother gave me her name, my name was Jesse Burns 'til I was twelve. So I wouldn't have a blank space, she gave me a name. To hold me over. I understand when nobody knows your name. I understand when you have no name. I understand.
>
> —Jesse Jackson

Or, you may end several sentences with the same words.

> What remains? Treaties have gone. The honor of nations has gone. Liberty has gone.
>
> —David Lloyd George

Finally, for emphasis you can repeat key words or phrases within a sentence.

> But, in a larger sense, we can not dedicate—we can not consecrate—we can not hallow this ground.
>
> —Abraham Lincoln

Alliteration and assonance

These devices consist of saying the same sound in a sustained sequence. (Sorry about that silly sentence.) Whether it is with consonants (alliteration) or vowels (assonance), this repetition can make an idea more memorable, or at least charge it with a sense of poetry.

At his brother's grave, Robert Green Ingersoll said the following:

> He who sleeps here, when dying . . . whispered with his latest breath: "I am better now." Let us believe, in spite of doubts and dogmas, and tears and fears, that these dear words are true of all the countless dead.

Antithesis

When you want to contrast two ideas, certain sentence structures serve to dramatize the differences. Antithesis uses forms like:

> Not . . . , but . . .
> Not only . . . , but . . .
> Never . . . , unless . . .

> We live in a society that emphasizes military expenditures over education. We spend millions teaching young people how to kill and be killed, but we won't spend money teaching them how to live and make a living.
> —Harry Edwards

> It was we, the people; not we, the white male citizens; nor yet we, the male citizens; but we, the whole people who formed the Union. And we formed it, not to give the blessings of liberty, but to secure them; not to the half of ourselves and the half of our posterity, but to the whole people—women as well as men.
> —Susan B. Anthony

(3) Use fresh language.

The power of figurative language lies in the image stimulated in the listener's mind. After too many repetitions the original psychological impact is lost. "Fresh as a daisy" at first summoned a picture of a clean, bright, dew-studded blossom. At the first turn of the phrase "it went in one ear and out the other," its aptness produced pleasant surprise. Now both expressions are likely to be processed as just extra, empty words.

Certain fad words attract a cult following. "Bottom line," "prioritize," and "networking" become overnight sensations and are used to the exclusion of many good (and fresher) synonyms. Purge your language of such flatulent phrasing. Invest the time to select original combinations of words and phrases that capture the image, mood, or thought you want to get across.

(4) Vary the rhythm of your sentences.

Although oral style is characterized by simpler, shorter phrases with fewer different words, you are not compelled to homogenize your sentences into dullness. The singsonginess associated with doggerel can creep into a speech if you fail to pay attention to how you are stringing your sentences and phrases together. Be sparing in your use of parallelisms and repetition.

> The association's annual convention should be user supported. The convention is attended by a core of regulars. The average association member doesn't benefit from the convention. These average members shouldn't have to bear more than their fair share.

The choppiness of this tedious passage results from the sameness of sentence length and structure. Recasting the sentences will create a more fluid and graceful paragraph.

> The association's annual convention should be user supported. Who attends the convention? A core of regulars. The average association members, who don't benefit from the convention, shouldn't have to bear more than their fair share.

Exercise 3. Use at least two different stylistic devices to enliven each of these phrases.

A cold, rainy day
An unworkable policy
A delicate, intricate procedure
A very stern leader
A huge crowd

Exercise 4. Identify at least three different examples of imagery or stylistic devices in each speech in the **Appendix.**

Exercise 5. Think of fresh ways to replace these overused phrases:

Like comparing apples and oranges
Caught between a rock and a hard place
Two steps forward and one step back
Always darkest before the dawn

15e. Synchronize your language with that of your listeners.

Language is not the sole possession of speakers. Our words are shared with our listeners, drawn from a common pool of possible utterances. As we have seen in **1b**, speech does not consist of messages sent, but of meanings jointly constructed within the context of a discourse community. When choosing from many possible ways to talk about a topic, the most effective way will be the one that overlaps and resonates with your listeners. When you use phrases and metaphors that are comfortable for your audience, you say, "I may not be exactly like you, but I am part of your discourse community." This creates a bond with them that goes beyond the literal definitions of the words you use and lays the foundation for more communication. This sort of bonding is particularly important with an unfavorable audience.

In the process of bonding, be very careful not to parrot phrases you do not understand, mock anyone's accent, or seem to talk down to your listeners in a way that clearly does not ring true to your own identity. As a speaker, you must be yourself. But you have many facets to yourself, and, without being artificial, you can choose to bring into your speech those aspects of your own language that best match your audience.

People who like each other and agree with one another come to talk like each other. And people who talk like each other come to like each other better and agree with each other more. This cyclical pattern reinforces itself; groups that spend time together pick up common phrases and sentence structures. Language can readily disclose the insiders and the outsiders. Within a couple of minutes of small talk you can tell if a new acquaintance is a true sports fan in the way you and your group define it, or if this person is a "guru" or a "wannabe" in your area of business expertise. With language being this potent an identifier, you want it to work *for* you.

Synchronizing your language with your audience involves close audience analysis. Listening to them and engaging in genuine dialogue will reveal the terms and categories that organize their reality. Every aspect of style can be subtly adjusted—level of formality, use of jargon or abbreviations, selection of figures of speech and metaphors. Matching words or phrases is important not for its own sake, but rather because paying attention to the audience's words will give you clues to how they see the world. If you respect your listeners, you will almost subconsciously scan for terms that show that respect. If you do not understand them, there is the potential to get off on the wrong foot and truly offend them. The board member of an orchestra who talks to the musicians about Beethoven's *Ninth Symphony* as a good "product" may alienate them irretrievably. Or the lack of understanding may not be as dramatic: Perhaps it sometimes is just a feeling of not really connecting, though neither speaker nor audience can quite say why.

Exercise 6. You are going to speak on the topic of why a two-day strategic planning retreat is a good investment for an organization. You visit three different departments of the organization to whom you will be making separate presentations. Based on the following observations, how would you characterize each audience and how might you adapt your topic and your language to establish a tone that is in sync with theirs?

Group A makes use of these terms: *the real go-getters, on the fast track, it's a rat race every day, pressure cooker.*

Group B makes use of these terms: *dotting the i*s and crossing the t*s, getting your ducks in a row, doing your homework.*

Group C makes use of these terms: *our family here, the team, touching base, backing each other up.*

Chapter 16

Attention and Interest

Adapt your speech material so it will capture your listeners' attention and retain their interest.

Think back to your most recent walk through a department store. Did you notice every single display, each ten feet from the last and all competing for your attention? Or did you pass most without a flicker, being brought to a halt by a few that drew you to them through color, or movement, or contrast, or an unusual juxtaposition of images?

Some attention factors are universal, and some are more idiosyncratic. Such things as sudden movement or bright color would catch almost anyone's eye, but *you* might stop by snow tires while your friend looks at computer games. Or you might linger in the food department on a day you are hungry, but rush by it on another day when your thoughts are on the fact that you have no luggage for the trip you wish to take.

Why is it that some things always catch attention and others will be noticed only by some people or only in some situations? And of the thousands of things that receive momentary notice, what causes a few to be chosen for closer scrutiny? As a public speaker, you can profit from giving some thought to questions like these. After all, when you give a speech or presentation, your words are competing for attention with every other sight and sound in the room and with every daydream or concern in the mind of each listener. The better you understand the psychology of attention, the more likely you will receive the compliment most sought for and appreciated by speakers: a sincere and simple "That was an interesting speech!"

16a. Engage your audience's attention by making extensive use of techniques that enliven your speech.

A common misconception is that once you have grabbed your listeners' attention with a snappy introduction, that attention is yours until you relinquish it at the end of the speech. Unfortunately, it takes more than a clever opening to keep an audience listening. People are easily distracted. Unless reengaged, their minds may wander off every half-minute or so. When composing a speech, take every opportunity to weave in materials and to phrase statements characterized by the factors that have been identified as most likely to gain attention. These are:

1. Activity or movement—appropriate physical mobility of the speaker and a lively treatment of the content that creates a feeling of something happening.
2. Reality—reference to actual people, events, places; being specific and concrete rather than abstract.
3. Proximity—drawing on what is close at hand; people in the room, current events, local references.
4. Familiarity—the use of recognized examples, well-known phrases, commonplace events.
5. Novelty—the opposite of the familiar; startling facts, odd turns of phrase, surprising images, unusual combinations.
6. Suspense—creating curiosity about what will happen next; posing puzzles or provocative questions.
7. Conflict—setting up pros and cons, opposing viewpoints, competing schools of thought.
8. Humor—playful remarks, silly or exaggerated images, amusing plays on words, ironic twists of fate, entertaining stories.
9. The Vital[1]—reference to something that is important to listeners; at its most intense this would be on matters of survival, but to a lesser degree

---

[1]Bruce E. Gronbeck, Kathleen German, Douglas Ehninger, and Alan H. Monroe, *Principles of Speech Communication*, 12th brief ed. (New York: Harper/Collins, 1995), 145–49.

also anything that saves them time, earns them money, makes their life more pleasant.

People are intrigued by things that are unusual or spark their curiosity. Paradoxically, they also respond to well-known, everyday references. Most of all, as in the case of the Vital, people attend to material they see as connected to their own self-interest. Do not worry about using plenty of these. Think of all the speeches you have heard labeled dull or boring. Did you ever hear a complaint that a lecture was too fascinating? The use of these factors can be made second nature without much effort or time.

Not:	A college athlete might be having trouble in one of his classes.
But:	Suppose Larry Linebacker can't tell the difference between Bizet and "The Bizarroes" in his music appreciation class. (Humor, Reality, Familiarity)
Not:	A number of technologies have made business communication faster and more efficient.
But:	As I walked into my office about two hours ago, the red light on my phone was blinking. I picked up four voice mail messages, forwarding one to my colleague. I next jumped online to see if there were any e-mail messages and found that our client in Atlanta had changed the specifications for the contract we are bidding on. I quickly generated computer graphics reflecting the new data and faxed them to Chris, who, as you all know, is making his presentation right about now. (Activity, Proximity, the Vital)
Not:	When time is short, a good executive takes action first and then worries about causes, procedure, and policy.
But:	If I told you people in the fourth and fifth rows that that chandelier's going to fall in ten seconds, what would you do? Darn right! You'd get out of the way! Later, we'd talk about why it happened, whose fault it was, and how to fix it. (Proximity, Novelty, Suspense, Reality)

Be guided by the following principles as you incorporate attention factors into your speech:

(1) Use materials that are concrete and close to home.

Examples are always more interesting when they are specific and real. Notice how these paragraphs from a speech by Edward Kennedy create pictures in your mind—more tangible and believable than vague references to "the victims of our economic crisis."

> I have listened and learned.
>
> I have listened to Kenny Dubois, a glassblower in Charleston, West Virginia, who has ten children to support, but has lost his job after thirty five years, just three years short of qualifying for his pension.
>
> I have listened to the Trachta family, who farm in Iowa and wonder whether they can pass the good life and the good earth on to their children.
>
> I have listened to a grandmother in East Oakland, who no longer has a phone to call her grandchildren because she gave it up to pay the rent on her small apartment.
>
> I have listened to. . .[2]

Never say "a person" or "one" if you can give a name. Use well-known figures, members of the audience, or hypothetical characters. Use place names, brand names, dates, details.

(2) Keep your audience involved.

If you have done a thorough audience analysis, you will already have many references to the audience built into the speech and will have made use of attention factors like proximity and familiarity. But there are always other chances to adapt to your audience once you start your speech. Be willing to throw out what you have if you can replace it with something "close to home." Here are some adaptations you might try:

Use the names of people in the audience.

Replace supporting material with items drawn from the audience's direct experience. Before giving a speech you will often have a chance to meet a few members of your audience. It is often effective to refer to them. Why say "Suppose a businessperson wants to obtain a loan" when you could say "Suppose Ms. Silver's [nodding toward a listener] hardware business is expanding so rapidly she decides to take out a loan to enlarge her store?"

Refer to the person who introduced you
and to other speakers on the program.

Listen to the comments of the person who introduces you and to the content of any speeches that precede yours. You might be able to return a compliment, engage in banter, or, best of all, forge an intellectual link

---

[2]Edward M. Kennedy, "Principles of the Democratic Party," *Vital Speeches of the Day* 46, no. 23 (1980): 716.

between their speech ideas and one of yours. For instance, an alert member of a speech class might include something like this:

> So now that we have examined the causes of stress, let us look at four ways of reducing it. The first of these is physical exercise. Nearly everyone can find an activity she or he likes. Hong was telling us about the joys of tennis. Similarly, aerobic dance is . . .

Refer to details in the immediate setting or from shared experience.

> "And all of that expensive atom-smashing machinery was housed in a room not half the size of this one." "Everyone in this class knows about *situational stress*. The five of us giving speeches today are especially aware of it."

Do not use a hypothetical example of a point or process if you can draw a more concrete example from something that has just happened to the group.

Create an active rather than a passive role for your audience. Even though it is your show when you speak, you can still stimulate a sense of interaction in your listeners. Use audience participation techniques. Ask for shows of hands if pertinent, have listeners provide examples, ask questions of them.

> How many people here had breakfast this morning? Ah, I see about half of you raised your hands. What did you have, sir? Bacon and eggs? Over there? Coffee and a donut. I hear juice and toast, yeast shake, Cheerios, and yogurt. Would anyone care to hazard an answer to this question? What percentage of elementary school students go to school with no breakfast at all?

When you do not want to relinquish control or when overt audience participation is impractical for some other reason, you can still keep your audience mentally involved and active. Ask rhetorical questions. Have your listeners visualize examples. Ask them for nonverbal feedback and respond to it.

> Are there any Monty Python freaks here? Great, I can see there are. Well, do you remember the sketch about the cheese shop?

> There is yet another problem with home repairs. I'll bet this has happened to everyone here . . .

I have one colleague who always gives me feedback at the wrong time and place. Do you know people like that? Several of you are nodding. Isn't it frustrating?

We can learn from our mistakes. Think of the last mistake you made. Take a minute to recall a big one. Do you have it in mind? OK. Now I want you to think about how you felt.

An even less complicated technique to maintain attention is the liberal use of the word *you:*

You've probably seen . . .
Do you sometimes wonder . . .
In your morning paper . . .
Now, I'll bet you're saying to yourself . . .
You could undoubtedly give me a dozen more examples.
In your city here . . .

Be careful not to overdo the use of these techniques. In our experience there have been a number of occasions (mostly banquets and awards) where the presenter got so caught up in introducing oblique references to historical (and allegedly amusing) events with members of the organization's old guard that it became indulgent and annoying to even longtime members.

(3) Keep the energy level of your speech up through variety and movement.

Change attracts attention. Sameness is dull. One visual aid may add interest to your speech, but a succession of visual aids can drag a speech down if they are not used judiciously. If your content or delivery becomes totally predictable, minds in the audience will start to wander.

Vary forms of support—do not rely on just statistics or just testimony. Draw examples from many domains. Three political illustrations of one point are less interesting than a single political illustration combined with a sports example and an example drawn from a popular film. Similarly, repetition of the same sentence constructions and overuse of a word or phrase should be avoided. See **15d**.

Whenever possible, give the speech a sense of movement. Create images of activity. Use verbs with vivid connotations and stay in the active voice as much as possible. For instance, instead of saying "Five new businesses can be seen downtown," say "Drive down First Street and you will see five new businesses." If you need to point out the features of a piece of equipment, describe it in use, with fingers flying over the keyboard or gears turning or shutters clicking or even electrons crackling.

In your delivery, too, remember the importance of variety and movement. A deadpan speaker monotonously delivering a presentation while standing on a particularly adhesive spot on the floor certainly would benefit from reading section **25c** and Chapter **26**.

(4) Use humor in appropriate situations.

Integrate humor into your speech. Make sure it is appropriate to your personality and to the situation.

Of the many factors of attention, humor is so powerful and at the same time so tricky that it deserves a careful look. An infusion of humor into any speech can break tension, deflate opponents, enhance the speaker's image, and make points memorable. You need not consider yourself a humorous speaker or your speech a humorous talk to benefit from this unique attention factor.

Developing your use of humor is not a matter of collecting jokes and gags that have limited usefulness. What is important is the ability to spot a potentially humorous idea in your speech and to develop it into a genuinely funny moment.

Draw humorous material from a variety of sources.

Look for the humor in your everyday experience. Most of us have days when one disaster follows on the heels of another, and there comes a point where we have to take an objective look at the humor of the situation—or crack. "This will make a good story . . . someday" is an utterance that bears witness to the fine line between tragedy and humor. The boring, frustrating, and mundane aspects of life all have their humorous elements.

Take note of the everyday things that make you laugh: on your job, in your relationships, on television, in the paper. Decide which of these humorous items have any bearing on potential speech topics. Some are just amusing; some are both amusing and instructive. Jot them down, clip them out, and establish some sort of filing system so that you do not say to yourself six months later, "Now, what was the funny phrase that the judge used?"

Be selective when you draw on collected humor. A speaker can definitely benefit from reading books *on* humor, but care should be taken when using books *of* humor. Timeliness and original twists are so important to humor that the lag time involved in publishing renders stale much of the content of such books. Nevertheless, topically organized books of humor can sometimes yield just the gem you need. Better than jokebooks or magazine joke pages, though, are the works of genuine humorists. Read Mark Twain, Will Rogers, Robert Benchley, and contemporary columnists like Dave Barry and Molly Ivins. They introduce you to comic points of view that are more useful than jokes.

Exercise 1. Think over the spontaneous laughs you have had in the last few days in unstructured interpersonal interactions. Can you describe what your friends or acquaintances did that amused you? Do these people have uniquely funny approaches to life or ways of responding to events? Turn this around: can you describe what you've done to amuse your friends and acquaintances?

16b. Convert attention to interest.

Prehistoric people quickly discovered that keeping a campfire burning continuously was easier than laboriously rubbing two sticks together to light a new fire for each individual task. You will be working altogether too hard as a speaker if you must constantly light new fires under your audience with a succession of attention getters. If, however, you can kindle a sustained *interest* in your topic, your job becomes easier. When an audience member becomes more than merely attentive, but actually interested, then he or she starts to take a more active role. The listener puts forth effort to stay with you even through complicated lines of thought or technical material—focusing concentration and pushing distractions aside.

When you have gained attention, through the methods recommended in **16a,** you need to use those moments to demonstrate how and why your topic is worthy of your listeners' interest.

(1) Emphasize the link between your topic and the listeners' self-interest.

Most times when people say, "So what?" they are really saying, "What's it to me?" Do not assume that the benefits of your particular approach are obvious; motivate your audience to listen by spelling out the rewards. Do careful audience analysis and tie into as many of your listeners' needs and values as possible. See **18.**

> If you take the time to learn the basics of car maintenance, you'll no longer be at the mercy of a mechanic. You can shop around for the most economical and reliable car care and have the added peace of mind of knowing that you'll be able to spot potentially dangerous conditions.

> I know that many of you work in the helping professions—as teachers, social workers, counselors, and nurses. Learning to read the subtle cues of body language will help you interpret messages your clients may be unable to transmit in words.

> You don't have to be a vegetarian or a gourmet cook to benefit from these menu ideas. By serving just a few meatless meals a week, you can save thirty to one hundred dollars on your monthly grocery bill and also provide a healthier diet for your family.

(2) Incorporate some of the techniques of effective storytelling.

A reader will innocently open a book at bedtime to read a few pages before turning out the light. Dawn comes and the bleary-eyed reader is still engrossed, even if the subject is not one that normally produces any interest or relates to a part of the reader's life. A well-constructed story, whether it deals with elves and hobbits or secret agents in the world of international financial intrigue, commands the interest of nearly everyone. The raconteur who can take the chaos of everyday experience and produce a compelling narration will never have trouble attracting an audience.

People are fascinated by human interest stories, as well as by hard news of matters that concern them directly. Notice how excellent feature articles and documentary films share many of the qualities of good fiction or drama. A speech, even if it is an annual report, can capture an audience if it unfolds in a narrative fashion with suspense, conflict, intriguing characterizations, lively bits of dialogue, and a moment of climax leading to the denouement. Your speech need not promise to make your listeners rich or famous if it takes them outside their experience in an engaging way.

Exercise 2. Identify the attention factor or factors in each example:

A good accountant can help you avoid paying extra taxes.
You've all heard the phrase, "the bottom line."
Our own accounting department has developed some new techniques.
I was trembling when I went into the tax auditor's office. Could Melvin's ledgers save me or was I ...?

Exercise 3. Describe how you could use at least five of the attention factors from **16a** in a speech on each of these topics:

Computers
Art frauds and forgeries
Federal regulatory agencies

Exercise 4. Identify at least four attention factors in each speech in the **Appendix.**

Exercise 5. Select one speech from the **Appendix** and discuss how the speaker transforms attention to interest.

16c. Avoid these attention pitfalls.

(1) Avoid inappropriate stories, humor, and other attention "grabbers."

Don't risk losing the good will of your audience by using questionable material. It is a safe bet that ethnic jokes, sick humor, and coarse vulgarities will offend someone in every audience. Sensitive audience analysis should cause you to revise or eliminate stereotypical treatments of women, homosexuals, mothers-in-law, and senior citizens. Knowledge of your listeners will also help you make a judgment about the inclusion of a slightly risque remark or politically loaded story. Insults or ridicule—unless stylized as in a "roast"—should be avoided unless you are very sure that the object of your putdown genuinely enjoys public teasing.

(2) Don't let a story or joke consume your entire speech.

It is easy to spend so much time getting attention there is no time left to deliver your substantive points. Every bit of supporting material in a speech has to make a direct contribution to the thesis. A string of unrelated jokes and stories or aimless clowning pulls the focus away from your topic. Constructing a transition that huffs and puffs with exertion to tie in an unrelated joke is a waste of time.

(3) Do not tell jokes unless you have mastered the techniques of joke telling.

Everyone is funny, but not everyone can and should tell jokes. Telling a joke takes skill, and telling a long, complex joke with voices, intricate timing, dialogue, and physical movement takes consummate skill.

If you do choose to use jokes, you should expect to do more precise planning than that necessary in the more conversational parts of your speech. To be successful requires you to draw on the writer's attention to word choice and the performer's sense of presence and voice. An excellent public speaker should not impair his or her image of competence by bungling a joke in these all-too-familiar ways:

- Inadequate lead-in or setup
- Fizzling midseries in a climactic joke ("So anyway this same thing happens four or five more times.")
- Not committing oneself actually to telling the joke. Describing the nature of the joke and delivering the punch line, but never getting into the storytelling aspect
- Overintroducing your humorous material, using tedious and empty lead-ins like: "Now here's a real funny story my cousin told me. It really points out what I'm talking about and you're going to love it."

(4) Be careful that audience participation does not cause you to lose control.

A half-hearted attempt to get listeners involved can result in awkward silences. At the other extreme, too responsive audience members can turn a speech into a group discussion.

Chapter 17

Credibility

Establish your credibility, both before and during your speech, by projecting the qualities of competence, concern, trustworthiness, and dynamism.

Your content and delivery determine to a great extent whether or not your listeners believe what you say. However, there is a force at work independently that can doom even the most exquisitely wrought speech to failure. Beyond what you say and how you say it, your audience is influenced by who you are—or, more accurately, who they think you are. Your *credibility* is that combination of perceived qualities that makes listeners predisposed to believe you. For centuries scholars have been fascinated by credibility—from classical discussions of *ethos* to contemporary investigations of concepts labeled *image, personality,* and *charisma*. What is it about some speakers that makes you want to accept what they say, while others make you want to reject what may be an identical message? Aristotle observed that audiences are most inclined to believe a person they see as having good sense, goodwill, and good character. Modern social scientists have tried to isolate the characteristics that distinguish the most credible speakers from others. Their lists include: competence, dynamism, intention, personality, intelligence, authoritativeness, extroversion, trustworthiness, composure, and sociability.

You can enhance your credibility and thus the chances of meeting your speech objective by projecting these qualities. You may build up your prior image or reputation going into the speech, and you can take steps to improve your credibility as you are speaking. The first step, though, is to assess your present image.

17a. Conduct an honest assessment of your speaking image.

While the perfect speaker would be seen as competent, concerned, trustworthy, and dynamic in discussing all topics with all audiences, most of us fall short of this ideal. One speaker might seem warm, charming, likable—but somehow have trouble being taken seriously on weighty issues. Another may have a demeanor that immediately inspires confidence—but suffers from seeming dull or distant, not human enough.

Before you can work on improving your credibility, you need to see where you stand now. Is your overall credibility high or low? Do people agree with you because of, or in spite of, the personality you put forth? Which components of credibility are strongest for you? Which need to be developed? If possible, have some friends or acquaintances help you with this appraisal. It is very hard to estimate how others see us.

As you answer the following diagnostic questions, you will see that they fall into three areas: your image *prior* to the speech, your *content,* and your *delivery.* Suggestions for improving your credibility in each of these areas are provided in **17b, c,** and **d.**

(1) Are you perceived as *competent?*

Prior:	Do you have education, experience, or credentials to make you an expert on this topic? Does your audience know that?
Content:	Have you researched broadly and deeply? Does your speech reflect this with well-documented, factual information?
Delivery:	Does your delivery connote competence? Do you seem to be "on top of your information," well organized, and composed?

(2) Are you perceived as *concerned* about your audience's welfare?

Prior:	If you have a history of generosity or selflessness on relevant issues, is it known? (For example, have you sponsored a

scholarship, or volunteered your time, or made a sacrifice of some sort?)

Content: Do you stress the audience's needs and goals throughout the speech?

Delivery: Is your delivery warm, unaffected, friendly, and responsive to the audience?

(3) Are you perceived as *trustworthy?*

Prior: Is your past record one of honesty and integrity?

Content: Do you make a special effort to be fair in presenting evidence, acknowledging limitations of your data and opinions, and conceding those parts of opposing viewpoints that have validity?

Delivery: Is your style of presentation sincere and honest—not too slick or manipulative?

(4) Are you perceived as *dynamic?*

Prior: Is your image one of an active, fairly aggressive person—a leader rather than a follower, a doer rather than an observer?

Content: Does your speech have a sense of movement? Do the ideas build to a climax rather than dropping into a static heap? Is your language lively and colorful?

Delivery: Is your delivery animated, energetic, and enthusiastic?

Exercise 1. Complete your image inventory. In a few sentences describe your prior image as a speaker in your speech class or in a social or professional group you relate to regularly. Which is your strongest area: competence, concern, trustworthiness, dynamism? Which is your weakest?

Exercise 2. Consider how your credibility varies from topic to topic. Name three topics where you have high credibility and three on which you would have to work very hard to establish credibility.

Exercise 3. Rate the last four U.S. presidents' credibility as high, medium, or low on competence, concern, trustworthiness, and dynamism. Discuss your choices and reasons.

Exercise 4. Name a public figure who you believe is competent, concerned, and trustworthy but whose image suffers due to lack of dynamism. Can you think of a public figure of whom the opposite is true?

17b. Build your credibility prior to the speech.

(1) Provide the contact person with adequate information about your qualifications.

Do not be overly modest when asked for information for advance publicity. Send a résumé that lists your background and achievements. Include clippings, testimonials about your speaking, books or articles, and a photograph if appropriate.

(2) Help the person introducing you to set a favorable tone.

In addition to providing written information, be available to consult by phone or in person with whoever will introduce you. If there are aspects of your background you would like to have stressed for a particular speech, be sure to say so.

(3) Be aware of your image in all dealings with the group prior to the speech.

In a speech class you know that you have a certain image. You can tell if you are considered serious, funny, prompt, lazy, cheerful, argumentative, intelligent, informed, and so on just from daily classroom interactions. These perceptions will affect the way your first speech is received. A similar situation exists if you are to speak in front of the service group you belong to or your professional association.

Speaking before an unfamiliar audience is different. Since these people have little to go on to form an impression, recognize that just about all of your interactions with them will affect your credibility. Your friendliness, professionalism, and confidence in negotiating arrangements and even in making social small talk prior to the speech will be very influential.

17c. Bolster your credibility through your speech content.

As you prepare your speech outline and select your supporting evidence and examples, think about ways to communicate your competence, concern, trustworthiness, and dynamism. The following suggestions are especially relevant to the opening minutes of the speech, while first impressions are being formed (see **11a**), but many credibility boosters can be woven in throughout the entire speech.

(1) Present your credentials.

The majority of inexperienced speakers find it difficult to "blow my own horn" and do not do as much credibility building as they should. Do not be reluctant to provide information about your qualifications to speak.

> In my 15 years as a kindergarten teacher . . .

> The most common error I see in the twenty to thirty loan applications I look at each week is . . .

> I've had a special awareness of the barriers the physically handicapped face since 1991, when my brother Dave returned from the Gulf War . . .

Judgment and tact are important in deciding which qualifications to mention and how to work them into the speech. Our culture frowns on bragging and name-dropping, yet false humility is out of place. The too-humble speaker insults the audience by implying that if they knew anything at all, they never would have invited the person to speak. However, you can include many statements of your qualifications without seeming boastful, if you play it straight and present them matter-of-factly. Include only relevant qualifications. Do not talk about how many celebrities you know unless it relates to the topic. Do not expound on financial success unless the speech is specifically about making money.

(2) Demonstrate a thorough understanding of your topic.

To communicate a sense of expertise you must let the listeners know that you have done your homework. Mention the nature of your research when appropriate:

> The seven judges I interviewed all agreed on one major weakness in our court system.

> I read the minutes of all the committee hearings on this bill, and not one expert mentioned . . .

There is considerable disagreement on this point in the books and articles I read. Several scholars say . . .

Use concrete examples, statistics, testimony. Be sure you have your details straight. One obvious error early in the speech can ruin your credibility.

Just imagine what it would have been like for the Union soldier crouching in the trenches around Richmond, his jacket zipped up tight in a futile battle against the cold and the wet.

The people listening to this would probably think, "If this speaker doesn't know that the zipper wasn't invented until long after the Civil War, I wonder what other information is all wrong?"

(3) Be sure your material is clearly organized.

A sense of competence depends on being in command of the material and seeming to know where you are headed. Listeners will label you as uninformed rather than unorganized if you wander from topic to topic or if you must apologetically insert, "Oh, one thing I forgot to mention when I was discussing . . ."

(4) Make a special effort to present a balanced and objective analysis.

To demonstrate that you are fair, trustworthy, of good character, go out of your way to acknowledge the limitations of your evidence and argument, if appropriate:

Now, I know there are some problems with relying on surveys, but this one was carefully conducted. It seems safe to conclude that at least *many,* if not *most,* working mothers are dissatisfied with the quality of child care available to them.

I'm not saying television is the only cause of these problems. I realize that's an oversimplification. But I do think that TV has had a pronounced effect on the imaginative thinking of the last two generations.

Also be sure to acknowledge the existence of opposing evidence and opinions:

There are some studies that indicate that an alcoholic can return to social drinking, but . . .

I recognize the contributions the administration has made to social welfare programs, but it has failed in so many other areas that I still maintain it is time for a change.

Acknowledge self-interest when it exists, to prevent the audience from thinking you are trying to hide something from them. If they discover later that you are more partisan than you made it sound, then your credibility would be dealt some powerful blows.

It's true I'm a Realtor and I stand to profit by having folks invest in real estate. But that's not my main reason for urging you to invest.

(5) Explicitly express your concern and goodwill toward the audience.

Let them know that your speech is offered to serve their interests.

I'd do anything to save your families the headaches and heartaches that go along with having a relative die without a will.

Taking up tennis has added so much to my life I'd love to see some of you share in that fun.

17d. Use your speech delivery to increase your credibility.

Too many expert and well-prepared speakers lose effectiveness because they cannot *transmit* these qualities to their audience. Dropping cards, reading in a shaky voice, fumbling with whatever is at hand, all suggest lack of competence. An unexpressive face and voice might be interpreted as disdainful and detract from perceived goodwill. Hesitancy and uncertainty are sometimes falsely seen as shiftiness or dishonesty. Listless, monotonous, colorless speaking is the very opposite of dynamism. To be seen as a believable source of information and opinion, continue to work on all aspects of delivery covered in Chapters **25** and **26**.

Exercise 5. How does each speaker in the **Appendix** directly establish his or her credentials to speak? Which example do you find effective? Are there any that strike you as heavy handed or arrogant?

Exercise 6. Find an example of how each speaker in the **Appendix** explicitly establishes concern for the welfare of the audience.

Exercise 7. What sections of the speeches in the **Appendix** seem to present the speakers as fair, objective, honest people?

Chapter 18

Motivational Appeals

Motivate your listeners toward your speech purpose through appeals to their emotions, needs, and values. Be sure that these appeals supplement, but do not replace, the sound logic and evidence upon which you base your speech.

This book stresses the role of clear analysis in support of ideas, but it also emphasizes making those ideas meaningful to an audience. A good speaker is constantly aware of the humanness of the audience. To be human is to be rational, but it is more than that. Love sometimes overrules logic, reverence transcends reason, emotion contradicts evidence. Understanding the humanity of your audience means reaching them as total persons—packaging your essentially logical case so that it touches the listeners' feelings, needs, and values.

18a. When developing the content of your speech, be conscious of the emotional impact you want to create or avoid.

Keep in mind that everything you say has the potential to trigger some sort of emotional response in your audience. Generally, you can strengthen your speech by selecting main points, supporting material, and language that can engage your listeners' feelings. Positive emotions— hope, joy, pride, love—are surefire motivators. Negative emotions like fear, envy, disgust, and contempt can also motivate; witness the popularity of roller coasters and horror films. The motivational effects of negative emotions are less predictable, however, and can sometimes boomerang. While moderate levels of fear appeal enhance persuasion, higher levels may work against the desired effect. Some presentations feature gory films of traffic accidents, vivid visual aids showing cancerous lung tissue, or detailed descriptions of the plight of a family whose breadwinner had no insurance. These either cause the audience to tune out the unpleasantness or just seem too extreme to be statistically plausible fates for the listener to worry about. When adding emotion to your speech, remember the old adage, "although some is good, more is not always better."

Devoid of Emotion

A dose of 600 rems produces acute radiation illness. Japanese A-bomb victims experienced a variety of physical symptoms and usually died within two weeks of exposure.

Moderate Emotion

A dose of 600 rems or more produces acute radiation illness. Thousands of Japanese A-bomb victims died from this sickness within two weeks of the bomb explosions. Such exposure to radiation kills all actively dividing cells in the body: Hair falls out, skin is sloughed off in big ulcers, vomiting and diarrhea occur, and then, as the white blood cells and platelets die, victims expire of infection and/or massive hemorrhage.[1]

Excessive Emotion

The bomb has fallen, and you're unlucky enough not to have been killed immediately. There's nothing you can do except sit there dumbly, in your own vomit and excrement, while the omnipresent radiation kills off the process of life. With no cell growth, your skin becomes leprous and detaches from your body in great clumps; but you don't notice because your white blood cells have died and dark swelling has overtaken all of your body, immersing you in a pain that will not subside until a weakened artery in your brain bursts in a final geyser of black blood.

On any topic there are these three levels. What you have to do very early is discern where your audience draws the dividing lines. Try to

---

[1]Helen Caldicott, *Nuclear Madness* (Brookline, MA: Autumn Press, 1978), 29.

include the optimal amount of emotional appeal—not so little that you fail to touch them, not so much that you turn them off.

18b. Relate your speech to the needs of your listeners.

The most well-known way of classifying human needs is the hierarchy devised by Abraham Maslow.[2] See Figure 18-1.

In this hierarchy the lower needs have to be met or satisfied before an individual can become concerned with the needs on the next-higher level. For instance, if speaking on the topic of physical fitness, you could appeal to your audience at any of the following levels:

- The effect of exercise in reducing cardiovascular disease appeals to the survival need.
- Security might be drawn in by mentioning how physically fit people are more likely to be able to resist or evade attackers.

FIGURE 18-1   Maslow's Hierarchy

Self-Actualization Needs
Personal Fulfillment, Knowledge, Creativity

Esteem Needs
Self-Image, Approval, Recognition

Belongingness Needs
Friendship, Love, Acceptance

Security Needs
Safety, Shelter, Protection

Survival Needs
Food, Water, Air

[2]Abraham Maslow, *Motivation and Personality,* 2nd ed. (New York: Harper & Row, 1970), 35–58.

- The need for belonging can be linked to becoming trim and attractive as well as to making friends through physical activity.
- Esteem needs can be tied into the current popularity of fitness and the social desirability of an active image.
- Finally, a speaker might relate fitness to the need for self-actualization—the highs of exercise, the mental and physical challenge of reaching one's potential.

The significance of Maslow's hierarchy to the speaker is apparent. You must analyze your audience well enough to determine which need is most salient for them. Listeners whose jobs are in danger and who are struggling to feed their families do not want to hear you contrast local economic programs in terms of the implications drawn from Keynesian theory. They want to know which one will create jobs—being absorbed with their security needs, they are not likely to respond at the self-actualization level.

It is ineffective to aim your emotional appeals too high. It is unethical to aim your appeals too low. Take a speaker who wants to convince colleagues to adopt a different software system than the one currently in use in that department. If the company is healthy and the colleagues are satisfactory employees, then it would be inappropriate to use a fear appeal with visions of the organization going out of business and people being tossed into the street if the new system is not adopted. The more ethical approach would be to build a case related to the colleagues' needs for efficiency, productivity, success, and prestige (esteem and self-actualization levels).

To be fair, you should respond to existing needs, not create a new and artificial sense of insecurity in your listeners. Speakers who abuse their influence in this way falsely assume that the most primitive needs are the strongest. We disagree. Altruism is an extremely effective motivator. In fact, we might place another pyramid beside Maslow's, illustrating our belief that every person has a basic need to *protect* others' survival, to *give* security, to *spread* love, to *build* esteem, to *nurture* self-actualization. Appeals to the idealistic, caring sides of human nature can be at least as powerful as self-oriented appeals.

18c. Relate your speech to the values of your listeners.

When, in a presentation, you use the argument "and this procedure will speed up your assembly line," you are actually unveiling only a part of the following syllogism:

Anything that speeds up your assembly line is good.
This procedure will speed up your assembly line.
Therefore, this procedure is good.

You assume that your listeners share increasing production speed as a value, and as a result, you do not feel it is necessary to burden your talk with the other parts of the syllogism. As it turns out, however, these particular listeners are currently satisfied with the speed of production, but are more concerned with the accuracy of assembly. A little audience analysis could have alerted you to the fact and you might have worked from the following syllogism:

Anything that improves accuracy is good.
This procedure improves accuracy.
Therefore, this procedure is good.

Both arguments are logically sound (and, we hope, both are true), but the second is psychologically more effective because its underlying premise reflects the dominant value of the listeners.

We hold a certain value if we believe that a particular thing is either good or bad, in the broadest sense of those terms. Specifically, we *evaluate* concepts, people, objects, events, or ideas every day as we label them just or unjust, wise or foolish, beautiful or ugly, and so on. Whereas emotions and needs are considered to be innate (and therefore consistent across cultures, societies, and individuals), values are judgments or choices made by individuals. Looking at two people in isolation we could predict that they both feel fear and the need for status, just on the basis of their humanness. We could not easily predict if one hated homosexuals or if the other was a passionate supporter of the free enterprise system.

(1) Incorporate appeals to the general values of the culture.

Although values are individually chosen, the choice is not often a totally conscious and rational one. Culture has a strong influence, shaping values through families, schools, media, and peers. Moreover, values are rarely formed in isolation; they are organized and structured into related clusters. By knowing the culture of your listeners, the influences on them, and perhaps some of the other values they hold, you can make an educated guess how much particular values might shape their attitude toward your speech topic.

Look at one popular classification of contemporary American values.[3]

- A comfortable life (a prosperous life)
- An exciting life (a stimulating, active life)
- A sense of accomplishment (lasting contribution)
- A world at peace (free of war and conflict)
- A world of beauty (beauty of nature and the arts)
- Equality (brotherhood, equal opportunity for all)
- Family security (taking care of loved ones)
- Freedom (independence, free choice)
- Happiness (contentedness)
- Inner harmony (freedom from inner conflict)
- Mature love (sexual and spiritual intimacy)
- National security (protection from attack)
- Pleasure (an enjoyable, leisurely life)
- Salvation (saved, eternal life)
- Self-respect (self-esteem)
- Social recognition (respect, admiration)
- True friendship (close companionship)
- Wisdom (a mature understanding of life)

Sometimes identifying values in your own culture can be extremely difficult. With the constant currents of change, predominant values and trends often do not become clarified until a decade later, much too late to do a speaker any good. However, there is always at least one writer or commentator who captures the essence of the changes while they are occurring. Your audience analysis will be enriched by awareness of the changes in mainstream values caused by economic and technical trends, countercultural movements, and liberation movements. Pay attention to the editorial writers and news commentators who help you get a clearer picture of the "national mood." Be aware that many public opinion polls on specific issues like abortion, school prayer, capital punishment, and women's rights contain a few questions specifically addressed to values. One resource for poll information is the Inter-University Consortium for Political and Social Research (ICPSR) data bank in Ann Arbor, Michigan.

---

[3]Sandra J. Ball-Rokeach and Joel W. Grube, *The Great American Values Test: Influencing Behavior and Belief Through Television,* (New York: The Free Press, 1984), 90.

(2) Identify and relate to the core values of your audience.

If the members of a culture share common values, why do we not see lockstep agreement on every issue? Obviously, not all members of a culture give equal importance to the common values, nor is there a standard ranking of them. Values are very general, and any particular issue can touch on many values, both on the pro side and the con side. Examples of this value conflict can become common around election time. Say that there is a proposed bond issue to build an expensive fine arts complex. A person may be drawn toward approving the bond as a result of holding the values of *a world of beauty* and *a sense of accomplishment,* but this individual may also have reservations about taking on a greater tax burden because of belief in the values of *a comfortable, prosperous life* and *family security.* The resolution of this conflict is a function of how he or she has prioritized these values.

Because nearly every topic stirs up such value conflicts, a list of audience values would not be useful unless it were supplemented by some estimate of the relative ranking. One way to map this prioritizing is to imagine a series of concentric circles, with the deepest-held values at the *core,* the degree of importance of the other values determining their distance from the center. (See Figure 18-2.) The innermost circle contains *core values,* the ones so central to a person that to change one of them would amount to a basic alteration of that person's self-concept. The next band out from the center contains the *authority values,* the values that are influenced by and shared with groups and individuals most significant to the person. *Peripheral values* form the outer band.[4] These are the more-or-less incidental evaluations, easily made or changed.

Say that over the course of several political campaigns Rodney developed a distaste for the kind of content-free commercials that are normally done. This value, though peripheral, can be strong enough to influence Rodney's voting behavior in contests where, other things being equal, he has not taken a position. Other things are rarely equal, though. In a race between a Republican who uses content-free commercials and a non-Republican who does not, Rodney's values would come into conflict.

---

[4]This approach to values is adapted from Milton Rokeach's method of classifying beliefs by their centrality. Milton Rokeach, in collaboration with Richard Bonier and others, *Open and Closed Mind* (New York: Basic Books, 1960).

FIGURE 18-2   Ranking of Values

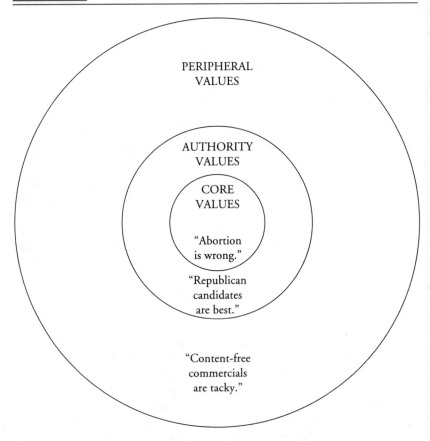

PERIPHERAL
VALUES

AUTHORITY
VALUES

CORE
VALUES

"Abortion
is wrong."

"Republican
candidates
are best."

"Content-free
commercials
are tacky."

Since his preference for Republican candidates is tied to an authority value and therefore closer to the core than a peripheral value like esthetic dislike of content-free commercials, he would normally resolve this conflict in favor of the Republican. However, the non-Republican opponent supports a constitutional ban on abortion while the Republican views such an amendment as an unwarranted government imposition on the individual. Rodney's opposition to abortion is one of his most deeply held moral principles. Again, he would experience conflict, but would resolve it in favor of the core value over the authority value—to do otherwise would require a thorough rethinking and reevaluation of his ethical system.

Understanding this, you should try to make reasonable inferences about your listeners' core values and stress them in your speech or presentation. For example, suppose you have an educational innovation you would like the local school system to adopt. In speaking to the school board, you might stress the values of practicality, efficiency, and local control of education. In speaking to the teachers, you might stress the more idealistic value of progress in education. While your approach in these two cases is different, this does not mean you assumed that teachers are impractical or that school board members care nothing about educational progress. The members of both groups probably hold each of these values. However, as a speaker you made a decision to stress those values that are likely to be closer to the core in each audience.

(3) Forge strong, logical links between the issues of your speech and the values of the audience.

The *issues* of your speech are the questions that must be resolved in your listeners' minds before your speech purpose can be met. See **3d**. Decisions about what is worth knowing, what should be done, or what touches our spirit often depend on the prior acceptance of certain values. Not only do people differ in what values they hold and how they prioritize them, but people also differ in how they perceive connections between particular values and particular issues. Even when listeners share almost identical values and priorities, it is possible for them to perceive links differently. Take two audience members who value creative freedom and efficiency, with efficiency being closer to the core. If your issue were the abolition of tenure, one listener might link that issue to creative freedom and be antagonistic to your speech goal, while the other might link it to efficiency and look upon your proposal favorably. It is not enough, then, to know what values your audience holds. You must try to discover which values they see linked to your topic. Often you will need to spell out for them new issue-value links that are logical but perhaps not readily apparent. As you prepare a speech, draw out as many *valid* links to values as you can discover. One of the less obvious ones may be just the connection that strikes through to a core value. See Table 18-1.

TABLE 18-1   Issues and Value Links

Issue	Obvious Value Links	Less Obvious, but Probably Valid, Value Links
Equality for women and marginalized groups	Justice, fairness, compassion	Increased productivity, avoiding waste, patriotism (world image)
Buying laptop computer	Efficiency, speed, scientific advancement	Creativity, expressiveness, economy (in the long run)
Deregulating small business	Lack of government interference, pioneer spirit of small entrepreneur	Honesty, trust of fellow citizens, dislike of red tape and paperwork
Welcoming delegation of foreign businesspersons	International harmony, U.S. hospitality, pooling of information	Efficiency, progress, pragmatism

(4) Use motivational appeals to broaden your listeners' sense of history and community.

Understandably, when people first encounter an issue they tend to analyze it from a perspective that is close to them in time and space. They ask, how does this affect me and my immediate circle now and in the near future? In contrast to this impulse, a Native American proverb suggests that every decision should be evaluated in terms of its impact on the seventh generation in the future; John Donne's statement that no man is an island has been amended by contemporary thinkers to state that today no person is even a peninsula. One of the most powerful ways that public speakers can use motivational appeals is to draw people outward and refocus their awareness on larger frames of reference.

This broader awareness is there and available to be tapped. When the U.S. public really saw and felt the suffering of Romanian orphans, there was an outpouring of financial support and a series of adoptions. Pictures of fish disfigured by discarded pop-top rings contributed to beverage companies' using a different system for opening aluminum cans. Speakers can create powerful pictures with words to remind listeners of their interdependence with other people and creatures, and to transport us into the past and the future. You can use your words to show people the historical and cultural meaning of endangered objects and places. You can take listeners into the future and reveal the effects of our environmental policies or our national debt on unborn generations. Link your speech topic to your audience's values in ways that tie in to the broadest sense of community and situate the present in relation to the past and the future.

18d. Avoid excessive and inappropriate use of emotional appeals.

Throughout this chapter we promote the effective use of appeals to the emotions, needs, and values of your listeners. We must end with a caution about the overuse and misuse of these appeals. A speech with too much emphasis on feelings can embarrass and offend the audience. If these listeners perceive that the speaker is playing on their emotions to the exclusion of sense and logic, they can become infuriated. It is always a mistake to underestimate the intelligence of an audience. Aside from the issue of effectiveness (advertisers and politicians show us that many times these appeals *can* be effective), there is the question of ethics. See **21**.

Exercise 1. Which needs are appealed to in each of these examples?

1. Following the dress-for-success formula has helped countless people advance in their careers.
2. Every home should have an electronic alarm system.
3. Meditation will enhance your understanding of the universe.
4. Some of the marijuana available on the street is laced with deadly chemicals.
5. This shampoo makes your hair more touchable.

Exercise 2. Identify at least three appeals to needs in each speech in the **Appendix.**

Exercise 3. Of the eighteen values in the Great American Values Test, which three or four would you designate as your core values?

Which do you think are most salient in the value system of the United States today?

Which values do you see as undergoing the greatest change in the past few years?

Exercise 4. Return to the items in Exercise 1. Rewrite each statement on the same general topic so that it relates to at least two of the values listed in **18c(1)**.

Exercise 5. Analyze an audience you speak to regularly (speech class, professional association, study group) in terms of their probable responses to a speech on the problems of mental illness.

What needs could you appeal to?
What core values could you appeal to?
What authority values could you appeal to?
What new value-issue links could you forge?

Chapter 19

Informative Strategies

For informative speaking, plan a strategy based on an understanding of information processing. Use clear explanations to aid your audience's comprehension.

A large part of speaking is merely explanation—stating an idea and then restating it in a way that develops or expands upon the basic notion. Unfortunately, some explanations do more to confuse than to clarify, usually when the speaker has lost sight of which of the many details of a complex process or idea are the essential ones. It is a real challenge to select the most significant details and present them in the clearest order. How can you most economically create the mental picture that will aid your listeners' understanding?

According to an old saying, *those who can, do; those who can't, teach.* This seems to imply that it is much easier to teach another to do something than to do it yourself. In fact we find the opposite is often true. People can perform a task very competently, but cannot describe to another what they have done. (Frankly, we find it much easier to give effective speeches than to write this book explaining the process.) However, a knowledge of the way people learn can make teaching both easier and more effective.

19a. Base your speech on an understanding of how people acquire, process, and retain information.

(1) Avoid information overload.

When you speak on a topic that you know a great deal about, there is a tendency to want to bring your audience up to your level immediately. When you give out too much information in too short a time, the result is information overload. The consequences of this condition—usually in this order—are anxiety, confusion, irritability, anger at the source, and finally, just tuning out. Do not engulf listeners with a tidal wave of facts or bury them under an avalanche of data. The job of the informative speaker is to manage a large mass of information and to deliver it to the receivers at the right pace and in the right-sized chunks to be useful and meaningful. This means being selective. Your audience does not necessarily know what is important and what is not. You are the expert, and you must pick out the important points for them. Bear in mind the information-processing principle known as *seven plus or minus two*. Research suggests that this is how many points the average person can comprehend at one time, so select just a handful of points to develop.

(2) Give listeners a framework for organizing the information.

Have you ever tried to put together a jigsaw puzzle without looking at the picture on the box? What you have is a jumble of unrelated pieces. Once you see the big picture you have some idea of how things are supposed to fit together. This is the same principle that makes you want to look at a map before starting off on a trip or to skim the table of contents before diving into a complicated text. Do not plunge directly into a part of the topic before giving your audience some sense of the whole.

(3) Move from the simple to the complex.

Even at the risk of temporary oversimplification, it is advisable first to lay out the most basic concepts and later to introduce qualifiers, exceptions, and interesting tangents. Think of each listener as the newcomer to town who would first want to learn the basic route from home to work, and only after mastering that would want to learn about shortcuts and scenic detours.

(4) Move from the familiar to the unfamiliar.

Any group can learn about any subject if you start where they are and move along at the proper rate. Teachers will attest that learning proceeds best when they are able to adjust the focus of their instruction to a point just beyond the knowledge level of the group. If the instruction duplicates what the group already knows, the material will not be challenging. If the focus is two or three levels beyond them, the members of the group will get discouraged.

This fourth principle, even more than the others, ties directly to audience analysis. A creative speaker will be able to think of examples and analogies that tie directly to the experience of a particular group. Hearing references to familiar topics builds their confidence that they can understand the new material.

19b. Adhere to these principles of clear explanation.

(1) Use organizers.

Provide your listeners with cues as to how they should structure the information.

Signposts

> First, I'll show you how to make a simple white sauce, and then move on to three more elaborate sauces that start with the basic recipe.

> So, from this short description of one novel and three of her poems, you can see once again the two themes that permeate Sylvia Plath's work.

Enumeration

> The many steps in building an apartment complex can be grouped into these three phases:

> > One: Finding attractive sites with the proper zoning.
> > Two: Negotiating for the purchase of a piece of property.
> > Three: Contracting with architects and builders.

Acronyms

When you want to show empathy through nonverbal cues, remember to SOFTEN your listening style:

Smile
Open posture
Facial expression
Touch
Eye contact
Nodding

Slogans, catchwords, and memorable phrases

So, look at those files in your drawer that you haven't used in a year, and assess their real value. Keep in mind Peg Bracken's advice about leftover food: "When in doubt, throw it out."

Try to do something decisive with each piece of mail as you open it. Apply the "Four D's": Drop the item, Delay the item, Delegate the item, or Do the item.

(2) Use emphasis cues.

Underline and highlight key points with phrases like "this is very important," "if you don't remember anything else . . ." and "here's what it all comes down to . . .".

You can also emphasize points by vocal or physical cues. When you want an idea to stand out, speak much louder, or occasionally much softer. Pause before and after the big idea. Step forward. Let your facial expression forecast the seriousness of a point.

(3) Use examples liberally.

When an audience is feeling confused, nothing reassures them like the appearance of a concrete example.

Begin with a simple, even whimsical, example—

A "win-win" negotiation has occurred when both parties achieve their important goals without perceiving that they have had to make a major sacrifice.

Phil and Dave are roommates, and they both think the other needs to do more around the apartment. After talking about it, they agreed that Dave would do all the cooking and Phil would do all the cleaning. Each thinks he got off easy.

—move to a more complex and realistic example—

Or suppose that you have a used car for sale and your neighbor wants to buy it but does not have all the cash now. You offer to carry an interest-free note due in six months if your neighbor will take care of your pets and plants for three weeks while you are on vacation. You are happy because you will receive the asking price for your car and not have to worry about arranging for a housesitter. Your neighbor is happy because she can have the car now and does not have to pay finance charges on a loan.

—and finally to an example sophisticated, subtle, and complex enough for your audience to transfer to situations they may actually encounter:

Now, let's see how these principles apply to a typical real estate negotiation. On this chart you will see the seller's prioritized needs and bargaining chips listed in Column 1 and the buyer's prioritized needs and bargaining chips in Column 2. Let's start with the original offer that was made . . .

Sometimes one example can be extended and elaborated on throughout an entire presentation to provide unity.

(4) Use analogies.

Continually compare the known to the unknown.

Start with a simple analogy—

A nuclear power plant is like a steam locomotive. The fireman shovels coal into the furnace, where the heat it gives off turns the water in the boiler into steam. The steam travels through pipes to pistons, where the energy is converted and carried by driving rods to the wheels, pulling long trains of cars down the rails. Substitute a nuclear pile for the coal, a turbine for the pistons, and an electrical generator for the drive wheels, and you have a nuclear power plant.

—then clarify the points of dissimilarity:

> Of course, where in the locomotive you'd see a grimy engineer squinting at a pressure gauge with a pop-off valve, in the plant you'd see a large number of scientists and operators presiding over banks of sensors, controls, and computers, each with triple-redundancy safety telltales. The biggest difference, as we know, is that a lump of plutonium contains 240 million times the potential heat energy of a similarly sized lump of coal.

To reinforce points and reach more listeners, draw analogies from many areas: sports, movies, nature, history, other cultures.

(5) Use multiple channels and modes.

The message will be clearer if you send it through several channels. As you describe a process with words, also use your hands, a visual aid, a chart, a recording. Appeal to as many senses as possible to reinforce the message. A good rule to follow: If a point is very important or very difficult, always use one other channel besides the spoken word to get it across.

(6) Use repetition and redundancy.

People learn and remember what they hear repeatedly. If a principle is important, say it over again, in the same words or different words. Repeat it. Paraphrase it. Reinforce it. Tie back to it. Then mention it again.

Exercise 1. How many analogies and metaphors are used in this chapter? Do they help clarify?

Exercise 2. How might you link the familiar and the unfamiliar when speaking to:

a motorcycle club about nutrition?
a group of engineering students about writing a résumé?
elementary school students about endangered species?

Chapter 20

Persuasive Strategies

Plan a strategy based on sound logical analysis and an understanding of audience attitudes. Select and arrange your content for maximum persuasive impact.

What gives one person the right to try to change the attitudes or behavior of someone else? Some would say that you earn the right by having a noble end in mind. But what aspiring persuader would claim any other kind of goal? We maintain that *inquiry* is a prerequisite to *advocacy*. You earn a license to persuade by "doing your homework," researching the topic fully, thinking about it deeply and analytically, examining the best evidence on both sides. Then and only then are you in a place to recommend your position to someone else. When you take on this challenge you will want to plan a unified persuasive effort according to some guiding principles. This requires an understanding of how and why people change their minds.

There are many theoretical frameworks for approaching persuasion, from Aristotle's *logos*, *pathos*, and *ethos*, through post–World War II models of social judgment theory and consistency theories, up to the contemporary cataloging of compliance-gaining strategies. An examination of these theories is out of place in a practical handbook, though we allude to several in the suggestions that follow.

Earlier, in the chapter on reasoning, we talked about the benefits of exposing your reasoning steps to your listeners, of showing how your data and your claims are linked. As it turns out, in the area of persuasion this is not only the ethical road to take, it is also the practical one, as studies have shown that when a person's attitude is the result of processing issue-relevant arguments it is more predictive of his or her actual *behavior*, it tends to last longer, and to be more resistant to counterpersuasion.[1] What this boils down to is that it is less useful to say, "do this [adopt/continue/avoid/stop] because Eddie Expert says it's the right thing to do and because everyone is doing it," and that it is more useful to say, "do this because my reasoned presentation of the relevant arguments shows that it is the right thing to do." So, if you have earned the right to be persuasive, through careful analysis, and you've invested the effort to construct and deliver a persuasive message, why not do it right? Stress the argument and its merits. True, it is usually easier to plant a weak suggestion at the periphery of the listeners' awareness and hope it has influence without being scrutinized. But the well-developed and well-supported position will usually work better and last longer.

20a. Clarify the goals of your persuasion.

A strong grasp of purpose is especially important in persuasive speaking. When you try to change people, not just educate or inspire them, you are more likely to run into resistance. It helps to know exactly what your goals are—and what they are not. You want to aim for a realistic target.

Some authorities distinguish between persuasive speeches that seek to change actual behavior and those that try simply to influence beliefs and attitudes. Although an attitude is a predisposition to respond in a particular way, holding a certain attitude does not guarantee certain behaviors associated with the attitude. People may say they believe in recycling, but never get up the energy to separate their trash. Generally, if you want action, you should set your goals in terms of action and tell the audience what to *do*, not what to think. An exception is a case where you will be speaking to an unfavorable audience (see **20c**). Here it is better to set a realistic goal of obtaining agreement with your views; you risk losing the audience if you ask for too much too soon. In any persuasive speech,

---

[1]Richard E. Petty and John T. Cacioppo, *Communication and Persuasion: Central and Peripheral Routes to Attitude Change* (New York: Springer Verlag, 1986), 5.

then, ask yourself if you are *primarily* trying to change people's minds or *primarily* trying to change their actions.

It is also important in setting goals to think carefully about the nature and direction of the impact you seek. There is a tendency to characterize persuasion as "getting people to start doing something": buy a product, vote for a candidate. This persuasive goal, known as *adoption,* is only one of four. You might also persuade a person to stop doing something *(discontinuance)*; to keep doing something *(continuance)*; or not to start doing something *(deterrence)*.[2]

On the general topic of physical fitness you could choose one of a number of persuasive tacks for your speech, such as persuading your audience to:

> *adopt* an exercise program
> *continue* eating healthful foods
> *stop* eating junk foods
> *avoid* taking up cigarette smoking.

To be purely technical, then, persuasion is not always geared toward change. The advocates of continuance or deterrence want "change" from what they fear is about to happen. These two persuasive goals make sense only if there is some jeopardy or pressure in the opposite direction. Exhorting an audience to *continue* breathing would not require much in the way of persuasion. The football coach asking the booster club to *continue* supporting the team knows that his audience has other demands on their time and money. If a speech admonished the audience to "avoid the instant gratification syndrome of credit cards," it would be relevant only in a Western culture, where there is great pressure in the opposite direction.

20b. Base your persuasive efforts on sound analysis.

Inquiry precedes advocacy for both ethical and practical reasons. Before you can get into designing a persuasive message that will achieve your goal, you need to spend time analyzing, or breaking down, the logical obligations you have taken on. In **3d** this process was described as finding within your thesis sentence the list of questions that absolutely must

---

[2]Wallace C. Fotheringham, *Perspectives on Persuasion* (Boston: Allyn & Bacon, 1966), 32.

be answered. In **14a,** the process was discussed in terms of the kind of reasoning needed to provide a link between the evidence you have and the major claim(s) of your speech. Here we pursue the analysis process more specifically from the direction of understanding the type of proposition you support and identifying the points at issue as you set out to prove your case.

(1) Identify whether your persuasive goal requires you to establish a proposition of fact, of value, or of policy.

The thesis of a speech and the claim of an argument are also described as propositions—in persuasion the speaker *proposes* something to the audience. There are three kinds of propositions: the proposition of fact, the proposition of value, and the proposition of policy. Discovering which kind of proposition lies at the heart of your speech is essential to discovering your obligations and planning your persuasive strategy.

1. Proposition of fact

It may seem that if something is a *fact* there is no need to use persuasion to establish it, but there are issues in the factual domain that cannot be verified directly. There either is or is not life on other planets. The question is one of fact, but, because we lack the means to find out, we must argue from the data we have, drawing the most logical inferences therefrom. For example:

> Lee Harvey Oswald did not act alone in the assassination of John F. Kennedy.
> More than two cups of coffee a day increases the chance of cancer of the pancreas.
> Converting to solar energy can save the average homeowner money.

2. Proposition of value

Persuasive speakers are often attempting to prove evaluative positions. Their goal is to judge the worth of something, to establish that it is good or bad, wise or foolish, just or unjust, ethical or unethical, beautiful or ugly, competent or incompetent. For example:

> It is wrong to try to avoid jury duty.
> The free enterprise system is the best economic model for the working class.
> Charlie Parker was the greatest sax player ever.

3. Proposition of policy

Most common and most complex among persuasive theses is the proposition of policy, which advocates a specific course of action. Here are some propositions of policy:

> The federal government should legalize marijuana for private use.
> You should vote for Dan Huboi for union president.
> You should send your children to private schools.

When you undertake to prove a thesis sentence that is a proposition of policy, you must be very specific about what plan or program should be adopted by what specifically empowered group or agency. Otherwise, although your thesis includes the word *should/should not*, it is really a disguised proposition of value. Tax loopholes should be closed, for example, is only another way of saying: The present tax system is bad. To be a proposition of policy it must read: Congress should change the present tax structure to reduce oil depletion allowances, vacation home deductions, and home office deductions.

The thesis of a speech is a claim that is supported in turn by subclaims. See **14a**. By the same token, notice that the types of propositions are cumulative: The proposition of value assumes certain propositions of fact, and the proposition of policy takes its direction from a proposition of value. Or, proving that something *should/should not* be done depends on proving that something is *good/bad*, which in turn requires establishing that something else *is/is not* the case. For instance, to establish the proposition of policy:

> Our local government should/should not commence the aerial spraying of Malathion to eradicate the Mediterranean fruit fly,

one has to prove at least this proposition of value:

> It is appropriate/inappropriate to risk some danger to human health in order to protect an important agricultural product.

To accept this proposition of value, three propositions of fact need to be established:

> The effect of Malathion on human health is/is not minimal or nonexistent.
> Malathion is/is not effective in controlling the Mediterranean fruit fly.
> The fruit attacked by the fly is/is not important to the agricultural economy of the area.

Propositions of fact: IS/IS NOT
Propositions of value: GOOD/BAD
Propositions of policy: SHOULD/SHOULD NOT

Exercise 1. Identify which of the following are propositions of fact, value, or policy.

The cost of maintaining NASA's space station will be astronomical.
Music on MTV is simplistic and tasteless.
Cats make better pets than dogs.
Children should learn a foreign language before fifth grade.

Exercise 2. Write a proposition of fact, value, and policy on each of these general topics:

Atheism
Nutrition
Women in the military

(2) Use stock issues, when possible, to help you analyze your topic.

Drawing on preestablished, "stock" issues can save you time and effort in preparing a speech. For the standard argumentative problem-solving approach, there is no need to reinvent the wheel. Central to understanding stock issue analysis is the concept of burden of proof drawn from the legal system and from formal debate. The individual or side that advocates change has specific responsibilities. For an extreme example, consider all the burdens on the British prosecutor in a murder case. In British law, *murder* is defined as:

<u>the unlawful killing</u> <u>of a reasonable creature</u>
       1   2
<u>who is in being</u> and <u>under the Queen's peace</u>
    3   4
<u>with malice aforethought, express or implied,</u>
          5
<u>the death following within a year and a day.</u>[3]
       6

---

[3]F. T. Giles, *The Criminal Law: A Short Introduction* (Harmondsworth, Middlesex: Penguin Books, 1967), 197.

We have underlined and numbered each of the six issues a prosecutor must prove. To lose even one issue is to lose the case. If the defense can show that any *one* of the conditions was not present—for instance: that there was no malice aforethought, *or* that the killing was not unlawful (as in self-defense), *or* that the victim survived a year and two days after the alleged act—then murder has not occurred. The burdens on the prosecutor are great, but they are publicly acknowledged and agreed to. Some kinds of speeches have such well-defined lists of requirements, or stock issues, that guide the speaker. Propositions of policy lend themselves to formal argumentative analysis, and here referring to a list of stock issues is very helpful.

Stock debate issues

In a formal debate on a proposition of policy, the speaker advocating a change is required to provide the audience with satisfactory answers to *all* the following questions:

Is there a compelling need for change?
Is that need inherent in the very structure of the present system?
Will the proposed solution meet the need presented?
Is the proposed solution workable and practical?
Do the advantages of the proposed solution outweigh its disadvantages?

You do not have to be a debater to use these stock issues—they serve as helpful guidelines in analyzing any persuasive topic.

Stock issues against a change

The examples in the previous paragraph apply to persuasive speeches where the primary objective is adoption. In a speech that argues against a policy—where deterrence or discontinuance is the goal—this list of stock issues can be turned around. Because burden of proof lies with the advocates of change, an opponent of change can succeed by establishing a negative answer to just one key issue.

Exercise 3. Which stock debate issue is being addressed in each of the following points?

1. Putting more money into the welfare program will not get at its underlying problems.

2. Adopting a voucher system for the financing of education will allow parents to choose the educational approach that is best for their children.
3. Violent crime has gotten out of control in our cities.

20c. Adjust your speech content in light of your audience's attitude toward your topic and you.

Section **4d** asks you to analyze your listeners' possible reactions to the thesis of your presentation. Based on surveys, observations, or inference, you can make some discrimination of their predisposition toward your topic. The following continuum classifies audiences according to that predisposition:

Types of Audiences

Unfavorable			Neutral	Favorable		
Strongly	Moderately	Slightly	Neither agree	Slightly	Moderately	Strongly
disagree	disagree	disagree	nor disagree	agree	agree	agree

Here are some suggestions on how to deal with such favorable, neutral, or unfavorable audiences.

(1) Favorable audience

A speaker facing a favorable audience is relieved of a number of burdens. In this situation as a speaker, you will rarely need to establish credibility: Your listeners, perceiving your position as identical to theirs, approve of you and your good taste already. Furthermore, you will find that a favorable audience will not be raising internal counterarguments for you to deflect or defuse.

Being relieved of a few burdens, however, does not release you from all responsibility as an effective champion of your position. A poorly prepared speech can actually erode audience support. On the other hand, if you realize and accept the challenge of speaking to a favorable audience, you can solidify or strengthen their attitudes, or cause them to move from theoretical agreement to positive action.

Make use of emotional appeals to intensify your listeners' support. The difference between intellectual agreement and commitment to some purpose, and the difference between commitment and action are usually a function of emotional arousal. Out of the vast number of positions you would say you agree with, there is a much shorter list of issues that you really *care* about. This list contains topics that appeal to your most basic needs, touch on your core values, or have a personal effect on your life.

To get your speech on your listeners' list, make extensive use of appeals to basic values such as patriotism, humanitarianism, and progress; appeals to basic needs such as survival, security, and status; and appeals to basic emotions such as fear, pity, and love.

Here is one example of how a position can be intensified (see Table 20-1). Look also at the examples in the appropriate sections of **18**.

When an audience agrees with you but is not taking action, they probably do not feel personally involved with the subject. A major task in speaking to a favorable audience is the creation of that personal involvement in two ways: First, be very specific about how their lives are affected; second, show them that their actions can make a difference.

Your ten dollar check can feed a Sudanese refugee family for a week.

If you can take that extra second to switch off the lights as you leave the room, you can save yourself fifty dollars a year.

For most audiences emotional appeals should be handled sparingly and cautiously, but for the favorable audience you can hardly be too vivid or personalized as long as you avoid bad taste and redundancy.

TABLE 20-1	Appeal to Basic Values
Logical Stem	Emotional Intensifier
It is only fair to allow groups with which we disagree to exercise their legal constitutional rights.	Where will it stop if we allow *selective* enforcement of the protection provided by the Bill of Rights? Today the flag burners or skinheads may be denied their rights as Americans; tomorrow it may be any of *us*. (appeal to fear, appeal to core value of civil liberties)

Get your audience to make a public commitment.

Invite your listeners to offer suggestions, sign a petition, raise their hands to volunteer, lend their names to a letterhead, or talk to others. People who have made a public commitment, either oral, written, or physical, are less likely to change their minds.

Provide several specific alternatives for action.

The following audience reaction is not enough: "Yes, somebody really should do something about that situation. I should get involved myself one of these days." Make it easy for them to take action by offering several very specific choices. Do not say to people who have shown up at a rally for a candidate: "Stop by campaign headquarters sometime." Instead say: "I'd like everyone here either to walk a precinct or to spend an evening making phone calls. Sign-up sheets are being passed around now. If you can't help out in either of these ways, Judy will be standing at the door and can tell you about other things that need to be done to ensure our success." With a favorable audience do not settle for urging them to do "something." Tell them what you want them to do, and make the execution easy and attractive: If you want them to write letters, give them addresses; if you want them to reduce their sodium intake, give them low-sodium recipes.

Present your arguments in abbreviated form so that audience members actively participate in the reasoning process.

Being free to use more motivational appeals with a favorable audience does not exempt you from building a strong argument with solid support. However, it does allow you to cast it in a special form. Because a favorable audience often shares your values and beliefs, it is not always necessary to spell out every step of your reasoning. In fact, classical rhetorical theory suggests that compact lines of argument (called *enthymemes*) are very powerful. When the audience members fill in part of the reasoning that you have not spelled out, be it major premise, minor premise, or conclusion, they are *actively* participating in making meaning with you. Just as members of a group feel bonded when they use special jargon or initials or shorthand lines of speech, favorable audience members will establish an "in-group" feeling of commitment when a speaker takes some things for granted.

> If we elect this candidate it will be like returning to the Carter years. (taking for granted that listeners agree that the Carter years were bad)

> We must support this bond issue, for if it fails, there will be no raises for teachers for five years. (assuming the audience agrees that raises for teachers are desirable)

To use these brief enthymematic arguments that create audience involvement, you must be sure that your listeners really do share your beliefs. Otherwise, the shortcut can backfire.

Prepare your audience to carry your message to others.

You can tap the potential of audience members as persuaders in their own right. Each of them may later discuss your topic with coworkers, neighbors, or friends who are neutral or hostile toward it. Give the less-facile listeners ammunition for these interactions, and make that material as memorable and quotable as possible. When, in front of a favorable group, you offer examples, arguments, and statistics that support your position, your goal is not the persuading of your immediate audience. Rather, you are aiming at the second generation of listeners. This second audience is a reason to consider not relying only on the compact argument of the enthymeme.

A part of this preparation is providing your audience with ready answers to refute standard counterarguments. See **20f.** This also serves to inoculate your listeners against the persuasiveness of those counterarguments.

> You may meet people who tell you that the administration's economic policy is designed to help the average worker. Just ask those people why the greatest tax relief goes to the rich. Have them explain to you why a person who earns $300,000 a year will have a 50 percent reduction in taxes, but a person making $18,000 a year will see a reduction of only 6 percent. They may say, "Ah, but we are creating new jobs." Ask them this . . .

(2) Neutral audience

An audience could be neutral toward your position for one of three reasons: They are *uninterested,* they are *uninformed,* or they are genuinely *undecided.*

Stress attention factors with an uninterested neutral audience.

An audience is uninterested in a topic or position because they do not see how it affects them directly. With this sort of audience draw on all the attention factors described in **16,** but give special emphasis to the *vital.*

Their interest and attention can be gained only through concrete illustrations of the impact of your subject on their lives.

> A lot of you are probably saying "So what? So what if somebody across the room lights up a cigarette? It's a free country, and *he's* inhaling the smoke, not me." Would you say "So what?" if I told you "secondhand" smoke can blacken your lungs just as badly as if you smoked two to twenty-seven cigarettes a day?

Be sure the facts and statistics you use are relevant to your listeners' experience. Sprinkle your speech with humor and human interest. Make a special effort to have a lively and animated delivery and style to stimulate them.

With an uninformed neutral audience, emphasize material that clarifies and illuminates your position.

Before you can expect people to agree with you, they must have some comprehension of the topic. When they lack that essential background, you must spend a significant portion of your speech filling them in, even if it means sacrificing time you would have spent making points to support your position.

The main concern is clarity: Use explanation, definitions, examples, restatement. See **19**. Visual aids can be helpful. Keep your language simple and your organization straightforward.

A direct persuasive appeal should be saved until the very end of the speech.

For an undecided neutral audience, establish your credibility by presenting new arguments that blend logical and emotional appeals.

The undecided neutral audience is both interested in and informed about your topic, but they find the arguments for each side equally compelling. Let them know that you understand their ambivalence. Grant the complexity of the issue and admit that there is truth on both sides.

Most audiences are uncomfortable with such uncertainty and seek to be rid of it. They would like to make a decision and are looking for a legitimate basis for one. Offer yourself as the vehicle for reducing their discomfort. Establish your credibility by communicating expertise and integrity. As you present the arguments for your side, stress any recent evidence or new interpretations that could justify a decision. By definition, this audience finds sense in some aspects of the opposing arguments. You must not ignore this fact. Acknowledge and respond to the major arguments against your position, using the techniques in **20f**. Similarly, you need to inoculate your audience against arguments they may encounter later. When unanticipated, these arguments may tip the scales back to the balance point of indecision, or worse. When anticipated, these arguments can be dismissed by your listeners as having been dealt with already.

In short, a well-documented, logical presentation works best for the undecided neutral audience. Appeals to emotions, needs, and values can be effective only if used sparingly and if clearly interwoven with the logical argument of the speech.

(3) Unfavorable audience

Murphy's Law: Anything that can go wrong, will. A corollary of this law, especially true for speakers with an unfavorable audience, is: Anything that *can* be interpreted wrong, *will* be interpreted wrong.

An unfavorable audience is by no means a belligerent one—remember that unfavorable is defined to encompass anything on the *disagree* side of neutral, starting with *slightly disagree*. However, the more intensely the audience disagrees with you, the more they will be predisposed to reject both you and your message. Any idiosyncrasies of appearance and style of delivery will allow them to dismiss you as the lunatic fringe. One joke that falls flat labels you a buffoon. Express yourself with conviction and you will be branded a fanatic.

At the same time, your audience realizes the disadvantage you are working under. If you are able to handle the situation with grace and aplomb, you can earn their grudging respect. The results can be gratifying when you approach the speech to an unfavorable audience as a challenge to your skill.

Set realistic goals for a single speech.

Do not try to do too much with an unfavorable audience. Attitude change takes place slowly. If most of your audience falls at the *strongly disagree* end of the continuum, do not expect your ten-minute speech to change them to strong agreement. Sometimes the measure of success is that they threw eggs and not bricks. Even if it means modifying your thesis sentence, set a goal that you have a reasonable chance of achieving, such as easing the *strongly disagree* over to *moderately disagree,* or *moderately disagree* over to *neutral.* Trying to do too much can alienate your audience and lead to a boomerang effect where the attitude change that occurs is in the opposite direction of that which you were seeking. Do not make an express call for action when such action is highly unlikely. It would be self-defeating to ask a pro-choice group to contribute money to the campaign coffers of a right-to-life candidate. Better to ask them to think about the issues you have raised, or to ask them to work together to find a compromise.

Stress common ground.

However great the difference between you and your audience on any particular issue, there are bound to be many places where your opinions and experiences overlap. When you think about the unfavorable audience you face, ask yourself what goals and values you share. Even the intensity of the disagreement between you and your audience over school busing reveals a common concern for your children's education. Or, if your opponents think unemployment can best be combated through government programs and you feel that private enterprise can deal with the problem successfully, it is still true that both agree that unemployment is "bad."

Common ground is important to every speech, but certainly crucial to the speech to the unfavorable audience. Stress it in your introduction and at several points throughout the speech. When you minimize the differences between you and your audience, you create the basis for communication to occur.

Base your speech on sound logic and extensive evidence.

The unfavorable audience is skeptical of your position and will reject most emotional appeals as manipulative. Your only chance to persuade them is to build an irresistible case supported by impeccable, unbiased evidence. With this audience you must clearly indicate every step of your reasoning—nothing can be taken for granted. Discuss and defend even those assumptions that seem obvious to you. Spell out the logical links and connections that hold your argument together. Do not overstate your points; be careful not to claim more than the data allow. Say: "These examples suggest" rather than "These examples prove"; "Smoking contributes to cancer" rather than "Smoking causes cancer."

Use factual and statistical evidence and always cite your sources completely. If you mention the results of a survey, for example, tell when, where, and how it was conducted, and where it was presented or published. When supporting your points with testimony, quote reluctant experts if possible or highly respected unaffiliated authorities. Quotations from your own partisans are hardly worth giving. See **14d**.

Confront directly the arguments that are foremost in your listeners' minds. Do not be afraid to concede minor points that do not damage your basic case. State the remaining counterarguments fairly and answer them forcefully, but never stoop to ridicule. In fact, it has been shown to be advantageous to state your opponents' view *even more elegantly than they have,* before proceeding to refute it.

Pay particular attention to establishing a credible image.

Nowhere is the careful establishment of good character, good sense, and goodwill more important than in a speech to an unfavorable audience. See **17b**. Plan every detail of your speech content and delivery to project an image of a calm, reasonable, fair, well-informed, and congenial person. The judicious use of humor can aid this image while releasing tension and putting the issue in perspective. Direct the humor at yourself, your position, a common enemy, or the ironic aspects of the confrontation. Never direct it at your audience and their beliefs.

Although you do not want to seem combative, do remain firm in your position. It is fine to build rapport by stressing common ground and granting minor points, but do not waffle or be overly conciliatory.

Resist the temptation to be snide, shrill, defensive, paranoid, outraged, arrogant, sarcastic, facetious, or patronizing.

Do not become frustrated by heckling or other indications that you are not getting through to them. See **27c**. Remember that attitude change is a slow process and that by maintaining your dignity and rationality you will not hurt and may help your cause in the long run.

Exercise 4. Examine the persuasive speech in the **Appendix.** Do you think the speaker perceived the audience as unfavorable, neutral, or favorable? What strategic decisions reflected in the speech content justify your conclusion? Name two specific adjustments the speaker should make if presenting this speech to each of the other possible types of audiences.

20d. Organize your points for optimal persuasive impact.

The speech organization patterns discussed in Chapter **8**—topical, spatial, and chronological—grow out of analysis of the speech content.

Other patterns can form from retracing the reasoning that led you to your conclusion—inductively, deductively, causally, or analogically (Chapter 14). Yet another way to think about ordering points is to consider how your speech unfolds for your listeners. So, if none of the familiar formats seems strategically adequate, here are some suggestions for alternative arrangements.

(1) Use the motivated sequence to engage your audience.

Developed by Alan Monroe several decades ago, the motivated sequence is one of the most widely used organizers for persuasive speeches.[4] This psychologically based format echoes and anticipates the mental stages through which your listeners progress as they hear your speech. Note that it includes the speech introduction and conclusion, unlike the sample outlines in the ORGANIZATION chapters.

Attention	The speaker must first motivate the audience to listen to the speech.
Need	Auditors must become aware of a compelling, personalized problem.
Satisfaction	The course of action advocated must be shown to alleviate the problem.
Visualization	Psychologically, it is important that the audience have a vivid picture of the benefits of agreeing with the speaker, or the evils of alternatives.
Action	The speech should end with an overt call for the listeners to act.

Here is an example of a speech that follows the motivated sequence:

Thesis: We need a light rail system in our country to reduce excessive commuter traffic congestion.

ATTENTION

Introduction

I was on my way to work, having left home earlier than usual so I could be there in plenty of time for my first important presentation. I heard

---

[4]Bruce E. Gronbeck, Raymie McKerrow, Douglas Ehninger, and Alan H. Monroe, *Principles and Types of Speech,* 11th ed. (Glenview, IL: Scott, Foresman/Brown Little, 1990).

screeching brakes. It turned out to be only a fender-bender a quarter mile ahead of me. Nevertheless, I sat in my car, and sat, and sat, while my mood progressed from irritation to outrage to despair. There was no way even to reach a phone. I arrived at work an hour and a half late, just as the meeting was breaking up.

NEED

I. Excessive reliance on automobile transportation to the county's major employment areas is causing severe problems.
   A. Major traffic jams
   B. Pollution
   C. Stress to commuters

SATISFACTION

ll. A light rail system should be constructed to alleviate these problems.
   A. (Definition of light rail)
   B. (Proposed route)
   C. (Proposed funding)

VISUALIZATION

III. The new system would be a vast improvement.
   A. (Scenario with the light rail system)
   B. (Scenario without the light rail system)

ACTION

Conclusion

Support the county initiative for a light rail system. Urge your friends to vote for it. Write to members of the county board of supervisors on this issue. Ask your employer to commit to providing free shuttle service from the proposed light rail station to your place of business.

This organization is rather similar to a standard problem solution speech, but the presence of the visualization step makes all the difference. Instead of providing just a logical need satisfaction in Main Point 2, this speaker has added another psychologically powerful step in Main Point 3. Two detailed narratives drive home the case for the listeners. The actual wording of the speech might go something like this:

If this proposal is adopted, picture yourself parking at a spacious parking lot, dropping your child off at the child-care facility right at the light rail station and settling back in your comfortable seat. You can enjoy a cup of coffee, read the paper, review materials for your first business meeting, and arrive at work relaxed.

But, if this proposal is not adopted, picture your commute lasting longer and longer until you are spending nearly one working day a week driving to and from work. The smallest incident will cause gridlock. The pollution will become worse. Your stress-related health problems, such as high blood pressure and headaches, will increase.

It is essential that the attention step be engaging and that the action step be concrete. This does not preclude using the other parts of introductions and conclusions discussed in **11** and **12** if they enhance clarity.

(2) Compare the advantages of two alternative proposals as a way of organizing your speech.

Sometimes your persuasive task boils down to convincing an audience to choose between two alternatives. It may be that the need to do something is acknowledged, or that the choice is "go/no go." In any event, your job is to show the comparative advantage of one choice over the other, which pretty much dictates that you organize your speech around a sequence of head-to-head comparisons of the components of each proposal. You might have to compare energy policy based on conservation to energy policy based on expanding access to fossil fuel; or compare cost benefits for the long term and the short term. You are not compelled to say one is perfect and the other awful. Rather, you strive to tip the scale toward your position. That is why a recurrent and highly effective phrase in comparative advantage persuasive arguments is "on balance."

20e. As a general rule, place your strongest points first or last.

Ideally, all of the arguments and support for your thesis statement should be strong. In reality you will find you must use materials of varying strength. These should not be arranged randomly. Be aware that people will remember what you say first (the primacy principle) and what you say last (the recency principle). In light of this, it is logical that arranging your arguments either from weakest to strongest (climax) or from strongest to weakest (anticlimax) would be more effective than placing your best points in the middle (pyramidal).

The research on which one is stronger, primacy or recency, is far from conclusive. Our best advice in deciding what to say first and last is that you should consider the importance of your topic to your audience, their attitude toward it, and your credibility. Also, remember that previews and summaries are essential in developing any complex line of argument. If you use these, your listeners will hear *all* your most significant points both first and last.

Exercise 5. Which of the speeches in the **Appendix** follow a climax order? An anticlimax order? Can you justify choices made by each speaker in terms of primacy or recency?

20f. In addition to presenting your own viewpoints in a persuasive speech, you may often find it advisable to deal with opposing arguments.

When time is limited, it is hard to decide whether to present just your own side of an issue or to bring up opposing arguments and answer them. In the first instance you run the risk of appearing to have a weak position. In the second instance you take time away from developing your own arguments and there is always the chance that you might introduce a point against your case that would not have occurred to your audience otherwise.

Generally, it is a good idea to address counterarguments. On widely debated topics, these ideas will already be on listeners' minds, and they expect a response. Even on less familiar subjects where you may have the first word, you probably won't have the last. At the end of a straightforward pro speech your audience may agree with you, but if a few hours or a few days later they become aware of powerful opposing arguments, they may discredit your entire position. Speakers often inoculate their audience by presenting a few counterarguments and answering them. Then, when these points are brought up later, the listener will say, "Oh, yes, I was warned about this." Inoculation has created "antibodies" to resist the opposing position.

(1) Address the opposing arguments directly, using refutation techniques.

If you choose to respond to a point, you may follow these steps of refutation:

1. State the opposing view fairly and concisely.
2. State your position on that argument.
3. Document and develop your own position.
4. Summarize the impact of your argument and show how the two positions compare.

Here is a distilled example:

1. Many people argue that flexible work schedules lead to reduced productivity.
2. I challenge the underlying assumption that most people work only for money and will do as little as possible. Employees who are treated like responsible partners take pride in their work and are dependable and productive.
3. There are several research studies that support my point of view: [Speaker introduces and explains the studies.]
4. So, these examples refute the position that flextime will lead to decreased productivity. I have shown you how that argument is based on a false assumption about why people work.

Effective refutation can take various forms. In a speech against capital punishment a speaker might follow the points supporting the thesis with this main point:

IV. Arguments in favor of capital punishment do not justify its continuation.
    A. It is argued that capital punishment deters crime: The facts do not support this.
    B. It is argued that it is very costly to provide life sentences for serious offenders: This is true, but expenditure of money is not a justification for collective murder.

C. It is argued that dangerous criminals are released on parole and endanger lives: This may be a problem, but we can respond with stricter parole policies rather than execution.

Note that counterarguments may be handled in different ways. Point A is denied directly. Point B is conceded but labeled unimportant. Point C is partly conceded, then analyzed in a different light. Responding to a counterargument does not mean utterly obliterating it. You may concede it, minimize it, dismiss it as irrelevant, attack the supporting evidence or underlying premise. Even if you grant the existence of a problem you can differ on the best solution.

(2) In most cases, answer counterarguments after developing your own position.

Pro-to-con order is almost always more effective than con-to-pro. The only exception to this rule applies to when you know the audience is so preoccupied with an opposing position that they may not listen to you. In that case, respond to the point immediately.

Exercise 6. Do any of the speeches in the **Appendix** address opposing viewpoints directly? Identify the paragraphs that serve this function. In terms of what you know about the audiences of all of the speakers, evaluate the decision of each speaker to answer or not to answer counterarguments.

Exercise 7. Select a position you believe in strongly. Consider one widely used argument against that position. Write out your refutation of that point exactly as you would present it in a speech, following the four steps in **20f(1)** and including evidence and support.

Chapter 21

Speaking Ethics

Commit yourself to a set of ethical principles that will guide you as a public speaker.

This handbook serves primarily to help you plan and present public speeches that are effective—that is, that allow you to achieve your goals in speaking. Every speech also has another dimension. Sometimes a speaker succeeds in getting a point across or persuading an audience, but does so in a manner that is manipulative, exploitative, dishonest or otherwise offensive. These cases raise questions about the ethical obligations of all speakers. Ethical questions are not about "what works?" but "what is right?"

Fortunately, most of the time effective speaking and ethical speaking go together. The speaker who plays games with statistics or quotes authorities out of context frequently commits fallacies of reasoning in the process. The heavy-handed use of emotional appeals often boomerangs. Credibility suffers when listeners perceive an overly ingratiating style of speaking as insincere. There are no guarantees though that audiences will always respond best to those speakers who take the moral high ground; history is replete with examples of speakers who used all sorts of questionable tactics and were rewarded with great success. Ultimately, the question transcends the simple yes/no choice of "can I get away with it?" and moves to the more complex realm of personal values, where each speaker has to decide what is ethically justifiable.

Your approach to the ethical choices involved in public speaking grows out of your more general philosophical and moral beliefs about such basic matters as how people treat one another and what counts as honesty.

In one sense ethical beliefs are so individual that they almost seem to be a matter of each person's private conscience. Yet our beliefs about right and wrong are highly influenced by other people. Professional groups such as doctors and lawyers have formalized codes of ethics. Other less formal codes of ethical conduct come to us through family, religion and culture.

21a. Be aware of the ethical implications of all human choices and the way these play out in public speaking.

Every action has an ethical dimension.

No decision that a speaker makes is morally neutral. We speak because we believe that what we say makes a difference. And it does. The results of a speech can be as serious as persuading others to follow a dangerous course of action or as apparently harmless as wasting their time with a scattered and unprepared message. Every time you speak you exercise power and take on some responsibility for the consequences of what you do or do not say.

Ethical decisions are rarely clear cut.

The answer to questions about what works in public speaking is often "it depends." Questions about what is the right or ethical course of action are just as complex. Ethics grow from our values, and values sometimes conflict with each other. Classic communication dilemmas in everyday life deal with choices about whether to be honest (and hurt someone's feelings) or tactful (and be not quite truthful). Rarely are there black or white choices. The best we can do most of the time is to select the lighter shade of gray. As communicators we are obligated to think hard about each case, and to develop our judgment through experience and reflection. As time goes by we should be more discerning about the nuances of a situation and more skilled in using language and nonverbal communication in sensitive and responsible ways.

Ethical decisions vary with context.
In a speech tournament, a debater might argue for legalized prostitution at 9:00 and argue against it at 10:30. In this context, it is understood that the rules of the game are to defend the assigned side of a topic as vigorously and skillfully as possible. This is considered no more unethical than the football team that defends the north goal in the first quarter and then just as vigorously defends the south goal in the second quarter. However, if a candidate gets caught taking one position when speaking to voters in Oregon and the opposite in Kansas, we judge that to be very unethical. That is because, as critical listeners in the political arena, we view a public speech in those circumstances as not part of a game but as a sincere statement of the speaker's true beliefs.

What you can use as your own words varies also. A political leader is assumed to have speech writers draft many of the speeches he or she gives. This is considered ethical because the demands of a person in public life make it impossible to personally prepare each speech that must be given. However, in an academic speech class, it is well understood that each person is expected to create and deliver his or her own speech because the learning experience depends on receiving an assessment of skills. To use your friend as a ghostwriter is clearly plagiarism in that context. See **21d.**

21b. Respect the integrity of your own core values.

As a public speaker you are not just a transmitter of messages, you put yourself (your *self*) in contact with an audience. Though you may adapt and adjust and accommodate in order to meet your goals, you have an ethical obligation to be true to yourself. When you've finished a speech, regardless of how anyone else responds, you should always feel good about what you said and how you said it. Never be reluctant to speak from your heart and express your passion and conviction on a topic.

21c. Respect the integrity of your audience.

An important tenet of many ethical systems is the recognition of each human being as a unique individual with free will and autonomy. Within this value system, those who have power over others do not have the right to use people as means to their selfish ends. Public speakers have a special kind of power. When audience members entrust you with their time and attention, you take on an obligation to treat them with fairness and concern. You have every right to pursue your own reasons for speaking, but not at the expense of your listeners' welfare. An ethical speaker would not underestimate their intelligence or try to trick them into making decisions that endanger their health, safety, financial security, or other interests. At the end of each speech, an ethical speaker should feel confident that the listeners are better off than before. Whether or not they agree with the speaker's points, they have had a chance to consider ideas without coercion or manipulation so they can make rational decisions.

21d. Respect the integrity of ideas.

(1) Don't plagiarize.

Besides yourself and your audience, there are others, not present, to whom you have some ethical obligations. These are the people whose ideas and words you draw into the speech situation. Some individuals who would never steal another person's property seem to think it is somehow acceptable to steal a scholar's solution to a problem or to borrow a friend's outline for a speech. The ethics of public speaking generally proscribe using another's major ideas or exact words—including the close paraphrasing of them—without giving credit to the source. Plagiarism is a serious offense in academic institutions and in the world of publishing. Careers have been ruined when public leaders have been exposed as plagiarists.

To avoid even the appearance of unethical appropriation of speech content, form the habit of taking careful notes of the sources of your ideas, statistics, and evidence. And when you hear a wonderful anecdote, story, or turn of phrase you might like to quote someday, make a note right then so you will remember to give credit to the source. See **5e**.

(2) Don't lie.

Nothing that could be written here can stop the blatant lies of the pathological liar or the ill-intentioned person. For the majority of us, the questions surrounding honesty are much more subtle. Our courts require an oath to tell "the truth, the whole truth, and nothing but the truth." Rarely do we live up to that in everyday interactions, and even in court, testimony far short of that is not always deemed perjurious. Out of kindness, one may compliment a friend's new outfit although it may really not be very attractive. Acting on the best information available, a presidential candidate promises there will be "no new taxes." A nurse tells a child that the shot "will only sting a little bit." You exaggerate a funny story to better entertain your listeners. The phrase "it depends" always enters conversations about what counts as a lie, a white lie, a fib, a prevarication, or tactful phrasing.

In public speaking, we think that most people would consider that at least the following categories of behavior cross the line between honest and dishonest speech.

Making statements that are completely counterfactual

I have no financial interest in this fitness center . . . I just care about your health. (When you receive a commission for every new member you sign up.)

I put my life on the line in the defense of this country. (When your military service consisted of clerical work in San Diego.)

Playing word games to create a false impression
Sometimes a speaker can use words with great precision of definition, being technically correct although totally misleading.

One thing I learned in my many years of study in Berkeley. (When those many years of study consisted of reading books in your living room, not coursework at the University of California at Berkeley.)

In response to allegations of illegal drug use, let me say that I have never broken the laws of this country. (When the drug use was in another country.)

Leaving out some part of "the whole truth" which if known would completely reverse the impact of the statement

There are no convicted child molesters on the professional staff of this day care center. (But one of the five professional staff has been formally charged, and one of our nonprofessional staff has been convicted.)

None of the studies in the dozens I reviewed show that smoking causes lung cancer. (But many show it is strongly linked to it.)

(3) Don't oversimplify.

Another dimension of the integrity of ideas has to do with a faithfulness to the facts and realities of your subject matter. While it is hard to say that there is one "real truth" on any complex issue, it is not hard to say that some accounts are so shallow or oversimplified as to provide a basically false picture. Before you stand up to speak in public, thus contributing to and shaping the public discourse on a topic, you have an ethical obligation to do your homework, to look beneath the surface, to weigh evidence carefully, and to explore a variety of viewpoints.

21e. Understand that ethical decisions often involve weighing complex factors and competing goals.

As a speaker, you perform a delicate balancing act in many of the decisions you make. Be especially aware of the ethical impact of choices you make about language, emotional appeals, and persuasive strategies.

(1) Balance the value of using language in a lively and forceful manner against the risk of causing pain and offense.

We take issue with the old saying "Sticks and stones can break my bones, but words can never hurt me." No doubt it was born of bravado on some schoolyard where, as each of us can recall, incredible emotional wounds are inflicted through verbal abuse. When occupying a public platform, holding audience members hostage in one sense, speakers can cause similar pain by making some segment of the audience endure exposure to words they find demeaning, racist, sexist, or obscene. Some speakers do not use language to offend those present, but have routinely use violent and hateful expressions to make their points stronger. Language, especially in its cumulative effect, has the power to heal or to divide. In being respectful and responsible, a speaker does not have to rely on bland or wishy-washy terminology. The wonderful richness of vocabulary, metaphor, and style provide ways to be colorful, precise, and sensitive.

(2) Balance the importance of appealing to your audience at an emotional level against the risk of abusing emotional appeals.

For centuries the mainstream rhetorical tradition has been that the speaker's first responsibility is to present a logically sound, well-documented argument. If you agree with this ideal, then you will not be tempted to substitute pseudological emotional appeals for the logical foundation of your speech. Appeals to your listeners' feelings are legitimate ways to support and emphasize your points. We would not undertake to set a precise ratio of emotional appeals to logical analysis. Nor would we judge any speaker who became a bit carried away now and then when presenting a deeply held belief. It seems, however, that a heavy reliance on appeals to needs, emotions, or values is highly suspect under the following conditions:

1. When a need is created that the listener had not perceived before, *and* the awareness of the need causes considerable pain or discomfort, *and* the action required in response to that need directly benefits the speaker.
2. When extreme emotional appeals are made to listeners at a time of great emotional susceptibility or are related to an area of their lives in which they are particularly vulnerable.
3. When emotional appeals are part of a sustained, systematic effort to make an audience feel more confused, dependent, insecure, or helpless rather than more independent, autonomous, and powerful.
4. When the basic logical argument underlying the emotional appeal would not be validated by dispassionate and informed observers—particularly if the speaker is unwilling to withstand such scrutiny.

(3) Balance the right to use compelling persuasive appeals against the obligation to avoid simplistic persuasive techniques.

By definition, when you are persuading you are not neutral. You have decided that one point of view is worth advocating. Using persuasive strategies as outlined in **20** helps you succeed. In the zeal of putting across your point of view, there is a need to remember that the good speaker never shortchanges the role of logical arguments supported by sound evidence. To use peripheral, edge-of-awareness methods to persuade someone to buy a certain brand of deodorant or to drive you to the airport may or may not be justified; but to try to change other people's minds about important questions of fact, value, or policy on the basis of fuzzy thinking or irrelevant claims just cannot be defended. The classic list of propaganda devices identified by a group of journalists some decades ago sets forth the techniques that an unethical speaker could use to short-circuit an audience's rational processes.[1]

Name-calling

By attaching a negative label to an idea or person, a speaker can raise fear or hatred in an audience. Highly charged words such as "sexist," "terrorist," and "unprofessional" are used to short-circuit a listener's critical faculty. The speaker hopes this tide of emotion will gloss over the lack of substance to his or her position. See **14f(1)**.

Glittering generalities

At the other extreme is the creation of a positive response to a concept or statement through the use of words or phrases that represent some abstract virtue. This technique attempts to convert listeners, not on the merits of a position, but because adopting the position would be patriotic or good for motherhood and such.

Testimonials

Another way to generate positive emotions is to link a popular figure with some cause or product. Here sound argument is replaced by the inappropriate extension of a person's credibility. An actor may become admired in his role as a doctor, but when he is used to endorse a headache remedy, he is way beyond his qualifications, and the testimonial is based on a misleading impression.

Plain folks

It is fine to build identification with your audience so that they will be receptive to your ideas. This process goes too far, though, when the speaker implies: "You should believe me, not because of the inherent validity of what I say, but because I'm just like you." Some examples of the "we are all plain folks here together" technique are the politician whose entire platform is "I'm just a farm boy myself," or the speaker who

---

[1]Alfred McClung Lee and Elizabeth Briant Lee, *The Art of Propaganda* (New York: Harcourt and Institute for Propaganda Analysis, 1939), 23–24.

discounts the theories and findings of educational psychologists on the grounds that "those of us who are parents know how kids really are." This device is often anti-intellectual in that it makes an unwarranted distinction between the "common sense" of the audience and the harebrained reasoning of experts, academics, and opponents in general.

Card-stacking

In this method a speaker carefully uses only facts or examples that bolster her or his position, and the highly biased selection is passed off as representative. An opponent of hiring more police officers might stress accounts of police sexual misconduct and reports of pilferage of confiscated drugs and ask: "Do we want to spend money to put *more* of that kind of person in positions of responsibility?"

Bandwagon

This technique is useful to a speaker who wishes to discourage independent thinking. The "everyone is doing it" approach appeals to the need for security and plays on fears of being different or left out. Speakers frequently cite public opinion polls to support their position. The fact that many people are in favor of some proposal does not necessarily make it right. A proposition should be sold on its merits, not on its popularity.

Transfer

To make some unfamiliar thing more acceptable (or less acceptable) to an audience, many speakers will ascribe to it characteristics of something familiar. Often there is no true relationship between the two. For example, a local perennial candidate's last name is the same as that of a famous golf professional, and although this candidate does not play the game, he always files with "Golf" as his nickname on the ballot. Characterizing video games as a "cancer spreading through our society" plays on the knowledge that probably every audience member has had firsthand or secondhand experience with that fearsome disease.

This list is far from comprehensive. Effective modern persuaders also use such techniques as *snob appeal* (the opposite of plain folks) and *stand out from the crowd* (the opposite of the bandwagon). Such persuasive appeals are questionable whenever they serve to:

> distract listeners from important issues
> cloud important distinctions

introduce irrelevant factors in the decision making
use emotional appeals inappropriately or excessively

Exercise 1. Here are some clichés about right and wrong that have come up again and again over the centuries. Relate each of these to problems a public speaker might face in trying to be ethical and fair.

What would the world be like if everyone did that?
Do unto others as you would have others do unto you.
Above all else, do no harm.
Can you look yourself in the mirror every morning?
The ends do not justify the means.
Two wrongs don't make a right.
Would you want your mother (favorite teacher/clergy member/most admired friend) to know that you did this?

Exercise 2. What can a listener reasonably expect from a public speaker? Write "an audience bill of rights" that you would like to see adopted.

Exercise 3. Evaluate these uses of emotional appeals according to the principles suggested in **21e(2)**.

If you can pinch an inch of flesh at your midriff, you are disgustingly fat and should buy a membership in my health club.
We need a space-based defense system to defend our country from outside aggression.
If I don't raise $8 million by April 1, the Lord will call me home. Please send in your contributions.
I know how shocked you are by the death of your two classmates last week. They would certainly want you to write your congressman today demanding stricter penalties for drug pushers. You can show your love for them and save others from going through the pain you are experiencing.
You can make $50,000 a year in your spare time by becoming a distributor for our organization. But you must do exactly as I say. Put yourself in my hands, and I will make you rich.

Chapter 22

Guidelines for Special Occasions

Research the specific demands that special occasions place on speakers. Adapt your speech to the specialized formats and expectations of these occasions.

This chapter looks at a potpourri of public communication settings that differ in varying degrees from the persuasive, informative, and evocative speeches emphasized throughout the book. Some of these, such as chairing a meeting or being interviewed by a group, may not seem like speech occasions. We want you to see how concepts from the handbook, such as audience analysis, introductions, and conclusions, can enhance your performance in these settings. Other situations described here, debates or television speeches, for example, clearly call on all of the public speaking skills covered in previous chapters, but require mastering a number of particular techniques as well.

22a. On ceremonial occasions, follow the traditional patterns but adapt them so they are immediate and personal.

Some speeches, classified in this book as evocative, are designed more to fill a ritualistic function than to transmit information or change behavior. When you are asked to present an award, welcome delegates to a convention, propose a toast, nominate a candidate, and so on, be aware that there are standard forms. And as with all ritual, the familiarity of the form is one source of the emotional satisfaction participants derive. Happy moments like winning an Olympic medal or sad ones like mourning a death take on added meaning when accompanied by traditional, familiar ceremony. Certain words, gestures, acts are expected—the Olympic athlete would undoubtedly be disappointed if the medal, three-tiered platform, and national anthem were replaced by a gift certificate presented at a pizza house get-together. As you might imagine from the preceding, you are by necessity forced to tread near that line separating tradition and triteness when you give a ceremonial speech.

Cover the expected bases no matter how predictable they are. Do not be *too* creative. At the same time, you must strive to find ways to make these ceremonial moments special and fresh. Above all, this means avoiding overused phrases and constructions. Unless you prepare carefully, you will hear yourself ad-libbing clichés you would never use otherwise:

> On this auspicious occasion . . .
> It is indeed an honor and a privilege . . .
> . . . this small token of our esteem.
> With no further ado . . .

Information exchange is of secondary importance in these speeches; style becomes crucial. Because the two or three ideas you transmit will be pretty basic, you should expend your energy crafting ways to express them, polishing your language and timing. This is made easier by the fact that ceremonial speeches are usually short. Frequently a memorized or partially memorized mode of delivery is best. See **23d**. Your language should be more elevated than in everyday speech, but not so formal as to seem stiff or unnatural.

In preparing all ceremonial speeches consider the following two questions:

What are the needs of the person to whom or about whom I speak?

Although as company president you give a safety award each year and for you it is old hat, it is a special moment for the recipient. What can you say that he or she will remember with pride? Address the *uniqueness* of that person. While the form of the speech may be stylized, the content should be personalized.

What are the needs of the people for whom I speak?
In most ceremonial or ritualistic addresses you can think of yourself as speaking on behalf of some group or community, not just for yourself. People have come together to share emotions as well as—or instead of—information. Yet, these emotions may be unfocused. When you deliver a thoughtful and moving speech, you symbolize the feelings of the audience, thus bonding them. You also help them achieve perspective and find deeper meanings in their experiences. Early in the preparation for this sort of speech, envision yourself as a vehicle for group expression. The following internal monologues are examples of this search for group motivations: "All of us feel such affection for Gary. What is the best way to say what each of us would like to tell him as he retires?" Or: "So many people in our city have worked hard to arrange a successful visit for these exchange students. What words can I choose to portray that warm welcome?"

(1) Follow these guidelines when presenting an award or honor:

- Unless a surprise is part of the tradition, announce the person's name early in the speech.
- Explain how the person was selected for the honor, and by whom.
- Besides listing achievements or qualities, try through a brief anecdote or description to capture some unique qualities of the person.
- If a tangible object—plaque, certificate, key to the city—is presented, explain what it symbolizes.

(2) Follow these guidelines when delivering a eulogy or memorial address:

- Do not accept this assignment unless you feel able to keep your composure.
- Acknowledge shared feelings of sadness, loss, and anger, but do not dwell on these.
- Highlight and celebrate the value of the one being eulogized. Some people present may have known the person only professionally or only socially, only long ago, or only recently. Touch on several aspects of the person's life. Do not be reluctant to share light, even humorous, moments.
- Use phrases that bond the group together.
  All of us who cared for Eleanor . . .

I see many people here who . . .
We all know how persistent she could be when she believed in an idea.

- Try to place the loss in some larger, optimistic perspective. Themes of the continuity of life, appreciating each moment, and growing through pain are timeless and universal. These philosophical concepts are still a source of comfort.
- Do not play on the grief of a captive audience to promote a specific religious belief or social or political cause.

(3) Follow these guidelines for a toast:

- If the toast is a formal part of the event, make arrangements ahead of time so that everyone will have a beverage in hand at the proper point. Be sure that nonalcoholic alternatives are available so that everyone can participate.
- Refine your basic idea into a short message of goodwill and memorize it.
- Choose the words carefully. Humor, wordplay, rhymes, metaphors, proverbs all find their way into toasts. If no witty inspiration comes to you and if the toasts in books all seem corny and contrived, then there is absolutely nothing wrong with taking a sincere thought and stating it gracefully.
- If the toast is more than a few sentences—really a short speech—do not make listeners hoist their glasses the full time. Start out as a speech. Then at the end say something like, "Let's raise our glasses to our new laboratory director. Sheila, we wish you luck, success, and may all your troubles be microscopic!"

(4) Follow these guidelines when accepting an award or tribute:

- Unless asked in advance to prepare a major acceptance speech, limit your remarks to a few sentences.
- Accept the honor with pride.
- Do not let humility and embarrassment make you seem to reject the gesture.
- Share the honor with those who deserve it. But do not get into an endless thank-you litany of the sort that always makes the Academy Awards presentation run overtime.
- Give a gift back to the audience. Can you offer them a genuine tribute, an insight, even a funny story related to your relationship with them?
- End with a future-oriented statement about what the honor means to you.

22b. When participating in a panel, symposium, forum, or debate, tailor your individual presentation to the group format.

(1) Be sure of the format of the program, and clarify expectations about your responsibilities.

There are many versions of group presentations, and too often their standard labels are used interchangeably and inconsistently. You may be invited to be part of a "panel," prepare accordingly, and discover that the organizer has actually set up a debate. Here are the definitions most commonly used by speech communication texts:

Symposium	A series of short speeches, usually informative, on various aspects of the same general topic. Audience questions often follow.
Panel	Composed of a group of experts publicly discussing a topic among themselves. Individual prepared speeches, if any, are limited to very brief opening statements.
Forum	Essentially a question-and-answer format. One or more experts may be questioned by a panel of other experts, journalists, and/or the audience.
Debate	A structured argument where participants speak for or against a preannounced proposition. The proposition is worded so that one side has the burden of proof, and that same side has the benefit of speaking first and last. Speakers assume an advocacy role and attempt to persuade the audience, not each other.

Do not assume that the person arranging the program uses the terms this way. Find out as much as possible about the program, asking such questions as:

What is the purpose of the group presentation?
Who is the audience?
How much time is allotted? How will it be divided among speakers?
Will there be discussion among participants? Will there be questions from the audience?
Who are the other speakers? What will they talk about? In what order?
Is there a moderator or discussion leader?

(2) Prepare as carefully for a group presentation as for a speech.

Do not be lulled into thinking a group presentation is just a conversation. Even if you already know your topic very well, brush up on your research, plan a general outline, and bring along notes with key facts and statistics. Prepare visual aids if appropriate. Plan an introduction and conclusion for your formal part of the session.

Be prepared to adapt, however, in your best extemporaneous style. Since you are in a group, do not give your talk in isolation—make frequent references to the other panelists. "Ms. Larsen has pointed out some of the reasons mental health care is so expensive," and "I won't get into the medical details. Dr. Nguyen is the expert on that." Also, unless the panelists coordinate beforehand, overlap is inevitable on related topics. When you hear your favorite example or best statistic being presented, quickly reorganize and substitute the backup material you wisely brought along. Review the principles in **29** for use in the question-and-answer exchange.

(3) Be aware of your nonverbal communication throughout the entire group presentation.

When you speak in a group you should still follow the guidelines for effective delivery. The fact that you might be seated does not give permission to be offhand and overly casual. On the contrary, you may need to project a little more energy to compensate for lack of visibility and movement.

What far too many speakers seem to overlook is that they are "on stage" during the whole presentation. While other speakers are talking, look attentive and be courteous. Nod and respond facially in ways sufficiently subtle that you do not upstage the speaker. Above all, do not distract the audience by whispering, fidgeting, or grimacing in disbelief. Do not hurt your own credibility by looking bored, or by frantically going over your notes.

The previous suggestions, combined with general speaking skills, should get you through most group situations. The public debate presents some additional challenges.

(4) Follow these guidelines for a public debate:

Formal academic debating and competitive tournament debating require skills beyond the scope of this handbook. Excellent texts and classes are available. Any good public speaker, though, can handle informal debates—such as are held during election campaigns or at public meetings or club functions—by remembering and applying the following prescriptions.

Prepare by considering the opposing point of view.

Research both sides of the topic to see what evidence you will encounter. Get outside yourself and look at the strongest points of your opponent's case and the weakest points of your own. This helps you anticipate the arguments and prepare for them.

Organize your ideas, arguments, and evidence into three general areas:

1. Your own best case for your position. This will be your opening statement or constructive speech.
2. Attacks on or challenges to the opposing position, which you will use to respond to or refute their case.
3. Defense material, which you will probably need to answer challenges to your position.

Prepare your opening speech with particular attention to organizational clarity (see Chapters **8** and **10**) and sound support of assertions (see **13**).

Follow the general suggestions for speaking to an unfavorable audience. See **21c(3)**.

In the refutation phases of the debate follow the guidelines in **20f(1).**

Time is usually limited, so address yourself to major issues. Explain the argumentative impact of your points. Show what damage you have done to the underlying logical structure of your opponent's argument.

When you weaken an opponent's case, drive home the point by issuing a specific challenge.

Save time for a clear and persuasive summary of the argument.

Debates can be confusing, with points flying back and forth. So, even if you have to skip some additional specifics, take the last few minutes to focus the controversy, interpreting how it has emerged during the discussion. End with a persuasive closing statement and clincher that capitalizes on your strongest point.

Maintain a calm and professional demeanor throughout the debate. As with sports, card games, or any competitive activity, emotions can sometimes get out of hand. Do not lose perspective: Getting the last word on every single point is less important than maintaining your long-term credibility. Even if the other debater distorts or misleads, you should remain courteous and unflappable. Your tone may be vigorous, but never hostile. Address your arguments to the audience, and refer to the other speaker by name, not as "my opponent." Treat her or his arguments respectfully, grant good points that are made. Always assume the honesty and decent intentions of the other speaker. Never say, "That's a lie," but rather, "I think those figures are inaccurate. Here's what I found."

22c. Prepare carefully when you chair a program or meeting. Clarify the format, coordinate the participants, and anticipate contingencies.

(1) Plan the agenda carefully.

Determine what will occur and in what order. In some cases you will find that a format is already set by bylaws and custom. Regardless, try to establish mechanisms whereby all potential agenda items are submitted to you well in advance. How many business meetings and banquets have been thrown off schedule by the surprise request to make a "brief announcement"—one that turned into a fifteen-minute speech followed by a half-hour debate? It is your responsibility to manage the communication so that the group's goals are met efficiently. Be firm in sticking to the agenda and moving the proceedings along.

Generally, an agenda should follow a climactic order. Take care of routine reports, announcements, or introductions early and lead up to the major speaker, presentation, or discussion.

A Sample Agenda for a Banquet or Ceremony

1. Greeting: Brief Statement of Purpose by Emcee
   *Invocation, song, patriotic ritual, group ritual
   *More extended theme-setting remarks by emcee
   *Formal welcome (from mayor, governor, etc.)

---

* indicates optional

   2. Introduction of Honored Guests
      At platform or head table
      *In audience
      *Telegrams, messages from those not present
   3. Ceremonial Event
      *Thanks to committees, planners
      *Announcements of elections, etc.
      *Awards, presentations
   4. Introduction of Featured Speaker or Event
      Featured speaker or event
   5. Closing by emcee
      *Quick announcements
      *Benediction, song, ritual

Light entertainment—comedy, skits, musical interludes—may be interposed before 2, 3, or 4. When a ceremony is the very purpose of the event, as in presenting the Heisman Trophy, 3 and 4 are usually reversed.

A Sample Agenda of a Parliamentary Session

   1. Call to Order
      *Check credentials; call roll; introduce observers, parliamentarian; any ceremonial functions
   2. Approval of Agenda
   3. Reading (or Distribution) and Approval of Minutes of Previous Meeting
   4. Treasurer's Report
   5. *Reports of Other Officers
   6. Reports of Standing Committees
   7. *Reports of Special Committees, Task Forces
   8. Old Business
   9. New Business
 10. Announcements
 11. Adjournment

(2) Be sure all participants in the meeting or program understand the agenda and the roles they are expected to play.

Give a *written* copy of the agenda to all participants in a formal business meeting. Confirm how and when they will participate. "I'll call on you for the treasurer's report right away. Save your idea for fund raising, though, and introduce it under new business." For a decision-making session, let every participant know what to expect, so each can come prepared with the right information and some prior thoughts. For an informal program such as a banquet, you might not write out the agenda, but you should still apprise each person of your plan. "Right after the ventriloquist performs, I'll introduce you for the presentation of the Scholarship Award."

(3) Be prepared for all contingencies.

As chair of any event or session, you are a coordinator, facilitator, and host. You are not the "star," but are there to serve the group by helping them meet *their* goals efficiently and pleasantly. To this end, prepare by visualizing the event that you will chair. Anticipate the issues that may arise. Will the group need information for its discussion? Perhaps you should bring minutes, policies, reports, and data for reference. Prepare handouts, slides, or charts to put key information before the group. Consider the comfort and convenience of those assembled. At a business meeting are there writing materials, name tags, refreshments, scheduled breaks? At a banquet or public program, oversee or delegate even such small details as seating arrangement, water at the speaker's table, or audiovisual equipment.

Carefully plan your opening and closing statements. Try to develop coherent, even graceful, transitions to bridge the parts of the program so that you do not fall back on "moving right along" or "last, but not least."

(4) Follow these guidelines when moderating a forum, panel, or debate:

- Be sure the format and ground rules are clear to all participants well in advance. Let them know who the other speakers are and what they will cover.
- Plan an introduction. Engage and motivate the audience toward the topic to be discussed. See **11**.
- Make a *brief,* one- or two-sentence transition between each segment of the presentation.
- Strictly enforce time limits. Emphasize the importance of this to speakers before the program and arrange an unobtrusive signal for when the time is almost up. If a speaker goes way overtime, you should interrupt politely but not apologetically.
- Moderate discussion aspects of the session by keeping the participation balanced. If one topic, speaker, or audience member is consuming far too much time, again interrupt politely and move the discussion along. Do not, however, take over the discussion to develop your own ideas.

- Wrap up the parts of the presentation with a conclusion. See **12**. The logical closure should be an extemporaneous summary of the points that have actually emerged.

(5) Follow these guidelines when acting as emcee of a ceremony or banquet:

- Plan opening remarks that establish an appropriate mood. Whether the occasion is a solemn one, a celebration, or a regular monthly luncheon, make guests feel welcome and set the tone for the events to follow.
- Make gracious and concise introductions. Learn to control and invite applause at appropriate times. When you introduce people, you will not have applause cards to regulate audience response. Direct it by asking them to "hold their applause" or by signaling for it through your phrasing and inflection.

(6) Follow these guidelines when introducing a main speaker:

- Get current and accurate information about the speaker and his or her topic.
- Stress those aspects of the speaker's background and qualifications that will establish credibility for this audience on this topic.
- Avoid the biographical recitation as an organizational pattern. An introduction is itself a short speech and should have an attention-seizing opening, should develop a couple of main ideas, and end with a clincher that clearly signals for applause.
- Keep the introduction brief, but do tell the audience something they do not already know. In the majority of cases, one to three minutes is adequate. A featured speaker deserves a more personal send-off than an introducer who simply reads off the paragraph from the printed program while the audience reads along.
- Avoid long strings of empty and embarrassing adjectives. Be complimentary, of course, but not fatuous.
- Talk about the speaker, not yourself.

22d. Prepare for a group interview as if it were a public speech.

Traditionally, the job interview consists of an applicant and a personnel director, with a desk as a prop. However, more and more interviews are being done in a group, with a number of people from different departments and levels talking with the applicant. Other interview-like events are the news conference and the sales presentation to a committee. In any of these situations, you may not be successful if you come prepared only to answer questions. When you speak to a group, even a small group, you should apply several public speaking concepts, of which the following are the most important.

(1) Analyze your audience.

Learn all you can about the people who will be interviewing you. If possible, get a list both with their names, so you can learn to pronounce them, and with their positions, so you can think about the various perspectives and interests they represent. When you are introduced, you can quickly associate faces with the names and roles you have studied. Throughout the interview you can adapt your answers to their perspectives: "That brings up the whole question of the cost effectiveness of surveys. I'm sure that you confront that issue all the time, Mr. Keenan, being director of marketing research."

(2) Prepare an opening statement.

It is predictable that the first question will be, "Well, tell us a little bit about your background, how you got to where you are now, and how you describe your orientation to our field." Hearing this, you do not want to seem startled or reluctant. Do not chastise them for the breadth of the question. Seize the opportunity to set the tone. Make a brief statement that serves the purpose that a speech introduction does: gets their attention, creates rapport, and establishes a framework for the main content to follow. Do not assume that on the day of the interview your résumé or sales brochure is fresh in the interviewers' minds. They may have read it a week ago and need a little memory jogging. Besides reiterating what you sent earlier, you can also update it, if further developments would be of interest to the group.

You may use your opening statement to develop a general philosophy or position. Sometimes you set a vocabulary and theme in your initial remarks that you can keep referring back to as you answer questions. You may highlight aspects of your experience to show trends or directions that led you to the present interview. Whether you are selling yourself, a service, a product, or an idea, use this opportunity to establish credibility.

It almost never hurts to compliment their organization. Be as specific as possible to show your knowledge of it and its workings.

(3) Answer questions directly and concisely.

Before any interview, review the guidelines for answering questions in **29**. Try to tie questions together in a group interview. "This question spotlights another side of the training issue Ms. Herman raised a few minutes ago." You can demonstrate your powers of synthesis by pulling through certain common threads and relating them back to your opening position.

(4) Maintain effective delivery skills throughout an interview.

Just as in the panel discussion, you are "on stage" the entire time, even though you are seated and in an informal setting. Look at **25** and **26** for a review of delivery skills.

When you answer a question from one group member, be sure to include the entire group in your eye contact.

Part 4

Presentation

23 Modes of Delivery
24 Practice Sessions
25 Vocal Delivery
26 Physical Delivery
27 Adapting to the Speech Situation
28 Visual Aids
29 Answering Questions

Introduction

A face-to-face speech puts heavy demands on speakers and listeners. However, "keynote handouts" have not replaced keynote speeches at conventions, nor have memos usurped the role of conferences. This is because information transmission is but a small part of the total communicative event. People meet in public spaces to affirm their sense of community and to act collectively. The combination of voice, body, and personality—as well as on-the-spot chemistry—makes speech a form of communication with compelling vitality. It is exciting to listen to a good speaker.

By *good speaker* we mean someone who has something to say and says it well. Too often, when people describe a speaker as good or poor, the reference is to the speaker's delivery only. "He didn't have anything to say, but he was a very good speaker" is a contradiction that points up how necessary it is for speakers to have strong presentation skills if they expect to have their message heard. An audience will listen avidly to a well-delivered speech, even if at the end they discover there was little of substance in it. They will not afford the same consideration to a poorly delivered speech, no matter how exciting or important the content.

Recognizing the importance of the performance aspects of a speech, some speakers prepare as actors do: blocking out each movement, planning every vocal change. Carried to its extreme in a movement known as *elocution,* this approach led to the detailed marking of a manuscript or outline so that a typical sentence might look like this:

You and I must work/ together/ to *solve* this *dreadful* problem.//

It is almost impossible to find the words among all the stage directions! When voice and bodily action are consciously orchestrated to this degree—whether or not they are written down—the ideas of the speech are lost to both the speaker and the listeners.

As we explained in Chapter 1, borrowing too directly from the performative repertoire of the actor can be inappropriate because being in a play and giving a speech are fundamentally different. As an actor you assume the role of someone else, speak words written by another person, and strive to perform each line exactly as rehearsed. As a speaker you present your own personality, speak your own words, and try to adapt to the response you receive. Thus public speaking is far more like conversation than like acting.

We advocate an approach to speech delivery called the *natural theory of delivery,* which emphasizes speech as an interaction of ideas as opposed to speech as a performance. However, this does not deny the performance aspects of a public speech. It *does* claim that the performance will be most effective when conceptualized as amplified conversation (rather than as a whole new kind of speaking.)

Your consciousness can be directed—consciously—toward your speech goals rather than yourself. Paradoxically, the less you think about your speech delivery the more effective it becomes. Perhaps you have heard a speaker go through a speech presentation stiffly and mechanically, then heave a sigh of relief and ask for questions. Suddenly a great transformation occurred! In the question-and-answer period the speaker had more facial expression, more variety of tone, more body language while clarifying points. It was as if the speaker had thought, "I'm through with 'my speech.' Now I can really talk to these people." The delivery became much better as the speaker's attitude toward the situation shifted from a performance orientation to an interaction orientation. There is an explanation, if oversimplified, for this change. We all have had more practice communicating than performing. The natural theory of delivery is based on the assumption that you communicate well many hours of every day without consciously thinking about speech mechanics. When you are intensely involved in conversation, you do not stop and think, "Now I'll furrow my brow and point my finger." Changes in your voice and action just happen naturally when you are wrapped up in communicating your message. If you are similarly wrapped up in the content of your speech, your delivery should take care of itself. The single most important delivery goal for any speaker is to internalize this conception of speech as conversation. Once you feel the sense of interaction with an audience—the sort of give-and-take contact you experience in other conversations—your enjoyment of speaking will increase along with your confidence and skill.

Now, are we saying that a successful speech will result from talking just as you do every day? Certainly not, if your everyday speech is listless, ungrammatical, and marred by distracting habits. What we are saying is that this natural theory of delivery ought to ensure that your public style is *no worse* than your private style, but ideally your speech delivery should be lively and unobtrusive. This can be difficult: A conversation with fifty people is very different from a conversation with three. Projecting your voice and personality in this setting may seem and sound strange at first. But you can amplify and exaggerate your conversational style without acting like a different person. Be yourself. There are many sides to a person's self, of course, and different ways of speaking associated with each. Neither the intimate shorthand of lovers nor the lazy, rambling style of a telephone conversation between best friends would be an appropriate model for public speaking. We suggest you picture the way you describe an exciting event to friends, or picture yourself as you talk about a strongly held opinion. That is, imitate yourself as you are in your liveliest and most animated conversation. Disregard for now the more reserved and introspective aspects of yourself. You have chosen to be (or have been thrust into) the center of several people's attention, so call on that side of you that is most outgoing and expansive.

This may not be easy, since the fears surrounding public speaking can put you in touch with the facets of yourself that are shy, apologetic, and self-protective. Thus a lively delivery may not feel really "natural"—hiding under the podium could feel more in character. Nevertheless, learn to assume a role as you speak, and the role you assume is yourself: the most confident, poised, and expressive side of yourself. Quite literally, call up past triumphs of lively and effective speech. "I want to communicate as I did at lunch the other day telling about my trip. I don't really feel comfortable here, but that's the sort of speech personality I want to try to project."

Effective, natural delivery is also unobtrusive. Your audience should be thinking neither "what an awkward gesture" nor "what a beautiful voice." They should attend to *what* you are saying. If you do have problems of a vocal, verbal, or physical nature, work on them, by all means. Be realistic, though, about how many goals you can set for conscious competence at one time. It is a good idea to select one goal in the area of physical delivery and one goal in the area of vocal delivery to work on at a time. When these are mastered, and you become unconsciously competent, entrust them to habit and then move on to another area of improvement. That way, most of your conscious attention during a speech can be directed where it belongs—to your message and your audience.

Chapters **23** through **29** deal with the diverse aspects of speech presentation. Depending on the situation, you will find yourself using one of four standard *modes of delivery. Practice sessions* help you shape your presentation and sharpen your message. Whatever the mode, to transmit your message effectively you must understand the dynamics of *vocal delivery* and *physical delivery.* Another skill in this effective transmission is being able to *adapt to the speech situation* and modify your presentation to account for differences between how you envision a given speaking event and how it really turns out. The successful speech will have even greater clarity and impact if you also support it with *visual aids.* Finally, if you go about *answering questions* properly in the question-and-answer period, you can have more chances to reinforce your message.

Chapter 23

Modes of Delivery

Select a mode of delivery that is appropriate to your topic, audience, and occasion.

Decide early if your speech will be: off-the-cuff—*impromptu;* given from notes—*extemporaneous;* written out and read—*manuscript;* or *memorized* word for word. Settle on the predominant mode you will use, but be aware that no speech is purely *one* mode. As we've seen, each speech is a unique blend of conversation, writing, and performance. Even in an extemporaneous speech, for example, it is often advisable to write out the introduction and conclusion and partially memorize them. And any speaker who encounters hecklers must expect to engage in some improptu retorts.

23a. For most speaking situations use the extemporaneous mode.

Extemporaneous speaking is the most common mode of delivery, and is the one you should use in all but a few special cases. This mode is sometimes confused with impromptu. Although it shares some aspects of spontaneity with impromptu, the extemporaneous mode is considerably more structured. In this mode you prepare extensively: constructing the progression of ideas with the aid of an outline, planning your content thoroughly, practicing until you are comfortable and conversational, but never committing yourself to a rigid, exact sequence of words. Preparing a set of ideas rather than a set of verbatim paragraphs is the only practical and realistic method for most teachers, trial lawyers, salespersons, and others engaged in speaking for hours at a time or for large portions of the day. But even for the occasional public speaker, the extemporaneous mode, once mastered, gives a sense of power and confidence. You will sound more natural and conversational if you phrase your sentences as you go along. Your mind will be on your ideas and on your audience's reaction to them—so you are less likely to go blank than if you were focusing on recalling certain words. Finally, you will find that speaking extemporaneously is flexible. You can adjust to audience response. If you find your listeners nodding knowledgeably at points you thought would be confusing and in need of clarification, you can drop your extensive examples and move on. Conversely, you can spend more time on points where you have hit unexpected resistance or do not get the response you anticipated.

Prepare an extemporaneous speech in four steps.

1. *Begin with a fully developed outline.* Follow the recommendations in **7**, **8**, and **9** to arrange your material in a logical and effective manner.
2. *If you have used a full-sentence outline, convert it to a key word or phrase outline.* The full-sentence outline is a tool to ensure that you develop your speech content adequately and logically. The full-sentence outline is *not* the written version of the words you will use in your speech, however. The declarative sentences that characterize a full-sentence outline are written English, not spoken English, and if you follow them too closely as you develop the wording of your speech, the result may be dull and lifeless. In other words, you may find your expressiveness being limited by what you see on the page. For this reason we suggest that you convert the full-sentence outline to a key word or phrase outline. For instance, Main Point IV of the full-sentence outline in **9b** is "During World War II and after, women were used as a dispensable and secondary source of labor." This could be converted to "WWII—dispensable labor." An outline constructed of such phrases retains the structure derived from the full-sentence outline while enabling you to innovate as you proceed through Step 3.
3. *Word the speech.* Speaking from this brief outline, practice putting your ideas into words. Listen to yourself carefully to hear what sounds clumsy

or to remember an exciting turn of phrase. The second time through, some of the clumsy phrases will have disappeared (and some of the exciting ones, maybe) as you play with sentence structure, rhythms, and so forth. Third time, fourth time, fifth time through—your topic is becoming more and more familiar, giving you the freedom to relax and to allow yourself to really experiment with construction. You will also discover that no one way of expressing a set of thoughts is necessarily better than another: You have said the same thing five times, differently each time, but all of the last three ways work equally well.

4. *Convert your brief outline to speech notes.* See **24c** for directions on how to transfer your content to a format that provides easy visual cues to which you can refer.

23b. Avoid impromptu speaking. But learn to cope with the situation if it is thrust on you.

No one should set out to give an important speech in the impromptu mode. Those good speakers who seem to be able to speak fluently on the spur of the moment are usually speaking extemporaneously, stringing together practiced "bits" to fit the subject that has been dropped into their laps. Do not let this illusion of spontaneity mislead you into under-preparing.

There are three sets of circumstances that can result in impromptu speaking.

No excuse
A lazy or overconfident speaker may decide to "wing it" even though there has been plenty of time to prepare. The resulting shoddy word choice, lack of organization, repetition, generalities, and unsupported assertions will be a monumental waste of the audience's time.

Should have seen it coming
Many impromptu speeches could have been extemporaneous if the speaker had analyzed the requirements and potentials of the situation. An expert caught flat-footed by a question at a news conference probably could have seen it coming by visualizing the event and anticipating the varied perspectives of the questioners. The best man at a wedding who has not prepared a toast is guilty of failing to investigate his responsibilities.

Legitimately unexpected

There are some instances where no realistic amount of preparation or anticipation would lead one to think that he or she would need to speak. The executive who finds fifty demonstrators in the boardroom could be excused for not having a prepared statement. Similarly, it would be a bit conspicuous if the recipient of a surprise award proceeded to give a two-hour speech of acceptance. In a meeting you innocently agree to a whispered request to nominate a colleague, and to your dismay the chair then announces: "Now we will have the nominators make statements about their candidate's qualifications."

If you too often find yourself speaking in the *no excuse* or *should have seen it coming* scenarios, the solutions lie in other chapters of this book, especially **2**, **5**, and **9**. The suggestions that follow pertain to the third, *legitimately unexpected,* case.

(1) Keep your composure.

Do not apologize. Knowing the situation is truly a surprise, the audience will have realistic expectations of you. You should have realistic expectations yourself and not fall apart if what comes out is not your most polished performance. Speak slowly and confidently. Remind yourself that you speak all the time without extensive preparation. In any casual conversation not only are you speaking, but you also are planning what to say next. You do mental composition *all the time.* Do not let the stress of a speaking situation make you forget that!

One important benefit of maintaining your composure is that you can take full advantage of the time between the surprise announcement of your speaking and the actual beginning of that speech. Whether you have the thirty seconds that it takes to walk to the podium, or the ten minutes after hearing that the featured speaker is caught in a snowbank in the next county, use the time to go through an accelerated speech preparation. However short the period, the steps should be the same: pick a theme, an organizational pattern, and a beginning and ending sentence.

(2) Select a theme.

Very quickly list several possible approaches to the topic. Do it mentally, but if time permits, with pencil and paper. By thinking beyond the most obvious approach, you may discover a way to link your topic to a subject you are conversant with.

(3) Select an organizational framework.

You will not have time to make an extensive outline, obviously, but that does not mean you are justified in bouncing erratically from point to point. You can hook your topic to a simple framework like one of the following:

> Past-Present-Future
> Pros and Cons
> Problems and Prospects
> Concentric Rings (Main points progress from immediate concerns to universal concerns, for example: In the Home, In the School, In the Community; Locally, Regionally, Nationally, Internationally)
> Domains (Develop the different spheres touched by the topic, for example: Politically, Socially, Economically; or Practical Implications, Theoretical Implications, Moral Implications)

After you have divided your topic along the lines of one of these frameworks, find one means of support or development for each idea, such as an explanation, an example, a story, a fact, or a statistic.

If time permits, make a rudimentary outline. Even a few key words on a napkin can reassure you and keep you on the path once you have started to speak.

(4) Whenever possible, plan your first and last sentences.

The beginning and ending are the most difficult parts of any speech, and this is especially true in impromptu speaking. Even the simplest attention getter can propel you through that awkward first moment. When you know there is a concluding sentence ready to slap on, you will avoid the panicky feeling that comes with looking for an ending when you run out of steam. Having introductory and concluding sentences averts the aimless rambling so characteristic of impromptu speaking. When you know your task is to start with Sentence A and work your way to Sentence B, you will have a ready reference against which to judge ideas that occur to you as you are speaking.

23c. Speak from a manuscript when precise wording and exact timing are essential to the situation. Maintain oral style and conversational delivery.

There is a widespread misconception that speaking from a manuscript is the easiest and safest mode of delivery. "I'm not an experienced speaker, so I'd better write it out." This is no excuse for avoiding the extemporaneous mode. A bad manuscript speech is much worse than a bad extemporaneous speech. Stilted phrasing, monotonous vocal delivery, and lack of eye contact are all perils facing a novice speaking from a manuscript.

Limit your use of manuscripts to the following situations.

The time allotted is specific and inflexible.

This is mostly the case in the broadcast media. Short free speech replies to editorials need to be precise and compact with only a few seconds of leeway in the scheduling.

The wording is extremely critical.

The section on extemporaneous speaking makes the point that many ways of phrasing a thought are acceptable. But, there are occasions when slight differences in phrasing are *not* acceptable. Exact word choice, or lack of it, can have severe consequences. The most visible examples of this are the public statements made by world leaders during a crisis. As the crisis deepens, the wording of these statements becomes more and more precise to forestall the misinterpretation that could trigger holocaust. Closer to ordinary experience, there are times where the lack of precision in speaking can lead to lawsuits. On some sensitive and emotionally charged topics the consequences of an ill-chosen word can be hostility, hurt feelings, and loss of business. A speaker would also be best advised to use a manuscript for technical or research reports where there is a lot of complex data and specialized denotations for many words.

The style is extremely important.

There are occasions where, although World War III is not a possible result, precision is required all the same. The necessity of precision springs from matters not so much of content but of style. It is expected that your language should be more compact, elevated, witty, or elegant than your everyday speech. For instance, though you still want to sound conversational in a major speech of tribute, the desire for the best possible word choice, sentence rhythm, and polished tone might lead you to use a manuscript.

(1) Prepare an easily readable manuscript in the oral style.

Do not let the fact that you are writing out a manuscript lure you away from the tenets of good organization and composition. Work from a full-sentence outline as described in **9**. Remember that the sentences of the outline are meant to be logical guides and not the actual wording of the speech. To get from the outline form to the manuscript, talk the speech out and onto the paper. You need to check your composition against your ear more than your eye. As you write, and rewrite, keep saying it aloud, listening for the rhythms of oral style. See **15**.

A tape recorder would be a good aid here. Listen to yourself and find the stiff, unwieldy phrases that need revision. To get a second opinion, have a friend listen.

When you have settled on the final version of your speech, produce the copy you will read from, following these guidelines:

- Don't write it out by hand; print it out on a printer. Triple space with wide margins. Some speakers prefer to use oversized type.
- Use capital and lowercase letters in standard sentence format. Text done using all capitals is more difficult to read.
- Produce it on heavy paper. Avoid crinkly or flimsy paper.
- Produce it so the letters are dark and legible. Do not counteract the benefit of typing or printing something out by then having the product too faint to read easily.

Figure 23-1 gives an example of a manuscript page prepared along these lines.

In some speaking situations you will not have your manuscript in your hands, but will be reading it from a TelePrompTer or similar machine.

(2) Be familiar enough with your manuscript to look and sound as though you are speaking extemporaneously.

The two biggest problems in delivering a manuscript speech are:

- Lack of conversational inflection
- Lack of eye contact

| **FIGURE** 23-1 | Easy-to-Follow Manuscript |

①

Everybody knows it: if you want to get
anywhere these days you've got to have a

58
specialty. And when, at the age of fifty-eight,
you become associated with a large and active

B of R
Naples
Board of Realtors like the one at Naples,
Florida, and you're making an entirely fresh
start in what is for you a new and challenging
business, you have a problem.

acreage
One man is a specialist on acreage. One   (**Names**

m & h
knows all about motels and hotels. A woman I   **from**
audience?)

? condo
know has picked condominium apartments.
Waterfront houses are the principal interest of
another. Everywhere I looked someone was
there before me. Reluctantly, I accepted the
truth: all of the good specialties were taken.

/ **min.**

Even though every word is written out for you, you should not be sight-reading. Practice your manuscript out loud often enough that you are comfortable with it. Do not memorize—but be familiar with the flow and rhythm of the words. If you have followed the hints for composing in oral style, you should not find yourself slipping into a singsongy cadence or gasping for breath between overlong sentences.

The typed, easy-to-follow page mentioned in **23c(1)** is essential to maintaining good eye contact during a manuscript speech. The spaces and visual cuing make you less likely to lose your place while looking out at the audience regularly. Only through sustained eye contact will you reap its benefit: feedback. An occasional neck-snapping glance up from the page will not provide you with much information about what is going on in your audience, and that jerky movement can be just another distraction. If you have practiced your speech enough, you will have time to raise your head and engage the audience with unhurried and unchoppy motion.

Never read your first or last few sentences. Have them memorized so that you can start your speech holding eye contact with your audience. Never read your punch lines.

23d. Memorize a short, important speech only on those occasions when holding a manuscript would be out of place.

By definition, giving a memorized speech would entail the delivery of a manuscript speech—without the manuscript. The only times you should give a memorized speech, therefore, are the same as put forth in **23c**, with the added limitations that the speech should be a short one and the situation inappropriate for reading. These occasions are most often ceremonial: giving a toast, presenting a plaque, or accepting an honor.

(1) Memorize the structure of the speech before memorizing the speech word for word.

Learn a few key words that will help you internalize the main sequence of ideas. For example, if you were presenting an award to your company's salesperson of the year, you might learn this outline for your brief speech.

   I. Selection process for the award
   II. Chris Welch's sales record for this year
   III. Chris' qualities as a successful salesperson

Or even more simply:

Process
Record
Qualities

(2) Read the speech aloud several times and then work on learning it paragraph by paragraph.

Always keep your mind on the meaning. Do not try to learn sentences in isolation, but rather work on whole paragraphs at a time, reinforcing their logical and conceptual unity.

(3) As you practice, visualize giving the speech.

Avoid thinking of your speech as lines of text in a social vacuum. You do not want to be startled and lose your concentration when you realize that you are actually facing a roomful of people.

(4) Do not go into a trance when delivering the speech.

Once again, be comfortably familiar with your material so that you can maintain eye contact and rapport with your audience, instead of having your eyes glaze over and your voice and body tighten with concentration.

(5) If you go blank, switch to the extemporaneous mode and recall the structure of the speech rather than groping for the next word.

Speaking along the general lines of the point you know you were trying to make, you can collect your thoughts and soon click back into that which you have memorized.

Chapter 24

Practice Sessions

Use practice sessions to help compose and polish your speech. Allow time for three stages of practice.

Start practicing your speech aloud well before the presentation; this allows time to finalize your points, get feedback from others, and polish the delivery.

24a. Optimize your sources of effective feedback.

(1) Whenever possible, form a support group of other learners or a network of colleagues and friends.

Although you can get feedback from a number of sources, it is most desirable to establish an ongoing relationship with people who have similar goals. In a speech class, this may be a group of students who meet to discuss ideas and practice speeches. The value of peer collaboration is acknowledged in business and professional settings and by politicians and citizens' groups. The most effective speakers routinely test their presentations with one another throughout the phases of development.

(2) Set guidelines for effective feedback and speech criticism.

Within any group of speakers it is desirable to establish some ground rules for giving comments on each other's speeches. Often, the speaker can lead the discussion, asking for comments on the areas of greatest concern to her or him as recommended in **24b(2)**. To be most helpful, good criticism balances honesty with tact. The supportive critic bears in mind the fragility of partially formed ideas and the close connection between one's speaking personality and one's self-image. The following guidelines are for the listeners who have been asked to give feedback:

Start with the positive.
Acknowledge what the speaker has tried to do and the ways that it has succeeded. (In working on the current edition of this book we have relied on readers' suggestions of what to keep as well as what to change. Without their help, our attempts to "improve" this book might have boomeranged.)

Make important comments first.
Try to communicate some sense of priority. There is no profit in refining the style of a sentence if the whole point is going to be thrown out of the speech. Think first about whether the message makes sense, if the overall strategy is effective. When those issues are settled, move on to the refinements.

Be specific.
It is more helpful to say, "You were discussing causes of the problem in Point 1 and then again in Point 3" than "This speech was disorganized." With positive comments as well, better to say, "Comparing the greenhouse effect to the atmosphere inside a closed car really had an impact" than "The speech is great."

Give suggestions, not orders.
Your comments should acknowledge the fact that your response is the reaction of just one listener and that others may differ. Also, recognize that some wonderful ideas can and should be rejected by a speaker because they just do not fit her or his style. Bearing these things in mind, you might make a suggestion along the lines of "I have never cared for a big dramatic introduction, though I know it works for some people. Have you considered . . .?"

Be realistic about the amount and kind of feedback
a speaker can receive.
Always consider the speaker's feelings when deciding what to say and
how to phrase it. There is no need to comment publicly on aspects of a
person's speech style that are tied to cultural identity. Some delivery problems are so obvious that viewing a videotape is a less embarrassing way to
confront them. Others are so complex that a speech professional rather
than a peer audience member could better address them.

Be aware of the time constraints a speaker faces. If you are giving
feedback early in the development of the speech, you can make some
major suggestions for revision. If the speech is in final rehearsal, it may be
pointless to suggest going back to the drawing board. Try to find a few
suggestions that can improve *this* speech, rather than make the speaker
wish there were time to prepare a different speech.

Use the 90/10 principle.
This principle, developed by one of the authors in teaching interpersonal
communication, states that people's weaknesses are rarely the opposite of
their strengths. More often they are the excesses. This awareness suggests
a way of phrasing feedback that communicates "90 percent of quality X is
a positive addition to your speech, but the last 10 percent of quality X
begins to work in the opposite way." You are not suggesting that speakers
eliminate a characteristic behavior, but that they hold it in check. Feedback phrased this way might sound like, "Your informal conversational
style works wonderfully for most of the speech, except that at one or two
points it becomes so colloquial and casual that your credibility suffers a
bit" or, "Generally, the use of evidence is what makes this speech so compelling. Sometimes, though, the statistics are so dense that I find it hard
to concentrate and wish that you would just insert a down-to-earth
example or a little of your own interpretation."

24b. Use three stages of practice sessions to convert your speech from outline to finished product.

Your practice sessions need a timetable. It is not necessarily true that
more is better. In the case of your speech or report, too much practice
may make your delivery stale, and you run the risk of becoming bored
with your topic. Most speakers err in the opposite direction, however,

TABLE 24-1		Possible Practice Schedules	
Type of Speech	Commitment Made to Speak	Preliminary Analysis, Research, and Outline Completed	Early Practice Sessions (Development)
Major policy address	Several weeks before	One week before	Two to one weeks before: Discuss ideas with colleagues. Six to five days before: Talk through speech once a day.
Classroom speech	Ten days before	Four days before	Ten to four days before: Talk about speech with friends. Four days before: Read outline several times. Practice aloud twice.
Routine oral report in a business meeting	Twenty-four hours before	Evening before	Afternoon or evening before: Talk through basic ideas with friends or colleagues. Evening before: Practice aloud one to three times.

and the result is even more disastrous. To avoid falling into either of these traps, you should plan your practice sessions, write down a timetable of steps and phases, and adhere to it.

Your speech is not going to be static during these sessions. The creative process, as outlined in **2a**, will continue, and the practice timetable should not be so rushed that the periods of incubation between sessions are squeezed out. Doing a stand-up, full-scale practice once in the morning and once in the evening for three days is immeasurably better than running through the speech six times in a row. With your practice sessions spread out, you are more likely to benefit from the illumination and refinement that follow incubation.

There is no one, arbitrary timetable to adopt. The variations in type of speech and lead time given for preparation make it impossible to prescribe an exact number of practice sessions. Table 24-1 shows possible timetables for three speeches where the advance notice is different for each. This can be used as a guide to help you make a schedule unique to your circumstances.

A practice timetable can also be influenced by personal differences in speaking ability. For instance, an experienced speaker giving a classroom

Middle Practice Sessions (Feedback)	Final Practice Sessions (Refinement)
Four days before: Give speech on videotape, review with advisers, repeat.	Beginning three days before: Practice aloud once a day. Read notes or outline once a day. Day of speech: Practice aloud once. Review notes just before speaking.
Three days before: Give speech to friendly critic, receive feedback, practice aloud one other time.	Beginning two days before: Practice aloud one to three times a day. Read over outlines and notes several times. Day of speech: Practice aloud once. Review notes just before speaking.
Morning of meeting: Give report to colleague, if possible.	Day of presentation: Practice aloud once. Review notes just before leaving for meeting.

speech may not need three final practices a day—one may suffice. Adapt the timetable to an honest evaluation of your speaking skills.

(1) Use early practice sessions to flesh out your outline.

During these early developmental sessions you will be transforming your set of ideas into your speech by adding the elements of language and delivery to the logical framework erected by your outline.

Begin by internalizing your outline. Read it over a number of times, becoming familiar with the flow of the logic. Sit at your desk or a table and mumble through the outline. Try to explain the ideas to yourself—half-thinking, half-talking it out.

At this point pick a quiet spot and start to put together the speech as it will actually be given. Stand up and give the speech out loud in your speaking voice. Include everything. Do not say to yourself, after making a point, "and then I'll give you a few examples." Give them. Awkward phrases, construction, and word choice should be discovered sooner rather than later. Visualize the speech situation and mentally put yourself there. Do not think "this is a practice session." Make it real—see the faces out there and talk to them. Do not consciously worry about your hands and voice. Sometime during this stage you will have made the first draft of your speech notes. Do not carve them in stone. They are mutable according to how things shape up as you play with the wording. Remember that you do not want to lock yourself irreversibly into one exact sequence of words.

(2) Use one or more middle practice sessions for receiving feedback.

After you have become comfortable with your material but before the final polishing, there is a point where you should seek feedback on your speech. This is usually sometime in the middle of your timetable. If you start looking for feedback on content, style, and delivery too soon, when you have not finished shaping your basic speech, you will miss getting help on those parts that have not yet been crystallized. If the feedback comes too late in the schedule, you will not have the time to incorporate comfortably the useful information you have received.

Practice your speech in front of others and ask for their feedback.
Just as people are good sounding boards for the development of your ideas, as stated in **24a(2)**, so are they the best source of feedback. Seek a variety of responses from others—colleagues, family members, or groups of friends. Take what you can get, but, if possible, move beyond your support group and find critics as close to being representative of your potential audience as possible. If you are going to speak to a high school audience, for instance, ask your teenage cousin, niece, or friend to listen to a practice session. Give your speech exactly as if you were in front of your actual audience, no nervous clowning around. Do not make it more informal just because they are friends. Do not leave things out and say, "You've heard this story." Tell it. Do not talk about your speech. Give your speech.

Ask for honest feedback on content and delivery, but do not necessarily take any single person's comments as the last word. He or she has quirks and prejudices just like everyone else. This is why a group of people would be better, giving you a sampling of responses.

You should not ask, "How'd you like my speech?" Answers like "It was nice," "I thought it was OK" certainly do not help you much. Lead your critics with a few questions and seek clarification of their answers. Here are some specific questions you can ask:

"What did you see as the single most important thing I was trying to say?" If they do not come up with your thesis sentence, then you must look at your structure again.

"What were the main ideas I was trying to get across?" They should answer with your main points.

It is important to get answers to these first two questions before moving on to finer points of development and delivery. You are speaking for a specific purpose, and everything else is insignificant if your whole reason for speaking is not being understood. If you are satisfied that your purpose is clear, then you can ask questions along these lines:

> "Did you think ideas flowed in a logical sequence?"
> "Did the speech hold your attention? What parts were boring? Confusing?"
> "Did I prove my points?"
> "Did my introduction show you where I was going?"
> "Did the conclusion tie the speech together?"
> "Did I sound natural?"
> "Did I have any distracting mannerisms?"

Record your practice session on audiotape or videotape and analyze your performance.

A videotape is the next best thing to a human critic. If you don't own a video camera, there are sources for the casual user. Video clubs usually have rental equipment available. If you are taking classes, the school may own a machine to which you can have access. Some speech consultants offer a videotape service. Your company may have videotape equipment for training.

When you view your performance on playback, try to get outside yourself and see the image as that of a stranger. In this case you may shift your consciousness, but only temporarily, from your message and your imagined audience to yourself as a speaker. Become the audience and ask yourself the same questions that are raised above. You might not believe it when a friend tells you your "I mean's" start every other sentence and you are always picking at your sweater. The evidence is inescapable when you watch yourself do it on tape. A hazard to avoid here is being too self-critical. Seeing yourself on tape can be devastating if you notice only the aspects that need improvement. Look also for things you are doing right. Do not get caught up in examining physical attributes, worrying about the shape of your nose or the fact that your ears stick out or that your taped voice sounds different from the way you normally perceive it. This is where it can be helpful to watch the tape with a friend or coach who can give you a more balanced perspective.

If a video camera is not available, your next best help is, of course, the tape recorder. You will not receive the visual information, but you certainly will be able to get feedback on content, pacing, voice, and so on. Occasionally you may want to use a tape recorder earlier in the timetable, especially if you are blocked creatively. This is a different use of the machine: It helps you remember good ideas and possible wordings, and it complements talking your ideas out with friends.

Practicing in front of a mirror should be limited to a single session, if done at all.

It is our opinion that practicing in front of a mirror often does more harm than good. The methods described in (1) and (2) above allow the feedback to be *delayed:* After speaking you can shift your focus away from ideas to a more detached assessment of the details of your presentation. With a mirror, however, you are constantly compelled to divide your attention between what you are saying and how you are saying it. If you have no other way to get a general check on the visual impact of your posture, gestures, and facial expressions, it may be worthwhile to practice before a mirror just once.

(3) Use the last few practice sessions for refinements of style and delivery.

By this time you should be committed to a basic version of your speech, while maintaining the looseness of the extemporaneous mode. You should not be making radical changes right up to the deadline.

Make the final practice sessions as realistic as possible.

If you are going to use visual aids, they should be ready early enough that you can include them in your final practice sessions. The same holds true for the final draft of the notecards. Check yourself against your time limit. Practice your speech, standing up, at the rate and volume you will be using. Speaking with rudimentary mechanical amplification to a large audience, for example, will use more breath than will the conversational volume used in early practice. You need to unabashedly boom out in the final practice sessions, if that is what it will take to be heard when you actually give the speech.

Continue reading through your notes and outline, but do not think of these activities as a substitute for the formal practice sessions.

24c. Prepare speech notes to act as a guide and a safety net.

You should not confuse speech notes with your outline, as they serve different functions. An outline is used to ensure that the speech is prepared in accordance with a logical organization. Speech notes, on the other hand, are used as an aid while you are actually speaking.

Like your outline and wording, your notes can go through several drafts. Work on them, doodle on them, then copy them over. Do not feel committed to the first thing you write. Just the kinesthetic act of copying over your notes is an excellent way to firm up your speech in your mind.

(1) Speech notes should consist of key words and phrases and material that is to be cited directly.

Unlike your outline—in which your points must be parallel, mutually exclusive, and in full sentences, with "no *A* without a *B*"—your speech notes do not have a rigid, regulation form. A point can be represented by a word, a sentence fragment, or an actual sentence or two. What goes into your notes depends on what you find you need during practice.

For example, perhaps one point of your speech, which in your outline was developed to the second level of subordination, with all its accompanying *A*'s and *B*'s and *1*'s and *2*'s, is one with which you are so familiar that it can be represented in speech notes resembling those in Figure 24-1.

While practicing you may also find that you want more than just a key-word reminder to get through an important but tongue-twisting sentence or to ensure that you remember an especially eloquent turn of phrase that has a delicate rhythm. Your notes may also contain material that you will be citing exactly as written out: quotations that are too long to commit to memory or complicated statistics, for instance.

Keep in mind, however, that your notes should remain *notes*. If you make them too extensive and detailed you risk moving out of the extemporaneous mode and into delivering a manuscript speech. Your notes should be referred to, not read from.

FIGURE 24-1   Speech Notes

> B. Recurring experiments with Protectionism
>   1. Just doesn't work
>   -- F Co's absorb, cut profits
>   2. Pass to consumer
> $66 B   Gary Hufbauer
>   (Prof of finance GT U)
>   3. Hurt US Co's
>   15% imports multinat.
>   need cheap F mat'ls & components
>   4. Retaliation
>   McFadden (Fortune)
>   trade war —→ recession —→ depression
>
>   CHECK TIME *(about 8 min)*

(2) Prepare your notecards in a format that aids your delivery.

Generally, most speakers prefer to put their notes on 4" × 6" or 5" × 8" cards. The 8 1/2" × 11" sheet of paper has the disadvantage of being large and floppy, inhibiting your gestures and limiting your movement by effectively tying you to the lectern or table. While the 8 1/2" × 11" sheet is too large, the 3" × 5" card is too small. If you make your notes on them properly, large enough to be read, you will end up with a huge stack of cards through which you are constantly flipping.

A few medium-sized cards can easily become an extension of your hand as you gesture and move about. They will not be distracting to your listeners if you seem comfortable with them. Do not be coy about using your notecards—refer to them honestly. A surreptitious peek at protectively cupped hands will not fool your listeners into believing that you are speaking without aids.

Do not go to the other extreme and get lost in your notes. You should be able to look down, see what is next, then talk about it. If you find yourself burying your nose in your cards, you have not prepared them correctly. The words and phrases should be large, well spaced, and uncluttered. There should be a lot of visual cues—large card numbers, underlining, indenting, stars, highlighting, different colors—all for the purpose of making it easy for you to find what you want at a glance. Speech notes should also be cued to choices you will make during the speech. Time notations are essential. You might write at one point "if more than 8 minutes, skip to card 6." You might use a special color to mark optional sections of the speech. Examples highlighted in yellow could mean: *Include this if the audience seems uncertain about my point. Otherwise omit it.*

24d. Fit your speech into the time limit.

The section on preparation admonishes you to limit your topic according to the time allowed. Often you cannot tell for sure how much time your speech will take until you have gotten well into the practice sessions. In extemporaneous practice you will experience variations in length as you work with the form of your ideas and the style and rhythms of your speaking. This, again, is where envisioning audience response is helpful. Most first-time speakers practice at a speaking rate faster than the one they find necessary for clarity during the speech itself. The more realistic your practice the less likely you are to misestimate your time.

To clock your speech do not glue your eyes to the sweep hand of your watch. Merely note the time when you begin and again when you finish. A sweep hand can induce unnatural behavior like speaking twice your normal rate for the last minute if you think you are going too long, or, in the opposite case, slowing your delivery to a tired shuffle. There are more-sensible ways to address problems of length. The first step is to time the parts of your speech. Two possible ways of doing this are to have a helper jot down the times of your main points on your outline as you practice or to do it yourself with a tape recorder.

Look at the relative proportions of the parts of your speech: introduction, body, conclusion. Generally, the body should comprise 75 percent of your speech. Does an extended story make the introduction too long? Look, too, at the relative proportions of your main points. Are you spending half your time on just the first main point? Is it worth it?

If Your Speech Is Too Long

1. Consider cutting out an entire main point. (Adjust your thesis accordingly.)
2. Look at your supporting evidence and examples and cut those that duplicate effort. (But save the ones cut as they may be needed for the question-and-answer or discussion period.)
3. Turn some of your illustrations into examples. (Instead of telling the whole story, toss off a one-liner that capsulizes it.)
4. Eliminate any long stories, jokes, narrations, unless they are absolutely essential to the theme of the speech.
5. Consider using means other than speech to transmit technical or detailed information. Handouts and visual aids are two examples.
6. Polish and tighten your language and phrasing. Speak simply.

If Your Speech Is Too Short

1. Find if there are important ideas that are not getting enough development relative to the other points.
2. See if you are too concise for your own good. As is explained in many other places in this handbook, the spoken word is fleeting and needs repetition and embellishment and illustration to bring home to each and every member of the audience the emphasis that you want to deliver.
3. Make sure you have proved all your points. Double-check your evidence to make sure that you have not assumed too much or made some logical leaps that are not justified.
4. You may have given up too soon at the library. Have you really researched enough?

In a speech class there may be penalties for not reaching a minimum time limit. In most other settings no one is going to be awfully upset if you take only fifteen out of the twenty minutes you have been given. However, taking forty minutes when you have been allotted twenty can disrupt the schedules of countless other people.

The experienced speaker always knows the duration of each element of the speech. Even if the first clocking run-throughs show that the speaker meets the time requirement satisfactorily, she or he still wants to have a point-by-point time breakdown. This knowledge aids adaptation to changes that might crop up in the speech situation itself. See **27**.

When you reach that point in your practicing where the speech consistently comes out the same length, mark the cumulative times of the parts of your notes. For example, you might print "2 mins" at the bottom right of your notes on the introduction, "5 mins" after the first main point, "8 mins" after the second, and so on. See Figure 24-1.

Here, as examples, are two situations where knowing the timing of the elements of your speech will help you adapt without panic.

You planned to spend five minutes on your first main point. Feedback from the audience convinced you to use eight minutes to make certain they were getting it clear. You decide to drop anecdotes from your second and third points to make up the three minutes.

You are on a program that is running late but can't go overtime because of scheduling conflicts. The moderator asks you if you can trim your presentation from thirty minutes to ten. You begin doing mental arithmetic, subtracting combinations of points until you arrive at a plausible shortened version of the speech.

Some people have internal clocks that are accurate enough that these speakers do not need external cues. If yours is not that well developed (and most of ours are not), feel free to take off your watch and lay it where you can see it, or have a colleague in the audience give you arranged signals. Avoid excessive reliance on the clock, though. Become comfortable with your presentation by practicing and timing your speech.

24e. Save the hours just before the speech for one final run-through and for getting into the proper, relaxed frame of mind.

Imagine that you are giving an important speech one afternoon or evening. You should have planned your practice sessions so that, by the night before, your speech is polished and you are comfortable with it. Remember that it is never a good idea to compress your practice into a few frantic hours. On the morning of the event, allow for one unpressured practice session. As you go about the day's activities, you may want to look over your outline or notes one time. If you feel yourself becoming anxious, try some of the relaxation or visualization techniques recommended in **6c** and **d**.

The last quiet, private moment before the speech is the time to go through your notes and outline once again.

This could be done just as you leave your home or office or as you sit on a bench outside the building. In the final minutes before your presentation, go through your introduction and conclusion. Visualize the gross structure of the speech, a macroview of the ideas.

Throughout the constructing of your speech, you should keep in mind what preparation it would take to get yourself to the podium in a relaxed frame of mind. Take time well before the speech to think about those possible situations that could throw you off your pace, and set up strategies to avoid or dilute them. Try to arrange your day so that you are not rushing around picking up dry cleaning or cashing a check. Get the logistics of your life in order early. If you have a meeting just before the speech, one that you know is usually tense and upsetting, do not go. Be conscious of your idiosyncratic responses to a number of stimuli. If you know you do not function well on a full stomach, do not eat the rich banquet—have just the salad. In short, be a little selfish and take care of yourself in the ways you have learned work best. You owe it to your audience and to yourself to be feeling comfortable, confident, and composed when you present the speech you have worked so hard to prepare.

24f. Avoid these practice pitfalls.

(1) "Mental" practice rather than oral practice

Sitting and thinking about your speech, or reading over your outline or notes is not substitute for rehearsing the speech aloud. This is essential to get comfortable with phrasing and to check your timing. Do not let "speaker's" block make you put off working orally until the last moment.

(2) Too many critics

Some speakers seek feedback from everyone they know, and most of these friends will be happy to oblige. While it is good to get a variety of opinions, it can be confusing to receive contradictory advice. "Make it longer." "Make it shorter." "You seem too serious." "You seem too casual." It is *your* speech; after receiving comments from a few people whose judgment you trust, *you* decide what advice to take, and move on to finalizing your speech.

(3) Overpreparing

This is rare, but some speakers rehearse their speech so much that it becomes mechanical. As noted in **1c(5)**, by drawing too heavily on writing, or on performing, or on both, speakers can lose all sense of the original meaning of the words and ignore audience reaction.

(4) Self-consciousness rather than audience-consciousness

Except for a few middle practice sessions where you receive feedback from others or from recordings, try to keep your attention off yourself as a speaker and rather on your message and the audience response you desire. Remember to visualize *them* when you practice. Again, don't let the performer upstage the conversationalist.

Chapter 25

Vocal Delivery

Speak clearly, correctly, and conversationally. Vary your vocal delivery for interest and emphasis.

As important as preparation, organization, content, and style are, the essence of speech is still your utterings. What a waste of time and brainpower if that which you have to say cannot be heard or understood at the critical moment of speaking. You must be aware of the mechanics of transmitting sound: articulation, breath control, projection, and so on. At the same time, your most important goal is to develop a style of vocal delivery that sounds natural and conversational. The "orator," with trilling *r*'s and shuddering pauses, can really set one's teeth on edge. Except for the stylized chants of the auctioneer and revival minister, most public speech should sound like private speech, only exaggerated to fit the size of the room.

Voice prints are as distinctive as fingerprints. "Finding a voice" is a powerful metaphor for social identity. Your way of speaking reveals your ethnic and cultural heritage, as well as your personality. In a multicultural society, the sounds of everyday speech are always changing to include new voices. As you develop your public speaking skills, stay attuned to your distinctive sound.

25a. Identify and eliminate distracting characteristics of your vocal delivery.

Your reason for speaking is defeated when your listeners begin to pay less attention to what you are saying and more to how you are saying it. "That's the fifteenth time she's said 'quite frankly'." "Why doesn't he clear his throat?" "That repetitious inflection is really irritating." Your voice and speech style should be unobtrusive vehicles for your ideas.

Distracting speech habits are difficult to identify and even more difficult to change. Vocal mannerisms become so familiar to you and your closest associates that they are overlooked and cease to distract, but to a new audience they are blatant. Follow the suggestions in **24** for receiving feedback. Use videotape, audiotape, and critics to get some objective distance on your performance. When you isolate a problem, do not view it as just a public speaking problem. An overused phrase, a harsh, raspy voice reduce your effectiveness in daily conversation as well. Resolve to correct problems gradually and permanently by modifying your *everyday speaking habits.*

(1) Identify problems of voice quality.

The resonant, musical voice you view as an ideal may be beyond your reach, but there is, of course, no one perfect voice for effective speaking. There is a range of pleasing voices, and although the quality and timbre of your voice are determined to a great extent by your larynx and the size and shape of your nasal cavities, you can find yourself within that range unless you are hampered by one or more of the following problems:

Harshness, hoarseness, or stridency
These qualities are caused by constriction of the throat or by tension or damage to the vocal folds. The voice may sound husky, rough, or shrill and often gives an impression of anger or gruffness.

Breathiness, thinness, or weakness
These qualities are caused by having an inadequate airstream, by releasing excessive air, or by speaking in an unnaturally high falsetto. The effect is a soft, often childish-sounding voice that lacks authority and power.

Nasality and denasality

Incorrect flow of air through the nasal passages creates these problems. Too much air escapes through the nose in the former case, too little in the latter. These problems primarily affect *m, n,* and *ng* sounds, and produce either whiny or stuffed-up qualities.

(2) Identify problems of articulation.

Many people have speech problems that are not severe enough to be considered disabling, but are still sufficiently distracting to impede good communication. A stutterer will certainly be aware of her or his condition, whereas the people with lesser problems are usually not conscious of the particular misarticulations that occur in their speech.

Listen closely to your own speech for irregularities in the way you produce consonant sounds or blends of consonants. Many articulation errors take the form of *substitutions,* such as "*th*olution" for "solution," or "*dese*" for "*these.*" Also common are sound *distortions:* the slushing, hissing, or whistling *s* or the lazy *l* or *r.* Less frequently encountered articulation errors are *additions* ("ath*a*lete" for "athlete," "Real*a*tor" for "Realtor"), and *omissions* ("doin'" for "doing," "reg*l*ar" for "regular"). If you discover any of these errors, notice if they occur every time you make the sound or if they happen at the initial, middle, or final positions in a word. For instance, a lazy *r* may show up in the middle position but not in the initial position: You can say "*r*abbit," but "tu*r*key" comes out as "tuw-key." Also, consonant sounds you produce well in isolation you may tend to distort in consonant blends: That same *r* sound may give you trouble only in *cr, gr,* or *dr* combinations.

The real distraction caused by these misarticulations is not the minor aural irritation it may arouse in your listeners. Rather, these speech problems can create a contradictory message that works against the credibility that you want to project. Sound substitutions are a part of a child's language development and disappear after the child learns to discriminate more precisely among sounds. An audience listening to a speaker who says "wange of pothibilities" will experience conflict between the image of competence and intelligence conveyed by the words and the image of incomplete development triggered by the sounds. Similarly, sound distortions can produce an image of sloppiness that conflicts with an otherwise crisp and concise presentation. Consider the image discord created by the accountant who presents precise facts while slushing his *s*'s in phrases

like "the projections for the next fishcal year sheem to shupport our pre-
diction of sholid growth potential." It may be illogical and unfair to associate certain articulation errors with baby talk and drunkenness, but you
had best be aware of the unconscious tendency of listeners to do so.

(3) Identify vocalized pauses and other irrelevant sounds and phrases.

Do not be afraid to pause between sentences or thoughts when you
speak. But avoid filling those pauses with distracting and meaningless
sounds and phrases. When a speaker is nervous, a one-second pause can
seem like a ten-second stretch of dead air, and the temptation to fill it
with something can be great.

Do you use vocalized pauses: "uh," "um," "err"?

Do you fill pauses with other nonspeech sounds: lip smacking,
tongue clicking, throat clearing, snuffling? Some speakers unconsciously
insert a giggle after every sentence.

Do you repeat to excess certain words or phrases in nonsensical
places? Some may have originated as requests for feedback. The coherent
question, "Do you know what I mean?" following a complicated idea
turns into "y'know" tossed in whenever the speaker feels uncertain. From
there it is a short step to using it as just another pause filler. In the following example, the phrase "y'know" has no more meaning than "uh."

> One of the, y'know, advantages of joining a credit union, y'know, is the low-
> interest auto loans, y'know.

Other irrelevant repetitions may have grown out of an unconscious need
to apologize for inadequacies of expression. Tacking on "or whatever" on
the end of every sentence is an example.

Here is a list of words and phrases that lose their original meanings
when allowed to spread cancerlike through a speech:

> OK?
> y'know
> see
> like
> I mean
> or whatever

and so on and so forth
et cetera
in other words
so to speak
you might say
right?

(4) Identify repetitious patterns of inflection.

While growing up and listening to other people, you learn very early that there are logical and natural places in sentences to vary the pitch of your voice. For instance, in English it is usual to have your voice go higher in pitch at the end of a question or to have it deepen for an emphatic statement. In normal conversation we use a variety of inflection without having to think about it. In public speaking, however, there can be a tendency to deliver every sentence with the same inflectional pattern regardless of the sentence's meaning or grammatical structure. This happens when the speaker is not thinking about the content of the speech, but is nervous, or is reading from a manuscript or recalling a memorized text. A singsong, hypnotic pattern of inflection can easily lead to drooping eyelids in the audience.

(5) Eliminate your distracting habits through a systematic self-improvement program, or by seeking professional help.

Self-improvement
When you identify a problem and your motivation to correct it is strong, you may devise a simple plan of action, as Demosthenes did when he was troubled by problems of articulation and enunciation. His solution was to practice being understood while speaking over the roar of the ocean with his mouth full of pebbles. This may not suit many modern speakers, especially if they live in Kansas on sandy soil, but there are other sources to tap. Books and recordings are available to provide exercises in breathing and projection. These also have exercises, like tongue twisters, that make apparent the muscle groups used to produce certain sounds properly. You can start with such books as:

Hahner, Jeffrey C., Martin A. Sokoloff, and Sandra L. Salisch. *Speaking Clearly: Improving Voice and Diction*. 4th ed. New York: McGraw Hill, 1993.

Modisett, Noah F., and James G. Luter Jr. *Speaking Clearly: The Basics of Voice and Articulation.* 3rd ed. Minneapolis: Burgess, 1988.

Wells, Lynn K. *The Articulate Voice.* Scottsdale: Gorsuch Scarisbrick, 1989.

For a deeply ingrained habit you may choose to map out a program of behavior modification. This approach, which has been quite successful in helping people to lose weight or quit smoking, is based on the premise that habits that develop gradually are best eliminated gradually. New behaviors are substituted for old ones and the new behaviors are rewarded. The steps are simple:

1. Assess your present behavior. Quantify the exact frequency of the distracting habit.
2. Set a specific, realistic goal. If you say "OK?" after nearly every sentence, perhaps twenty times in a ten-minute speech, resolve to cut down to ten times in a ten-minute speech.
3. Monitor your behavior. Do not just estimate your progress. Have a friend tally the occurrences, or tape each speech yourself. Keep a written chart of your progress.

For most motivated adults, knowledge of results is an adequate reward. Just seeing the progress in quantified form keeps you working toward the goal. Feel free, though, to use more tangible rewards. You can promise yourself a special treat of some sort when you reach your goal, if you think that such an added incentive would be useful in helping to keep you on track.

Professional help

Some problems of vocal delivery are difficult to diagnose or solve without professional help. In seeking help, consider the nature and seriousness of your vocal problem, as well as the time and money you are able to commit. Then consult the appropriate professional person from the following list:

Speech therapists are the best source of help for fairly serious or persistent articulation and voice problems.

Voice coaches may be affiliated with theater, radio, or television. They can help you improve voice quality, diction, and pronunciation. If you also want to work on regionalisms or accents and want to develop greater variety and expressiveness, consider a course in voice and diction or oral interpretation. An acting course will help in these areas and also improve your physical movement.

Public speaking teachers and *consultants* can provide help with voice, articulation, emphasis, and expressiveness within the context of public speaking. Usually, work on speech delivery is integrated with the development of speech content.

25b. Speak so that you can be heard and understood.

(1) Speak loud enough to be heard by the entire audience.

For the inexperienced speaker just about *any* volume level will sound too loud. This is understandable. There are few occasions for speaking above a conversational level, and even on such occasions, as when we scream our heads off at a football game, we rarely care if we are being understood. For the most part, being loud and conspicuous is, in Western cultures, considered boorish behavior. This adds another dimension of difficulty to being able to use your voice properly when you speak before an audience.

The only thing that will make loud speaking more comfortable and natural is, of course, practice. In the early stages you will have to ignore the feedback on volume that you receive from your own ears and rely on a friend or perhaps a tape recorder set some distance away. What you are aiming for is a louder voice that retains the rhythms and inflections of your normal conversation. You want to be loud, but not yell like a drill instructor. As you practice, you will discover that this takes more wind for each phrase and that you will need to develop breath control to permit you to keep your breathing pauses in normal patterns.

Maintain a mental image of broadcasting or propelling your voice to the far corners of the room. You will then find yourself doing those things that naturally aid projection, such as keeping your head up and opening your mouth wide.

Know how large an audience you can address without sounding strained. Can you speak for an hour at an outdoor political rally, or do you reach your limit speaking to twelve people in a boardroom for ten minutes? (Insist on a microphone if you know that the audience or room will be too big for your voice.) Continue to practice increasing your speech volume. A good goal for the average person would be to be able to speak conversationally, without amplification, to fifty or sixty people in a room with average acoustics.

(2) Speak at a rate your audience can follow.

While there are speaking-circuit veterans who have a 250-words-per-minute rate as one of their gimmicks, most people lose intelligibility far short of that. An average rate of speaking is around 150 words per minute. To check your rate, select a fairly easy newspaper or magazine article. Then time yourself for three or four minutes of reading aloud. Next, count the number of words in the passage and divide by the number of minutes you read. Be sure to read in as natural and conversational a manner as possible. If you speak faster than two hundred words per minute or slower than one hundred words per minute, you may be endangering your comprehensibility by overworking your audience. The extremely fast speaker asks his or her listeners to decode and process information more rapidly than is their custom. The plodding speaker, who seems to avoid phrases and slowly lays out each word as if it were unrelated to any other, keeps the audience in bored suspension as they wait for the words to gel into some sort of context.

Generally, when giving a speech, plan to speak a little slower than you do in daily conversation. The need to speak a little louder and a little more distinctly will require extra breath. It will be more natural to pause to breathe between phrases than to rush through the last few words of a sentence and gasp noisily for air. To be sure you have timed the speech realistically, practice at the rate and volume you will actually use.

(3) Enunciate words distinctly and naturally.

Even people who have no chronic articulation problems of the sort discussed in **25a(2)** rarely enunciate *every* sound in *every* word. The phrase "jeetyet?" can be deciphered as "did you eat yet?" by a friend who is standing by the person speaking and who has a context for the remark. In public speaking settings much information can be lost due to distance from the speaker and distracting noise. Thus it is important to work on crisp, precise articulation. Use your tongue, teeth, and lips to pronounce every sound. Be sure you say "government" rather than "goverment" and "hundred" rather than "hunnerd." Do not mumble, slur words together, or swallow whole phrases.

You can enunciate properly and still sound natural. It just takes the practice that comes from incorporating precision into your normal conversation instead of creating a separate "speaking persona." Some people, in a misguided attempt to sound more formal or "literate" during a speech, will overarticulate words or take on affected mannerisms or pronunciations. The result is quite the opposite of what they wish. Rather than sounding erudite, they, with their grimaces and popping consonants, appear patronizing, melodramatic, and just a little silly. Do not say *thee* in a place where *thuh* is natural. Do not use "would not" where "wouldn't" feels right. (Just be sure to say "wouldn't" rather than "*wunt*.") Standard usage dictates that some syllables are truncated. Do not reverse this procedure. "*Con grat you lations*" is an overly precise pronunciation of "congratulations," which most speakers say like "*con grad ja lations*."

(4) Make special adjustments, if necessary, to compensate for having an accent that your audience may have difficulty understanding.

If you have a regional accent or if you are not a native speaker of American English, you may be concerned about being understood. Do not try to eliminate or hide your accent. Your manner of speaking is part of your unique personality. The differences can add interest and charm to your presentation. To ensure comprehension, follow these suggestions:

1. Do not start out with the most important material. Use your introduction to let the audience adjust to your pronunciation and patterns of emphasis that differ from their own. Usually this will take just a few minutes.
2. Speak more slowly and distinctly than you do in conversation.
3. Be very alert to feedback. If you see confused faces, repeat ideas slowly. Unclear vocabulary or mispronunciation of one key word may mystify your listeners. Try several synonyms for important words.

If you are a nonnative speaker of English, you may find these two simple tips useful in increasing your intelligibility.

1. Prolong your vowel sounds. In contrast to many other languages, spoken American English carries more meaning in vowels than consonants. It will sound odd to you, but make a conscious effort to extend your vowels. Maaaaake eeeeeach laaaaaast a loooooong tiiiiiime.

2. Also blend the end of one word into the beginning of the next so that each phrase sounds like one long word. This reduces the perceived choppiness of much accented English.

For more detailed suggestions, refer to:

Porter, Patricia A., Margaret Grant, and Mary Draper. *Communicating Effectively in English: Oral Communication for Non-Native Speakers.* Belmont: Wadswork, 1985.

Dale Paulette, and Lillian Pons. *English Pronunciation for International Students.* Englewood Cliffs, NJ: Prentice-Hall, 1993.

25c. Reinforce meaning and make your speech more interesting through vocal variety.

The speaker who has a clear speaking voice devoid of vocal tics wastes these good qualities if she or he speaks hypnotically, with no variation in pitch, rate, or volume. Change and movement are intrinsically more interesting than the static or predictable, and, in Chapters **15** and **16,** we stress the importance of variety of word choice and variety of examples in maintaining a high level of audience attention. Vocal variety is equally important, and the need for it goes beyond mere desire for novelty. Your voice should not just transmit words; you can use it to underscore and reinforce your message. Suppose your speech on air pollution contained these two sentences:

When the pollution levels are high, my hair feels gritty and I have to wash it more often.

and

Every time pollution reaches the Alert level in our city, more people with chronic respiratory problems die.

Delivering these sentences in the same tone of voice could imply that they were of equal importance. Changes in pace and emphasis show your audience what is significant and can signal humor, seriousness, irony, and a range of emotions.

(1) Vary your pitch.

Speaking in a monotone says this to an audience: "I have little interest in the subject or confidence in my ability to interest others in it." A listless vocal performance will negate any dynamism that ordinarily would spring from your word choice and content. Varied inflection implies a high energy level and self-confidence, and generally aids your credibility. The pitch you use for the delivery of a word or phrase can underscore its meaning or imply its opposite. For instance, it is common to indicate disagreement with an assertion or statement merely by speaking it in the inflection used for questions.

If you can sing an octave, on key or not, you can speak an octave. Do not be afraid to use the full range of your voice.

(2) Vary your rate of speaking.

The average pace of your delivery should be geared toward comfortable listening. However, changes in rate at different times during the speech can be effective in establishing moods or in adding emphasis. Speaking slowly can make you seem thoughtful and deliberate, or can impart a sense of drama. Similarly, an extended pause at the end of a sentence will signal to your audience that you consider what you just said important and worth some thought on their part. Rapid delivery shows excitement and activity. A climactic effect is achieved by presenting a series of ideas or examples at a rapid clip, as in the following example:

> [slow] Since we adopted this management system, [fast] absenteeism is down, productivity is up, morale is up, sales are up, profits are up.

The preceding example also demonstrates that the shift in rate (in this case, slow to fast) is as important to creating a climactic effect as the rate itself. The following passage shows what one can do with a fast-to-slow shift. Were you to read this aloud you would speak faster and faster through the first sentence, but would speak the second sentence very slowly:

> In the next hour they looked in her room, checked the tree house, went over to the playground, called several of her friends, drove around the block,

asked all the neighbors. No one—had seen—Emily—since—she—got off—
the school bus.

The accelerating pace of the first sentence shows mild concern turning to
frantic searching, which leads to the sudden moment of grim acceptance
contained in the measured delivery of the last sentence.

(3) Vary your volume.

You should speak loud enough that you can drop your voice for effect
and still be audible to the people in the far corners. At the same time, you
should hold some volume in reserve so that you can raise your voice for
emphasis.

Notice how a drop in volume (the sentence below in italics) can pique
interest by evoking an air of confidentiality:

> I was having an awful week. Few prospects, no sales. It was hard on a
> young, eager guy just out of school. On the other hand, I never saw old
> Jones without a customer at his side or a signed contract in his hand. I guess
> he saw my hangdog look and took pity on me, because he walked over and
> said, "Smith, you've got the makings of a great salesman, but you're doing
> one thing wrong."
> *Now, this is what he said: . . .*

Here is an example of raising one's voice for emphasis:

> The city council has approved yet another halfway house in the neighbor-
> hood. The university is using our streets for its parking lot. The state parole
> board dumps its parolees downtown. Prostitutes from miles around converge
> each night on Second Street.
> **Do you want to know what's coming next?**

25d. Use standard, acceptable pronunciation.

(1) Identify words that you habitually mispronounce.

Some differences in the ways people pronounce words are inevitable and
cause no problem for public speakers. A person from New England will
say "I went to a pahty," a Pennsylvanian may have "cot a cold," and a

Texan may tell you to come "ovah heah." Unless they have strong biases against some part of the country, listeners rarely make negative inferences about the speaker on the basis of regional pronunciations like these. If, however, a person says "warsh" instead of "wash" or "ax" for "ask," many listeners will consider this substandard and draw conscious or unconscious conclusions about the speaker's educational level, competence, and intelligence. This sort of linguistic snobbery can be unjust and inaccurate, but a speaker can change some pronunciations more easily than everyone else's attitudes.

Look over the list in Table 25-1 and see if you make any of these pronunciation errors.

If you found on the list one or two words that you mispronounce, you can easily work on correcting them. If you found five or more, you may need more extensive help in the form of coaching or coursework. Due to factors in your background or perhaps a lazy ear for the finer distinctions of speech, you probably are also mispronouncing several other words and impairing your effectiveness in communicating with certain groups of

TABLE 25-1   Pronunciation Errors

	Proper	Improper
Get	get	git
Just	just	jist
Across	a cross	a crost
Nuclear	nu clee ar	nu cyou lar
Perspiration	pers pir a tion	press pir a tion
Strict	strict	strick
Escape	es cape	ex cape
Compulsory	com pul sory	com pul so rary
Recognize	rec og nize	reck a nize
Library	li brar y	li berry
Mischievous	mis che vous	mis chee vious
Theater	*thee* a ter	thee *a* ter
Picture	pic tchure	pit chure
Surprise	sur prise	sup prise
Comparable	*com* per able	com *pare* able
Larynx	lar inks	lar nix
Relevant	rel a vant	rev a lant
Drowned	drown'd	drown ded
Et cetera	et cet era	ek cet era

people. Here, too, feedback from your practice audience can alert you to errors of which you were unaware.

(2) Check the preferred pronunciation of unfamiliar words.

Your reading vocabulary and your speaking vocabulary are different. There can be words you frequently see and understand yet rarely speak or hear spoken. Without exposure and feedback you might develop your own silent way of saying such a word that involves a mistake like adding a sound or reversing sounds. The incorrect pronunciation will feel right to you because you have said it to yourself so often as you read and did research. If you give a whole speech about the Electorial College (instead of Electoral), your listeners might just wonder how knowledgeable you really are. Or, they may be confused or amused if you constantly refer to the need for a counselor to listen "emphatically" when you think you are saying "empathically," a word that means something entirely different. Check words you encounter in research, but do not use regularly, to be sure you have them right.

As a child you may have been taught to "sound out" unfamiliar words. You also discovered the perils of this technique the first time you pronounced *island* "iz-land," and wrestled with *pneumatic*. You learned then that it was unwise to make assumptions about unfamiliar words; that is still true, especially for the speaker.

Place names are always an area for careful investigation. Looking at the word *Beaulieu* one would expect to say it "Bowl yew." However, the village by that name in Britain is pronounced "Byew lee." Similarly, Leicester is "Lester." The Cairo in Egypt we call "Kie row"; the Cairo in Illinois, "Kay row." Houston Street in New York City is "How ston," but Texans have "Hyew ston."

There are minor differences in pronunciation that can be troublesome. "*A*pricot" or "*ay*pricot"? "Har *rass*" or "*har* rass"? Which pronunciation of *Vietnam, Peking,* or *Caribbean?* A dictionary is not much help when there are several correct pronunciations, or changing ones, or when words become more or less anglicized, or when unusual proper names like Nagorno-Karabakh spring upon the scene. It has been said that the arbiters of the most current acceptable pronunciation are the anchorpersons of national news programs. You are usually safe to follow their lead or that of other such models as the most articulate and respected leaders of the community.

Refer to these sources for questions of pronunciation:

Lass, Abraham, and Betty Lass. *Dictionary of Pronunciation.* New York: Quadrangle/The New York Times, 1976.

Prator Jr., Clifford H., and Betty Wallace Robinett. *Manual of American English Pronunciation.* 4th ed. New York: Holt, 1985.

Dauer, Rebecca M. *Accurate English: A Complete Course in Pronunciation.* Englewood Cliffs, NJ: Prentice-Hall Regents, 1994.

Chapter 26

Physical Delivery

Use your physical delivery to create a visual effect that complements the content of your speech.

Much of how your audience responds to you is a result of what they see rather than what they hear. The words may be confident, but trembling legs and fidgeting fingers tell another story. Slumped posture and a sour expression can give the lie to the statement, "I'm so happy to be here!" When practicing and delivering your speech, be aware of the visual image you are creating. As with vocal delivery, the goal is to be natural and to avoid any actions that would distract your audience from your message.

26a. Be conscious of your appearance.

What kinds of first impressions do people have of you? Are they initially intimidated by you because you are football player big and burly? Do people dismiss you because you look ten years younger than you are? Obviously, you cannot trade in your body; but if such impressions get in the way of your speech goal, you can try to compensate. Correct false impressions, especially in the opening minutes of your presentation, by using speech content and all those physical characteristics you have control over.

As you get ready for a particular speech, consider what your hairstyle, grooming, and clothing might say to your audience. You do not need, or necessarily want, to mimic the dress of your audience. Regardless of differences in sense of style, you should show that you took *care* in preparing, that you consider the event important enough to expend some energy in trying to look good.

Ideally, your clothes should provide a tasteful and unobtrusive frame for your personality and your remarks. Be aware of regional, cultural, and occupational norms. In some parts of the country and in certain professional or social settings jeans and a sport jacket can be considered formal enough for a presentation. When in doubt, though, lean toward conservative, businesslike clothes. There is no need to be drab, but remember that your audience could be distracted by gaudy colors, busy patterns, eye-catching jewelry, unorthodox combinations of apparel, and any clothing they associate with seduction or courtship.

26b. Eliminate distracting mannerisms.

Distracting mannerisms fall into two categories: those you have all the time (pushing your glasses up your nose, tucking your hair behind your ear, cracking your knuckles), and those you have only when giving a speech (noisily fanning and squaring up your notecards, rocking back and forth on your heels, tapping your pencil on the lectern). These are physical equivalents of saying "y'know . . . y'know . . . y'know." Few acts are inherently distracting—it is the repetition of that act that becomes distracting. As with vocal mannerisms, you are unaware of the frequency of the act until someone points it out. Thus, the biggest step toward eliminating the problem is becoming aware of it; sometimes this awareness is sufficient to resolve it. Commit yourself to using the practice techniques laid out in **24a** to get feedback on your delivery.

A distracting mannerism did not spring up overnight, and it would be unrealistic to think that it could be eliminated overnight. The primary goal should be a reduction of the frequency of the mannerism by adapting the behavior modification techniques described in **25a(5)**.

26c. Stand or sit with a relaxed but alert posture.

As a general rule, you should stand when speaking. This focuses the attention on you and gives you a better view of your audience. There are exceptions, of course. In an intimate setting, such as a circle of a dozen people, you might choose to speak seated. As a member of a panel discussion, you may be constrained to follow the sedentary lead of the moderator. If, however, you can learn to be comfortable speaking without a lectern, with your weight evenly distributed, your notes grasped casually in one hand at waist level, supported by no props of any kind, then you can easily adapt to any setting. Appropriate variations might include leaning across the lectern to show deep involvement or sitting on the edge of a desk or table to signal the shift to an informal mood. Draping yourself across the lectern, lounging at the side with one elbow extended, or standing in an off-center posture are never compatible with the energetic and controlled image of a polished public speaker. But avoid also the rigid, petrified stance of a military academy cadet. Specifically, be careful never to lock your knees—you risk becoming lightheaded or even toppling over.

26d. If you move about during the speech, make the action purposeful and relevant.

You can give a perfectly good and proper speech standing behind a lectern. However, most speeches can be aided by movement at appropriate times. Taking a few steps to the left or right, or moving closer to your listeners can add variety or emphasis to your speech. You also establish contact with that segment of the audience that you have moved toward. Moreover, physical movement during a speech is a constructive way to release tension.

Make your movements purposeful. Pacing nervously around the room is distracting. So are the tentative dances of the speaker who cannot really decide whether to move or not. This speaker shuffles, rocks to either side, extends a toe as if testing the temperature of the water, and then darts back, chilled. If you are going to move at all, be decisive. Take at least two or three normal paces diagonally or directly forward. When you stop keep your body orientation and eye contact toward the most concentrated part of your audience.

The timing of your movement can reinforce your ideas. Generally, it is not effective to move around when explaining complex material or when delivering your most emotional examples or powerful arguments. Physical movement works best at transitional points, where it signals a change in mood, content, or form.

26e. Keep your hands free so you can gesture if it feels natural.

"I don't know what to do with my hands" is perhaps the most frequently expressed concern about delivery. People who use their hands to gesture quite naturally and comfortably in everyday interaction stare with consternation at the two frying pans below their wrists when it is time to give a speech. What you should do with your hands in a speech is exactly what you do with them in normal conversation. For some people, using their hands in this manner means hardly using them at all. For others, this means gesturing a great deal. Whether we gesture a little or a lot, we do it to describe, to point out, to enumerate, to emphasize, to entreat.

There is no need to plan what gestures go with your speech. If you have ever seen a speaker who had prepared a gesture for nearly every word in the speech, you probably began to feel you were watching a game of charades or a person signing for the hearing impaired. Inevitably with such a scheme, the carefully planned gestures get a little ahead of or behind the words, the unfortunate result resembling a movie with its sound track out of sync.

If you are absorbed with your topic and with communicating it to your listeners, the gestures will emerge spontaneously at the appropriate points. But this will happen only if your hands are free to move. Too many speakers immobilize their hands completely, both out of the panicky need to cling to something and the desire to prevent uncontrolled movement. Do not lock yourself into any of these gesture-inhibiting stances:

The Bear Hug	Arms across chest, is one of the most common ways of getting a grip on yourself
Ten-Hut!	Arms stiff, wrists firmly nailed to pelvis
The Flesh Wound	One arm hangs useless at the side, the other hand serves as a tourniquet above or below the elbow
The Firing Squad	Legs slightly spread, hands tied behind back
The Choirboy/Girl	Hands clasped at waist level, every finger entwined with several others
The Supplicant	Same as the Choir, but higher: at chest level
The Fig Leaf	Demurely crossed hands, strategically placed

Actually, all of these are perfectly acceptable transitory postures. The problem with them lies not in the position of the hands but rather in the temptation to remain in one stance, statuelike, while concentrating on what is coming out of your mouth. As you become more involved in your message and the audience's response to it, your natural gestures will come back to you. When these natural impulses collide with the unnatural posture you have locked yourself into, the results are bizarre:

- The Supplicant, who cannot get her fingers untangled when she wants to forcefully jab a finger in emphasizing a series of points, looks like she is holding a pistol in a two-handed police grip and taking potshots at the audience.
- Another speaker, trying to describe a complex process while in the Ten-Hut! position, finds himself flapping his hands uselessly at his thighs, like a penguin trying to fly.
- The Choirboy starts a dramatic elevating gesture to emphasize his point on the rise in inflation and discovers that since he cannot unclench his hands they have come to a stop against his chin and his elbows are twitching out in the vicinity of his ears.

So, what *do* you do with your hands? First, nothing distracting like nervously shredding notecards, drumming on the table, or other kinds of unproductive hand movements:

The Lady Macbeth	Hands wrung compulsively and continuously to wash out the stain of having to speak
Happy Pockets	Keys, change, and other pocket articles are set to jingling by restless hands, the sound competing with the speaker's voice

Second, nothing contrived, no rehearsed gestures. A hand can be at your side, be holding cards at waist level, resting lightly on the other, *gently* grasping the lectern, or casually in a pocket (no change jingling). What matters most is that your arms, wrists, and fingers are relaxed so that your hands can move if you find a need for that movement arising naturally.

26f. Maintain eye contact.

Be familiar enough with your material that you can look at as many members of your audience as possible, as often as possible. In our culture, looking into another's face connotes openness and interest, while looking away or down is interpreted as a sign of insincerity or shiftiness. People would much rather look at your face than the top of your head. Moreover, it can distract them from what you are saying if you stare fixedly out the window or up at the ceiling. After a while the audience's attention begins to shift in those directions, wondering if cue cards are taped to the rafters, or if a major crime is in progress outside. But more essentially, maintaining eye contact allows you to read your listeners' faces to get feedback on how your message is being received. Advice to fake eye contact by looking between heads or looking just over the heads of the people in the back row misses the whole point.

At the beginning of your speech, when you have not yet gotten into your stride, find a few listeners who are responding supportively with nods and positive facial expressions. Look at them and use their support to help you through this uncomfortable period, but as soon as you start to roll, widen your eye contact to include everyone.

Actually look into the eyes of the individual audience members, and hold that contact for at least three seconds. Do not skim across rows of faces. Move your eye contact randomly throughout the room. Do not fall into a head-bobbing pattern: left, center, right, center, left . . . Have a friend or colleague observe and tell you if you scan mechanically or if you have a tendency to neglect any one segment of the audience.

In any speech, even a manuscript speech, you should have eye contact 85 percent of the time, looking down only to read technical material or to refer briefly to your notes. Most importantly, be sure you have eye contact throughout your introduction and conclusion and during the most telling points and pivotal arguments.

26g. Use facial expression to reflect or forecast mood and tone.

Do not let the tension of a speaking situation force you into a deadpan face. Your natural facial expressions can add one more channel for effective communication. Generally, changes in facial expression precede and forecast shifts in tone or mood. Replacing your cheerful countenance with a concerned frown can be a better transition than that hoary old cliché, "but seriously, folks."

You should not plan a series of mugs, smiles, and grimaces—all you need do is exaggerate slightly those expressions that arise normally. The subtle nuances that work in face-to-face contact will not show up in the back row.

The *one* expression that has the same meaning in every culture is the smile. Most public speakers underuse or misuse this powerful tool. A constant, fixed, jaw-aching grin is as bad as a deadpan expression. A smile at a sad or serious moment is inappropriate. However, remind yourself to smile genuinely whenever it can reinforce your message. It is one of the easiest ways to establish rapport, show your goodwill, and put you and your audience at ease.

27

Chapter 27

Adapting to the Speech Situation

Anticipate that the actual speech situation may be different from your visualization of it. Be prepared to take advantage of the good variations and to cope with the bad ones.

What would you do if twenty people show up for your speech when you were told there would be three hundred? What if you expected a homogeneous audience and find a mixed one waiting, or assumed an audience to be favorable but discover they are unfavorable instead? How would you handle distractions or hecklers during your speech? To cope with these turns of events you must resist the temptation to go on automatic pilot and spew out the speech exactly as practiced. Do not stop thinking the second you start speaking. Despite all your hours of preparation, the actual creation of the speech occurs *now*, as you talk. Dozens of strategic choices cannot be made until during the speech. But you can avoid some unpleasant shocks if you spend some time thinking about the contingencies you face. When you prepare for and practice a speech, consider not only the probable but also the possible.

27a. Adapt to the audience response as you give your speech. Plan alternative strategies for reactions you may receive.

The give-and-take between speaker and listeners is one thing that makes a good speech more than reading aloud. A speaker can present the same report twelve times and not become boring and flat, because she or he experiences the excitement each time of interacting with a new and different audience. The changes and adaptations sustain the vigor of the speech. Adaptation is not a new skill you must laboriously learn; it is nothing but a more structured version of the mood sensing and editing you do all the time in ordinary conversation.

What follows are some common adjustments you might make.

(1) If your audience seems bored or restless, consider the following:

- Use more humor and novelty.
- Use more concrete examples.
- Use more direct references to the audience.
- Invite direct participation—by asking them to give examples or to raise their hands to denote agreement, and so on.
- Cut out or simplify technical descriptions and statistics.
- Make your delivery more animated.
- Make a physical change; for example, walk around the lectern and sit on a desk.
- Cut it short. The program might be running late—cut out subpoints, drive home your thesis sentence, and stop.

(2) If you are not getting the agreement you expected, consider the following:

- Stress common ground.
- Modify your goal; do not try to do so much.
- Spend extra time on establishing your credibility.
- Appeal to your listeners' sense of fair play: "Whether you agree with me or not, I'm sure you will hear me out."

(3) If your audience is less informed than you expected, consider the following:

- Check your perceptions. Ask questions like, "How many of you know the difference between fission and fusion?" . . . "the secret of Damascus steel?"
- Use more supporting materials that are geared toward clarification: definition, explanation, examples, illustration, restatement, and analogies that compare the unknown to the known.
- Delete the more technical materials.

(4) If your audience is more informed than you expected, consider the following:

- Condense your basic material and call it a review. "As most of you know . . ."
- Recall and insert the more technical or abstract materials you encountered in your research.
- Introduce the questions and issues that you see as unresolved aspects of the topic.
- Cut the speech short and invite discussion of your topic.

(5) If your audience is more heterogeneous than you expected, consider the following:

- Gear your supporting material and language to what seems to be the typical audience member. Identify the predominant ethnic group, for example, or estimate the average age.
- Add materials that acknowledge the presence of the full range of listeners, but do not change the main thrust of your speech. Add a reference to a television show that children in the audience can relate to, or spend a few minutes establishing your credibility for the 10 percent of the audience that disagrees with you.

Caveat: Do not overreact in categorizing your audience. Give your listeners time to adjust to you and give your speech room to make an impression on them. Keep in touch with the mood of the audience and do not play to the extremes.

27b. Take several steps to prevent distractions. If distractions do occur, be familiar with the strategies to deal with them.

Murphy's Law is an especially potent force to reckon with in facing the physical setting and the mechanical apparatus of the speech situation. Here are some suggestions on how to avoid or mitigate its effect.

(1) Check your presentation's setting and equipment to detect possible sources of distraction.

Arrive early and survey the room where you will speak. Make whatever changes necessary to ensure that attention will be focused on you and your message. For instance, if the room has windows, you may have to draw the blinds or modify the seating arrangement to prevent sunlight from blinding your listeners. An obtrusive object or chart should be covered or turned around. The chairs should be shifted to suit your type of presentation. Test the acoustics to see if you need to close windows against outside noise or need amplification to counteract an undercurrent of environmental sounds.

If you are using electronic aids, find the outlets in the room and actually test both your aids and the outlets for proper functioning. Have backups for your equipment or, if you are being provided with equipment, insist that it come with spare bulbs, batteries, and so on. Now, and not after being introduced, is the time to check the sound level of your microphone.

If you are using a computer, make sure it is compatible with the projection system.

Inevitably, there will be some sources of distraction that cannot be controlled. The FAA would doubtless not approve of canceling all commercial flights over the building in which you will be speaking, but you should take every opportunity to change what you can: Katharine Hepburn, during the run of the musical *Coco,* was able to convince the construction workers across from the theater to cease riveting during her big solo each matinee.

(2) Fleeting or low-level distractions during your speech are best dealt with by not acknowledging them.

The first rule of dealing with distractions is, naturally, that you yourself must not become or seem distracted. At the same time, though, you should subtly raise your energy level to keep your listeners' attention. When all heads turn as a latecomer enters through the door behind you, do not legitimize the interruption by turning your head also. Do not appear to be flustered when a fluorescent bulb starts to flicker over-head—just speak a little louder, become just a bit more animated, add some extra attention devices such as humor or storytelling.

(3) Sometimes distractions can be turned to your purpose by incorporating them into your speech.

One frequently told story is of the politician whose campaign speech was interrupted by a crying baby. "I can't blame that youngster," he remarked. "She's just thinking about four more years of a Republican administration." In another instance, a speaker had to pause when a waiter noisily dropped a tray of dishes. He continued with, "That's about how the inter-collegiate athletics' department came crashing down when the scholarship scandal hit the press. Guess who got elected to pick up the pieces?"

(4) When it is actually necessary to interrupt the continuity of your speech, do so as quickly as possible and then draw your listeners back in.

Your job is to give the speech, not close doors, answer telephones, adjust the thermostat, and so on. If no one seems to want to take care of a problem, then you must interrupt your speech and deal with it so that everyone can quickly return to the business at hand.

There are two levels of interruption. In the first, you do not stop speaking: ". . . which would justify that course of action. Would someone please unlock that door? There are people wanting to get in. For my second point, I would like you to consider . . ."

In the second case, circumstances require that you stop speaking while certain actions are taken by you or members of the audience. After you are satisfied with the result of that action—as, for example, when a victim of heat prostration has been cared for and led from the room—you may continue, backing up in your organization to summarize the progression of your points prior to the interruption: "Thank you for handling that so competently. Now, as you remember, I was just a moment ago talking about . . ."

27c. Do not hand control of the situation over to the verbal or nonverbal heckler. Respond to such interruptions calmly and firmly.

The worst distraction a speaker can face is the intentional interrupter. The problems can range from the listener who has had a little too much to drink and has delusions of wit, to the person who makes a systematic attempt to undermine your speech goal or even to prevent you from speaking. Generally, respond to them by progressing through the steps from **27b**: Ignore; if you cannot, incorporate; if you cannot, confront.

Always keep in mind your credibility with the audience and remember that you do not want to do anything that will interfere with achieving your speech purpose. You never want to lose your composure, dignity, or temper; you do not ever want to sink to the heckler's level.

(1) The verbal heckler

If you start justifying yourself to a heckler, you have lost control of the situation and have put it in his or her lap. Do not get into a defensive posture. For example, do not defend yourself against name-calling. "You're a crook!" "You don't care about the environment." Do not waste time with denials. Deal with the substance, not with the accusations.

First-level tactics
Establish an image or tone of reasonableness or fairness. Make it clear that you are not opposed to dialogue, even if the heckler is disregarding the polite convention that gives the floor to you. Give the heckler the benefit of the doubt in terms of her or his sincerity.

Appeal to fair play. "I base my opinions about China on my three months travel there. Will you hear me out while I describe those experiences? *Then* we'll listen to your objections."

Build on common ground. "We both want the best schooling for our children. If we didn't think it was vitally important, neither of us would be here."

Never seem to close down the heckler or his or her point of view completely. Each does represent a point of view, and you want the audience to view you as a reasonable person. Of course, if you believe that the heckler, though sincere, has adopted a vastly oversimplified analysis of a complex issue, you communicate that to your listeners.

Second-level tactics

In the course of being polite, you do not want your audience to think that you are glad that you have been interrupted and are enjoying the byplay. There comes a time where you have to shut the person off and get on with the speech.

Enough is enough. If the heckler has not been mollified or deflated by your reasonableness, then you can say something like, "I think you've made your point. Now I really must ask you to sit down and let me continue my speech." Even if the heckler does not, this will give the audience permission to tell the person to shut up, or security permission to remove her or him.

The zinger. As a last resort it is sometimes appropriate to flatten a heckler with a pithy and pointed comeback. Effective use of the "zinger" depends on two factors: your ability to think of a wise and witty retort (*not* one of the "your mother wears combat boots" variety), and your correct reading of the audience. If your listeners are irritated and impatient with the heckler, they will welcome your initiative. If you have misjudged their mood, however, you run the risk of seeming nasty.

(2) The nonverbal heckler

These are the hecklers you will run into more frequently. Rolled eyes, fidgeting, sighs, whispering, note-passing are their trademarks. They do not have quite the nerve to heckle you out loud, but they want you to know that they disagree or are bored. If you focus on their behavior, your self-confidence may start to erode. These people can absorb all your attention as you start playing to them.

By and large, the usual way to deal with the nonverbal heckler is to ignore him or her. Sometimes you might have to cut off eye contact completely with that section of the audience. Instead, make eye contact with the people who are displaying positive signs, and avoid allowing your eyes to drift back to the heckler.

If you find it difficult to ignore the heckler, you may want to try one of the following:

- If you know the person by name, throw the name, in a complimentary sense, into the speech. This may either get the heckler's interest or embarrass her or him into being polite.
- If you are sufficiently self-assured, maintain eye contact with the nonverbal heckler until he or she defers.

If the heckling is an ongoing problem, in a class, say, or in a series of business meetings, it may be advisable for you to talk to this person privately and ask for feedback. He or she may be gratified enough by the attention to modify the annoying behavior.

You should avoid, however, projecting your own interpretations too freely onto the members of the audience. Often, teachers have been surprised when the student who has been sitting in class all year with crossed arms and a sour expression comes up at the end and says, "This was the best class I've ever had." The frown in the audience may be the result of a headache, or poor dinner, or merely concentration. Do not be too eager to leap to conclusions about the nonverbal messages your audience is sending you.

Chapter 28

Visual Aids

Use visual aids appropriately and effectively.

There are places in a speech where a visual aid can help you make a point more clearly and in a shorter time than if you were forced to use words alone. Conversely, visual aids poorly used or overused can make your ideas obscure and slow the pace of your speech. Relying too much on visual aids will cut into time that should be spent on analysis or development of points and ideas.

A visual aid is best used in two places: when you are attempting to explain a complex or technical idea, and when you want to reinforce a particular message. For example, a geneticist might find it useful to have a model of the DNA double helix when talking about how that remarkable molecule duplicates itself. Or, the speaker wishing to impress upon his or her audience the importance of stiffer drunk-driving penalties may choose to reinforce a recitation of traffic fatality percentages with a "pie" graph that demonstrates the overwhelming predominance of drunken driving over other causes of traffic deaths.

28a. Select a visual aid appropriate to the point you wish to illustrate or clarify.

We can put visual aids into three categories.

(1) The object or a physical reproduction of it

While demonstrating the superior simplicity of a new lens-to-camera attachment system, a speaker can put force behind her or his words by using the actual camera and lens to show the ease of coupling. It would take many more words by themselves to convey the same message. With a large audience, however, this sort of demonstration might not work, because of the smallness of the equipment. In this case, the speaker could use larger-than-life-size models to make sure the message was clear. Other objects are obviously too small or large to use, like a microchip or the actual *Queen Mary,* so scaled-up or scaled-down reproductions are necessary.

There are other considerations when deciding between an object and its reproduction. Most audiences (other than groups of medical professionals) would be grateful if the speaker explained valve structures and their functions by using a plastic replica of a human heart rather than the real thing.

(2) Pictorial reproductions

These can include photographs, sketches, plans, pictures, slides, computer animations, film clips, videotapes, and the like. If the mechanical device that makes the lens-camera coupling so easy is in itself complex, perhaps the speaker would use an "exploded" three-quarter-view schematic drawing to show the interaction of all the pieces. A large photograph of the human heart may be preferred by the speaker wishing to show the musculature. As in **(1)**, size of object and size of audience are important factors in determining which to use.

(3) Pictorial symbols

These are used with more abstract concepts and can include graphs, charts, diagrams, and lists of important words and phrases.

Bringing a derelict in off the street would probably get an audience's attention, but it would not be as useful, when speaking on the declining state of the economy, as a line graph showing the buying power of the dollar through the last two decades. An aerial photograph of San Jose would not be as appropriate to a speech on local politics as would a map showing city council district boundaries. If a speaker wants a motto, inspirational phrase, or name of a product reinforced, then suitably lettered posters can help. (See Figure 28-1.)

FIGURE 28-1   Pictorial Symbols

Pie Graph

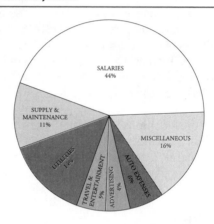

Line Graph

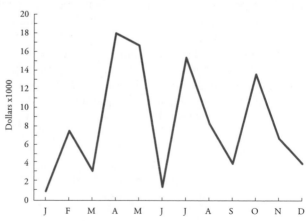

FIGURE 28-1 continued

Bar Graph

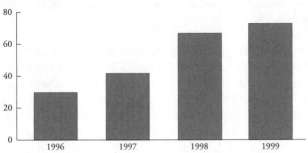

Annotated Map

Slogan or Memorable Phrase

THE "FOUR D's"

Drop it
Delay it
Delegate it
Do it

28b. Prepare clear and manageable visual aids.

(1) Prepare visual aids large enough to be seen by the entire audience.

The nature of the place in which you will be speaking and, as stated in **28a(1)**, the size of the audience determine to a great extent the type and size of visual aid. It will help to look over the facility in advance, if that is possible. Stand at the back of the room and envision the scene, or, if you already have a rough mock-up or draft of one of your aids, place it where you expect it to be when you speak. Obviously, if the aid is too small you will need to enlarge it. One option is to design transparencies to show on an overhead projector, or use presentation software. Reduce any aid that is larger than it need be, considering the size of the room, or that is so unwieldy you will have to wrestle with it.

Lines on charts should be thick and bold. Model parts should be large enough to be distinguished. Screens for slides, projected presentations, or filmstrips should be large enough for the size of the room, and projectors should have focal lengths great enough to fill the screen. If you are showing a videotape, make sure the monitor can be mounted high enough to be seen by the back row, and that there are enough monitors for everyone to get a good view.

(2) Keep your visual aids simple and clear.

Do not construct overelaborate aids. They should contain just enough detail to allow your listeners to distinguish easily one part from another. Look at the two cutaway drawings of a car engine in Figure 28-2. The one on the right would be the better one to use if you wanted to demonstrate the ignition system. It provides information on where the ignition system is in relation to the rest of the car's engine, without subjecting the audience to the eyestrain of trying to distinguish it from the fuel system, the cooling system, the air conditioning system, and so on. Similarly, do not crowd maps, charts, graphs, models, and photographs with so much data that your audience ends up confused about which part you are referring to. For instance, you should have one map showing only city council districts and another only county supervisorial districts in the city. Avoid having so many lines on a line graph that an audience will "take a wrong turn" while following one line across. For photographs, try to find one

FIGURE 28-2   Keep Visual Aids Clear

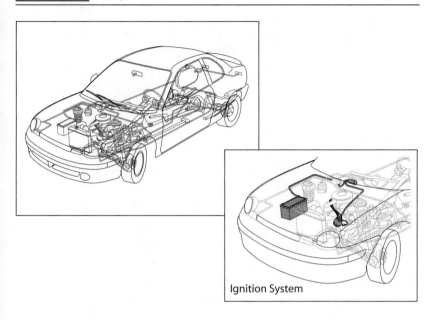

Ignition System

that shows the object in isolation, or in sharp focus in relation to other objects.

Keep the wording on any visual aid simple and familiar, printed in clear block lettering if you letter by hand. Use no more words than strictly necessary to label parts and ideas.

Maintain continuity when you spread your information out. If you have used a pie graph for your first aid, any following aids dealing with similar or related information should also be pie graphs.

Use color to delineate different aspects of the object or symbol. A large model heart with bright blue, red, and yellow parts may not look totally realistic, but the audience will find it a lot easier to keep the parts separate in their minds as they follow the explanation.

Presentation software packages enable you to create slides that you may print and project, or project directly from a computer projection system. Keep the following suggestions in mind to ensure that the overheads and projected slides you create are effective.

- Use simple typefaces. Do not mix more than two typefaces on a sheet. Avoid ornate or showy type, and stay away from drop shadows, outline fonts, and other decorative type modifications that add visual noise.
- Use uppercase and lowercase letters in the titles and text. Sentences printed exclusively in capital letters are harder to read.
- Use a lot of white space. Do not crowd too much information on one sheet. Keep the information simple; use your speech to fill in the details.
- Maintain continuity throughout the transparencies. Settle on a design theme and carry it out for each sheet. For instance, if you use a border, put it on all sheets; if you use bullets for a list on one sheet, do not use dashes for a list on another sheet.

(3) Design visual aids for maximum audience impact.

The design and form of your visual aids can sometimes enhance your credibility, add humor, provide information beyond the data presented, or just maintain the interest level of your listeners.

A professional-looking aid can do much to lend a polished tone to an entire speech. You need not hire a professional to prepare one, however, nor do you need a computer. Art supply stores stock transfer letters, stencils, colored plastic in various geometric forms—all sorts of simple graphic materials that even the unartistic can use to produce a neat and attractive visual aid.

If you do use a computer to make a two-dimensional aid, there are a number of presentation software packages that offer templates with predetermined design attributes: colors, borders, typefaces, and the like. These are handy to ensure continuity between sheets, and to ensure that the type will be large enough to read. The manuals describing these templates will usually categorize them by method of display: There will be some suggested if you plan to make overheads off a laser printer, others if you are looking to produce 35mm slides, and others if you are going to present the material on-screen. Follow the guidelines; a laser print of an overhead produced from a 35mm-type template will probably be dark and hard to read, with murky graphic elements. Within a particular category, choose one of the simpler designs. Many of the templates can be overly complex—and some have design elements that detract from the material presented—the visual equivalent of a dog barking at your feet while you speak.

For whatever type of visual aid, basic, unexotic colors are best to use, unless there is a color that is popularly associated with the object or idea being depicted. And, of course, there are standard uses, like green for forests, blue for water, and so on.

Along this line, you can construct your visual aids in a manner that underscores the theme of your speech. Consider, for instance: Instead of using bar graphs to indicate yearly differences in logging revenues, substitute tree outlines with the proper relative dimensions (be careful here: if you go by relative height alone, the relative volume of the objects will be out of scale and the graphic will be misleading). Or, compare rows of objects—houses, missiles, stick figures with dunce caps—where each object represents a certain number of housing starts, strategic warheads, or failing high school students. A particularly subtle way of using visual material to drive home a verbal message was demonstrated by President Reagan when he went on television to present his tax plan to the American public. He displayed a line graph depicting the projected government spending that would result from his plan and the spending that would result from his opponents' plan, explaining it by saying, "Our plan, shown here by the *solid* line . . ." and ". . . the Democrats' proposal, which is the dotted line . . ." Using a solid line on the graph invested his position with the semblance of stability and careful planning, while the insubstantial dotted line represented the lightweight, disjointed thinking of the opposition.

28c. Introduce your visual aids so that they blend smoothly into the speech.

(1) Practice with your visual aids.

Your aids should be prepared early enough that you can practice with them several times. See **24b(3)**. This will alert you to any changes that might be necessary. Become comfortable with them so you do not fumble around during the presentation.

(2) Maintain eye contact.

Be so familiar with your material that you can look at your listeners while explaining the visual aid. Often a speaker will turn his or her back on the audience and talk directly at the visual aid. This deprives the speaker of feedback and will strain the listeners' hearing.

(3) Keep talking.

Avoid long pauses when demonstrating a process. If there is some complexity, or if many steps are needed to produce your desired result, you might be wise to take a hint from television cooking shows and prepare a series of aids to demonstrate various phases. Doing this will eliminate those periods when both you and the audience are waiting for something to happen. For example, a speaker could say: "Then you apply glue to the two blocks, press them together like this, and let the bond dry. Here are some that have already dried, and I'll show you the next step . . ." When you cannot avoid a time lag introduced by some process, have a planned digression—some bit of history related to the process, perhaps—to fill the gap.

(4) Do not let your visual aids become a distraction.

Keep your visual aids covered, out of sight, turned off, or turned away from your audience until you are ready to use them. Remove or re-cover them immediately after they have served their purpose. If you are using a projector, turn it off when you can to eliminate the cooling fan noise.

Refrain from passing objects through the audience, as that will cause a ripple of inattention over the next few minutes. This rule is flexible, especially when you are dealing with an unusual object and a small audience, but still it is probably best to share the item *after* the speech, say during the discussion period. By the same token, handouts should be distributed after a speech. You want the audience to listen now and read later.

Finally, visual aids are most distracting when you are clumsy with them. Be sure your charts are in the right order, your models are set up, your equipment is in perfect working order. Avoid visual aid fiascoes by practicing carefully, arriving in plenty of time for setup, and being pessimistic enough to carry with you pins, tape, extension cords, extra projector bulbs, floppy backups, and the like to ensure that what you envision will come to pass.

28d. Understand the benefits, constraints, and perils of using presentation software.

Presentation software can be considered a mixed blessing to the speaker. One the one hand, it is possible to create transparencies and handouts that are consistent and attractive. On the other, it is possible to be put in a position where you are narrating your outline rather than giving a speech.

(1) Keep your text slides simple.

The templates that come with the presentation software application are designed to keep your slides simple. That is, if you use the typefaces in the sizes that come as the default, it will be difficult for you to clutter up a slide with too many words and ideas. This is good; avoid the temptation to finesse your way around the constraints of the type size. Instead, look for better ways to organize your material, and pare down your language to the minimum. See **7** and **8**.

You may use animation effects or "builds" to expose certain elements of a slide in a particular order for dramatic effect or to keep the focus on the most immediate point. If you do take advantage of this capability, do so with restraint; the efficacy of the effect will diminish with overuse.

(2) Maintain consistency.

If used properly, presentation software can help you maintain a consistent look throughout your slides. While templates work for keeping the type consistent, the program's settings for color schemes, slide backgrounds and patterns, and so on, work to keep other elements consistent. Even with this help, though, you need to review your slides to make sure no discrepancies have crept in. Look at the captions, are they all in burgundy 14 pt bold Helvetica? Or has one somehow ended up in green 14 pt Arial Narrow? How about placement of elements? Click through the slide show quickly to see if elements seem to jump from place to place in relation to other instances. Also, check other features, like transition effects and builds, for consistency. Sometimes, especially if a presentation is being created from a number of earlier ones, these may get mixed up, so that you end up with most slides using a "fade through black" transition and a few using a "wipe right."

(3) Be judicious in your use of clip art.

Avoid the temptation to "pretty-up" your slides with a lot of clip art graphics from the libraries that come with the software. Since the popular software packages have such wide exposure, the use of a familiar clip art image like, for example, business folks standing around a table will make your message seem less unique. Additionally, too many images will be distracting. Images in different styles (line drawing of person followed by cartoon image of person, for instance, or a low-resolution bitmap image followed by a sharp PostScript image) will be distracting as well. See **28c(2)**.

(4) Do not become secondary to your slides.

It is a common picture in conference and convention settings: one or two large screens in a room holding hundreds of people; dwarfed by the screens, a speaker is partially hidden behind a bank of computer monitors where he or she is hunched over in the dim light, clicking away at the mouse while talking into the body mike, the commentary often on some glitch with the system. Obvious problems here are lack of connection with the audience because of the darkened room and the focus on the machine, confinement of the speaker to the space in front of the computer, and the "aid" becoming an impediment.

If you are in a situation where this sort of projection will be taking place, take steps to counteract the potential difficulties. Enlist a colleague or assistant to work the program on the computer (make sure you have practiced enough, see **28c(4)** and **27b**) so that you are free to move around and to make what eye contact with the audience is possible. If you cannot get away from working the equipment, or if you must compensate for dim lighting, use vocal variety to counterbalance immobility and lack of visibility. See **25c**. If possible, use the slides for key illustrations and points, but have the screen blank at other times.

Exercise 1. Suggest three different kinds of visual aids that might be used for speeches on each of these topics:

Car pool lanes
How a check is processed
The workings of a lock
Instituting mandatory national service

Exercise 2. Rank order the speeches in the **Appendix** by the need for visual aids. Explain your decision in terms of audience, occasion, and topic. If you decide that visual aids would complement some of the speeches, recommend what kinds of aids, and indicate where in the speech they should go.

Chapter 29

Answering Questions

Use the question-and-answer period to ensure that your message was understood by as many people as possible. Prepare fully, answer questions directly, and maintain control of the interaction.

The question-and-answer period is a great opportunity to further the goals of your speech. While you spoke, you attempted to address the needs of your audience, and now you can see how close you came. From your listeners' questions you can learn what points are unclear or what arguments and objections they have. Do not approach the question-and-answer period as if facing a firing squad. Communicate an eagerness to interact with the audience and to hear their ideas on your subject. Express your enthusiasm through such reactions as, "I'm glad you brought that up," "That's a good question," "That's intriguing. I never thought of it quite that way."

Do not lose your delivery skills just because the speech is over. Keep eye contact, avoid fidgeting or mumbling. Actually, some speakers' delivery improves during the question-and-answer period because they become more relaxed.

29a. Come prepared for a question-and-answer period.

Keep in mind the importance of the question-and-answer period throughout the stages of preparing your speech. Anticipate the questions that will arise naturally from each of your various points. One aid to this would be to have the friends who listen to your practice sessions ask you questions afterward. Although you can never predict the exact questions that will come up, there are certain ones that are more probable than others. Rehearse aloud possible answers to the most complicated and difficult ones. This is how public figures prepare for news conferences.

Ideally, your research has been so extensive that you have much more material than you were able to use, considering the time constraints surrounding your speech. You should not shove this extra material into a closet and forget about it. Continue to review it so you will be familiar enough with the content to weave it easily into elaboration and explanation in response to questions.

Think of possible applications of particularly effective evidence. For instance, for your speech on women in the labor force (see **9b**), you do not use a delightful story you found about a Japanese woman worker because your speech concentrates on conditions in the United States. The day before the speech, though, you go over the details of the story so you can tell it accurately should any of the audience question you about how your observations may relate to women in other cultures. Similarly, it takes a minute to memorize Flo Kennedy's wonderful insight—"I know we're termites. But if all the termites got together, the house would fall down."—which you realize might fit into a discussion of the need for women to use their potential power. The statistics used in your speech relating income differences between men and women in Woodside city government jobs may seem vulnerable to some in the audience, so put together a backup notecard that (1) explains the sampling frame for the survey, (2) breaks the statistics down by occupation group, and (3) lists comparable statistics for eight other major cities.

29b. Invite and answer audience questions in a straightforward manner.

Do not worry if there are not any questions immediately, or if at first there are long pauses between questions. It usually takes your listeners a moment to collect their thoughts. In some cases you can start the ball rolling yourself by asking a question of the audience. "What problems have you encountered setting up affirmative action programs in your companies?" can generate counterquestions.

Call on questioners in the order they sought recognition and maintain eye contact while the question is being asked. If you are not sure you understand the question, paraphrase it according to your own interpretation and ask the questioner if it is accurate. When both of you are satisfied, restate or paraphrase it for the entire audience and direct the answer to them.

Be sure you *answer* the question. To avoid oversimplification, you will want to elaborate, expand, or qualify your answer, but if your discussion becomes too diffuse you will appear to be avoiding the issue. Consequently, always include a one-sentence, direct answer in your response to a question. For emphasis, place this sentence first or last, as in these examples:

First	*"Yes, I do oppose building nuclear power plants,* at least until several safety questions are answered satisfactorily. My reasons include . . ."
Last:	". . . so, because of all these serious problems I see, my answer to your question would be: *Yes, I do oppose building new nuclear power plants* at this time."

What if you are asked a question for which you do not have an answer? Do not bluff. Say that you do not know. If you have some idea where the answer could be found, tell the questioner of the source. Ask other audience members to help you out by volunteering what they know. Or, you might promise to look it up if the listener would like to get in touch with you later.

29c. Do not allow self-indulgent questioners to distort the function of the question-and-answer period.

The purpose of a question-and-answer period is to clarify issues for the entire audience. When individual audience members attempt to use this time for detailed consultation on a specialized problem, or to get on their favorite soapbox, you have an obligation as the speaker to bring the interaction back on its true course.

Be prepared to keep control of the situation by dealing in a firm and tactful manner with the following types of distracting questioners:

(1) The person who wants to give a speech

This person may agree or disagree with you, or may have a favorite ax to grind that is only tangentially related to your topic. The distinguishing characteristic is that it becomes obvious that she or he has no real question to ask you, but rather is taking advantage of an assembled audience to hold forth. It is rarely effective to ask, "What is your question?" The person will just say, "Don't you agree that . . ." or "What do you think of the position that . . ." and take off for another five minutes. You must just jump in at the end of a sentence, manufacture a question somewhat related to the person's ramblings, answer it, and recognize another questioner on the opposite side of the room. "So, you're saying that there is so much inefficiency in government that you wonder how this or any other problem can be solved. That is a tough question to answer, but I am hopeful that the recent reorganization of our agency will permit us to be successful in our efforts. Next question over there?"

(2) The person who wants to have an extended dialogue

This person might start out with a genuine question, but will not relinquish the floor when you respond. Rather, he or she counters with follow-up questions, comments on your answer, or new lines of discussion. Sometimes this sort of person wants free professional advice or therapy and does not mind seeking it in public. Other times the person simply finds you and your ideas fascinating and wants to converse at length, as though you were both guests at a cocktail party instead of speaker and audience member in a formalized setting. The best way to deal with this sort of person is to end the exchange firmly but with a compliment and/or invitation. For instance, "Thank you, you've given me quite a number of interesting insights here. Maybe you can come up and talk to me about them some more later."

(3) The person who wants to pick a fight

Intellectual confrontation and probing, penetrating questions are to be expected, even welcomed from audience members who disagree with you. But sometimes questioners become inappropriately argumentative and mount hostile, personal attacks against a speaker. It becomes obvious that they are not really seeking an answer to a question, but are trying to destroy your credibility. Do not let them succeed by becoming angry, or by defending yourself against generalized name-calling. See **27c** on heckling. Pick out the part of such a person's diatribe that contains the kernel of a question, paraphrase it, and answer it calmly and reasonably.

Q: "What about all this poisonous junk that you greed-crazed despoilers dump into our river to kill our children and whole species of animals?"

A: "The questioner has brought up the valid and difficult subject of toxic waste disposal. What is our company doing about it? Well . . ."

In short, respond to these disruptive people diplomatically. Remember that, unlike hecklers, their participation has been invited. Do not take cheap shots or direct humor at them to shut them off. Likewise, when you are taken aback by incomprehensible questions, or questions that demonstrate gross ignorance or misinformation, you should react positively. Avoid language that embarrasses the questioner or points out errors:

Not: "Well, *as I said* in my speech . . ."
But: "Let me go over these statistics more slowly . . ."

Not: "You've totally confused fission and fusion!"
But: "Many of those problems relate to nuclear *fission*. The *fusion* reaction is quite different. It works like this . . ."

Try to find ways to dignify bad questions and turn them into good ones. Your listeners' empathy is with the questioner who may be nervous or confused. Your efforts to put others at ease will win you an audience's goodwill.

Appendix

The Centrality of Oral Communication in Secondary Education
By John Poulakos

About two hundred speech communication teachers from universities, colleges, and secondary schools gathered in Springfield, Missouri, for the 1989 convention of the Missouri Speech and Theatre Association. At an after-dinner meeting, John Poulakos, associate professor of communication at the University of Pittsburgh, delivered this keynote address. Although recognized as a scholar of classical rhetorical theory, Dr. Poulakos has devoted substantial time and energy to a task force of educators committed to enhancing the status of K–12 speech education in Pennsylvania.

1 When I first came to this country twenty-five years ago, my English was minimal. I only knew a few words and how to turn them into simple sentences. I could, for example, say such things as "This is my left hand," "That is a pretty flower," "That is an ugly house." I thought that my symbolic world was a bit limited, but at least it was safe. I soon discovered that it was very limited indeed and not very safe at all. One time I was driving a car taking directions from a friend in the passenger seat. I was doing quite well until we got to an intersection and he said, "Make a left right here." I almost had an accident. Another time, I found that a Mrs. Dibble was going to be my new English teacher. I asked an older fellow student to tell me what she was like. He said, "She is pretty ugly." I thought he was alluding to Plato's mind-body dichotomy, but I was too proud to ask for clarification. Another time, I was telling my uncle, who is from Mexico, that I could play intercollegiate football, work part-time after school, do volunteer work at the local hospital, and still get straight A's in all my classes. He looked me straight in the eyes and said, "I am from Missouri." "But," I said, "I thought you are from Mexico." He responded, "I am." Needless to say, I was a very perplexed young man.

But I was determined to find out how the English language works. It has been an interesting twenty-five years, and I am still finding out its secrets.

Today, I find myself committed to two paradoxical tasks: first, teaching American college students how to speak effectively, and second, promoting the expansion of oral communication in secondary education. The first task is paradoxical because English is not my native tongue. The second task is paradoxical because oral communication should need no promotion. It should already be at the very center of secondary education.

Unfortunately, it is not. Why not? Let's speculate for a moment on the reasons. To begin with, it is no secret that our culture is ambivalent about speech. On the one hand, we glorify the power of oratory to forge consensus and show us better versions of ourselves. On the other, we are afraid of its capacity to lead us to catastrophes. We envy the person with polished communication skills, but we also distrust him or her. A smooth talker evokes our admiration and arouses our suspicion at the same time. As a people, we are torn between a profound sense of logophobia and an equally profound sense of logophilia.

I don't think there is a way around this ambivalence. As the Greeks pointed out 2,400 years ago,

> The effect of speech upon the condition of the mind is comparable to the power of drugs over the condition of the body. Just as different drugs dispel different secretions from the body, and some bring an end to disease and others to life, so too in the case of speeches: some distress, others delight, some cause fear, others make the listeners bold, and some drug and bewitch the soul with a kind of evil persuasion.

Another reason why oral communication is not a central part of the secondary curriculum is that listening and speaking are often taken for granted. And what is taken for granted is generally ignored or left unattended. The thinking here is that children can speak and listen adequately even before they step foot in kindergarten. By the time they are in high school, they know the whats and the hows of oral communication. Therefore, we should teach them things they do not already know. Things that really matter. Useful things. Things like driver's education, health education, drug education, sex education, wood shop, auto shop, metal shop, and how to shop. Things like accounting, typing, computing, cooking, sewing, and farming.

6   A third reason for the marginal status of oral communication is that it is messy. Speech classes are noisy, full of students talking, discussing, arguing. Learning is supposed to take place in the mind, quietly, and should leave the sound waves undisturbed. Students should pay attention silently, and the only source of talk should be the teacher or the TV monitor, or the film projector. Besides, speech cannot be measured along true and false or right and wrong answers. And, as we all have been trained to think, evaluation should be objective.

7   A fourth reason is that the mastery of oral communication frees a person from seeing the world according to normative societal prescriptions. Masters of speech are accomplished artists whose vision of the world is subversive if only because it is new and unprecedented. Eloquent speakers are agents of change. And change is a mortal enemy to traditional vested interests. Effective spokespersons always demand more than the status quo can deliver. They always point to the indecency, the incompetence, and the corruption of the powers that be. They always offer more attractive options, they raise our level of expectations, and they promise higher levels of satisfaction. Because they are eloquent they can persuade us to believe otherwise, to think in other words, and to act in other ways. For all these reasons, master orators are regarded as revolutionaries and subversives.

8   There you have it. Oral communication has been marginalized because we are ambivalent toward it, because we take it for granted, because we cannot measure it with the tools of measurement we have devised, and because it can turn docile people into demanding, inquisitive, critical human beings. But despite its current marginalization, speech will not go away. It has been around for at least as long as we have, and it will be around as long as we are. That is the nature of the animal.

9   Consider what Isocrates said in 375 BC:

> In the powers which we possess we are in no respect superior to other living creatures; nay, we are inferior to many in swiftness and in strength and in other resources; but, because there has been implanted in us the power to persuade each other and to make clear to each other whatever we desire, not only have we escaped the life of wild beasts, but we have come together and have founded cities and made laws and invented arts; and generally speaking, there is no institution devised by man which the power of speech has not helped us to establish. Through speech we educate the ignorant and appraise the wise; for the power to speak well is taken as the surest index of a sound understanding, and discourse which is true and lawful and just is the outward image of a good and faithful soul. And if there is need to speak in brief summary of

this power, we shall find that none of the things that are done with intelligence take place without the help of speech but that in all our actions as well as in our thoughts speech is our guide. . .

Well, a great deal has changed since 375 BC. However, at least two things remain the same. First, orality still remains an indispensable part of literacy. Second, the ideal of participatory democracy continues to be, at least in principle, a significant goal of this country. Regarding the first continuity, it is self-evident that all people are born into language. Among other things, this means that they are spoken to even before they can speak. Soon, they join the perplexing, exhilarating, debilitating, empowering, depressing, and joyful world of discourse. But they will never come to know what they can do with language. Nor will they ever come to know what language is doing to them. Malcolm X was the exception.

As I have already suggested, speakers are not born. They are made. And if this is so, it is we, their teachers, who must make them. This means that we must instruct students in the properties of language, the rules of its operation, the possibilities of its structure, and the conditions of its impact. Our mission, as I see it, is to reclaim speech for all students. Not just the academic kind. The time has come, ladies and gentlemen, when we can no longer be accomplices in the conspiracy of the electronic media to take from our students their voice. The time has come for us to enable the young people of this country to tell it like it is, to speak their minds, to voice their objections, to say what they have to say, and to say it well. The time has come to help our students listen not to the Heartbeat of America, but to those around them who have something to say, and who can say it well. The time has come to make students understand that they are part of an immense discursive network, a network that they can affect and that affects them profoundly.

Of course, the scary thing about this idea is that it is we who must take the initiative and serve as their example. But serving as an example of eloquent speech is no mean task in a culture that says: "Talk is cheap," "Actions speak louder than words," "Speaking is silver but silence is golden," "A picture is worth a thousand words," "If you don't have anything nice to say, don't say anything at all." In my judgment, this string of cliches betrays an ideological predilection intent on manufacturing unreflective human beings, compulsive consumers of discourse trained to look at things uncritically and to follow directions quietly. In short, this string of clichés is intent on keeping people silent regardless of the state of affairs in their life. But we all know that to be reduced to silence is to be humiliated, to be gagged, to be cut off from one's vital connection to the world of other people. We also know that to be a member of a silent majority is to belong to a population that is ignored and left out of account. By contrast, a vocal minority always gets attention and, in many cases, results. Significantly, those who are vocal are hard to control. And the powers that be prefer time and again silent subordinates.

13   Let's turn now to the second continuity since the time of Isocrates: participatory democracy. We all know that the Greeks were the first people in Western history who tried to govern themselves democratically, by the will of the people. This meant most fundamentally that all the citizens of the city-state were both free and obligated to partake of political decision making. In turn, this meant that all citizens had to have some training in public speaking. Today, we are supposedly the carriers of the promise of democracy and political freedom. However, it is simply hypocritical to tell students that they are guaranteed the freedom of speech in this country and then leave their potential for speech uncultivated. What good is freedom of speech if one is brought up to believe that one has nothing to say? What good is freedom of speech when one has something to say but does not know how to make it count? I would contend that when the speaking and listening faculties of our students are left uncultivated, the result is despair in the private domain and apathy in the public domain.

14   Now I do not mean to suggest that instruction in oral communication will turn all our students into John Kennedys, Mario Cuomos, and Jesse Jacksons. Nor that it will reverse, overnight, public apathy toward this country's political affairs and social issues. Nor that it will put an immediate end to the widespread feeling of alienation, aimlessness, and disorientation among today's youth. However, it can provide students of all walks of life with a few good hints: that all people are capable of and subject to persuasion; that language has the capacity to liberate them from the bondage of political, social, and religious institutions. Furthermore, instruction in oral communication can make them realize that in a humane society there has to be tolerance for individual differences, allowance for the thoughts we most despise, and respect for even those with whom we disagree. Moreover, instruction in oral communication can show them that conflict, which is inherent in a pluralistic society, must be resolved not through automatic assault weapons but through debate, negotiation, and compromise. Finally, instruction in oral communication can compel them to reflect on themselves as speakers and listeners, to see

themselves in relation to those they address and those by whom they are addressed. In short, education in speech can help students break out of their confining walls of egocentricity and enter the circle of their interlocutors. I offer you these potential benefits, ladies and gentlemen, not as guarantees but as articles of faith tested by 2,500 years of human experience and reflection.

5   What I am proposing here tonight is not original. During the last decade, a host of task forces, commissions, and foundations have argued the same thing: Good listening and speaking skills are essential for everyone. In their 1983 report, *A Nation at Risk*, the National Commission on Excellence in Education addressed "the essentials of a strong curriculum," thus: "The teaching of English in high school should equip graduates to . . . listen effectively and discuss ideas intelligently." Also in 1983, the Task Force on Education for Economic Growth recommended speaking and listening competencies as part of their plan for improving education in this country. Specifically, they highlighted the following: 1) the ability to engage critically and constructively in the exchange of ideas; 2) the ability to answer and ask questions coherently and concisely, and to follow spoken instructions; 3) the ability to identify and comprehend the main and subordinate ideas in discussions and to report accurately what others have said; and 4) the ability to conceive and develop ideas about a topic for the purpose of speaking to a group; to choose and organize related ideas; to present them clearly in standard English. Also in 1983, the College Board of New York published a volume entitled *Academic Preparation for College: What Students Need to Know and Be Able to Do*. In its report, the board listed speaking and listening among the basic academic competencies. For the most part, the board endorsed the specific recommendations of the Task Force on Education for Academic Growth. Also in 1983, the Carnegie Foundation for the Advancement of Teaching published *High School*. Its author, Ernest Boyer, said among other things:

> The high school curriculum should . . . include a study of the spoken. As humans, we first use sounds to communicate our feelings. Very early, we combine phonemes orally to express complex ideas. In our verbal culture we speak much more than we write. We use the telephone more frequently than we send letters. Talk is everywhere. Throughout our lives we judge others, and we ourselves are judged, by what is said. We need to be as precise in speaking as we are in writing. Therefore, we recommend that high schools give priority to oral communication, requiring all students to complete a course in speaking and listening.

16   There you have it. Arguments. Recommendations. Suggestions. Solutions. Proposals. It's all there. And that is precisely the trouble. Millions of dollars and millions of hours have been spent by prominent people to publish millions of copies of their work. And where is it? In the bookshelves, under piles and piles of paper, somewhere in a corner, silent and neglected. Exactly where the opponents of oral communication would like to see it. But as I have suggested throughout my talk, arguments that are written down and stay written down are useless. The only way they can make a difference is when they are spoken up. And who is going to speak them up? We are the ones. We are the ones who must call attention to the urgency of oral illiteracy in our country. If we don't, nobody else will. Yet, it simply is not enough to agree passively with great ideas. It is not enough to contemplate weighty matters and feel indignant that the world is not as good as it could be. Activism is where it's at. And activism means speaking out.

17   At the risk of sounding presumptuous, let me say that in the state of Pennsylvania I am one of a group of five people who have been speaking up for four years now. We have left no stone of the educational establishment unturned. We have contacted every speech teacher, every principal, and every superintendent in the state. We have spoken to bureaucrats, administrators, legislators, decision makers, opponents, proponents, money holders, influence peddlers, you name it. And we have just started. We have traveled from coast to coast and have given talks, workshops, presentations, debates, addresses, lectures, the works. It should be obvious that we mean business. To show you how committed we are, we came to the "Show Me" state to tell our story. Tell the people of the "Show Me" state. What could be more challenging?

18   Well, we have come, and we have given you the word. We now hope that you will pass it on.

19   Clearly, ladies and gentlemen, I am happy to be here tonight.

The Assault on Your Ears
By Patrick Kan Wong

Patrick Wong gave this speech at San Jose State University. For the second assignment of the semester in public speaking, instructor Linda Hervey asked these beginning students to present a five-to-seven minute informative speech on a significant topic.

1 How many of you have ever left a musical event like a concert and found that your ears were ringing when it was over? I know I have, especially after a major gig with the deejaying group I belong to. A couple years ago when I first started working these events, my ears would ring constantly, sometimes for as long as three days afterward. I had trouble going to sleep. I'd lie there and hear this sound like *eeeeee* all the time; it's like, God, right? Since I've been working around amplified music for a while, it seems that loud noise doesn't affect me anymore. I thought that I was just getting used to it, but in reality, I never did get used to it. Instead, after doing some research, I now realize that what I've experienced—what I am still experiencing—is a slight case of hearing loss. This is not unusual today, even among people our age. The same technology that makes our modern lifestyle so nice also puts our hearing at risk. Not everyone is aware of how much noise is around us and what it may be doing to our ears. So that's what I am going to talk about today.

2 Every day all of us experience some type of noise, whether it's the alarm clock that we have to turn off in the morning or the speech I'm giving to you right now. It's not the noise that really hurts our hearing, but rather it's the loudness or the volume that can damage our ears. Scientists express the different levels of noise in terms of units called decibels, abbreviated as dB. On this chart [Chart A] I display some data compiled by OSHA (which stands for Occupational Safety and Health Administration) to give you an idea of the decibel levels of some different sources of noise. For instance, right now I'm probably talking to you at about a sixty-two decibel level. As you see, that's a little bit louder than a conversation, yet it's lower than freeway traffic noise. If you own a convertible and you're driving down a freeway with the top down, the noise level would probably be around ninety-five dB. And if you've ever fired a gun the magnitude of the noise could have been as great as 140 decibels.

3 Basically anything over ninety decibels can be damaging to the ears, so all of us need to be aware of the noise level around us. Surprisingly enough, even the government cares about our ears. In the workplace, the Department of Labor, or specifically OSHA, is charged with monitoring the environment that we work in. In a work setting where the noise level is around eighty-five decibels, the employee must be provided with hearing protection devices and/or rest periods. The requirement of a rest period makes an important point about how noise affects our hearing. The overall risk of damage is based on the interaction between the intensity of the sound and the duration of the exposure. That's what this other

Chart A	Typical Sound Levels	
Sound Level, Decibels (dB)		Source
140		Gunshot
130		Air Raid Siren
120		Live Rock Music
110		Auto Horn (3 feet)
100		Diesel Truck
95		Ride in Convertible
90		Motorcycle
80		Hair Dryer
70		Freeway Traffic
60		Conversation
50		Light Auto Traffic
40		Quiet Office, Home

Visual aid taped to wall behind speaker

chart [Chart B] shows you. These are the lengths of time that OSHA says that it's safe to be exposed to various sound levels. Notice that if you work in an environment that's around ninety decibels, you could be in that area for a period of eight hours. But look at the last line here. If you're where the noise level is 120 decibels, you should only be in that room or environment for seven and a half minutes. Now most concerts—referring back to this first chart—play at around 120 decibels. And everyone knows that a concert doesn't last for seven and a half minutes! It's usually more like two hours. So you can imagine what kind of damage is being done to your ears.

4   Even everyday things like driving your car with the window rolled down can produce a little bit of hearing loss. The ear that is closest to the window suffers a slight hearing loss just due to wind noise and road noise. Listening to your Walkman with the headphones on could produce up to 110 decibels, and that's pretty much equivalent to an auto horn three feet away. When you see people around campus with their Walkmans blasting they may think that they are acting real cool, but what they're actually doing is ruining the "hair cells" in their inner ears. That brings me to a real simple and brief explanation of how ears react to the different noises or sounds.

5   According to Dr. Maurice Miller of Lenox Hill Hospital, we have 20,000 hair cells in our cochlea, the spiral, fluid-filled tube in our inner

Chart B	Permissible Noise Exposure According to OSHA	
Daily Duration, Hours		**Sound Level, Decibels (dB)**
8		90
6		92
4		95
3		97
2		100
1 1/2		102
1		105
1/2		110
1/4		115
1/8		120

Visual aid taped to wall behind speaker

ear. It's from the nerve endings here that the sounds we perceive get transmitted to our brain. When the sound reaches this part of the ear, it sweeps across the hair cells, and if the sound is intense enough the hair cells in your ear can bend or collapse. If the noise is really intense, the sound can either stiffen or permanently incapacitate the hair cells. Right now you are thinking, "Oh, yeah, well, if I have 20,000 of these hair cells, I can lose a couple here and there, right?" In fact, if you lose just a small number of them, you'll begin to notice a difference in your performance in hearing. But, your ears are kind of nice because they give you a warning sign to let you know whether you're in an environment that's too loud. You'll get that ringing sensation in your ears that most of you said you have experienced. It's called tinnitus.

5   This ringing sensation can last for an indefinite amount of time. It all depends on how severely your ears were exposed to a loud volume. So, if you're lucky enough, the ringing will soon be gone. The range of sounds that you can hear, or your auditory threshold, has returned to its normal level. The medical term for what you have experienced is Temporary Threshold Shift or TTS. But, if you're not so lucky, and you don't recover from the hearing loss in from seven to fourteen days, you've probably lost some of the hair cells in your ear. If the threshold of what you can hear is irreversibly altered, then you suffer from Permanent Threshold Shift, which is called PTS.

7 Permanent hearing losses are of two main types: conductive loss or sensorineural damage. An article written by Lee Silverman in *Audio* magazine explains the difference. The first, conductive loss, has to do with how well the sounds are passed through the outer and middle ear. But sensorineural loss affects the nerve endings in the inner ear, and that's the kind of problem I just described to you when hair cells get damaged. Sensorineural hearing loss is generally more serious. This is not only a matter of having people talk louder. The actual reception of sounds is limited, not just the way they are conducted through the ear: No matter how loud people talk, you will have trouble discriminating the sounds. You might not hear the difference between "laugh" and "gaffe" or "cake" and "bake." Even more distressing than any cake and bake confusion is not being able to tell the difference between the sounds coming from the dishwasher, the TV, and a person talking to you.

8 In order to prevent words from sounding the same, or from blending into the background, or to avoid tinnitus, every one of you should be aware of the noise levels around you. It helps to remember the general decibel levels of these noise sources from this chart and to relate those to the lengths of time that it is safe to be exposed to various levels, indicated over here. If you work in a place that is dangerously noisy, that is a problem for OSHA. But they cannot monitor levels or enforce standards outside the workplace. It's up to us as individuals to be really careful when participating in recreational activities such as drag racing or listening to amplified music. The hearing loss I have is not too bad, but it could have been avoided. I hope you remember that your ears are a very delicate part of your body and that once you lose your hearing you can't get it back. So don't take it for granted.

Rainforests Are in Need of Defense
By Karen McNeil

In a persuasive speaking course at San Jose State University, Professor Laura Gadke's students were required to develop a ten-minute persuasive message that was adapted to the specific audience in the class. Karen McNeil had given previous speeches on environmental topics to this class. Based on that experience and through an audience survey she concluded that her listeners were generally favorably disposed to these issues but were not extremely well informed.

1   "Save the Rainforest!" But for what and from whom? The rainforest issue has had great media coverage, and we are all too familiar with this slogan. I'm not sure, though, that we're actually aware of what is at stake. I know I wasn't, even being really concerned about the environmental issues that face this planet, until I came across the orangutan. I'm an anthropology minor, and this semester I'm taking a class that details the habitats of primates. This is where I got to know more about the orangutan, the threats they face, and what it means to the rest of us.

2   Do you know where orangutans live? In the wild, these great apes live on two Indonesian islands: Borneo and Sumatra. Their habitat is exclusively tropical rainforest. They are frugivorous, which means that they rely on fruit as their source of nutrition. Because of this, they need a wide range of habitat to provide them with fruit year-round. Orangutans used to free-range in Southeast Asia, but development has pushed them out of these areas. The primary threat to these animals is habitat destruction, destruction of the tropical rainforests. I was alarmed to see that almost all of the primates live exclusively in tropical rainforests. Suddenly I had a new perspective on what we stand to lose as we continue to destroy these tropical zones.

3   These, then, are the questions that I want to address today: What are we saving when we save the rainforests? Who are we saving them from? What can we do that can actually make a difference? First, I'll briefly outline the threats to the ecology of the rainforest and then detail some of the investment policies of the World Bank, which is the institution that contributes to major destruction of the tropical rainforests. And then finally I have some suggestions of what you can do to ensure the well-being of our planet.

4   To understand the seriousness of the current threat to the rainforests, we need to recognize what they represent ecologically, culturally, and economically. These elaborate ecosystems are a kaleidoscope of biological diversity. The vegetation in these towering forests is divided into dozens of layers, each of which provides a distinct habitat for different plants and animals, literally thousands of species. Within the tropical belt that circles the equator there exist more plant and animal species than in the rest of the world combined! The rainforests are also home to millions of indigenous people. Thousands of tribal groups exist in rainforests throughout the world. Most of these peoples live as hunters and gatherers or they conduct small agricultural projects that fit the cycle of the land. Their centuries-old cultural practices have grown up in harmony with their

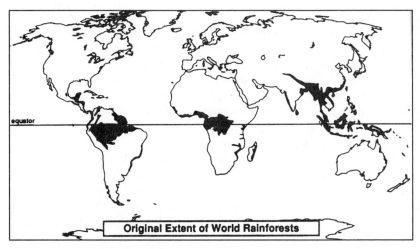

Original Extent of World Rainforests

Visual aid mounted on board and placed on easel

environment. Another value of the rainforests is the important role they play in our weather patterns, both locally and globally. In fact, they are often referred to as the lungs of our planet. Economically, these regions are a bountiful source of rubber, hardwood, food products, and essential medicines for heart disease and cancer.

5   Although lush, these ecosystems are really quite fragile. Similar to the old-growth forests that run from the northern part of our state up through the Pacific Northwest, these interdependent biological systems took centuries to develop. Without the constant renewal of the protective overgrowth and dense canopies the inhabitants of the lower levels— plants, animals, birds—die from exposure to the sun. The laterite soil on which the forests are built turns to clay and erodes quickly when cleared, as many farmers and ranchers are beginning to discover. Topsoil is swept away by floods. Sediment flows into the rivers and affects fishing. Most of the damage is irreversible. You can see why deforestation for farming, ranching, and logging has such a devastating effect.

6   Yet it goes on, and worsens, even as we speak. To give you some sense of the scope and urgency of the situation, let me cite some statistics from *The Rainforest Book* by Scott Lewis. Half of the earth's rainforests have already been destroyed. Thirty-five million acres a year are eliminated. That's an area the size of New York State gone forever. The rates of

deforestation have doubled in the last decade and they are continuing to rise. In the name of progress, the industrialized Western world destroys these irreplaceable plants and animals. It alters the environment of the region and the climate of the world. It wipes out indigenous cultures of rainforest peoples without even realizing the rich traditions that they have to offer us. These tribal people are not in a position to resist change that others define as progress. Imagine what it would be like if you had to defend your own home against lawyers of a multinational logging firm. Would you have any chance of winning? If it would be an uphill fight for someone like you, think what it would be like for someone from a community that has no grounding in Western-style law and that has no connection to the Western economic system.

Profits are the major factor that lead to rainforest destruction. My next point highlights the destructive investment practices that lead to environmental ruin. One investment institution that can be credited with funding a majority of the environmental devastation is the World Bank. After World War II the world community assembled the World Bank to help war-torn countries rebuild. After they completed that work, they turned to the Third World. The Rainforest Action Network of San Francisco argues that the World Bank has turned the Third World into a resource colony for the Western industrialized nations. The World Bank has become a power that dictates what's developed and created by countries, and also even at times how governments treat their own people. The World Bank is an organization that is funded by money that is borrowed on international markets and also money contributed by 148 member nations. The United States is the most influential of these members. We have 20 percent of the overall vote. The president of the World Bank, Barber C. Conable, is a United States citizen. U.S. members of the World Bank are given direction by the United States Department of Treasury and the Congress. The money the United States supplies to the World Bank comes from the taxpayers. The World Bank prefers to finance huge megaprojects: hydroelectric dams, massive relocations and resettlements, agricultural and industrial projects that involve building roads into areas that have previously been inaccessible. Bruce Rich of the Environmental Defense Fund states that over half of the loans given by the World Bank and its three regional counterparts in recent years has gone to support projects in sectors that can seriously affect tropical forests. Survival International, an organization that advocates the rights of tribal people and serves as a watchdog of the World Bank, makes these recommendations for the bank's reform. First, they want public access to all information regarding the bank's projects. They want the World Bank's staff to include people that are trained in ecology as well as in socioeconomic analysis. Systematic involvement of organizations representing the environment and indigenous people should be a part of all projects. The bank should increase its proportion of ecologically beneficial programs. These Survival International recommendations reflect their analysis that the World Bank has been developing projects solely on economic criteria without regarding or understanding the environmental effects of their actions. If you're shocked that these practices continue, and with our country's support, I'm glad. I want you to see how important it is that we understand these issues. I have some recommendations that I want you to consider adopting in your own lives.

8   My suggestions begin with learning more about this complex problem and then taking action both individually and collectively. Education is the key to bringing about change. Read some of the books that discuss the rainforest. Here is one concise (and inexpensive) one: *The Rainforest Book* by Scott Lewis, published in 1990. Share your knowledge about environmental subjects with children and support them as they try to make sense of these issues. Take some classes that are offered here at San Jose State that promote a global perspective on environmental issues. For instance, I know that many of you are communication studies majors or minors. You might be especially interested in a course that Dr. Dennis Jaehne will be offering next fall called Communication and the Environment. I took it the first time it was offered and it was excellent! Whenever you possibly can, travel to other countries and see for yourself what's going on. I've traveled four times around the world, and I wouldn't trade those experiences for anything. It's one thing to understand intellectually that our industrially advanced lifestyle and Western values are not universal. But it becomes meaningful in a different way when you have the chance to experience firsthand the incredible diversity of this planet. You realize how privileged we are in terms of material goods and political freedom. Yet you also see that there are places in this world of unbelievable physical beauty and cultures of such depth and richness that they must be preserved and cherished. Travel, especially off the beaten path of the usual tourist spots, really dramatizes the choices before those of us who live in rich and powerful societies. We can either expand our consumerism more and more by exploiting other parts of the world or we can start evaluating the impact of our economic policies on the rest of the world.

Through education, as you continue to learn about how we are all complicit in the problems of the rainforest, you will want to take some direct action. There are several ways to do this.

First, you can boycott products that are known to cause destruction of the rainforest. A typical four-ounce fastfood hamburger that's been made from "rainforest beef" took fifty-five square feet of rainforest to produce. Is one hamburger worth that destruction? We can insist on clearer labeling of meat so that we know where it comes from. Disposable chopsticks are oftentimes made from tropical timber, or in some cases whole stands of rainforest are cleared to plant trees that produce a color of wood more popular for chopsticks. In 1979 Japan used enough disposable chopsticks to build 11,000 timber-frame family dwellings. You can imagine what those statistics would be today. You may not use many chopsticks, but you can be aware of the exotic wood products that are being stripped from these regions. I've included a list of these woods on a handout that I'll give you in a few minutes.

Next, you can support organizations that are involved with saving the rainforest. I've listed several of them on the same handout. It is only through collective action in organized groups like these that we have any chance of influencing the policies of government and of the World Bank. The decision makers will continue to listen to business interests unless we show them how many of us there are that value long-term social and environmental goals over short-term material gains.

Finally, I encourage you all to stop by the Art Quad before three o'clock today and buy a scoop of Rainforest Crunch ice cream. Representatives of Ben and Jerry's Ice Cream are going to be here today, and they are going to donate the proceeds of the ice cream sales to SAFER, Students Affiliated for Environmental Respect, the campus environmental group. Rainforest Crunch is made from Brazil nuts, thus making it advantageous for the trees in at least one rainforest to be left standing. You'll find the address of the Rainforest Action Network printed on every carton of rainforest ice cream they sell. This is just one example of how business organizations can take steps to be socially responsible while still making a profit and offering a quality product.

Since I began this presentation, 1,000 acres of rainforest have been destroyed or degraded severely. These fragile ecosystems need to be protected; once they're destroyed they're gone forever. My studies about the primates intensified my interest in the rainforest because I realized how fragile they are and that these precious creatures have become very close

---

Avoid buying tropical lumber products unless you can be sure they are not endangered species and have been logged using sustainable methods. The following tropical hardwoods all come from rainforests:

Apitong	Greenheart	Purpleheart
Banak	Iroko	Ramin
Bocote	Jelutang	Rosewood
Bubinga	Koa	Satinwood
Cocobolo	Lauan	Teak
Cordia	Mahogany	Virola
Ebony	Meranti	Wenge
Goncalo avles	Paduak	Zebrawood

From *The Rainforest Book*, page 89

Organizations involved in saving tropical rainforests:

GREENPEACE, 1436 U. St. NW, Washington, DC 20009
CULTURAL SURVIVAL, 11 Divinity Ave., Cambridge, MA 02138
WORLD WILDLIFE FUND/CONSERVATION FOUNDATION, 1250 24th St., NW, Washington, DC 20037
SURVIVAL INTERNATIONAL USA, 2121 Decatur Pl. NW, Washington, DC 20037
RAINFOREST ACTION NETWORK, 301 Broadway, Suite A, San Francisco, CA 94133

Handout

to extinction. It isn't the Brazilian or Malaysian or Indonesian farmers who pose the real threat to these areas. It is the governments of the developed countries in cooperation with multinational development banks that initiate large projects and create real havoc in these areas. As Americans we contribute to the problem in a number of ways. As we drive the world market through our obsessive consumption, we entangle developing nations in outrageous debts. As American taxpayers we're helping to fund the World Bank's destructive policies through the taxes we pay. There are other organizations worldwide that we could support, groups that are committed to grassroots development. These smaller projects often are far more beneficial to the local people in other countries. The only way that we can hope to get a realistic picture of this problem is through education and involvement. We can no longer afford to think merely on a local or national level. We must learn to think on a global level and feel that the well-being of humanity and this planet is a responsibility we all share.

Although the problem is a huge one, we as individuals should not feel powerless. By taking even a small step, you can begin to make a difference. Please, don't wait. Take a step now.

A Sample Speech Outline for
Rainforests Are in Need of Defense
By Karen McNeil

Here is a sample speech outline for the preceding speech. This is just one illustration of the sort of speech outline that helps a speaker get organized. Some outlines are more spare and compact, and others are more like argumentative briefs containing full citations of all evidence.

Notice that the main points listed here are never stated in precisely those words in the speech transcription. The outline is a logical plan, a place to set down your main points in propositional form, to fit the subpoints beneath the main points, and fit your support beneath the subpoints. Uncluttered with transitions and extra words, and properly indented, the outline allows the reader to see the basic speech development at a glance.

After the logical plan or skeleton is constructed the ideas are talked out in oral style as the speaker practices. Had McNeil read from this outline directly, the result would have been stilted, choppy, and dull.

This outline was written to meet the requirements of a particular assignment. The instructor required that the following information be placed before the introduction: the general purpose, the specific purpose, the primary audience outcome, at least three specific audience outcomes, and the thesis sentence. The speaker was required to include the complete introduction and conclusion, labeling their parts. In addition, the speaker had to label three different types of supporting material, two different attention factors, two different types of reasoning, one direct attempt to establish credibility, one appeal to audience values, and one appeal to audience needs. Karen McNeil's speech has more of these rhetorical devices than the bare minimum required; the clearest examples are the ones labeled. This instructor required complete sentences at the first (I, II, III, etc.) and second (A, B, C) levels of subordination, but allowed words and phrases at lower levels. A reference list of at least four sources was also required.

General Purpose: To Persuade

Specific Purpose: To persuade the audience that the tropical rainforests are important to the world in many ways, that they are being threatened with destruction, and that people in the United States have the responsibility and influence to protect them.

Primary Audience Outcome: I want the audience to take action to preserve the tropical rainforests.

Contributing Audience Outcomes:
I want my audience to:
>   understand the importance and beauty of the tropical rainforests.
>   understand the fragile nature of the rainforests.
>   realize the threats faced by the rainforests.
>   be aware of the role of the World Bank.
>   recognize the U.S. influence in the World Bank.
>   evaluate the impact our behavior has on the global ecology.
>   read books on the rainforests and ecology.
>   take classes that increase environmental awareness on the local and the
>   global levels.
>   boycott products that endanger the rainforest.
>   support efforts for reform of the World Bank.
>   stop by the Art Quad today and buy a scoop of Ben and Jerry's Rainforest
>   Crunch ice cream.

Thesis: The continuing and accelerating destruction of the tropical rainforests, due largely to the policies of industrialized nations, poses a serious threat to the global environment and community—a threat that must be met by immediate action from concerned individuals.

Introduction

Attention getter: "Save the Rainforest!" But for what and from whom? The rainforest issue has had great media coverage, and we are all too familiar with this slogan. I'm not sure, though, that we're actually aware of what is at stake.

Psychological orientation:

Crediblility:
Concern

I know I wasn't, even being really concerned about the environmental issues that face this planet, until I came across the orangutan. I'm an anthropology minor, and this semester I'm taking a class that details the habitats of primates. This is where I got to know more about the orangutan, the threats they face, and what it means to the rest of us.

Do you know where orangutans live? In the wild, these great apes live on two Indonesian islands: Borneo and Sumatra. Their habitat is exclusively tropical rainforest. They are frugivorous, which means that they rely on fruit as their source of nutrition. Because of this, they need a wide range of habitat to provide them with fruit year-round. Orangutans used to free-range in Southeast Asia, but development has pushed them out of these areas. The primary threat to these animals is habitat destruction, destruction of the tropical rainforests. I was alarmed to see that almost all of the primates live exclusively in tropical rainforests. Suddenly I had a new perspective on what we stand to lose as we continue to destroy these tropical zones.

Logical
orientation:

These, then, are the questions that I want to address today: What are we saving when we save the rainforests? Who are we saving them from? What can we do that can actually make a difference? First, I'll briefly outline the threats to the ecology of the rainforest and then detail some of the investment policies of the World Bank, which is the institution that contributes to major destruction of the tropical rainforests. And then finally I have some suggestions of what you can do to ensure the well-being of our planet.

I. Tropical rainforests, important to the well-being of the planet, are being subjected to rampant destruction, with irreversible effects.
   A. Rainforests are an important component of the planet.
      1. Ecologically complex systems

Appeal to value:
A world of beauty

         a. Towering forests divided into layers
         b. More plant and animal species than rest of world
      2. Thousands of tribal groups live there.
         a. Hunters and gatherers/small agriculture
         b. Irreplaceable ancient cultures
      3. Rainforests affect weather patterns.
      4. Economically important

Supporting
material:
Example

         a. Rubber, hardwood, food products
         b. Medicines for heart disease and cancer
   B. Rainforests are in serious danger.
      1. They are fragile.
         a. Need dense canopies to protect inhabitants of lower layers

Supporting
material:
Testimony

       b. When exposed, laterite soil turns to clay, erodes
       c. Topsoil swept away, affects rivers
       d. Damage is irreversible
    2. Rainforests are being destroyed.
       a. By farming, logging, ranching
       b. Half of world's rainforests already gone
       c. 35 million acres a year, size of New York
       d. Rate of destruction is doubling
       e. Tribal people powerless to resist

II. Short-sighted economic policies of the industrially

Causal
reasoning:
Policies
concerned with
the short term
can be harmful
in the long term

    advanced countries, carried out through multilateral
    development agencies like the World Bank, are
    responsible for the destruction.
    A. The World Bank's policies tend to serve the
       industrialized nations.
       1. History
          a. Formed to rebuild after WWII
          b. Later took on Third World development
       2. U.S. plays major role in the World Bank's policies

Supporting
Material:
Statistics

          a. Of the 148 member nations, U.S. funds 20
             percent
          b. President, Barber C. Conable, is U.S. citizen
          c. Directed by U.S. Department of Treasury and
             Congress
    B. World Bank policies are destructive to the rainforests.
       1. Tends to fund huge projects such as hydroelectric
          dams
       2. Half of its loans have gone to projects that
          endanger rainforests
    C. Reforms of World Bank have been suggested.
       1. Public access to records
       2. Staff should include ecologists
       3. Should collaborate with environmental
          organizations and representatives of indigenous
          peoples
       4. Should consider more than economic criteria in
          selecting projects

III. Concerned individuals can help save the rainforests
    through education and collective action.
    A. Education is a key to saving the rainforests.
       1. Read books
       2. Educate children
       3. Take courses

4. Travel

Attention factor: Familiarity (fast-food burger)

B. Boycott products that cause destruction to rainforests.
1. Need to label meat so we can tell if it is "rainforest beef"
2. Wood from tropical lumber
   a. Chopsticks from light wood could have built 11,000 houses
   b. List of exotic woods to avoid will be on handout
C. Support organizations to save the rainforests.
1. Several national and international groups listed on handout
2. Campus organization SAFER

Attention factor: Proximity

   a. Ice cream social today until three at Art Quad
   b. Ben and Jerry's Rainforest Crunch saves nut trees

Logical closure:

Since I began this presentation, 1,000 acres of rainforest have been destroyed or degraded severely. These fragile ecosystems need to be protected; once they're destroyed they're gone forever. My studies about the primates intensified my interest in the rainforest because I realized how fragile they are and that these precious creatures have become very close to extinction. It isn't the Brazilian or Malaysian or Indonesian farmers who pose the real threat to these areas. It is the governments of the developed countries in cooperation with multinational development banks that initiate large projects and create real havoc in these areas. As Americans we contribute to the problem in a number of ways. As we drive the world market through our obsessive consumption, we entangle developing nations in outrageous debts. As American taxpayers we're helping to fund the World Bank's destructive policies through the taxes we pay. There are other organizations worldwide that we could support, groups that are committed to grassroots development. These smaller projects often are far more beneficial to the local people in other countries. The only way that we can hope to get a realistic picture of this problem is through education and involvement.

Psychological closure:

Appeal to need: Survival

We can no longer afford to think merely on a local or national level. We must learn to think on a global level and feel that the well-being of humanity and this planet is a responsibility we all share. Although the problem is a huge one, we as individuals should not feel powerless.

Clincher: By taking even a small step, you can begin to make a difference. Please, don't wait. Take a step now.

References

Durning, A. "Cradles of Life." *Worldwatch,* May–June 1989, 30–40.

Lewis, S. *The Rainforest Book.* Venice, CA: Living Planet Press, 1990.

Myers, N. (ed.) *Gaia: An Atlas of Planet Management.* New York: Doubleday, 1984.

Rich, B. "Multilateral Development Banks and Tropical Deforestation." In *Lessons of the Rainforest.* Edited by Suzanne Head and Robert Heinzman. San Francisco: Sierra Club Books, 1990. 118–30

Survival International. "Financing Ecological Destruction." N.p., n.d.

Major An: Let's Not Forget This Man
By Jade Pham

When Jade Pham was a seventeen-year-old high school student in San Jose, California, she learned of the plight of Major Nguyen Quy An, who had been in a forced labor camp in Vietnam for about fifteen years. As a distinguished young helicopter pilot, An had saved the lives of four U.S. pilots and been decorated for his bravery and later lost both his arms in combat. It was because of his disability that he was not allowed to complete a full term in a "reeducation" camp and therefore had remained imprisoned due to a technicality.

Pham was deeply moved by Major An's struggles to be released and join his family in California. She began to write letters to Congress, circulate petitions, and speak before various Vietnamese groups in her community and on college campuses. The following speech is a composite of the basic appeal that she made in slightly different forms during her campaign to obtain the release of this man she had never met.

Although the Vietnam War stole innocence, it also instilled heroism. While some heroes were untimely honored in caskets, those remaining were honored with valuable insignias. Major Nguyen Quy An was one of very few Vietnamese soldiers to receive decorated recognition for saving the lives of American soldiers. At the direction of the president of the United States, An was presented with the Distinguished Flying Cross.

It is said that no one gives without thought of return. But once in a lifetime, there will be a story such as that of Major Nguyen Quy An which proves this theory to be false. Only once in a lifetime will there be a story so compelling that it has the power to move people to tears, making them appreciate things which before they had ignored.

In the midst of combat, An rescued a burning U.S. Army helicopter in enemy-held territory. Without thinking of the great risk to his own life, An made an expeditious dive, saved the lives of all four U.S. soldiers and guided them to safety.

Later on a mission, he managed to maneuver his own burning helicopter, which had been struck by enemy fire, to save himself and his entire crew. Because of this daring rescue, both of his arms were severely burned and had to be amputated by American doctors.

Although the Vietnam War has ended, the passion and bravery of An's deed cannot be forgotten. The medal he justly earned must be worth its value.

An now lives in Vietnam with his daughter. Years of imprisonment and deprivation have intensified his single wish to be united with his only son and his remaining friends in the United States. Listening to the poetry of this man's bravery, I and many others have realized that he must be recognized and thanked for heroically saving our soldiers. Unfortunately, I am ashamed that we have turned our backs to him and have ignored his one request.

The U.S. State Department's Orderly Departure Program has closed its doors to An. After inconsistent promises, they now reason that he is not eligible for their program because he is forty-three weeks short of serving the required three years in Vietnam's infamous reeducation camps. But this trite reasoning is an insult to the United States. What could possibly justify this country offering refuge to convicted criminals but denying assistance to a recognized hero?

The ODP has closed its eyes to the fact that An's actions saved numerous lives—American lives included. Is he to be trapped because the

Communists rendered him a useless amputee and threw him out of the camps? Must he be condemned to a life of pain because he saved countless lives?

9   Crediting Major Nguyen Quy An with bravery simply is not enough. To hand him a token of appreciation for confronting death by saving the lives of our soldiers cheapens the value of bravery and heroism.

10   I realize that my voice alone, as a seventeen-year-old high school senior, cannot change the situation as it is. Therefore, I have written a letter to voice the concerns of, among others, the thousands of Vietnamese-Americans. I will circulate this letter now, and if you will sign it for us to submit to our leaders in Washington, I pray that these words will be enough to help save a hero's life.

11   A brave man's selfless conviction must be rewarded. He must be made an example for the citizens of today that such valor is to be commended, not ignored.

Civility Without Censorship: The Ethics of the Internet
By Raymond W. Smith

Raymond W. Smith, Chairman of Bell Atlantic Corporation, delivered this address as part of a one-day symposium at the Simon Wiesenthal Center/Museum of Tolerance in Los Angeles, California in December of 1998. The symposium was entitled "Internet 2000: Promise and Peril," and included a series of presentations and discussions on the positive and negative potential of the new information technologies. The audience was composed of educators, law enforcement professionals, students, and interested members of the community.

1 Thank you, Rabbi Cooper, for the gracious introduction . . . and let me acknowledge the tremendous contributions the Museum and the Center have made toward harmonizing race relations and advancing equality and justice. We're truly honored that you would include us in today's program.

2   For the past two years, I've been using the "bully pulpit" to alert various civil rights leaders and organizations (like Martin Luther King III and the NAACP) of the dangers posed by cyberhate. If not for the early groundbreaking work by the Simon Wiesenthal Center, I doubt whether I would have even known of this growing threat. Thank you for warning

us—and now, for showing us—how extremists are using the Internet for their own purposes.

3   When thinking about this morning's topic, I can't help but mention a cartoon that recently appeared in the newspapers. Through the doorway, a mother calls out to her teenager—who is surrounded by high-tech equipment—"I hope you're not watching sex stuff on the Internet!" To which her son replies, "Naw, I'm getting it on TV!"

4   Until recently, the chief concern of parents was pornography—kid's access to it over the Web and the fear of sexual predators cruising cyberspace. Now, we're worried about hate mongers reaching out to our children in digital space.

5   As we have just seen and heard, Neo-Nazis and extremists of every political stripe who once terrorized people in the dead of night with burning crosses and painted swastikas are now sneaking up on the public—especially our kids—through the World Wide Web.

6   As cyberhate is nothing less than the attempt to corrupt public discourse on race and ethnicity via the Internet, many people see censorship of Web sites and Net content as the only viable way to meet this growing threat.

7   I disagree.

8   Instead of fearing the Internet's reach, we need to embrace it—to value its ability to connect our children to the wealth of positive human experience and knowledge. While there is, to quote one critic, "every form of diseased intelligence" in digital space, we must remember that it comprises only a small fraction of cyberspace. The Internet provides our children unlimited possibilities for learning and education—the great libraries, cities and cultures of the world also await them at just the click of a mouse key.

9   In short, we need to think less about ways to keep cyberhate off the screen, and more about ways to meet it head on: which translates into fighting destructive rhetoric with constructive dialogue—hate speech with truth—restrictions with greater Internet access.

10   This morning then, I would like to discuss with you the options that are available to combat cyberhate that don't endanger our First Amendment guarantees—and that remain true to our commitment to free speech.

11   That people and institutions should call for a strict ban on language over the Web that could be considered racist, anti-Semitic or bigoted is totally understandable. None of us was truly prepared for the emergence

of multiple hate-group Web sites (especially those geared toward children), or the quick adoption of high technology by skinheads and others to market their digital cargo across state lines and international date lines at the speed of light.

12   One possible reason some people feel inclined to treat the Internet more severely than other media is that the technology is new and hard to understand. Also, the Internet's global reach and ubiquitous nature makes it appear ominous. As Justice Gabriel Bach, of Israel, noted, this ability makes it especially dangerous. "I'm frightened stiff by the Internet," he said, "billions of people all over the world have access to it."

13   My industry has seen all this before.

14   The clash between free speech and information technology is actually quite an old one. Nearly a century ago, telephone companies, courts, and the Congress debated whether "common carriers" (public phone companies) were obligated to carry all talk equally, regardless of content. And in the end—though some believed that the phone would do everything from eliminate Southern accents and increase Northern labor unrest—free speech won out in the courts.

15   Whatever the technology, be it the radio or the silver screen, history teaches us that white supremacists, anti-Semites and others will unfortunately come to grasp, relatively early on, a new medium's potential.

16   We simply can't condemn a whole technology because we fear that a Father Coughlin or a Leni Riefenstahl (early pioneers in the use of radio and film to advance anti-Semitism or Hitler's Reich) is waiting in the wings to use the latest technology to their own advantage. Nor can we expect the Congress, the federal government or an international regulatory agency to tightly regulate cyberspace content in order to stymie language we find offensive.

17   The wisdom of further empowering such organizations and agencies like the FCC or the United Nations aside, it is highly doubtful even if they had the authority, that they would have the ability to truly stem the flow of racist and anti-Semitic language on the World Wide Web.

18   Anybody with a phone line, computer and Internet connection can set up a Web site—even broadcast over the Net.

19   Even if discovered and banned, online hate groups can easily jump Internet service providers and national boundaries to avoid accountability. I think cyber guru, Peter Huber, got it right when he said, "To censor Internet filth at its origins, we would have to enlist the Joint Chiefs of Staff, who could start by invading Sweden and Holland."

0   Then there is the whole matter of disguise. Innocent sounding URLs (handles or Web site names) can fool even the most traveled or seasoned "cybernaut."

1   As for efforts on Capitol Hill and elsewhere to legislate all so-called "offensive" language off the Internet, here again, we can expect the courts to knock down any attempts to curtail First Amendment rights on the Internet. As the Supreme Court ruled last year when it struck down legislation restricting the transmission of "indecent" material online: (To Quote) "Regardless of the strength of the government's interest, the level of discourse reaching a mailbox simply cannot be limited to what is suitable for a sandbox."

2   In short, although the temptation is great to look to legislation and regulation as a remedy to cyberhate, our commitment to free speech must always take precedent over our fears.

3   So, cyberhate will not be defeated by the stroke of a pen.

4   Now, this is not to say that, because we place such a high value on our First Amendment rights, we can't do anything to combat the proliferation of hate sites on the Internet or protect young minds from such threatening and bigoted language.

5   Law enforcement agencies and state legislators can use existing laws against stalking and telephone harassment to go after those who abuse E-mail . . . parents can install software filtering programs (such as the Anti-Defamation League's HateFilter, or the one Bell Atlantic uses, Cyber-Patrol) to block access to questionable Internet sites . . . schools and libraries can protect children by teaching them how to properly use the Internet and challenge cyberhate . . . and Internet Service Providers can voluntarily decline to host hate sites. (Bell Atlantic Internet Services, for, instance, reserves the right to decline or terminate service which "espouses, promotes or incites bigotry, hatred or racism.")

6   Given that today's panel has representatives from state government, law enforcement, the courts and the Internet industry, we can discuss these initiatives later in more detail. The point is, there are other ways besides empowering national or international oversight agencies, or drafting draconian legislation, to lessen the impact of cyberhate.

7   Freedom, not censorship, is the only way to combat this threat to civility. In short, more speech—not less—is needed on the World Wide Web.

8   In fact, the best answer to cyberhate lies in the use of information technology itself. As a reporter for the Boston Globe recently concluded,

(quote) "the same technology that provides a forum for extremists, enables civil rights groups and individuals to mobilize a response in unprecedented ways."

29   We totally agree.

30   Our prescription to cyberhate is therefore rather simple, but far reaching in its approach:

31   The first component is access: if we're to get to a higher level of national understanding on racial and ethnic issues—and strike at the very roots of cyberhate—we must see that no minority group or community is left out of cyberspace for want of a simple Internet connection or basic computer.

32   At Bell Atlantic, we've been working very hard to provide the minority communities we serve with Internet access. Across our region, thousands of inner-city schools, libraries, colleges and community groups are now getting connected to cyberspace through a variety of our foundation and state grant programs. Also, our employees have been in the forefront of volunteering their time and energy to wire schools to the Internet during specially designated "Net" days.

33   Internet access alone, however, won't build bridges of understanding between people—or level the playing field between cyber-haters and the targets of their hate.

34   The second thing we must do is make sure the Web's content is enriched by minority culture and beliefs, and that there are more Web sites and home pages dedicated to meeting head-on the racist caricatures and pseudo history often found in cyberspace.

35   While cyberhate cannot be mandated or censored out of existence, it can be countered by creating hundreds of chatlines, home pages, bulletin boards and Web sites dedicated to social justice, tolerance and equality— for all people regardless of race, nationality or sexual orientation.

36   Over the past two years, Bell Atlantic has helped a number of minority and civil rights groups launch and maintain their Web sites (like the NAACP, the Leadership Council on Civil Rights, and the National Council of La Raza), and we've done the same for dozens of smaller cultural organizations (like the Harlem Studio Museum and El Museo del Barrio).

37   We believe that kind of moral leadership can have a tremendous impact. Quite simply, we need more Simon Wiesenthal Centers, Anti-Defamation Leagues, and Southern Poverty Law Centers monitoring and responding to cyberhate.

If we're to bring the struggle for human decency and dignity into cyberspace, we must see that the two most powerful revolutions of the twentieth century—those of civil rights and information technology—are linked even closer together.

Finally, we need to drive real-time, serious dialogue on the religious, ethnic, and cultural concerns that divide us as a nation—a task for which the Internet is particularly suited.

Precisely because it is anonymous, the Internet provides a perfect forum to discuss race, sexual orientation and other similar issues. On the Internet, said one user, "you can speak freely and not have fears that somebody is going to attack you for what comes out of your heart." It's this kind of open and heartfelt discussion that we need to advance and sponsor on-line.

Already, a number of small groups and lone individuals are meeting the cyberhate challenge through simple dialogue between strangers. I'm talking about Web sites run by educators to inform parents about online hate materials . . . sites operated by "recovering" racists to engage skinheads and other misguided kids in productive debate . . . Web sites run by concerned citizens to bridge the gap in ignorance between ethnic, racial and other communities.

The "Y? forum," also known as the National Forum on People's Differences, is a wonderful example of a Web site where readers can safely ask and follow discussions on sensitive cross-cultural topics without having to wade through foul language or "flame wars."

As a columnist from the Miami Herald described the appeal of these kinds of sites: "As long as we are mysteries, one to another, we face a perpetuation of ignorance and a feeding of fear. I'd rather people ask the questions than try to make up the answers. I'd rather, they ask the questions than turn to myth and call it truth."

In closing, my company recognizes that the Internet doesn't operate in a vacuum. We agree that those who profit from information technology have a special responsibility to see that its promise is shared across class, race and geographic boundaries.

That's why we're working with the public schools and libraries in our region to see that they're all equipped with the pens, pencils and paper of the twenty-first century . . . why we're helping to further distance learning and telemedicine applications that serve the educational and health needs of the disabled and isolated . . . why we're helping minority groups and civil rights organizations use information technology to spread their vision and their values to the millions of people electronically linked to the global village.

46   And that's the way it should be.

47   Let me leave you with a personal story. . .

48   When growing up, my Jewish friends and I often swapped theology—tales from the Hassidic Masters for stories from the Lives of the Saints. I remember from these discussions that one of the great Rabbis noted that the first word of the Ten Commandments is "I" and the last word is "neighbor." In typical Talmudic fashion, the Rabbi was telling us that if we want to incorporate the Commandments into our lives, we must move from a focus on ourselves to others.

49   At Bell Atlantic, the more we grow—in both scale and scope—the greater the emphasis we place on being a good corporate citizen, and the more we're driven to see that digital technology is used for purposes of enlightenment and education.

50   The Internet will fundamentally transform the way we work, learn, and do commerce. It will also, if properly used and rightly taught, help bridge the gap in understanding between communities—becoming not a tool of hate, but one of hope.

51   Thank you again for the invitation join you this morning.

Index

References to sections of this book are printed in boldface type, and italic page numbers indicate where figures or other illustrative materials appear.

A

Accents and vocal delivery,
  25b(4):344–345
Acronyms, use of, **19b(1)**:260
Adapting speech to situation
  audience response, **27a**:359–360
  distractions, preventing,
    27b:361–363
  hecklers, **27c**:363–365
  overview of, **27**:358
Ad hominem, **14f(1)**:194
Age of audience, **4b(1)**:48–49
Agendas for meetings or programs,
  22c(1):301–302, **22c(2)**:302–303
Alliteration and assonance, **15d(2)**:222
Alternative proposals and speech orga-
  nization, **20d(2)**:280
Altruism as motivator, **18b**:248
An, Major Nguyen Quy, 404
Analogy
  reasoning by, **14e**:190–193,
    14g(2):205–207
  use of, **19b(4)**:261–262
Analysis, definition of, 82
Antithesis, **15d(2)**:222
Appeals in conclusion to speech,
  12b(2):142–144
Argument
  extending to absurd lengths,
    14f(3):195
  presenting balanced and objective
    analysis of, **17c(4)**:242–243
Articulation, identifying problems of,
  25a(2):338–339

Attacking person rather than argument,
  14f(1):194
Attention
  converting to interest, **16b**:233–235,
    20c(2):273–275
  overview of, **16**:226–227
  pitfalls of, **16c**:235–236
  techniques to engage audience's,
    16a:227–233
Attitude, **20a**:264. *See also* Audience
  analysis, attitude toward topic
Atypical time frame, fallacy of,
  13c(2):162
Audience. *See also* Motivating audience
  adapting speech to response of,
    27a:359–360
  attention, techniques to engage,
    16a:227–233
  converting attention to interest,
    16b:233–235
  engaging with introductions,
    11:124–125, **11a**:125–126
  logical orientation of, **11c**:132–136
  narrowing topic for, **3b(1)**:32
  organizational patterns of speech and,
    8a(5):101
  orienting to approach to topic,
    11c(2):135–136
  primary outcome of speech and,
    3c(3):35–37
  psychological orientation and,
    11b:127–132
  reconceptualizing role of in fear of
    public speaking, **6a(2)**:75
  respecting integrity of, **21c**:286–287

Audience (*continued*)
  selecting topic appropriate to,
    3a(2):28
  synchronizing language with audi-
    ence, **15e**:224–225
Audience analysis
  attitude toward topic, **4d**:54–55,
    20c:270–277
  demographic characteristics,
    4b:47–52
  expectations, **4e**:55–57
  job (group) interview and,
    22d(1):305
  meaning and, **4c**:52–54
  overview of, **4**:44
  resources for, **4a**:45–47
Authority values, **18c(2)**:251–252
Average, fallacy of, **13c(2)**:161
Award
  accepting, **22a(4)**:297
  presenting, **22a(1)**:296

B

Boolean operators, **5c**:64
Brainstorming technique for selecting
  topics, **3a(1)**:26–28

C

Causal reasoning
  explaining claims, **14d(3)**:189–190
  linking evidence to claims,
    14g(2):204
  oversimplifying, **14d(2)**:187–189
  overview of, **14d**:185
  relationships, testing validity of,
    14d(1):186–187
Cause-effect pattern of speech arrangement, **8a(3)**:99
Central idea. *See* Thesis statement
Choice, ethical implications of,
  21a:285–286, **21e**:289–293
Chronological pattern of speech

arrangement, **8a(1)**:97, 103
Circular reasoning, **14f(5)**:196
Citing sources in speech, **13e(1)**:167
Claims
  definition of, **14a**:170–171,
    20b(1):267
  linking evidence to, **14a(2)**:171–173,
    14c:179, **14d**:185, **14e**:191,
    14g:200–207
Clarity in language
  economy, **15b(3)**:213–215
  precision, **15b(1)**:211–212
  specificity and concreteness,
    15b(2):213
Classification schemes for main points,
  7d:90–92
Clichés, use of, **21e(3)**:293, **22a**:295
Clinching speech, **12c**:144–145
Cognitive restructuring, **6d(2)**:78–79
Cohesion of audience, **4e(3)**:56
Common ground, establishing with
  audience, **11b(1)**:128, **20c(3)**:276
Communication, meaning-centered
  view of, **1b**:4–6
Communicative resources, **1c**:6–11,
  2d:22–23
Competence, assessing, **17a(1)**:238
Complexity of public speaking,
  1d:12–13
Compositional skills. *See* Writing skills
Concept mapping, **7b(2)**:86, 87
Conceptual placement of topic,
  11c(1):134
Concern for audience
  assessing, **17a(2)**:238–239
  expressing, **17c(5)**:243
Conclusions. *See also* Inductive pattern
  of reasoning
  clinchers, **12c**:144–145
  logical closure in, **12a**:139–142
  pitfalls of, **12d**:145–146
  psychological closure in,
    12b:142–144

Confidence. *See* Fear of public speaking
Consciousness, role in skill learning,
    1e:13–16
Context for speech
    establishing in introduction,
        11c(1):132–135
    reestablishing in conclusion,
        12a(2):140–142
Contextual meaning of communication,
    1b(2):5
Contingent meaning of communication,
    1b(2):6
Conversation skills
    overreliance on, **1c(4)**:10–11,
        1e:15–16
    overview of, **1c(1)**:7–8
    speech preparation and, **2d**:23
Coordinate points, **7f(2)**:95, **7f**:93
Core values
    audience analysis and, **4c**:53–54,
        20c(1):271
    description of, **18c(2)**:251–253
    ethical issues and, **21b**:286
    as speech topics, **3a(1)**:27
Counterarguments, addressing in per-
    suasive speech, **20f**:281–283
Creativity
    four phases of, **2a**:17–18
    organization and, 81–82
Credentials, presenting, **17c(1)**:241
Credibility
    assessing speaking image,
        17a:238–239
    bolstering through speech content,
        17c:240–243
    building prior to speech, **17b**:240
    establishing with audience,
        11b(1):128, **20c(2)**:274–275,
        20c(3):277
    increasing with speech delivery,
        17d:243
    overview of, **17**:237–238
Critical path, determining, **2b(2)**:19–20

Criticism of speech, guidelines for,
    24a(2):322–323

D

Data collection. *See* Statistical evidence
Deadlines, setting intermediate,
    2b(3):20–21
Debate
    definition of, **22b(1)**:298
    guidelines for, **22b(4)**:299–301
    moderating, **22c(4)**:303–304
Deductive pattern of reasoning
    formal syllogism of, **14c(1)**:179–181
    linking evidence to claims,
        14g(2):203–204
    modified form of, **14c(2)**:181–182
    overview of, **14c**:178–179
    premises of, laying out,
        14c(3):182–185
Defining terms
    in body of speech, **13a**:151–155
    in introduction, **11c(1)**:134–135
Definition
    by authority, **13a(5)**:154
    by example, **13a(6)**:154–155
    by negation, **13a(4)**:153
Degree of probability of claim,
    14b(2):175–176
Delivery. *See also* Physical delivery;
    Vocal delivery
    extemporaneous mode of,
        23a:311–313
    impromptu mode of, **23b**:313–315
    manuscript mode of, **23c**:316–319
    memorized mode of, **23d**:319–320
    natural theory of, 308–310
Demographic characteristics of audi-
    ence
    age/generation, **4b(1)**:48–49
    overview of, **4b**:47–48
    race/ethnicity, **4b(3)**:51–52
    sex/gender, **4b(2)**:49–51

Dialogue, creating sense of, **11b(1)**:127
Difficulty of good speaking, **1d**:12
Distractions
    during speech, preventing,
        27b:361–363
    habits, eliminating, **25a(5)**:340–342
Dynamic qualities, assessing,
    17a(4):239

E

Economical lines of argument,
    14c(3):183
Economy in language, **15b(3)**:213–215
Electronic information retrieval,
    5c:63–65
Elocution, 308
Emcee, acting as, **22c(5)**:304
Emotional impact of speech,
    18a:245–247, **18d**:255,
    20c(1):271, **21e(2)**:290
Emphasis cues, use of, **19b(2)**:260
Encyclopedia of Associations, **5d(1)**:66
Energy level of speech, **16a(3)**:231–232
Engaging audience, **11**:124–126
Enthymemes, definition of, **14c(3)**:183,
    20c(1):272
Enumeration, use of, **19b(1)**:259
Enunciation, **25b(3)**:343–344
Errors. *See* Pitfalls
Ethical issues
    audience, respecting integrity of,
        21c:286–287
    choice, implications of, **21a**:285–286,
        21e:289–293
    core values and, **21b**:286
    ideas, respecting integrity of,
        21d:287–289
    overview of, **21**:284–285
Ethnicity of audience, **4b(3)**:51–52
Etymological and historical definition,
    13a(2):152
Eulogy, delivering, **22a(2)**:296–297
Evidence, linking to claims,

14a(2):171–173, **14c**:179,
    14d:185, **14e**:191, **14g**:200–207
Evocative speech
    description of, **3c(1)**:33–34
    thesis statement and, **3d(1)**:38,
        3d(2):40
Examples, including in speech
    concreteness and relatedness,
        16a(1):228–229
    detail, determining amount of,
        13b(3):157–159
    factual, **13b(1)**:155–156
    hypothetical, **13b(2)**:156–157
    liberal use of, **19b(3)**:260–261
Expectations of audience, **4e**:55–57
Experts
    people as sources of topic informa-
        tion, **5d**:65–69
    testimony of, **13d**:163–167
Explicit previews, **11c(2)**:136
Extemporaneous mode of delivery,
    23a:311–313

F

False dichotomy, **14f(7)**:197
Familiar to unfamiliar, moving from in
    speech, **19a(4)**:259
Favorable audience, **20c(1)**:270–273
Fear of public speaking
    accepting fear as normal, **6a(1)**:73
    analyzing fear, **6a(2)**:74–75
    building confidence, **6b**:75–76
    conversation skills and, **1c(1)**:7
    positive self-suggestion for, **6d**:77–79
    professional help for, **6e**:79
    relaxation and tension release tech-
        niques, **6c**:76–77
Feedback on practice sessions, obtain-
    ing and using, **24a**:321–323,
    24b(2):326–328
Flattering audience, **11b(1)**:129–130
Formality of language, **15c(1)**:215–216
Forum, description of, **22b(1)**:298

Framework, providing for listeners,
  19a(2):258
Free text search, 5b(2):62
Fresh language, use of, 15d(3):222–223
Full-sentence outline, 9b:109–114

G

Gender issues of audience,
  4b(2):49–51
General purpose of speech, 3c(1):33–34
Generalization, 14f(9):198–199
Goals of persuasion, 20a:265
Group (job) interview, preparing for,
  22d:304–306
Group presentation format,
  22b:298–301

H

Hecklers, 27c:363–365
Hierarchy of needs (Maslow),
  18b:247–248
Historical development pattern of
  speech arrangement, 8a(1):97
Historical placement of topic,
  11c(1):133–134
Humor in speech, 11b(1):130,
  16a(4):232–233, 16c(3):236
Hyperbole, 15d(2):220

I

Ideas, respecting integrity of,
  21d:287–289
If-then statement, faulty reversal of,
  14f(8):197–198
Imagery, employing, 15d(1):219
Impromptu mode of delivery,
  23b:313–315
Inclusive language, 15c(4):218
Indentation in outlines, 9a(2):107–108
Inductive pattern of reasoning
  cost/reward analysis, demonstrating,
  14b(3):176–178

degree of probability of claim,
  14b(2):175–176
linking evidence to claims,
  14g(2):203
sufficient and representative instances,
  selecting, 14b(1):174–175
Informative speech
  description of, 3c(1):33, 19:257
  learning model, basing on,
  19a:258–259
  principles of clear explanation,
  19b:259–262
  thesis statement and, 3d(1):38,
  3d(2):39–40
Interest, converting attention to,
  16b:233–235
Internet, researching topic on,
  5c:64–65
Inter-University Consortium for
  Political and Social Research,
  18c(1):250
Interviewing, 5d(2):67–69
Introductions
  engaging audience with,
  11a:125–126
  logical orientation and,
  11c:132–136
  of main speaker, 22c(6):304
  overview of, 11:124–125
  pitfalls of, 11e:137–138
  psychological orientation and,
  11b:127–132
  time and subject limits on,
  11d:136–137
Involving audience in speech,
  16a(2):229–231
Issues of speech, 18c(3):253–254

J

Jargon, use of, 15c(2):216
Job (group) interview, preparing for,
  22d:304–306
Joke telling, use of, 16c(3):236

K

Keyword search, **5b(2)**:62

L

Language
appropriateness of, **15c**:215–219
clarity in, **15b**:211–215
ethical issues in choice of, **21e(1)**:289
overview of, **15**:208
selecting to show linkage of evidence
to claims, **14g(2)**:202–207
synchronizing with audience,
15e:224–225
vivid and varied, use of, **15d**:219–224
Lead-ins for supporting materials, varying, **13e(2)**:168
Library and topic research, **5b**:61–63
Logical closure, **12a**:139–142
Logical definition, **13a(1)**:151–152
Logical orientation to topic,
11c:132–136
Logical relationships, showing,
14g(1):200–202

M

Main points
arranging in patterns, **8a**:97–101
forecasting subpoints in outlines with,
9c:114–116
language of, in outlines, **9d**:116–118
mutual exclusivity of, **7d**:90–92
number of, **7e**:93
relationships among, **7f**:93–95
thesis statement and, **7c**:88–90
Manuscript mode of delivery,
23c:316–319
Maslow's hierarchy of needs,
18b:247–248
Mastery of skills, **1d**:12
Meaning
audience analysis and, **4c**:52–54
construction of, **1a**:4

creating with evidence and interpretation, **14a(2)**:172
in speaking events, **1d**:12–13
Meaning-centered view of communication, **1b**:4–6
Meetings or programs, chairing,
22c:301–304
Memorized mode of delivery,
23d:319–320
Misconceptions about public speaking,
1d:11–13
Moderating forums, panels, or debates,
22c(4):303–304
Modes of delivery
extemporaneous, **23a**:311–313
impromptu, **23b**:313–315
manuscript, **23c**:316–319
memorized, **23d**:319–320
Motivated sequence, **20d(1)**:278–280
Motivating audience. *See also* Persuasive
speech
emotional impact of speech and,
18a:245–247
needs, relating to, **18b**:247–248
psychological orientation and,
11b(2):130–132
values, relating to, **18c**:248–255,
20c(1):271–273
Multiple channels and modes, use of,
19b(5):262

N

Names, use of, **16a(2)**:229–230
Narrowing topic, **3b**:30–33
Natural theory of delivery, 308–310
Negotiation of meaning in communica-
tion, **1b(2)**:6
Neutral audience, **20c(2)**:273–275
90/10 principle, **24a(2)**:323
Nonverbal communication, **22b(3)**:299
Notecards, use of in research, **5f**:70–72
Notes for speech, preparing,
24c:329–331

O

Occasion. *See also* Adapting speech to situation
  ceremonial, adapting patterns to, **22a**:294–297
  demands of situation, considering, **1c(4)**:10
  expectations of audience and, **4e**:55–57
  formality of language, suiting to, **15c(1)**:215–216
  group (job) interview, **22d**:304–306
  group presentation format, **22b**:298–301
  meetings or programs, chairing, **22c**:301–304
  referring to in introductions, **11b(1)**:129
  selecting topic appropriate to, **3a(2)**:28
Opening sentence, **11a**:125–126, **22d(2)**:305–306
Operational definition, **13a(3)**:152–153
Oral and collaborative process of speech preparation, **2c**:22
Oral versus written style, **15a**:209–211
Organization, bolstering credibility by demonstrating, **17c(3)**:242
Organization of topic. *See also* Outlines
  arranging main points, **8a**:97–101
  assembling ideas and information, **7a**:84–85
  grouping subpoints, **8b**:102–104
  logical relationships, showing with, **14g(1)**:200–202
  main points and thesis statement, **7c**:88–90
  motivated sequence, **20d(1)**:278–280
  mutually exclusive main points, **7d**:90–92
  number of main points, **7e**:93
  overview of, 81–83
  relationships between points, **7f**:93–95
  strongest points, placing first, **20e**:280–281
  tools for, **7b**:85–88
Organizers, use of, **19b(1)**:259–260
Orientation to topic
  logical, **11c**:132–136
  psychological, **11b**:127–132
Outcome, **3c(3)**:35–37
Outlines
  conventional format of, **9a**:106–109
  example of, 399–404
  full-sentence type, **9b**:109–114
  language in, **9d**:116–118
  main points, forecasting in, **9c**:114–116
  margin notes on rhetorical devices in, **9e**:118
  overview of, **9**:105–106
  topic outline as tool for organizing, **7b(1)**:85–86

P

Panel, description of, **22b(1)**:298
Parallel language
  in outlines, **9d**:116–118
  in speeches, **15d(2)**:220–221
Paraphrased ideas, example of, **5f(1)**:71
Past-present-future pattern of speech arrangement, **8a(1)**:97
Pauses and irrelevant sounds and phrases, identifying, **25a(3)**:339–340
People as sources of topic information
  interviewing, **5d(2)**:67–69
  locating, **5d(1)**:65–67
Performance skills
  natural theory of delivery, 308–310
  overreliance on, **1c(4)**:11, **1e**:15
  overview of, **1c(3)**:8–9
  speech preparation and, **2d**:23, 308
Peripheral values, **18c(2)**:251–252

Personality and speaking style, **1c(4)**:10
Personification, **15d(2)**:220
Persuasive speech
adjusting content based on audience
attitude, **20c**:270–277
analysis of topic for, **20b**:265–270
clarification of goals for, **20a**:264–265
description of, **3c(1)**:33
ethical issues in, **21e(3)**:290–293
opposing arguments, dealing with,
20f:281–283
organization of, **20d**:277–280
overview of, **20**:263–264
strongest points, placing first in,
20e:280–281
thesis statement and, **3d(1)**:38–39
topical arrangement of, **8a(5)**:101
Pham, Jade, 404
Physical delivery
appearance, **26a**:351–352
eye contact, **26f**:355–356
facial expression, **26g**:356–357
gestures, **26e**:354–355
mannerisms, **26b**:352
movement, **26d**:353
posture, **26c**:352–353
Pictorial symbols as visual aids,
28a(3):367–369
Pitch of voice, varying, **25c(1)**:346
Pitfalls
of attention, **16c**:235–236
of conclusions, **12d**:145–146
of emotional appeals, **18d**:255
of introductions, **11e**:137–138
of planning, **2e**:23–24
of practice sessions, **24f**:334–335
of reasoning, **14f**:193–199
of statistical evidence,
13c(2):161–162
Plagiarism, **21d**:287
Planning and preparation
communicative resources and,
2d:22–23

creativity, four phases of, **2a**:17–18
as oral and collaborative process, **2c**:22
overview of, 1–2
pitfalls of, **2e**:23–24
timetable, making realistic, **2b**:18–21
Positive self-suggestion for anxiety,
6d:77–79
Post hoc, ergo propter hoc, **14f(10)**:199
Poulakos, John, 382
Power of words, 147–148
Practice sessions
early, use of, **24b(1)**:325–326
hours before speech, use of,
24e:333–334
last, use of, **24b(3)**:328–329
middle, use of, **24b(2)**:326–328
notes, preparing, **24c**:329–331
optimizing feedback, **24a**:321–323
pitfalls of, **24f**:334–335
time limit, fitting into, **24d**:331–333
timetable for, **24b**:323–325
Precision in language, **15b(1)**:211–212
Preparation. *See* Planning and preparation
Presentation, 307–310
Presentation software, **28d**:374–376
Previews
explicit type, **11c(2)**:136
transitions and, **10b**:122–123
Primary audience outcome of speech,
3c(3):35–37
Probability statements and demographic
data, **4b**:48
Problem-solution pattern of speech
arrangement, **8a(4)**:99–100
Pronunciation, **25d**:347–350
Propositions in persuasive speech,
20b(1):266–268
Psychological closure, **12b**:142–144
Psychological orientation to topic,
11b:127–132
Public speaking
communicative resources for, **1c**:6–11

Public speaking (*continued*)
  description of, **1a**:3–4
  misconceptions about, **1d**:11–13
  teachers and consultants for,
    25a(5):342
Purpose of speech, clarifying
  desired outcome, **3c(3)**:35–37
  general purpose, **3c(1)**:33–34
  specific purpose, **3c(2)**:34–35
  thesis statement, **3d**:37–41

Q

Quality of voice, identifying problems
  of, **25a(1)**:337–338
Question-and-answer period
  audience participation, inviting,
    29b:378–379
  control of, maintaining, **29c**:379–381
  overview of, **29**:377
  preparing for, **29a**:378
Questions, use of, **16a(2)**:230–231
Quotations or citations, example of,
  5f(1):71

R

Rate of speech, **3b(1)**:31, **25b(2)**:343,
  25c(2):346–347
Reasoning
  by analogy, **14e**:190–193,
    14g(2):205–207
  causal type, **14d**:185–190, **14g(2)**:204
  deductive pattern of, **14c**:178–185,
    14g(2):203–204
  fallacies of, **14f**:193–199
  identifying point where needed,
    14a:170–173
  inductive pattern of, **14b**:174–178,
    14g(2):203
  overview of, **14**:169–170
  unfavorable audience and,
    20c(3):276–277
Reductio ad absurdum, **14f(3)**:195

Reference formats, **5e**:69, **5f(1)**:72
Refutation techniques, **20f(1)**:282–283
Relaxation and tension release techniques, **6c**:76–77
Repetition
  in patterns of inflection, identifying,
    25a(4):340
  and redundancy, use of, **19b(6)**:262
Research strategy
  analysis questions and, **5b(5)**:61
  electronic information retrieval,
    5c:63–65
  general to specific approach,
    5a(2):59–60
  library, use of, **5b**:61–63
  notecards, use of, **5f**:70–72
  overview of, **5a**:58–59
  people as information sources,
    5d:65–69
  record of sources, maintaining, **5e**:69
  terminology of topic, **5a(3)**:60–61
  time allotment and, **5a(1)**:59
Resources
  accents and vocal delivery,
    25b(4):345
  pronunciation, **25d**:350
  vocal delivery, improving,
    25a(5):340–341
Respectful language, **15c(4)**:218,
  16c(1):235
Rhythm of sentences, varying,
  15d(4):223

S

Selecting topic
  appropriateness for audience and
    occasion, **3a(2)**:28
  overview of, **3a**:25
  sources of subjects, **3a(1)**:26–28
  timely and timeless subjects,
    3a(3):28–30
Semantic fallacy, **14f(6)**:196–197

Sequence, confusing with cause,
14f(10):199

Seven plus or minus two principle,
19a(1):258

Signposts, use of, **19b(1)**:259

Simile and metaphor, **15d(2)**:220

Simple to complex, moving from in
speech, **19a(3)**:258

Skill learning, role of consciousness in,
1e:13–16

Skim reading and researching topic,
5a(2):60

Slang, use of, **15c(2)**:216

Slippery slope, **14f(4)**:195

Slogans, catchwords, and memorable
phrases, use of, **19b(1)**:260

Smith, Raymond, W., 406

Social meaning of communication,
1b(2):5

Sources, maintaining record of, **5e**:69

Spatial pattern of speech arrangement,
8a(2):98

Speaker
good, description of, 307–308
misconceptions about, **1d**:11–12
power of, 148
role of, **1a**:3–4

Speaker's block, **2e(3)**:24

Specific purpose of speech, **3c(2)**:34–35

Specificity in language, **15b(2)**:213

Speech Structure Flowchart, 83

Speech therapists, **25a(5)**:341

Speeches, examples of
Assault on Your Ears, The, Wong,
388–392

*Centrality of Oral Communication in
Secondary Education, The,* Poulakos,
382–388

*Civility Without Censorship: The Ethics
of the Internet,* Smith, 406–412

Major An: Let's Not Forget This Man,
Pham, 404–406

Rainforests Are in Need of Defense,
McNeil, 392–399

Statistical evidence, including in speech
accuracy, checking, **13c(1)**:159–161
expert testimony, **13d**:163–167
making information clear and meaningful, **13c(3)**:162–163
pitfalls of, **13c(2)**:161–162

Step by step pattern of speech arrangement, **8a(1)**:97

Stock issue analysis, **20b(2)**:268–270

Storytelling techniques in speech,
16b(2):234, **16c(2)**:235–236

Straw figures, setting up, **14f(2)**:194

Style, **15**:208–211

Stylistic devices, use of,
15d(2):220–222

Subordinate points
definition of, **7f**:93
importance of, **7f(2)**:95
outlines and, **9a(2)**:108
patterns of grouping, **8b**:102–104
relationships among, **7f(3)**:95
role of, **7f(1)**:94

Substandard language usage,
15c(3):217–218

Summarizing in conclusions,
12a(1):139–140

Supporting materials
defining words and concepts,
13a:151–155
expert testimony, **13d**:163–167
including as examples, **13b**:155–159
overview of, **13**:150–151
statistical evidence, **13c**:159–163
weaving into speech, **13e**:167–168

Symbols in outlines, **9a(1)**:106–107,
9a(4):108–109

Symposium, description of, **22b(1)**:298

Synchronizing language with audience,
15e:224–225

Synthesis, definition of, 82

T

Taping practice sessions,
24b(2):327–328

Task analysis and setting timetable, **2b(1)**:19

Techniques, overview of, **1d**:13

Testimony in speech
credibility of sources, checking,
13d(1):164–166
editing and distortion of meaning,
13d(2):166–167
overview of, **13d**:163–164

Thesis statement
as list of questions, **3d(2)**:39–41
organizing main points around,
7c:88–90
as single declarative sentence,
3d(1):37–39

Time limit, fitting speech into,
24d:331–333

Timely and timeless topics,
3a(3):28–30

Timetable
making realistic, **2b**:18–21
for practice sessions, **24b**:323–325

Title, selecting, **3e**:41–43

Toast, presenting, **22a(3)**:297

Tools for organizing
concept mapping, **7b(2)**:86, 87
manipulating moveable components,
7b(3):86–88
topic outline, **7b(1)**:85–86,
9b:112–114

Topic
audience attitude toward, **4d**:54–55
clarifying purpose of speech,
3c:33–37
conclusions and, **12b(1)**:142
credibility, bolstering by showing
understanding of, **17c(2)**:241–242
linking to listeners' self-interest,
16b(1):233–234
motivating audience toward,
11b(2):130–132
narrowing, **3b**:30–33
orienting audience to approach to,
11c(2):135–136

research strategy for, **5a**:58–61
selecting, **3a**:25–30
thesis statement, developing,
3d:37–41
title, selecting, **3e**:41–43

Topic outline
compared to full-sentence outline,
9b:112–114
as tool for organizing, **7b(1)**:85–86

Topical pattern of speech arrangement,
8a(5):100–101, 102, 104

Transitions, **10**:119–123

Trustworthiness, assessing, **17a(3)**:239

U

Unfavorable audience, **20c(3)**:275–277

Unknown base, fallacy of,
13c(2):161–162

V

Values of audience, relating to. *See also*
Core values
incorporating appeals to general values of culture, **18c(1)**:249–250
linking issues to values,
18c(3):253–254
motivational appeals and,
18c(4):254–255
overview of, **18c**:248–249

Visual aids
categories of, **28a**:367–369
impact of, **28b(3)**:372–373
introduction of, **28c**:373–374
overview of, **28**:366
presentation software, **28d**:374–376
simplicity and clarity of,
28b(2):370–372
size of, **28b(1)**:370

Vocal delivery
accents and, **25b(4)**:344–345
distracting characteristics and,
25a:337–342
enunciation, **25b(3)**:343–344

Vocal delivery (*continued*)
  overview of, **25**:336
  pronunciation, **25d**:347–350
  rate of speech, **3b(1)**: 31,
    25b(2):343, **25c(2)**:346–347
  variety in, **25c**:345–347
  volume level, **25b(1)**:342–343,
    25c(3):347
Voice coaches, **25a(5)**:341–342
Volume level of speech,
    25b(1):342–343, **25c(3)**:347

W

Writer's block, **2e(3)**:24
Writing skills
  overreliance on, **1c(4)**:11, **1e**:15
  overview of, **1c(2)**:8
  speech preparation and, **2d**:23
Written versus oral style, **15a**:209–211

Y

"You," use of, **16a(2)**:231